The Army Staff Officer's Guide

The Army Staff Officer's Guide

**Colonel Glen R. Johnson
(USA Ret.)**

**Colonel Fred M. Walker
(USA Ret.)**

Gulf Publishing Company
Book Division
Houston, Texas

Copyright © 1975 by Gulf Publishing Company, Houston, Texas.
All rights reserved. Printed in the United States of America.
This book, or parts thereof, may not be reproduced in any form
without permission of the publisher.

Library of Congress
Catalog Card Number
74-11834
ISBN 0-87201-046-5

Dedication

To the many commanders, supervisors, and fellow staff officers
from whom we learned so much for so many years;
and to Delorean and Jo
who thought being married to professional soldiers was difficult
until they became the wives of aspiring military writers.

Preface

This book reflects the authors' belief that military staff members need a single, comprehensive reference to help them better understand their duties and appreciate the professional skills and personal qualities required of an effective member of the staff team. Many official references and the curricula of most service schools offer excellent instruction for accomplishing typical staff actions and solving the problems most frequently encountered by staff officers. However, no single available reference or course of instruction provides a detailed analysis of the staff—its reason for existing, functions, composition, the interfaces among its many parts, and the duties and responsibilities of its members.

In preparing this material, we have adhered to the standard practice of referring to all members of the staff who advise and assist the commanders as staff *officers,* or action *officers.* We are certainly aware that many of those "officers" are enlisted men and women or civilian employees of the Army. Our goal is to help all who serve in military headquarters, regardless of their military status or the level of their duties and responsibilities. Although aimed primarily at the staff, the suggestions and advice we have offered apply as well to young commanders, concerned with eliciting maximum results from their staffs.

The Army is a dynamic institution. It must change with the times both to utilize contemporary scientific and technological developments and to meet the demands of fluctuating international situations. Obviously then, some details of this book will become outdated; organizations will change, new formats will evolve and new procedures will be developed.

Yet the principles upon which command authority and responsibility are based have withstood the test of time. These principles are permanent. Commanders will continue to be concerned with four primary areas of interest: sufficient numbers of qualified and motivated people; information about factors that could influence mission accomplishment; the adequacy of physical resources; and planning and supervising military operations. Titles may vary, but staff functions will always pivot on various facets of those four areas of command concern. Therefore, we believe that the advice, guidance and suggestions presented will remain valid. Similarly, the attributes of a good staff officer and the skills that he must master are fundamental and will change little over the years.

We have attempted to concentrate on those facets of staff operations, problem-solving procedures and personal techniques that will be most useful and enduring for the readers. We hope that we have succeeded in imparting to others, through our efforts and experience, lessons we learned the hard way during many years of experience as Army staff officers.

Contents

1. Introduction, 1.

2. The Staff, Its Purpose and Its Evolution, 4.

Headquarters, 5.
The Staff, 6.
The Commander, 7.
Staff Evolution, 11.

3. The Major Staff Elements, 21.

Modern Staff Organizations, 22.

Special Staffs, 23.
Personal Staffs, 24.
Organization Charts, 25.
The Commander, 27.
Aides, 27.
Command Sergeants Major, 29.
The Chief of Staff, 30.
Command Groups, 31.

The Major Staff Elements, 31.

Personnel, 31.
   Strengths, 32. Grades, 33. Skills, 33. Motivation (Recreation, Welfare and Morale), 34.

Intelligence, 37.
Operations, 43.
   Identifying Problems, 45. Mission Restatement, 46. Studying the Problems, 47. The Commander's Decision, 47. Planning, 47. Orders, 47. Staff Supervision, 48. Additional Functions, 48. Training, 49. Organization, 49.
Logistics, 49.
   Supply, 51. Maintenance, 52. Construction, 52. Transportation, 54. Food Service, 54. Property Disposal, 55. Miscellaneous Logistics Services, 55.
Civil Affairs (G-5), 56.
Comptroller, 58.
   Fiscal Management, 58.
   Management Specialists, 60.
Communications and Electronics, 60.
   Organization, 61.
The Special Staff, 61.
Headquarters Commandant, 62.
Adjutant General, 63.
   Military Personnel Administration, 65.
Provost Marshal, 66.
Surgeon, 67.
Chaplain, 70.
Management Information Systems Office, 70.
Weather Officer, 72.
The Personal Staff, 74.
Inspector General, 74.
Staff Judge Advocate, 75.
Information Officer, 78.
Miscellaneous Staff Specialists, 78.
Aviation Officer, 78.
Nuclear Weapons Officer, 78.
Emergency Operations Centers, 79.

Appendix to Chapter 3, 80.

Engineer Battalion Skills, 80.
Motivational Activities, 81.
Social Activities, 81.
Athletic Activities, 81.
Religious Activities, 81.

Educational Activities, 81.
Community Recreational Facilities, 81.
Personal Assistance, 82.
Infantry Division Equipment, 1923 (selected items), 82.
Weapons, 82.
Mobility, 82.
Communications, 82.
Infantry Division Equipment, Early 1970's (selected items), 82.
Weapons, 82.
Mobility, 83.
Communications, 83.
Communications and Electronics (sample duties), 84.
Headquarters Commandant (typical duties), 87.
Adjutant General (typical duties), 88.
Provost Marshal (sample duties), 90.
Army Surgeon (sample duties), 91.
Chaplain (sample duties), 91.
Weather Officer (sample duties), 92.

4. Procedures, 93.

Standard Procedures, 95.
General Approach, 95.
Staff Procedures Outline, 95.
Procedures, 96.
Step 1—Identifying the Problem, 96.
Step 2—Considering Available Information, 97.
Step 3—Issuing Initial Guidance, 98.
Step 4—Studying the Problem, 99.
Step 5—The Commander's Decision, 101.
Step 6—Planning, 101.
Step 7—Orders, 102.
Step 8—Supervision, 102.

5. Typical Major Staff Actions, 104.

Estimates, 105.
Preparing Estimates, 107.

Mission Statement, 107.
Situation, 107.
   Facts, 109. Assumptions, 109.
Analysis of Courses of Action, 110.
Comparison of Courses of Action, 112
   Judgement, 114.
Recommendations, 114.
Other Estimates, 116.
Intelligence Estimates, 116.
Support Estimates, 116.
Staff Studies, 117.
Staff Study Procedures, 117.
Problem, 118.
Facts and Assumptions, 118.
Discussion, 119.
Conclusions, 119.
Recommendation, 120.
Special Studies, 120.
Analysis of Area of Operation, 121.
Standing Operating Procedures (SOP), 122.
Summary of Major Problem Solving Actions, 122.

Appendix to Chapter 5, 124.

Staff Estimate Format, 124.
Intelligence Estimate (sample format), 124.
Support Estimate, 125.
Staff Studies (sample format), 126.
Analysis of Area of Operations (sample format), 126.
Standing Operating Procedures (sample format for a combat division), 128.
Standing Operating Procedures (sample format for a logistical office subelement), 129.

6. Plans, Orders and Reports, 131.

Planning, 131.
Planning Sequences, 132.
Step One—Forecast to Determine Probable Commitments, 132.

Step Two—Examine Probable Commitments and Developments
and Establish Planning Priorities, 133.
Step Three—Study the Implications of Commitments
to Determine the Scope of the Mission, 134.
Step Four—Analyze the Mission to Determine All
Included Tasks, 134.
Step Five—Determine Command Guidance, 134.
   Discussions and Comments, 135. Policy Statements by the Commander, 135. Standing Operating Procedures (SOP), 135. Directives and Orders from Higher Headquarters, 135.
Step Six—Preparing Planning Studies, 136.
Step Seven—Selecting the Courses of Action, 136.
Step Eight—Preparing Complete Plans, 136.
Step Nine—Developing Planning Programs, 137.
Plans, 138.
Formats, 140.
Orders, 140.
Warning Orders, 141.
Fragmentary Orders, 141.
Letters of Instruction, (LOI), 141.
   Miscellaneous Directives, 141.
Reports, 142.
Reports Control System, 143.
Reporting Formats, 144.

Appendix to Chapter 6, 145.

Operation Plan (sample format), 145.
Administrative Plan (sample format), 146.
Letter of Instruction (sample format), 147.
Report Format (sample), 148.

7. Other Typical Staff Actions, 150.

Correspondence, 150.
Incoming Correspondence, 151.
Outgoing Correspondence, 151.
Internal Correspondence, 152.
   Memoranda, 152. Summary Sheets (Abbreviated Staff Studies), 153.

Items of Command Interest, 154. Fact Sheets and Talking Papers, 155.
Conferences, 155.
Briefings, 156.
Research, 157.
Staff Supervision, 158.
  Meeting with Representatives from Subordinate Commands, 163. Liason, 163. Supervision by Correspondence, 164. Reacting to Supervision, 164.
Coordination, 164.
General, 164.
Intrastaff Coordination, 165.
Formal Coordination, 166.
  Coordination Protocol, 166. Where to Start, 167.
Informal Coordination, 167.
  Timing, 168. Coordination by Conference, 168.
Coordinating Other's Actions, 168.
Nonconcurrences, 168.
External Coordination, 169.

8. Command Policy, 173.

Keeping the Commander Informed, 174.
  Report the Bad as well as the Good, 174.
Decision Policies, 179.
Changes in Missions, 179.
Negative Replies, 180.
Changes in Resources, 181.
Changes in Organization, 181.
  Creative Thinking, 181.
Interheadquarters Relations, 182.
Chain of Command, 183.
  Suspense Dates, 184.
Support to Subordinate Activities, 185.
Contributing to Actions, 185.
Supervision, 186.

9. Staff Services and Internal Support, 188.

Administration, 189.
Correspondence, 190.

Distribution, 191.
Suspense Controls, 193.
Filing, 193.
Typing, 195.
Reproduction, 195.
Audiovisual Aids, 196.
Funds, 196.
Duty Rosters and Additional, Non-mission-oriented Duties, 197.
Routine Orders, 197.
Visitors, 197.
Personnel, 198.
Miscellaneous Personnel Functions, 199.
Communications, 200.
Postal and Messenger Services, 200.
Electronics, 200.
Telephones, 200.
Data Transmission, 201.
Radio, 201.
Data Processing, 202.
Counterintelligence (Internal Security), 203.
Management Engineering, 204.
Supply, 204.
Transportation, 205.
Facilities, 206.
Summary, 206.

10. Personal Skills and Techniques, 208.

Communications, 209.
Receiving, 209.
Listening, 210.
  Concentration, 210.
Reading, 212.
  Reading Speed, 212. Concentration and Comprehension, 212. Reading as a Professional Technique, 214.
Observation, 214.
Sending, 215.
  Know the Subject, 216. Organization, 216. Vocabulary, 219.
Speaking, 219.
  Official Conversations, 219. Formal Oral Presentations (except briefings and conference presentations), 220. Types of Speeches, 222. Mechanics of

Good Speaking, 226.
Writing, 227.
  Effectiveness, 228. Writing Techniques, 228.
Briefings, 232.
Purposes, 232.
Format, 233.
  Briefing Techniques, 233. Rehearsals, 234.
Conferences, 234.
Conference Planning, 235.
The Staff Officer's Functions in Conferences, 235.
Conference Leadership, 236.
  Follow-up Actions, 237.
Research, 237.
Maintaining Data, 238.
Memory, 238.
Working Files, 239.
Data Banks, 240.
Policy Files, 241.
  Sample Actions, 242.
Management, 242.
Staff Management Responsibilities, 245.
Completed Staff Work, 248.
Staff Supervision (Follow-through), 249.
Summary, 249.

11. Staff Assignments, 251.

Normal Assignment Pattern, 251.
Early Staff Assignments, 252.
Peculiarities of Staff Assignments, 253.
Preparing for Staff Work, 254.
  Reporting to New Headquarters, 257. Learning the Job, 258. Continuing the Learning Process, 259.
Policies, 260.
The Chain of Command, 261.
Social Duties, 262.
Characteristics of Successful Staff Officers, 263.
The Rewards, 266.

12. Staff Officers of Other Services, 267.

Interservice Relationships, 267.
Purpose of Separate Services, 268.
Service Similarities, 269.
    Missions, 269. Command Channels, 269. Legislative and Judicial Controls, 270. Command Philosophy, 272. Mission Orientation, 272. Organization, 272.
Comparison of Staff Organizations, 272.
    Flexibility and Deviations, 279. Common Policies, 280. Staff Actions, 280.
Joint Staffs, 283.
Combined Commands, 284.
    Assignments to Joint and Combined Staffs, 284.
Summary, 286.

Index, 287.

The Army Staff Officer's Guide

1.

Introduction

This guide is designed to help young officers with limited experience through their first staff assignments. It should be particularly useful to those assigned, early in their careers, to large complex, headquarters organizations.

Staff assignments are unavoidable and important in career development. Most officers can expect to spend at least fifty percent of their service in staff positions. Professional success, therefore, depends heavily on the proficiency demonstrated during those assignments.

Few officers seek staff duty. Most prefer the more active life and the direct personal involvement of service with troop units to the desk-bound tedium of the headquarters. However, experienced officers recognize that service with a commander's team of advisors and assistants presents unparalleled opportunities for professional reward and personal gratification.

Most commanders select as their key staff members officers with whom they have served successfully in the past, officers who have established reputations for outstanding productivity. Working with such recognized experts, observing their techniques and learning from their examples is a valuable experience for developing officers.

Equally important, staff assignments afford, even to junior officers, opportunities for demonstrating to fellow professionals, senior supervisors, and commanders their personal skills and abilities for functioning as productive staff team members. A reputation as an aggressive but cooperative "doer", gained in the course of a single staff assignment, can have long lasting favorable effects on an officer's career. Unfavorable impressions based on equally brief associations can have even longer lasting adverse effects.

The personal gratification of a job well done is directly related to the degree of achievement. Few military experiences can equal the personal satisfaction of having accepted and completed a difficult staff action and knowing that it has been a truly outstanding job.

The personal rewards of self-satisfaction and increased confidence are great for those who master the intricacies of staff work. Conversely, the sense of failure that accompanies knowing that one's work is inadequate can be long lasting and traumatic.

Unfortunately, many officers receive their first staff assignments before their military education and service background have prepared them either to reap the professional rewards or to enjoy the personal satisfaction of jobs well done. Too often, newly assigned staff officers arrive at their first headquarters with little understanding of the commander's mission or the reasons for the existence of their organizations and even less comprehension of the staff, its purpose and how it functions.

Normally, these young officers are assigned because they possess professional or technical skills, and most are eager to apply those skills to the Army's needs. First, they must overcome the handicap of inexperience—an effort which can be frustrating.

The most obvious sources of help, fellow officers and supervisors, are likely to prove inadequate. Those who have mastered the necessary skills and techniques and who understand the staff's function and their roles within that function are invariably swamped with work and beset by suspense dates. Almost always, newcomers will find these effective officers to be most cooperative, quick to offer advice and eager to assist. Unfortunately, demands on their time will not permit them to start from the beginning to educate and train completely uninformed new arrivals.

Those officers who have time available for detailed instructions may only compound the problem. The fact that they have leisure time could auger poorly for their ability to guide beginners. Chances are they are poorly informed. If not, they probably have chosen to avoid becoming involved in the difficult labor inherent in good staff work.

Advice received from well meaning but poorly informed co-workers is not likely to lead to full and productive tours of staff duty. At best, guidance received from these sources could lead to a measure of usefulness in assisting more productive co-workers and to a reputation as a "pencil sharpener" useful only to relieve other, more productive officers from simple, routine chores. Advice accepted from those who have chosen the security of anonymity by avoiding action could well lead to very pleasant tours of duty with regular hours, an improved golf score, a reputation as a "dud" and professional oblivion.

References on staff organization and functions abound, and some are excellent. They may at the same time be inadequate for the beginner. Most military references are aimed at experienced officers and concentrate either on advanced higher level organization and employment theories or on detailed instructions concerning assignments and specific functions within the staffs and formalized guidance for specific types of actions.

At the one extreme, many fine works discourse on national-level staff organizations and on the historical effects of staff employment by national leaders and military chiefs. Such publications are essential background reading for military professionals and indispensable references for history students. They offer little comfort to young officers, newly assigned to unmarked desks in major headquarters, whose apprehensions and questions have little in common with Adolph Hitler's use (or misuse) of his general staff during the last years of World War II or with the controversial conduct of the U.S. War Department staff during the American Civil War.

At the other end of the scale, whole libraries of regulations, manuals, pamphlets, circulars, and directives provide minutely detailed instructions and examples for completing individual staff actions such as studies, estimates, plans, orders and reports. Many headquarters supplement these with even more detailed local guidance to the extreme of publishing lists of words and phrases to be used (or avoided) by the staff.

To experienced staff officers, these references become virtual bibles by which they conduct their business. To the completely uninitiated newcomer they may be useless. Formats mean little to one who has not the vaguest idea of what to study. Blessed or condemned words are of little help to those with nothing to write.

This book addresses much of the same material found in existing reference and instructional material, but at a different level and with somewhat different objectives. Its goals are to prepare inexperienced staff officers to use and understand available reference materials by broadening their comprehension of staffs, their purposes and their functions and to explain to young officers their probable roles as individual action officers within a staff. Also emphasized are individual skills and techniques not stressed in the lower-level military schools which younger staff officers may have attended. No effort is made to duplicate the many fine existing works by teaching those skills and techniques. The thrust here is toward impressing inexperienced officers with their urgent needs for those skills as keys to success as staff officers.

As stated in the beginning, this work is intended to assist individual action officers by answering many of the questions they will face during the early days of their first staff assignments. Particularly emphasized are the types of actions that can be expected at the action-officer level. For individual orientation the first few chapters are devoted to the staff as an entity: its history, its major elements and its functions.

The Staff, Its Purpose and Its Evolution

Assignment to a large headquarters can be an unsettling experience for any officer, whatever his age or experience. To a young, inexperienced officer, the first encounter with a large staff organization can be traumatic.

Few officers ever completely overcome the twinges of apprehension aroused by orders to a new duty station. In later years these qualms concern the minor inconvenience of adapting to new working conditions and procedures, adjusting to new co-workers, and becoming used to the foibles of new supervisors. Doubts about personal qualifications tend to lessen with the passing years. Experience, study and military education will have answered most questions regarding the nature of the new job.

Seasoned officers can deduce with reasonable accuracy what their new duties will entail and can refine those deductions by reviewing familiar references. Also, older officers invariably have friends and acquaintances at the new station who provide firsthand information on working conditions, size and nature of the workload, and the temperament and peculiarities of the commander and his senior assistants.

Inexperienced officers enjoy none of these advantages. Their military experiences are unlikely to have been sufficient to inspire self-confidence or to acquaint them with the purposes and functions of the headquarters organization to which they are being assigned. They probably are unfamiliar with reference material which could assist them and do not know anyone at the new station who is sufficiently well informed to be helpful.

The apprehensions of younger officers are the same ones experienced by older professionals (greatly magnified) plus doubts about their personal qualifications. They approach first staff assignments worried about the nature of the tasks expected of them and about their own capabilities.

The newly assigned, inexperienced staff officer's concerns are personal. His interest centers around the tasks he must perform, the skills required, and his capability to meet the requirements. To understand and appreciate the importance of the tasks he can expect, the fledgling staff officer must first understand the role of the commander, the part played by the headquarters, and the functioning of the entire staff. Only then can he begin to identify his niche in the overall organization.

Headquarters

"Sir, do you know anything about headquarters Such-and-Such?"

Most senior officers have heard this question, or a facsimile, from shaken young men clutching sets of newly arrived assignment orders. The question reflects the inquirer's apprehensions, his lack of knowledge, and his desperate need for help. Too often, casual answers given with little thought do little to ease the apprehensions or to inform the youngster. They may hinder, rather than assist, in his adjusting to the environment of his first staff assignment.

Replies such as "Headquarters, United States Army Europe, is in charge of all US Army organizations and activities in the European area," or "Headquarters, US Army Tank Automotive Command procures and maintains tanks and vehicles used by the Army" would be correctly interpreted and understood by experienced military men versed in command responsibilities, the functions of the commander and the true purpose of the headquarters. Accepted literally by an inexperienced officer, they contain inaccuracies and false implications which could mislead him and make more difficult his efforts to understand his new surroundings.

To be precise, headquarters are inanimate. They are in charge of nothing, command nothing, and maintain nothing. Most importantly, headquarters are responsible for nothing. Each exists for only one purpose: to serve as a commander's operations and control center.

Headquarters, United States Army, Europe, is not in charge of US Army activities in the European area. It is not even the headquarters of Army activities in the European area. It is one thing, and that only. It is the headquarters for the Commander, United States Army, Europe. He is in charge of Army activities in the European area, he commands the Army personnel, and he is responsible for all that occurs or fails to occur.

Similarly, Headquarters, US Army Tank Automotive Command is the headquarters of its commander, nothing more. The headquarters itself is responsible for neither procurement nor maintenance.

The distinction may seem to be a hair-splitting and insignificant exercise in verbage. For experienced officers, perhaps it is. To young officers attempting to understand the concepts by which they must conduct business in their new assignment, these examples highlight the most basic tenet by which they must live. It is imperative that each person associated with any headquarters condition himself to, and maintain foremost in his mind, one overriding factor. The headquarters, the staff and the individual action officer exist only because the commander requires a center from which to conduct his business and needs assistants to help him accomplish his mission. If the commander's job were to be eliminated, his headquarters would likewise be eliminated.

These examples also demonstrate an important point that the beginner must grasp. Staff officers must express themselves in precise terms not subject to misinterpretation. It is always safe to assume that if anything can be misunderstood, someone will misunderstand it. Much more will be said later about the importance of precise expression.

More meaningful information for the young officer would have concerned the mission and allied tasks for which the commander of headquarters Such-and-Such is responsible. Such information would form the base upon which to build a firm understanding of the functions and purposes of his staff and the role of the individual officer within it.

The level of the commander's authority and the extent of his responsibilities dictate the size of the headquarters and the skills required by its members. Every headquarters will have one group of professional and technical experts whose function is to operate the physical plant and to provide administrative and housekeeping support to the commander. These experts are important, and their functions are essential to the success of the commander's mission.

Each staff officer must be familiar with the functions necessary to operate a headquarters physical plant and to support its internal operation. Although this book is primarily aimed at those people in the headquarters, the commander's staff, whose principle functions directly involve accomplishing the actions which constitute their commander's mission, almost all staff members must contribute to internal headquarters support activities.

The Staff

The stress on commanders may have given the false impression that they are capable of accomplishing their missions with little need for assistance except from their almost equally powerful subordinate commanders. This is obviously untrue, as even the most cursory observation of any headquarters will reveal. All commanders are surrounded by assistants and advisors. The complexities of today's Army, with its sophisticated equipment and scientific innovations, have placed the details of command functions far beyond one person's capabilities. Even the lowest levels of command now require experts to assist the commander and to advise him on the capabilities and limitations of the advanced gadgetry available to him.

At the higher levels of responsibility a commander must surround himself with scientific, professional and technical experts to assist him in understanding the many facets of the mission, the multiple approaches available to accomplish it and the most effective and economical application of the resources available. The use of assistants and advisors in no way dilutes the commander's authority or decreases his personal responsibility.

All missions and their requisite tasks are assigned directly to a commander. Responsibility for accomplishing the mission is his. At his discretion a commander may delegate certain portions of his authority to his staff and to his subordinate commanders. He cannot delegate the responsibility for his mission or for any included tasks and functions.

Regardless of the immensity of a mission or its geographical extent, despite the magnitude of the function the commander may head, all responsibilities remain his alone. He receives the credit for jobs well done and the criticism for less than satisfactory work produced by those who work under his control.

That commanders do assign responsibilities within their own authority to their staffs, to individual staff officers, and to subordinate commanders does not relieve them of these responsibilities in the eyes of their own superiors; but both praise and criticism received by commanders are shared with those whose work elicited the favorable or unfavorable reactions. The passing along of praise and criticism in no way lessens the favorable or adverse impact on the commander's reputation. Perhaps this apparent overemphasis on the commander and the singularity of his authority and responsibilities helps clarify the purposes of the staff—at least from the negative view of what the staff is not.

The staff is not an extension of the commander's authority. It does not share in the commander's responsibilities. The staff's purpose, and the purpose of each of its members, is to help the commander accomplish his mission and its included tasks. This purpose and the functions which the staff must perform become more apparent through closer examination of the commander's job.

The Commander

Each commander is assigned certain specific missions to be accomplished, to given standards and within given or implied timeframes. Concurrent with a mission assignment, each commander is given the authority needed to control and influence the actions and events that will govern his success. Each commander is also allocated resources with which to accomplish his mission. To accomplish this within the prescribed timeframe he must proceed in a fairly predictable sequence of processes.

First, the mission itself must be analyzed to determine the exact nature of the requirements and the exact results expected. As a part of this analysis, each included task must be identified and its relative importance to the overall mission established. Next, each task must be analyzed—much like the entire mission—to determine the individual jobs included and to determine the proper time-phasing of the task into the sequence of actions required to complete the mission. From this mission analysis will come the commander's first broad concept of operation, his general approach to accomplishing the mission.

Detailed methods of operations may change as additional information becomes available and as situations change. If carefully thought through, however, the general concept should change little.

Consider, for example, the analysis to be completed by an engineer unit commander directed to construct a bridge over a designated river at a specified point to be crossed by a tank battalion at an exact time on a given date. Analysis of the mission proper reveals several pertinent points. To allow the commander maximum flexibility for using his own professional judgement in selecting the best type of bridge to be used and the most advantageous methods of construction, the type of bridge has not been specified and no mention has been made of construction procedures. Yet certain limiting factors are intrinsic to the problem.

Because the bridge is to be used by a tank battalion, it must be of sufficient strength and dimensions to accommodate the weight and size of the tanks and other equipment assigned to that battalion. Although completion time is also omitted from the mission statement, the time for its use is specified, requiring that the bridge be functional before that time. Therefore, construction procedures must be selected to allow for meeting that deadline.

After this overly simplified analysis the commander's mission has taken more definitive shape: (1) build a bridge to meet certain minimum capacity and dimension criteria, (2) build it at the designated spot, (3) have the structure useable by a specified time and date.

An experienced commander will consider the vagaries of people, machines, and outside influences such as bad weather and possible overload weight of unusually large equipment. He will insert safety factors for unavoidable delays. The bridge he decides to build will exceed minimum criteria and he will meet a somewhat earlier, self-imposed deadline for completion than that required by the directive.

Now consider the separate tasks that are included but not identified in the mission statement. Assume that the spot designated for the crossing is some distance from roads on either side of the river and that the intervening terrain is not trafficable for tanks or other vehicles (a not unusual situation). Two included tasks become immediately apparent. Access roads must be constructed to the river and exit roads must be built on the opposite bank to permit the tank unit to regain trafficable terrain. In this simple analysis the order of priority is also apparent. The access road must be at least partially completed before the bridge can be started, and the bridge will be needed by the equipment and people to construct the exit road. The commander's general concept might be

> First, construct a rough trail sufficient for passage of the bridge material and construction equipment. When that is completed, move to the bridge site and commence construction of the bridge. While the bridge is being built, expand and improve the access road for the tank unit and its support vehicles. When the bridge will carry vehicle traffic, cross with the necessary equipment and start exit-road construction. As the access road and the bridge are completed, move all men and equipment to the exit-road-construction portion of the project.

After analysis of the mission and its included tasks, the commander's next concern is likely to be the possible impact of outside influences which he cannot control. To the combat commander, the most significant of these influences is the enemy's ability to influence the proposed action.

The commander must inform himself to the maximum extent possible on the enemy's strength, including not only the numerical size of his forces but also their competence and motivation, their disposition, and the quantity and capability of their weapons and other equipment. He must estimate the enemy's probable course of action and the impact of this action on his mission. To a more functional commander, such as one who commands a procurement, maintenance, storage or similar activity, more significant outside influences might be the availability of labor, the sufficiency of commercial transportation, the adequacy of utilities, and the nature and extent of other community support services.

Whatever the command, whatever the mission, outside influences exist and must be carefully weighed. Whether it be an enemy counterattack or a major strike by mechanics or warehousemen, an overlooked and unplanned for contingency can be devastating to a mission and to a commander's career.

After studying the mission and considering possible outside influences, the commander must establish his requirements for personnel and physical resources and evaluate the assets available. Resources usually consist of three general categories: people, things and services.

Each category must be considered separately for quantitative and qualitative sufficiency. The commander's staff organization is usually grouped by expertise in the separate categories, but the interdependence of the three areas is such that the commander must evaluate them as a single integrated process. Personnel requirements, for example, are directly linked to the quantities and types of equipment required and available.

No longer can the commander concern himself only with numbers of combat soldiers. He must now consider the hundreds of skills needed to operate and maintain the sophisticated equipment necessary for even the simplest military operation. The adequacy of the equipment must be considered in the light of the professional expertise needed and on hand to assure maximum output from the available items and the technical skills required to maintain and repair each item.

Having studied the mission, weighed the outside influences and compared resources with resource requirements, the commander arrives at the planning process. He must develop a detailed, time-phased plan for applying his resources to the best advantage against each task to be performed in order to assure that the overall mission is accomplished within the directed timeframe. This plan is the key to the effective and economical use of resources.

Lastly, he must implement his plan, actually performing the tasks which lead to mission accomplishment. This requires directives to subordinate commanders and supervision as they analyze, evaluate, plan and perform their portions of the overall mission.

Each of the processes mentioned should be considered to have two distinct phases: (1) the initial process of analysis, evaluation and planning accomplished upon receipt of the mission and (2) the continuing process of analyzing, evaluating, planning, directing and supervising as more information becomes available and as situations change. As the mission progresses, additional included tasks will be identified, and some of those originally identified may prove to be unnecessary. Outside influences may change, favorably or adversely, and both resource requirements and resource availability are sure to fluctuate. Each new factor must be analyzed; plans must be adjusted; new directives must be published; and their implementation, supervised.

From the duties and function of the commander the general form and requirements for a staff begin to emerge. Obviously, in today's Army the requirements of command far outweigh the capabilities of a single person unassisted.

The form of necessary assistance begins to take shape. A commander needs help in analyzing the mission, identifying the tasks involved and developing his concepts of operations. This demands help and advice from experts on the many possible outside influences on his activities, whether they be enemy-associated or resource-oriented.

Establishing resource requirements and evaluating the quantitative and qualitative sufficiency of available assets also requires many specialists. Planning, both initial and continuing, also requires assistants who understand the many facets of the mission and operational concepts and who know the capabilities and limitations of the resources available to accomplish them. Finally, the commander alone cannot hope to supervise the activities of his subordinate commanders, who also employ many sophisticated items of equipment.

The influences which create the need for a staff exist at all levels of command. The only difference is one of magnitude. At one end of the scale, company commanders are assisted by first sergeants and company clerks who are experts in personnel requirements and management as they apply at the company level. Supply sergeants and motor sergeants help with the management of physical resources; subordinate commanders (platoon leaders) assist the commander in mission analysis, planning and supervision. At the other end of the spectrum the President of the United States, in his role as Commander-in-Chief of all US military forces, is assisted by a military staff consisting of the Department of Defense, including Headquarters, Department of the Army, and its US Navy and US Air Force counterparts.

Whatever the level of command, the size of the staff or the grades of its members, whether they be company clerks or general officers, the staff and its members are important only as their functions contribute to the success of their commander's mission. As emphasized earlier, the staff's only purpose is to help the commander succeed in his mission. If the commander's job were to be abolished, the need for the staff would cease.

Staff Evolution

We have already emphasized the indivisible nature of command and the commander's sole responsibility to his superiors for all that happens or fails to happen in connection with the missions assigned to him. That responsibility cannot be delegated to or assumed by members of the commander's staff. Yet as technology has increased the complexity of the machinery of warfare, the business of planning, directing and supervising military operations has become more than any one man can manage alone.

To commanders, advances and improvements in weaponry, transportation and communication techniques have been mixed blessings. They have improved fighting and support capabilities, but they have increased the need for technical knowledge. At some point, possibly very early in the history of armed conflict, commanders found it necessary to surround themselves with advisors and assistants with specialized knowledge on the more technical aspects of military operations.

In the beginning, perhaps, commanders could plan operations and control their forces alone. No one knows exactly when men, or their predecessors, first took up arms against their own species. We do know that warfare has been with us from the earliest recorded history and was very much a part of the word-of-mouth legends passed along from generation to generation before history was recorded.

Perhaps early stone age or even more primitive men found it necessary to fight to gain access to better hunting areas or to take over particularly desirable territory for shelter and security. If such attacks occurred, the man selected to lead the assault probably needed little help from advisors and assistants.

Weapons most likely consisted of those already in daily use for hunting and defense, stones sharpened by flaking the edges and perhaps pieces of wood as well. Transportation was by foot, and communications probably consisted of very limited oral interchange of information.

Although staffs as we know them would not appear for thousands of years, the considerations that much later created them must have originated with the birth of warfare. Through the millennia those considerations have changed only in scope, magnitude and complexity. Early leaders must have been concerned with the same questions which confront the modern commander:

"Do I have enough people?"
"How strong is the enemy?"
"Do I have enough weapons?"

Prehistoric men gradually made innovations, some of which must have inspired awe in their time. At some point sharpened sticks were fitted with bits of chipped flint, and stone eventually gave way to metal. Drums or other signals supplemented oral communication, increasing the commander's information gathering capabilities and span of control. But as even these modest improvements caused problems, requirements for rudimentary military training must have begun to emerge.

Perhaps commanders began to seek advice and help from expert weapon makers and users or to discuss communications problems with one who was best at giving signals. There were not yet any formal staff organizations as normal appendages to command.

One ancient and not too successful venture in the use of a formal staff is described in Greek mythology. According to legend, King Priam, ruler of Troy, used his city council as a sort of staff on at least one occasion. When the Argyves, commanded by Agamemnon, landed on the Aegean Coast near Troy with the obvious intention of laying siege to the city, King Priam directed the council to prepare a plan for the defense of Troy.

The council labored diligently but displayed one weakness still detectable in some staff organizations. It deliberated the many possible methods of defense at such length that the Argyves completed their preparations unmolested and launched their attack before a defense plan had been decided upon. This demonstration of staff efficiency did not lead to immediate, universal adoption of staffs by ancient Greek leaders.

The earliest weapons probably required little resupply. Their short range and hand-to-hand use would mean that a soldier losing or breaking his weapon would have brief need for a replacement. It is likely that the weapons had a greater life expectancy than their users.

Combat mobility and support transportation had their first big boost from the introduction of horses, elephants, camels or other beasts of burden, which must have been among the most significant changes ever to occur in military equipment and tactics. Certainly it was one of the most lasting.

War chariots appeared in Southwest Asia as early as 2000 B.C. and were in central Europe by 1200 B.C. By 1000 B.C. they were in general use throughout Asia, Europe and what is now southern Russia. Encountered for the first time on the battlefield by opponents on foot, the destructive power and immensely superior maneuverability of chariot-mounted soldiers must have been terrifying.

Like all improvements, the coming of the horse as a military asset brought with it added command considerations and new fields of expertise. New depths were added to the analysis, evaluation and planning processes, and logistics with the addition of carts, chariots and harness and the necessity for feeding and caring for the animals.

Supply and resupply of mounts during battle probably required little staff work. It is likely that each soldier replaced his animal by taking one from whatever source presented itself—the local populace, fallen comrades or defeated enemies. This system was still used even in the nineteenth century.

During the Civil War, Major General Blunt followed a rather indecisive victory over the Confederates at the battle of Prarie Grove, Arkansas, with a devastating raid on the Texas Brigade at Fort Smith, where it had withdrawn after the battle. Resupply of horses was handled by the Confederate Generals in the age-old way. A member of the Texas Brigade wrote that the entire brigade was furloughed for thirty days and each member was directed to secure a new horse and other equipment before returning. While requiring little logistical staffing, this simplified supply procedure—which removed one brigade from action—must have created considerable activity among those staff officers charged with combat planning.

It is impossible to say when commanders first started to surround themselves with advisors and assistants. The first of these were probably relatives and trusted friends who extended the commander's span of control by acting as couriers, delivering orders and receiving reports from subordinate commanders. Later, assistants wrote down orders, decisions and reports for official records. Then, as now, they helped to free commanders from onerous administration tasks.

At some point commanders recognized a need for a more formal organization to help with the increasingly complex business of command. Again it must be emphasized that the requirement, then and now, was for experts to assist and advise, *not* to share the responsibilities of command.

Certain staff functions were performed for commanders as far back as the Egyptian pharaohs, 1600 years before Christ. Alexander the Great used a staff system developed by his father, Philip of Macedon. In his records, Alexander referred to his chief of staff, adjutant-aids, engineers, supply officers, provost marshals, hospitals, and communications. More than two thousand years later these same staff positions can be found in the headquarters of most senior commanders.

Our modern US staff organization and procedures can be traced to the seventeenth-century army of the Swedish King, Gustavus IV. The Swedish staff organization was copied by many foreign armies and eventually evolved into the Prussian staff system and, later, the famous Great German General Staff.

The US Army has used several different staff organizations. General George Washington entered the Revolutionary War with a staff of four major elements—an adjutant general, a quartermaster, a chief engineer and a commissary general of musters. In the Civil War, Generals Grant and McClellan appointed chiefs of staff to relieve them of the detailed tasks of supervising their expanding headquarters. In 1903, the US adopted the general staff system for use at the National Command level. Staff organization at the lower levels remained unstandardized. Then, during World War I, General Pershing directed the use of the general staff system for all American Expeditionary Forces down to and including division level. The division staff, which consisted of three major elements (personnel, supply, and operations and training) was headed by a chief of staff.

In 1921, the general staff system was officially adopted for division level command and above. Similar staff organizations have since been prescribed down to the battalion level. The general staff system is still used by the Army and, with some modifications, by the other services.

From the very beginning of organized warfare, technological advances must have caused some increases in the numbers of advisors surrounding commanders. However, technical knowledge expanded slowly in the civilian community and in the military. The growth of staffs through most of the nearly two thousand years of their known existence has been extremely slow. During the last one hundred years the expansion has accelerated.

The US Civil War could be called the world's first modern war. New equipment allowed commanders' to hit the enemy with greater firepower in greater quantities and from greater distances, and to support large operations farther from established logistical bases. Breech-loading rifles and cannon, machine guns and incendiary shells were added to the arsenals of both sides. Electrically exploded mines were introduced and searchlights became available to illuminate the battlefield. Armor was attached to warships, and submarines made a somewhat abortive appearance. Railroads were used for the first time to supply and resupply personnel and physical resources to the battlefront. Even this partial list of new equipment should imply the need for enlargement of the staff.

The staff expansion that began at the time of the Civil War, reflecting advances in weaponry and the introduction of more sophisticated equipment, was only the beginning of the staff explosion to come. The half-century between the end of the Civil War and the beginning of World War I was one of great scientific and technological advances. Most historians discuss that era in terms of the giant strides made in the industrialization of the United States. These advances were reflected to some extent in military equipment available during the first World War, but not to the point of completely replacing the old.

At the end of World War I, the United States Army was a mixture of the old and the new. The 1922 edition of the *Tables of Organization for Infantry Divisions* (1923 reprint) authorized 406 trucks of various sizes and 3557 draft horses and mules. Fifty-nine automobiles supplemented nearly 2000 riding horses, 191 motorcycles and 190 bicycles. The motorized age had arrived, but the horses had not departed and would not depart for another twenty years.

Among the new items shown in the 1923 Tables of Organization and Equipment, two were destined to change the course of ground warfare and to proliferate commanders' needs for advisors and assistants. The 1923 Infantry division had thirteen planes and twenty-four tanks.

This was a small beginning compared to the 88 helicopters and more than 200 tanks authorized in a 1972 division with four tank battalions assigned. It would be even less impressive when compared to the 150 to 250 tanks in the 1972 armored division, or with the fifty helicopters in a single Assault Support Helicopter Battalion in 1972. It was sufficient, however, to demonstrate the potential of these novel devices to increase firepower and, perhaps more importantly, to add to battlefield mobility. It also demonstrated the cost of armor and airpower in added support requirements.

Naturally, more advisors and assistants were needed to help commanders make maximum use of their new capabilities. Personnel requirements were expanded to include a completely new array of skills. Soldiers had to be trained to operate and maintain the new equipment and the weapons systems unique to air and track vehicles. The thirteen aircraft added about 230 personnel to the strength of the division: thirty-three in the division air service headquarters and its ancillary functions (photo, intelligence, etc.) and 200 in the single observation squadron.

The new skills demanded a new vocabulary—electricians, ignition mechanics, instrument repairmen, pilots and observers to name a few. The twenty-four tanks necessitated similar increases in personnel and support. Besides a handful of tank drivers, the tank company included mechanics and others with support skills, a unit strength of 151 men.

The added support personnel in the tank company were only part of the change. Additional skills were also added to the maintenance and supply elements of the division.

Still faced with the feeding and care of thousands of horses and mules, logisticians were now confronted with the insatiable appetites of petroleum-devouring animals. These mechanized beasts also had a weakness not found in horses and mules: their parts wore out and had to be replaced. As a new requirement placed upon a still largely horse-drawn logistics system, providing fuel and repair parts for the new mechanized equipment must have been a formidable problem indeed. Drayage vehicles, for example, still included nearly 1000 carts and wagons, as compared to only about 400 trucks. The trucks themselves, while adding to the transport capabilities, imposed significant added requirements of their own in the form of fuel and repair parts. The trucks also required trained maintenance personnel and operators. The arrival of tanks, airplanes, and other fuel-consuming vehicles multiplied commanders' combat capabilities but also multiplied the problems requiring advisors and assistants.

The added firepower and maneuverability provided by tanks and aircraft greatly increased flexibility. A commander could now choose from more courses of action to accomplish his mission. At the same time many new tasks associated with the equipment became pertinent to mission accomplishment. Now expertise was needed to analyze the mission, to determine the included tasks and to plan operations to maximize the advantages of the new equipment and use it to complement the old, conventional assets.

Resource evaluation also became more complex. Commanders had to consider, along with their requirements for the new items (aircraft, tanks and vehicles), the ability of the available personnel to operate and maintain them and the availability of fuel and repair parts to keep them moving. Plans exploiting the mobility of the tank and aircraft must still make full use of the slower infantry, horse-drawn artillery, and wagon-equipped support units.

The diversity of personnel requirements must have seemed staggering to the 1922 commanders. No longer was personnel a purely quantitative consideration. Besides the all-important riflemen, upon whose skill and numbers success and failure in war always ultimately depends, literally hundreds of technical and professional skills were required to operate, maintain and supply the equipment that supported them. Logistics had become an overridingly important factor in the commander's choice of courses of action and his plans for implementing the course selected. Staff expansion had begun in earnest.

Armies change little between wars, particularly when an army has just won "the war to end all wars". During the 1920's and most of the 1930's the United States Army changed to become smaller in numbers of personnel while its equipment dwindled and became obsolete.

In the late 1930's, with war impending, the trend reversed. Expansion of The Armed Forces was accompanied by concerted efforts to modernize equipment and tactics. Despite these belated efforts, World War II began with the Army equipped and staffed much as it had been at the end of the previous war.

Although the US Army had made only modest progress, worldwide scientific and technological advances had been swift. A vast array of new equipment and techniques was available and had been adopted by the armies of the major enemy countries, Germany and Japan. Both had taken advantage of new equipment and had developed powerful modern fighting forces. The US Army spent the early days of the war frantically trying to expand while at the same time introducing new equipment and training personnel in new techniques in an effort to catch up with the opponents and overcome their head start.

The Germans, in particular, had opened completely new vistas in warfare. *Panzer* (tank) forces were employed in highly mobile, massive *Blitzkrieg* (lightning warfare) tactics, striking deep into enemy territories, dividing and weakening opposing forces for more deliberate and systematic destruction by follow-on attacks on the fragments. The tank, a novel gadget little more than twenty years earlier during World War I, had come of age as probably the most decisive item of World War II ground equipment.

Both Germany and Japan had highly developed the other infant of the first World War, the airplane. There can be little doubt that the Japanese bombing of Pearl Harbor and the German raids on England and the Low Countries drastically influenced the war. The German *Luftwaffe* had expanded and extended the range of battlefield firepower and added to strategic mobility by delivering bombs to targets at great distances from the battlefield.

In the ground war both countries used close air support by bombers and fighter planes. The Germans used transport planes to deliver parachute troops in the successful vertical envelopment of fortified positions that would have taken months of seige to capture otherwise. The entire combat environment had changed, and the US faced gigantic tasks of preparation to cope with these new tactics.

Not only did staff requirements increase, but also many specialized commands were created to meet the needs for added equipment and new skills. Commands were organized to obtain and issue the flood of new items introduced into inventory. Commands also sprang up to train the personnel who would use and repair the items. Schools were organized to educate personnel in the many technical intricacies of the mechanized Army and to produce officer and enlisted leaders. Basic military staff considerations remained the same, however, despite their increasing complexity.

The commander's tasks of analyzing, evaluating, planning and supervising were still the same ones confronted by the very first military leader:

What is my mission, and what are the included tasks?
What are the outside influences?
Do I have enough properly skilled, motivated people?
Do I have enough physical resources?
What course of action best applies my personnel and resources most economically and with highest chances of success?

World War II added another dimension to military operations and new facets to the need for advisors and assistants. In the Pacific, Japanese forces were firmly entrenched on hundreds of islands stretched over thousands of miles and protected by strong air and naval support. The Germans held all of Western Europe and could be approached only by a water and airborne invasion over the beaches.

Only concerted and closely coordinated air, sea, and ground efforts could defeat such formidable enemies. It became essential therefore, that Army commanders have the assistance of staffs who understood not only their own ground equipment and Army tactics but also the equipment, techniques and capabilities of their sister services. Joint staffs of ground, sea and air experts were developed for the commanders of all US services and in some instances, for the military services of the allied countries. Even in single service units such as Army or Marine Corps divisions, this additional demand for professional qualifications resulted in larger and more varied expertise on the commanders' staffs.

Because the world enjoyed only brief interludes of peace in the twenty-five years between the end of the second World War and the 1970's, modernization of equipment and tactics continued, and the US Army remained relatively large rather than atrophying, as in previous eras of peace. Although no major outbreak of hostilities occurred between the world's major powers, with a few brief exceptions armed combat was in progress somewhere in the world during the entire period.

The United States engaged in the two major military operations in Korea and South Vietnam, each with its own peculiar operating environment, enemy capabilities, organization and tactics. The national interests reflected in the military objectives of each incident were quite different from the all-out warfare of the two world wars. There were new requirements for specialized equipment and revised tactics to meet the challenges of those new combat environments. The most important factor contributing to military progress was the advent of the nuclear age and the distrust and apprehension which developed between the western nations and the Soviet Union and its allies.

The Cold War, with its arms race between the United States and the Communist Bloc nations, caused constant additions of new equipment and techniques into the Armed Forces. Battlefield mobility took a major leap forward with the introduction of helicopters in sufficient numbers to move entire brigades and their equipment from place to place on the battlefield within minutes. These same aircraft also added to commanders' capability to observe the battle progress first-hand from airborne command posts and to make instant decisions influencing the action. This accelerated command reaction and increased maneuverability required faster and infinitely more accurate staff work to provide commanders with up-to-the-minute advice.

Other developments also have added to both the capabilities and the problems of command. Weaponry, in particular, has advanced; and along with it the communications devices needed to control the added firepower. The most terrifying new development is the possible use of nuclear warheads as part of ground command tactical arsenals and the introduction of extremely devastating strategic weapons. The destructive power of conventional weapons has also increased.

The bombing of cities during World War II seemed to have approached maximum destructiveness. By the close of the Vietnamese encounter, however, the bombing capabilities of World War II had been dwarfed. Relatively small numbers of US bombers could deliver greater explosive power in a very short period than was delivered by the aircraft of all combatants during the entire second World War. The close air support planes operating in support of our ground troops had more firepower than the largest bombers that existed at the end of World War II.

A wide variety of missiles and rockets have also been developed. Lighter infantry weapons with higher rates of fire have replaced the older heavier ones, and the ammunition is smaller and easier to supply. Computers, teletype, communications satellites and television have been added to the communications equipment necessary to control the accelerated combat pace, and radar and number of other guidance systems control the multiplied firepower.

Behind the tactical commander, the business of command has also grown more complex. Obtaining, transporting, repairing and maintaining the many items of sophisticated equipment and replacing those which become inoperable at the rate demanded by modern warfare caused the creation of logistical organizations of previously unimagined proportions. The commanders of these organizations require virtual corps of experts in the many items now in the Army inventory, as well as in the storage, transportation and issue procedures required by such mammoth operations. Teaching personnel in the constantly changing and expanding equipment field the techniques for employing physical assets is a major endeavor. It requires special command networks and highly expert staffs of advisors and assistants to assure the US Army's readiness to respond quickly to military requirements ranging from small "brushfire" actions in smaller countries to all-out-nuclear general warfare.

The business of the military has long since passed the simple stage of resources and tactics where commanders could supervise all aspects of their missions alone, making decisions on the basis of their professional knowledge of their equipment and their skill in applying resources to tactics. Despite commanders' increased dependence on others for their success, their authority has not been diluted, or their personal responsibilities lessened. It is to commanders that missions are assigned. They alone must make the decisions concerning methods of accomplishment, and they alone take responsibility for mission success or failure.

Foremost in the minds of officers approaching their first staff assignments must be the fact that the staff is an entity and that they, as members of that entity, exist only to assure the success of their commanders' missions. The staff and each of its members must direct its full energies to that goal.

In these days of complex equipment and sophisticated techniques, the commander's success rests almost entirely on the shoulders of those who advise and assist him. If the mission succeeds, the staff can feel justifiable pride in its achievements. If the mission is less than successful, each member must feel a sense of personal failure.

The individual staff officer must recognize the impact of his personal proficiency, and his ability to translate that proficiency into tangible results, on the command mission. The success of any commander largely depends on the skills of his individual staff officers. To fully understand this dependency and the skills and techniques which must be mastered to meet the challenge of this personal responsibility, staff officers must first understand the organization within which they work and how the elements of that organization must function together to extend the commander's professional capabilities. Without this broad understanding, no officer can bring his efforts to bear with full effectiveness on the problems facing his commander.

The Major Staff Elements

Four concerns are of overriding importance to every commander's mission: sufficient numbers of qualified and motivated people, timely and accurate information about factors that could influence the mission, adequate physical resources with which to do the job and planning and directing the operations involved. Basically, all Army staff organizations are built around those four areas of command concern: people, information, things and operations.

However, as armies became more complex, certain of these four major areas began to exceed the control span of single staff elements. Specialization, particularly in the area of resources, became so significant that new special staff elements were created. At the same time, increased complexity and sophistication of equipment, doctrines and procedures necessitated expansion of the commanders' offices and of their personal staffs, consisting of advisors and assistants reporting directly to the commanders. With this expansion came the need for assistants to help manage and control increasingly large and unweildy staffs. Collectively, these developments have led to fairly standard army staff organizations, usually consisting of the following elements:

1. the Commander and his assistants or deputies
2. the Commander's personal staff
3. the Chief of Staff
4. major staff elements (sometimes called the *coordinating staff*)
5. special staff elements. The organization, internal function, and mutual relationships of these elements and how they work together are vital to an understanding of staff operations.

Modern Staff Organizations

In 1903, the US Army reorganized at the national level into the general staff system, patterned after the famous "German general staff". During the first World War, General Pershing extended the general staff organization down to division level in the American Expeditionary Forces. The War Department later approved this extension of the system and directed similar staff organizations for all Army units down to and including battalions.

In its original form, the general staff consisted of four major elements: G-1 (personnel), G-2 (intelligence), G-3 (operations) and G-4 (supply). Special staff elements were added as needed. When the system was extended to units and activities commanded by officers below the grade of general, *S* was substituted for *G*. For instance, S-1, personnel; S-2, intelligence; S-3, operations; and S-4, supply.

These designations are still in use, but some commands have added major elements to meet modern requirements. Special, functional commands have altered the designations to better describe staff duties, relationships and authorities.

In Army tactical units, staff element chiefs retain the *G* or *S* titles, but joint commands consisting of more than one service normally substitute the letter *J* using the normal general staff numbering system to designate element responsibilities. Nontactical organizations may use several titles for their staff element chiefs and, depending on the functional nature of their missions, may consider as major staff elements areas of interest other than those included in the standard General Staff organization.

In some functional commands, staff element chiefs are appointed deputies or assistants to their chiefs of staff. This elevated status gives, or at least infers, greater authority to act for the chief of staff, with attendant increases in flexibility and independence. Even more authority is implied when staff element chiefs are designated directors. Usually some decision-making privileges are specifically delegated to them by their commanders.

Actually, titles matter little. Whether a personnel officer is called G-1, J-1, Deputy Chief of Staff for Personnel, Assistant Chief of Staff for Personnel, or Director of Personnel, the job remains the same: to assist and advise the commander on all matters concerning human resources. Special-purpose, functional commanders construct their staffs to fit their peculiar needs. Such staffs could consist of major elements normally included as subelements on most staffs. A commander responsible only for logistical support might well consider his engineer, transportation officer, supply expert and maintenance supervisor as major staff element chiefs.

In people-oriented commands, the personnel officer might be replaced with several more specialized experts in such fields as recruiting, morale and welfare, awards, reinlistments, etc. The possibilities are too numerous to mention here. However, two new major staff elements have now been added to virtually all major staffs: comptrollers, and communications and electronics. A third, Civil Affairs, is usually added to tactical staffs in combat situations. These additions were required to help commanders cope with the increasing complexity of military operations.

Comptrollers specialize in the control of funds and the scientific management of resources. Communications and electronics experts assist commanders with the vast array of modern communications services, and civil affairs experts specialize in one of the most sensitive areas of personnel management: local populations and their governments. In most large headquarters, the general staff consists of the four basic elements plus a comptroller, a communications and electronics/officer and in theaters of operations a civil affairs officer.

Special Staffs

As the designation indicates, special staff officers have narrower, more specialized areas of interest than those of the major staff elements. They are important members of the team and, like the general staff, are divided into elements keyed to certain fields of expertise. With rare exceptions, these specialities can be identified with one of the major areas of command interest: people, intelligence, operations or logistics. The term *special staff* in no way demeans these experts. To the contrary, it identifies them as professionals in difficult and complex fields such as medicine, law, engineering, law enforcement, administration, religion, etc.

Commanders differ in their methods of using special staffs. Although broken down into separate areas of specialization, most special staffs are concerned with the same activities and considerations that occupy the major staff elements. For example, religious experts, chaplains, are obviously people-oriented. Their advice and assistance concentrates on the soldiers' spiritual welfare and, properly used, can greatly enhance human productivity. Engineers and their professional and technical assistants are closely involved in the flow of material assets. They are responsible for the routes of communications over which flow materials of war, for housing, for storage and maintenance facilities.

Because of the close relationship between the special staff functions and the four basic command concerns, many commanders place each special staff office under the supervision of its related major staff element. This arrangement serves several purposes. For one thing it narrows the span of control. If each special staff element in a large headquarters functioned independently, the chief of staff could have as many as twenty separate elements reporting directly to him. This would be an almost unmanageable supervisory load. Also, concentrating all related actions under one supervisor assures coordinated efforts and unity of purpose.

Except when a specific organization is directed by higher headquarters, commanders have the prerogative of using their staffs as they choose. As missions change, situations fluctuate, and priorities shift, commanders often change the internal, reporting and supervisory procedures within their staffs.

Chaplains and engineers for example, are special staff elements that are often used differently in different commands. Depending on the significance of their actions in a particular mission, a commander might choose to place the chaplain under the personnel staff element chief and the engineer under the logistician: or he could choose to make one or both into separate special staff elements reporting directly through the chief of staff.

In extreme circumstances, such as a period of serious morale problems, or when a particularly sensitive construction project is in difficulty, a commander could pass over all intervening supervisors and have one or both report directly to him.

It must be stressed that coordination of the special staff is no less vital than coordination of the major staff elements. Whether acting independently or through the personnel officer, chaplains must coordinate with personnel. Their programs must mesh with other planned action for maximum moral and spiritual benefits. They must recognize the realities of mission requirements and the sometimes unpleasant surroundings in which military men must do their jobs.

Similarly, engineering resources must be used with maximum effectiveness and economy. Such effectiveness and economy can be achieved only through close coordination with logisticians, personnel staffs and operators to assure that construction capabilities and materials are allocated according to the priorities set for meeting many requirements: housing, warehouses, hospitals, airfields and landing strips, roads, etc.

Personal Staffs

One last portion of the staff must be considerd, the personal staff. These experts work directly under the commander and assist and advise him on those matters upon which only he can act. Their recommendations and the flow of information between them and the commander often concern sensitive matters that are of interest only to the commander and to such other staff members as he chooses to inform.

This does not mean that these staff experts are not members of the team. While the line of authority and the flow of information between a commander and his personal staff often bypasses the chief of staff and sometimes even deputy commanders, only in rare instances does a commander actually exclude the chief of staff from the flow of information or deny him the authority to direct the efforts of that portion of the staff.

A commander may, however, exclude the chief from certain types of actions. For example, inspectors general and staff judge advocates might be directed to bring all derogatory matters concerning general officers directly to the commander, completely skipping the chief of staff. The commander would then decide to what extent the chief and other staff members should become involved. On all matters not specifically excluded by command directive, the personal staff works within the same pattern of coordination and cooperation as the rest of the staff. They are also available to assist other staff elements.

Organization Charts

A favorite device of military men for graphic display of organizational structures, lines of authority, and internal relationships is the organization chart, commonly referred to as a wiring diagram. These easy-to-read guides are normally found on the top of almost every desk in all headquarters. Chart 3.1 shows the skeletonized staff structure discussed to this point. The black lines represent lines of authority and channels of information between the commander and each element of his staff.

Not shown, but assumed by all experienced officers, are the formal and informal channels for exchange of information and coordination among the staff elements. These are all-important. Each action, even seemingly insignificant ones, must be coordinated among all interested staff elements and among suborganizations within each element. Staff officers must constantly bear in mind that although the staff consists of several elements, subelements and many action officers, it is a single entity. Every action must reflect the best judgement of the entire staff, not the best judgement of a single element or even of several elements.

As the black line indicates, the major staff elements are equal in authority, and the flow information melds into a single line both to and from the commander. Directives, information and queries from the commander are addressed to the staff—singular. Information from the staff comes from the organization—not from its individual elements.

The sample organization chart also demonstrates three different methods used to control and supervise special staff elements.

1. The adjutant general's office is shown as subordinate to the personnel element. It is supervised by, receives direction from, and reports to the personnel staff element.
2. The engineer reports to two elements. He is supervised by and reports to the chief of staff, but because of his close relationship with all facets of physical resources and logistical services, he coordinates his actions with the staff logistician.
3. All other special staff officers are supervised directly by the chief of staff.

The chart shows only the major subdivisions of the staff. In practice, each element would be subdivided into smaller elements for closer supervision of detailed operations and to focus expertise on specific functional areas.

Chart 3.1
Typical Staff Organization

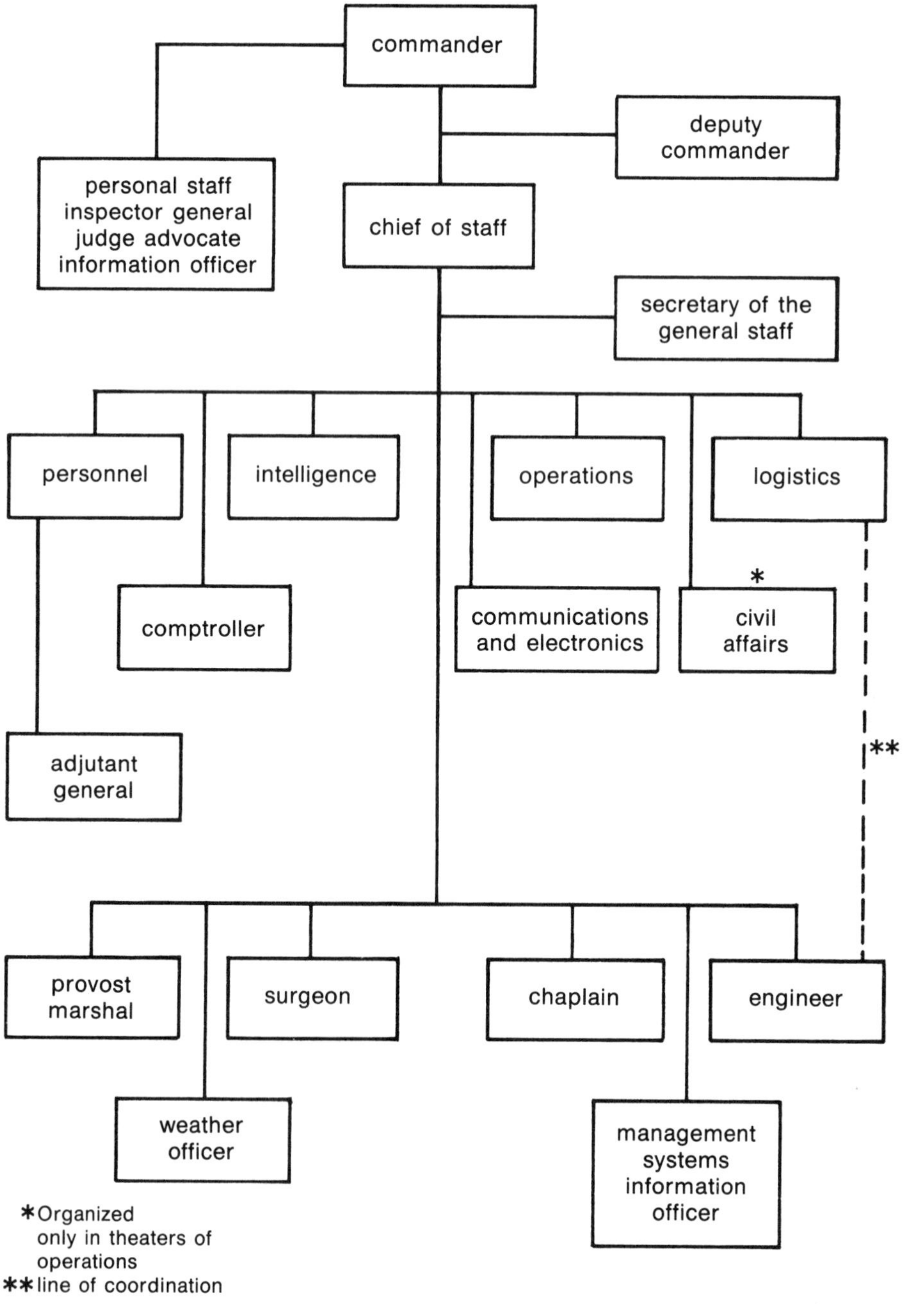

```
                              commander
                                  |
                    +-------------+-------------+
                    |             |             |
            personal staff        |        deputy
           inspector general      |       commander
            judge advocate        |
          information officer  chief of staff
                                  |
                                  +----- secretary of the
                                  |       general staff
                                  |
        +----------+----------+----------+
        |          |          |          |
    personnel  intelligence  operations  logistics
        |                       |           |
    comptroller            communications  civil*
        |                  and electronics  affairs ----+
    adjutant                                            |
    general                                             |**
                                                        |
        +----------+----------+----------+              |
        |          |          |          |              |
     provost    surgeon    chaplain   engineer  <-------+
     marshal       |                     |
                weather              management
                officer               systems
                                    information
                                       officer
```

*Organized only in theaters of operations
**line of coordination

In a theater of operations a commander responsible for extensive transportation activity might look to his logistician (G-4, J-4, Deputy Chief of Staff, Logistics, Assistant Chief of Staff Logistics, Director of Logistics, etc.) for staff supervision of transportation activities. The logistician would probably organize a transportation subelement (division, office, branch, etc.) with a transportation expert in charge.

Because of the complexity of the transportation problem, the transportation officer might further subdivide his shop into branches such as highway or motor transportation, sea movement, port operations, air movement, passenger service, household goods, etc. Some of these branches could even be further subdivided—*port operations* into *water* and *air,* for example. The movement of petroleum, ammunition and other sensitive items could require a special organization for each. Passengers could be divided into troop (or unit) movements and individual travel.

Chart 3.2 illustrates this detailed organization. For a thorough understanding of typical staff organizations, it is necessary to examine each element in considerable detail.

The Commander

The commander is not a member of the staff. However, the commander's block on an organizational chart, like other blocks, is occupied by more than one person. Except for the commander, these people are members of the staff. They are, in fact, important members, because they link the commander with the rest of the staff. These immediate associates of the commander who share his office are of different grades and skills and vary in their official and personal relationships to the commander and in their relationships with the rest of the staff.

Commanders of large organizations normally have at least one deputy, or assistant commander, who is empowered to act in the commander's name in most matters. To the staff, the policies, desires and directives of a deputy or assistant bear exactly the same weight as those of the commander. By the same criteria, the loyalty of the staff extends to deputies and assistants as it does to the commander.

Aides

Some official publications classify aides to the commander as members of the personal staff. While this may be technically correct, "members of the official family" would be more aptly descriptive. In the military profession, the official and personal lives of the members and their families often seem to meld practically into one.

(Text continued on page 29)

Chart 3.2
Sample Subdivision of Staff Element

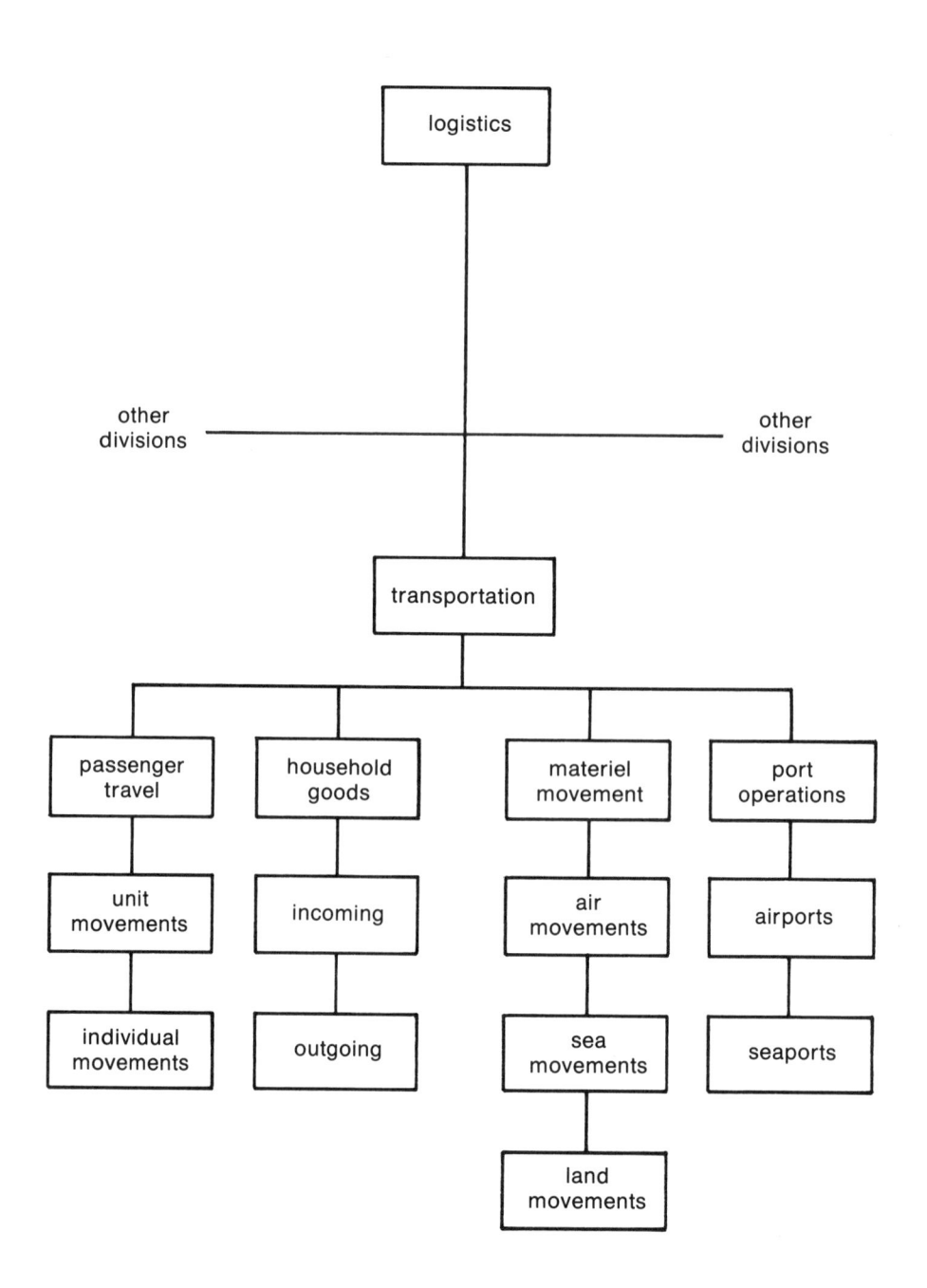

```
                        logistics
                            |
 other divisions ———————————+——————————— other divisions
                            |
                      transportation
                            |
        ┌───────────────┬───────────────┬───────────────┐
  passenger         household        materiel           port
   travel            goods           movement        operations
      |                |                |                |
    unit            incoming           air            airports
  movements                         movements            |
      |                |                |                |
 individual         outgoing           sea            seaports
 movements                          movements
                                       |
                                      land
                                    movements
```

Although some exceptions can be found, most military men, particularly those who become commanders, and their families share complete dedication to the service of their country. In the office, in the home, on vacation, on the golf course or at a party, the military mind (or conversation) seldom strays for long from official responsibilities and problems.

Aides, as the title implies, are closely associated with the commander both in the office and in his social life. In this position, they become intimately familiar with the commander's personal views, his likes and dislikes, his philosophy and his official and personal concerns with specific aspects of current and future actions. Because of this, aides occupy a special position in the staff structure. It would be oversimplification to group them with those personal staff officers who assist the commander only with his official duties.

A word, a hint from an aide can be of invaluable assistance to an alert staff officer. A chance remark by an aide that his general disliked formal briefings to the point of nausea led one of the authors to an enjoyable official relationship with a lieutenant general known throughout the Army as the military's most expert staff officer and as one of the Army's most capable and demanding commanders. Thereafter, briefings for the general were scheduled as informal office presentations. Hopefully, he never realized that the seemingly impromptu, relaxed, desk-side presentations were achieved only by greater research, more preparation, and longer hours of secret rehearsal than would have been needed for several formal presentations from the podium.

Other denizens of the commander's block are secretaries, special assistants for particular projects, drivers and in some instances, depending on the commander's preferences, the command sergeant major. Each of these people occupies a position of trust and enjoys the complete confidence of the commander. While their positions give them no additional authority, their opinions and advice often reflect the policies and personal preferences of the commander and would be ignored by only the least intelligent staff officer.

Command Sergeants Major

Commanders vary in their use of their senior enlisted advisor. A few commanders (hopefully, a disappearing type) relegate their command sergeants major to administrative positions or, even worse, set them up with well furnished, ornate offices and ignore them completely. Most successful commanders, however, recognize and make full use of the skills and experience of this valuable assistant. A young staff officer may find the sergeant major in his new headquarters functioning in any of several roles. A wise staff officer will take full advantage of the abilities of this senior enlisted man, regardless of his official role in the headquarter's hierarchy.

Consider the potential value of a sergeant major's advice and assistance in but a few situations of staff interest. To the personnel officer he represents a first-hand expert on the people who must accomplish the mission. He knows what they like and what they dislike, how much work they can do, what factors raise and lower their morale, and the conditions which build and destroy esprit. Above all he is a proven, on-the-ground manager of personnel resources. To the logistician the sergeant major is an equally valuable advisor on the supplies, equipment and services needed for the morale, welfare and recreation of the soldiers. In planning operations he is the leading expert on the temper and motivation of the most critical resource—people.

The Chief of Staff

Like the commander, the chief shares his organizational box with others: the assistant chiefs of staff, the secretary of the general staff, the protocol officers, the special project officers, the secretaries, the administrative assistants and others. Like the others who are closely associated with the commander, these assistants gain keen insight into the chief's methods of operation and his personal eccentricities concerning formats, words, phrases, briefings, etc. They also know which current actions he considers to be overridingly important. Their opinions are to be respected, their advice and assistance sought after and their confidence and respect treasured. Unlike the commander, however, the chief of staff is a staff member, albeit a very dominant one.

Early in the staff expansion, commanders began to realize that even the best staffs were difficult to unify. As a result, commanders were spending much of their time managing their staffs' efforts and attempting to identify best courses of action from conflicting recommendations of individual staff elements and from action officers within the staff elements. To overcome this problem and to maximize the staff effectiveness by eliminating long, unproductive "Yes, it is!" "No, it isn't!" type arguments, commanders began appointing an overall staff supervisor, the chief of staff.

As shown on the chart, the chief of staff is between the commander and the rest of the staff in the line of authority and the channel of information. Although most commanders use their chiefs in just that capacity, a word of caution might be appropriate at this point. Commanders differ in as many respects and are subject to as many idiosyncracies as are other humans. They employ their chiefs differently. Some conduct all actions and contact their staffs only through the chief, others sometimes skip him to work directly with staff members.

Staff members must understand and respond to their commander's desires and work according to his policies. They must also bear in mind the sensitive position of the chief of staff and his responsibilities for supervising the staff and managing its efforts. He can do this only if kept fully informed. Each staff member must see that he receives information. When the chief is skipped, the staff officers involved must be sure that he is informed after the fact.

Command Groups

While the command group is not shown on organization charts and is seldom referred to in official publications, it is important for staff officers to understand that the commander, his deputies and their assistants, and the chief of staff and his organization usually function as a single entity: the command group. It is from this group that missions, tasks, directives and guidance flow to the staff and to this group that the completed staff work returns.

Internal procedures vary within each headquarters, but in all headquarters those who work with the commander, his deputies, and his chief of staff form a united group, dedicated to making the commander's job easier. They also make the staff's job easier by providing clear guidance, relaying policies and keeping the staff informed. Such group operation could give the false impression that guidance and instructions emanate from comparatively junior personnel. Experienced staff officers know better.

Younger members should not be misled. Papers returned by a secretary, a noncommissioned officer or a junior officer for correction, revision, or complete rewrite should be accepted as if returned by the commander personally. In the first place, it may have been. In the second place, the corrections are probably required to meet standards set by the commander, his deputies or the chief of staff. In any instance, if the paper can be improved, it matters little who discovered its shortcomings.

The Major Staff Elements

Personnel

The general staff custom of numbering major staff elements from one through four in no way indicates relative importance among the elements. However, the number-one position of the personnel specialist (S-1, G-1, J-1) is not inappropriate. It indicates the key importance of people and commanders' awareness of their moral and regulatory responsibilities to care for this resource above all others.

Commanders are first responsible for accomplishing their assigned missions. This responsibility takes precedence over all other considerations. Second only to the mission, and far overshadowing all other considerations, is their responsibility for the welfare of the fellow humans who fire the weapons, operate the machines, build the roads and repair the equipment. This is an inviolate rule, scrupulously upheld by successful military leaders, commanders, staff officers, and noncommissioned leaders.

The job of the personnel staff officer has three major facets: (1) assuring that sufficient numbers of people are on hand to accomplish the mission, (2) making sure that the appropriate specialists are available to operate and maintain the many items of equipment required for even simple operations, and (3) maintaining the health, morale and welfare of the people who accomplish the mission. Each facet merits discussion. None of these responsibilities are simple. All require highly trained specialists.

Strengths. Just understanding personnel strengths is a challenge. Army units and activities are authorized specific numbers of people. The upper limits of those authorizations are established by two types of documents: (1) Tables of Distribution and Allowances (TDA) for some nontactical activities, such as headquarters, depots, and maintenance activities, and (2) Tables of Organization and Equipment (TOE) for most tactical military units.

TOE organizations consist of military personnel and normally have no civilian employees. Even so, maintaining them at full authorized strength is no easy matter. Normal enlistments are for three years, and officers seldom remain at one station for more than three years. Consequently, considering only normal rotation at least one-third of any organization's total officer and enlisted strength, would need replacement every year.

If this were the only factor to consider, the personnel officer's job would still be far from simple. Few industries could meet the challenge of replacing the entire work force, including supervisors, every three years. In the military, with its chain of personnel experts, the problem should theoretically be somewhat more manageable.

Consider an organization authorized 16,500 personnel. If the losses were envenly spaced, personnel experts could predict requirements for 5500 people each year, roughly 460 each month, or about 115 per week. In fact, these calculations could be made in Washington, D.C., and the replacement flow from recruiter to units could be automatic. Unfortunately, the process is less simple. Other factors must be considered.

The loss of personnel is far from an even flow and, with some exceptions, far from predictable. At the extremely high levels personnel experts with computerized data, can determine loss rates with some degree of reliability as they apply to the entire Army over long periods of time. Applying this general trend to specific small subordinate units is tricky.

Assume, for instance, that computerized data available to the Department of the Army indicates that 20% of the Army's strength will require replacement during a given one-year period. Barring unexpected changes in national and international affairs, the prediction probably would prove reasonably accurate. Army recruiters would know, within acceptable limits, their overall goals for that twelve-month period. At the high level in the organization, the overall requirement could be refined to monthly and even weekly requirements. At the lower levels, predictions become less precise. The many factors that cause losses apply unequally to different types of units and are affected by many influences. At the national level, experts could predict the extent that reinlistments would offset losses of young soldiers completing their first enlistment. An organization located in an undesirable area, undergoing extremely rigorous training or anticipating movement to a combat area might find the reenlistment rate well below the national average.

Other factors—illness, retirement, criminal convictions, unauthorized departures (AWOL and desertion), and requests for transfers—are also influenced by local conditions. Even so, personnel officers could master these challenges relatively easily in maintaining only the bulk requirement. The problem really only becomes difficult when qualitative factors are added.

Grades. A division personnel officer whose organization is located in an undesirable area (as divisions often are) might quite accurately predict 40% division losses during an approaching twelve-month period. But which forty percent? What grades? What skills? Even at the national level these are bothersome questions. At the lower levels they become extremely complex and are the real heart of the personnel expert's job of maintaining an effective force.

The infantry division's TOE includes nineteen separate grades, from major general to private soldier. This one qualitative factor adds entirely new dimensions to the personnel officer's problems. First-sergeant replacements would be of little use to units needing privates. Majors would be most unhappy as platoon leaders. Second Lieutenants, on the other hand, might be extremely happy as battalion operations officers, but their effectiveness probably would be less than perfect. The purely quantitative replacement requirement therefore must be considered not only as a total but by grades.

Actually, personnel experts can meet even this challenge with some degree of accuracy. Using historical data developed over periods of several years, they identify patterns which help to predict future losses and to estimate future needs for replacements by grades. Such errors as may occur are unlikely to cripple an organization. When necessary, junior personnel usually function with surprising effectiveness in positions designed for more experienced persons. However, the grade spread does make the problem more complex. Personnel experts must not only predict numbers of losses, they must refine their estimates by grade. And the complications have only just begun.

Skills. Commanders can no longer be concerned only with combat soldiers. Perhaps they never could. The most primitive weaponry required expert manufacture, repair and replacement. Today virtual hoards of experts are required to obtain, operate, maintain and replace the gadgetry of warfare.

The 1967 version of Army Regulation 611-201 lists various enlisted military occupational specialties in the US Army. Included are the old standards so familiar to commanders: infantry man, artillery crewchief, pioneer, cook, etc. Also included are many which would have been unrecognizable to Civil War commanders and personnel officers and some which would have been useless as late as the Korean War: missile technician, computer specialist, radar operator, etc.

The real challenge to the personnel expert in today's Army is not just to maintain the proper numbers of people of the proper grades but to obtain and maintain a force that includes the proper mixture of the many experts required for even the least complicated of military operations. Grade imbalances and even shortages in total strength become insignificant when compared to the frustration of having an organization that has 100% strength and good grade balance but is incapable of doing its job because essential skills are missing.

Consider once again the engineer commander directed to build the river crossing and its two roads. Assuming this to be an engineer combat battalion, part of an infantry division, it would be authorized roughly 800 people, ranging in grade from the lieutenant colonel battalion commander, to privates in the squads.

Grade imbalances would be extremely undesirable, but could be overcome. At considerable cost to morale, officers and noncommissioned officers could function in the lower grade jobs and, as has often been proven in warfare, junior personnel can rise to positions of considerable responsibility when forced to do so. Shortages, also undesirable, could be overcome by harder work. An understrength force with overages and shortages in certain grades could build the bridge and the roads, but the absence of essential skills could make tasks extremely diffiicult or, in extreme cases, impossible.

Engineer battalions in the infantry divisions were authorized some forty different enlisted skills in the 1970 TOE. The list appended at the end of this chapter demonstrates the diversity of those skills.

Obviously, road construction would be impossible if such skilled personnel as heavy equipment operators, truck drivers, etc., were lacking. The personnel officer's job then is to assure the assignment of the proper numbers of people in the appropriate grades and, of overriding importance, with the necessary skills. The commander's concern with people is the same today as it was 10,000 years ago:

Do I have enough people?
Are they proficient with their equipment?
Are they motivated to perform at their maximum capabilities?

The primitive warrior's equipment was simple. The necessary skills were those required by daily survival. Today a commander must consider many skills and the unity of purpose which might motivate a primitive culture cannot be counted on in the modern world. Fighting men have become as complex and individualized in their needs as the machinery they operate.

Motivation (Recreation, Welfare and Morale). From the beginning of warfare it must have been necessary to assure the welfare of the troops so that they would remain motivated to give their utmost to the job at hand. In recent years this facet of people management has become much more complex. The technological advances that have added equipment to the military inventory have been matched by the addition of new convenience, comfort and recreational items in American homes even at the lower income levels. Young men coming into the Army today expect to continue to enjoy those comforts, conveniences and recreational opportunities during their military service. The modern soldier requires much more in the way of morale, welfare and recreational attention than did his counterpart of even a few years ago—at least those requirements are now better recognized.

This is not to say that modern soldiers are incapable of or unwilling to endure austerity and hardships when necessary. The conduct of our soldiers in South Vietnam established beyond doubt that those young men were as good, perhaps better, than any generation that ever manned the United States Army. When possible, however, the modern soldier expects and deserves the amenities enjoyed by his civilian counterpart.

Soldiers who believe and can see evidence that their commanders are sensitive to their needs and are doing all that is possible to assure the soldier's comfort and well being are eager to put forth their very best efforts toward accomplishing the commanders' missions. Soliders who feel that their commanders are indifferent to their needs are unlikely to be deeply concerned with the mission. Personnel officers must, therefore, establish and supervise programs throughout their commands that promote maximum care of the people. At the same time they must be careful that in their concern with happiness they do not lose sight of mission requirements.

Morale, welfare and recreation have become a somewhat controversial area. At the one extreme are the bleeding hearts who would relax discipline to the point that the soldier's life would be completely unhampered by bothersome regulations. These well-intentioned persons would provide every possible comfort, creating virtual country club environments with each individual doing only those jobs which he considered pleasant. Obviously, this extreme would be quite popular with a large number of very junior enlisted men, and equally unpopular with commanders and supervisors trying to produce results.

Unyielding disciplinarians at the other extreme consider any concession to the troops beyond feeding, housing and pay to be coddling. These people would substitute work and training for recreation, minimize off-duty time and exhaust the soldiers to a point that comfort and convenience would hardly be missed. This approach may have worked well when the average soldier had lived much the same spartan life at home and when his education and training had prepared him to expect little more in the civilian community. It is now passé. Neither extreme can be accepted, but identifying the middle course is most difficult. It must balance the needs of the men with the realities of mission requirements and be economically feasible.

The optimum program differs with each situation and depends on work and training requirements and on the facilities available. Some aspects, however, are more or less standard. The activities appended are those found on most Army installations in the United States. Although most of them will also be found on overseas bases, their size and scope are likely to be reduced to match the conditions existing at the installation.

Morale and welfare activities demonstrate the interrelationship of responsibilities among the staff elements. Several staff elements contribute to this vital aspect of command responsibility. In addition to the services normally supervised by the personnel staff, other staff elements provide personal services that affect the morale, welfare and productivity of the people resource. Food, provided by the logistician, is a major consideration. In today's Army all commanders are vitally concerned with the quality and variety of food served and the environment in which it is served. Medical attention and the personal touch with which it is presented also concern commanders.

The recreational, welfare and morale aspects of the personnel officer's job may well be the most complex of his entire function in today's Army. Even a casual glance at the wide scope of activities which constitute the average program at an established installation indicates the large number of experts who must assist the personnel officer in this area of his job—athletic experts to plan and supervise sports programs, librarians to operate libraries, community affairs and social science specialists, plus innumerable other experts are essential to supervise these activities. Welfare and recreation become even more important and more challenging in remote areas where civilian community activities are totally missing.

The personnel staff's job is obviously a key one. Conceivably, a commander could accomplish his tasks with little or no equipment, depending only on the determination, strength and natural resourcefulness of the American soldier; but without people, the most sophisticated equipment is of little use.

The complexities of maintaining adequate forces of properly skilled and well motivated personnel and caring for personnel needs far outstrip a commander's capabilities. Even at the company level, first sergeants and company clerks serve primarily as the personnel staff. Additionally, company officers and noncommissioned officers are designated as athletic officer, voting officer, education officer and many other special duties related to the well being of the members.

At battalion level and above, personnel officers and their many assistants are invariably among the first staff elements to whom the commander turns for advice and assistance when new missions are received. As with the other elements, however, the personnel officer's work is inseparable from that of the rest of the staff.

The adequacy of personnel is meaningful to the commander only in terms of the mission itself, the plan of operation, the equipment to be operated and maintained, the outside influences and all the other aspects of the organization's activities. For example, a shortage of dump truck operators might have no immediate significance on a river-crossing mission for which little dirt or other material required hauling, while the full, authorized strengths of other skills such as bulldozer operators, demolition experts, etc., might be insufficient for the task at hand. Personnel officers and their assistants must constantly bear in mind that they are but a small segment of the complete staff, and that their efforts are wasted unless tied to the work of the entire staff.

Personnel staff members cannot hope to be experts on the many skills and professions which comprise the force for which their commanders are responsible. This expertise lies in other elements of the staff. For example, the personnel staff officer should be intimately familiar with the numbers, grades, and formal training requirements for the vehicle repairmen authorized in an infantry division TOE. He cannot hope to match the maintenance officers' detailed knowledge of what these technicians must know and their individual capabilities to perform the many necessary repair jobs. Neither can he match the maintenance experts' skills in predicting the rate of breakdown during a given operation, the manhours and skills needed to keep the equipment in operation and the number of maintenance personnel, by grades and skills, required to support an operation. Like all staff officers, a personnel officer must spend much time coordinating his efforts with those of his counterparts in other staff elements.

The personnel officer and his staff element are responsible for obtaining and maintaining an adequate force of trained personnel of the proper grades and skills necessary to operate and maintain the equipment needed by the commander to complete his mission. To meet these requirements a typical personnel staff element might be organized similar to that found in one Army headquarters in early 1973. See Chart 3.3.

Intelligence

Least understood and most controversial of all staff members are the intelligence experts, the specialists in identifying, analyzing and evaluating outside influences which could affect their commanders' missions. The uninformed often lump intelligence specialists together as snoopers, creeps, the cloak-and-dagger crew, and other equally derogatory but hardly descriptive epithets. Properly used, intelligence is one of the most valuable elements in any staff.

Upon receipt of a mission, a commander's first concern often is with the outside influences which could influence the assigned task. The concern is equally great whether the mission is to capture an objective in combat, to establish and conduct a training program, to build, stock and operate depots, to

(Text continued on page 39)

38   The Army Staff Officer's Guide

**Chart 3.3
Typical Personnel Office**

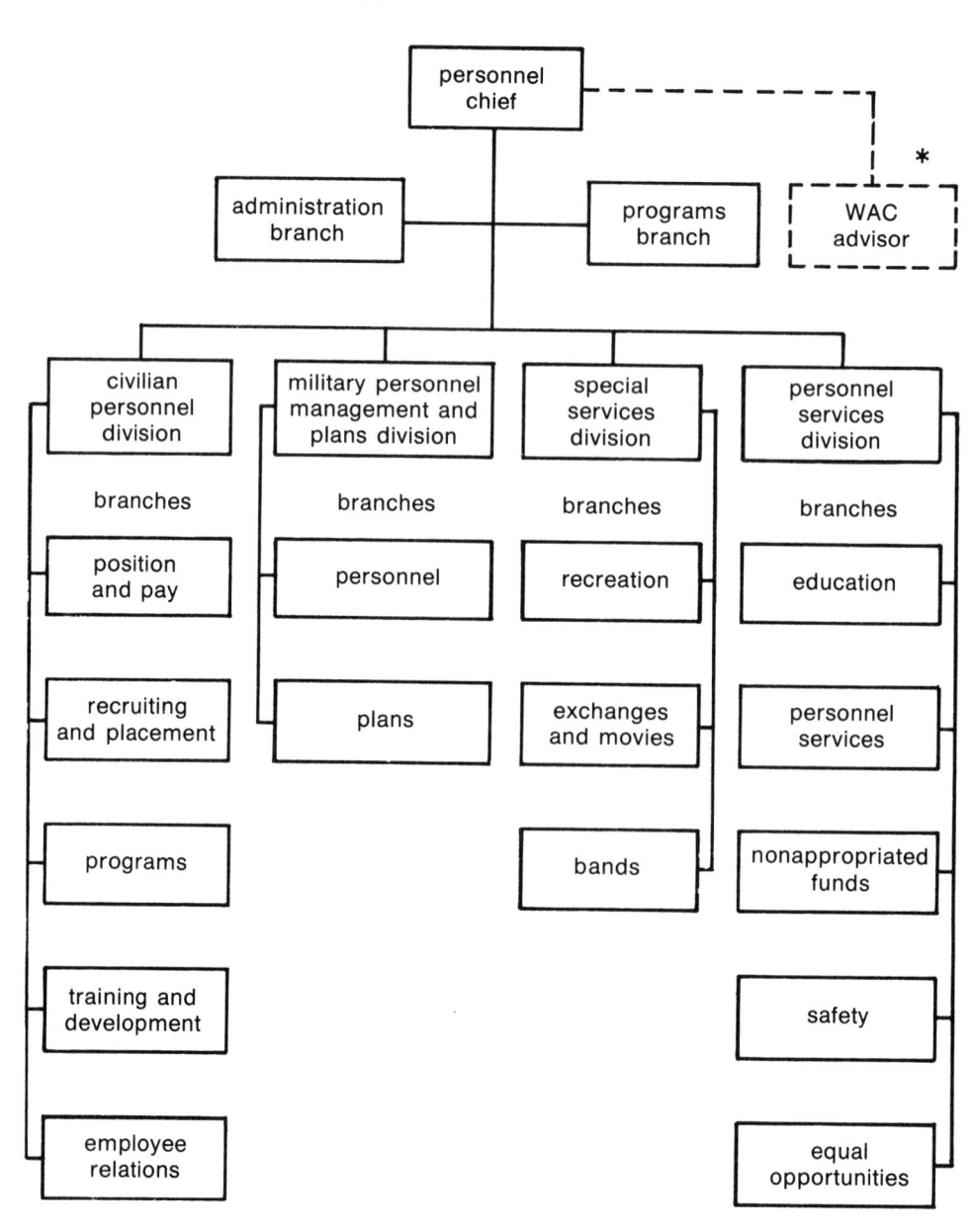

```
                          personnel
                            chief ─────────────────┐
                                                    │  *
    administration              programs         WAC
       branch                    branch         advisor
                                              (when Women Army Corps
                                               personnel are assigned
                                               to command)
```

- civilian personnel division
  - branches
    - position and pay
    - recruiting and placement
    - programs
    - training and development
    - employee relations

- military personnel management and plans division
  - branches
    - personnel
    - plans

- special services division
  - branches
    - recreation
    - exchanges and movies
    - bands

- personnel services division
  - branches
    - education
    - personnel services
    - nonappropriated funds
    - safety
    - equal opportunities

*when Women Army Corps personnel are assigned to command

undertake major maintenance actions or to conduct functional activities such as procurement. Whatever the job to be undertaken, outside actions beyond the commander's control are certain to influence his ability to meet his responsibilities. Some may work to his advantage; others may have an adverse impact on all or some of the tasks included in the mission.

To combat commanders and those who plan for combat operations to include long range contingency plans for wars that may or may not occur in the distant future, the enemy is a principle, but by no means the only, area of interest. Who is the enemy? Presumably, with the possible exception of extremely long range plans, the commander will know what country is or may become the enemy. His concerns are much more specific:

Who are the commanders of the enemy organizations?
Who are the soldiers in the organizations?
Are they seasoned soldiers or recruits?
Are they motivated and healthy?
What is the enemy strength?
How many divisions will be encountered? How much infantry, armor, artillery?
What sophisticated weapons has the enemy, and is he mobile?
Where exactly is he?
Where is each of his elements, including support activities?
Is he stationary and well barricaded in permanent positions?
Where has he been, and what have been his patterns of movement?
As a consequence, what are the probabilities that he will remain in his present location?
If he moves, which direction and how fast can he be expected to travel?
What will be the enemy's reaction to different possible methods of operation?
What are the time frames for his capabilities to counter the operation?
Why is the answer to each question as it is?

In considering outside influences, as in all staff actions, an essential part of good staff procedure is asking why. A good staff officer must constantly seek the answer to that question. It could be considered the quality control word in staff work, particularly for the staff intelligence officer.

After answering some of the questions listed, ask why. If, for example the opposing force is commanded by the enemy's most experienced and successful general, why? This could mean that a major counterthrust is planned that could be disastrous to the upcoming operation. The appearance of Field Marshal Von Rundstedt as commander of any particular German force during World War II would certainly have caused some very urgently apprehensive allied commanders to ask themselves "Why?" Identifying a relatively unknown commander at the head of opposing forces, however, might cause a commander to feel some degree of security. Perhaps the enemy does not anticipate the planned operation.

Why? applies with equal importance to all the elements of information the intelligence staff gathers about the enemy. Why is he armed as he is? Why are there (or aren't there) concentrations of armor? Why are the opposing forces manned by seasoned veterans only, with virtually no untested recruits? Or, why the opposite? In other words, bits of information are of little value unless their meaning and purpose can be understood.

If the intelligence staff can determine why each bit of information is true, or is likely to be true, the meaning of the information begins to be discernible. New staff officers must realize that most commanders and supervisors are very concerned with reasons for any proposed action. Very few recommendations will be accepted unless the action officer is able to satisfy in a very positive manner the query which is certain to come—why should we do this instead of something else?

As mentioned previously, enemy forces are not the only concerns facing combat commanders. Weather is an important influence to be reckoned with and one over which the commander exercises no control. He can, however, choose a course of action planned to minimize the adverse effects of extreme weather conditions.

The terrain must also be considered and its peculiarities identified. Commanders must adjust their plans to adapt to the terrain over which they will operate. Mountains, deserts, rivers, swamps, cities and other features can often be more effective obstacles than those deliberately prepared.

Natural factors (weather and terrain) are particularly significant with the dependence today on equipment that is, in many instances, most sensitive to weather and terrain. Tanks, although designed for rugged, roadless areas do have limitations. Sufficiently deep mud or nearly vertical mountainsides can completely immobilize even the most efficient armored vehicle, as can deep rivers and narrow, winding city streets.

Certain electronic devices essential to weapons guidance and to communications are highly sensitive to exteme weather conditions and to large land masses and tall structures which impair their transmission and receiving abilities. The effectiveness of aircraft for close-in tactical support and helicopters for troop movements is reduced by poor visibility and extreme terrain which make low level maneuvering difficult and dangerous. These factors equally influence the enemy and must be included in analyzing his capabilities and likely course of action.

Because enemy commanders also are vitally interested in information concerning the strengths, weaknesses and plans of their opponents, a major duty of the intelligence staff is to counter the efforts of enemy intelligence experts to gain useful information. Unlike the glamourous, spy-chasing adventure portrayed in fiction, this is just a common-sense program of safeguarding sensitive information which could be useful to an enemy. The intelligence staff assists the commander by establishing security programs to educate members of the command and subordinate organizations on the necessity for caution in handling sensitive material and by conducting inspections to assure that all precautions are being taken.

Intelligence is also important to the nontactical commander, but it may not be identified as an element of the staff. Whether or not intelligence is designated as a staff element, it is difficult to imagine an activity unaffected by outside influences. Such influences may be far removed from the enemy-oriented interests of the combat commander and his staff, but they exist, and they are significant. Commanders who must contract for construction, or who purchase materials and equipment, are faced with many unknowns related to situations and conditions over which they have little or no control.

Few sessions of the US Congress fail to take note of at least one major incident of *cost overrun,* a situation in which an item or structure actually costs far more than the original estimate. Presumably, the person responsible for the initial estimate did not deliberately establish a misleadingly low cost estimate. In some instances, careless, inexpert staff work may have failed to consider all facets of the project, leading to a faulty estimate.

Perhaps cases exist in which unscrupulous persons failed for selfish reasons to disclose all possible expenses. In the vast majority of cases, however, overruns result from outside influences beyond the control of the planners—increased material and labor costs, strikes or weather conditions which delay work and extend construction time, industrial accidents or acts of God that destroy materials and equipment, or combinations of these or other unpredictable events. That these imponderables have often caused great embarrassment to those who compiled initial estimates in no way indicates that their possibility was not recognized or that they were not studied by the staff responsible.

Intelligence gathering, analysis and evaluation are at best inexact. Engineers estimating the cost of a structure or contracting officers considering purchases of items or services certainly attempt to identify factors which may influence costs before the construction has been finished or the contract, fulfilled. Inflationary trends, for example, would normally be projected from the data of past years and applied to the estimated costs, but these data do not predict unusual acceleration of inflationary factors. During January, 1973, certain construction materials increased in cost by nearly 6%—more than half the increase which could have been predicted for that entire year. Fortunate indeed would be the engineer who could have predicted this spurt in costs.

Labor disputes are an outside influence which could have the same impact on the functional commander as an unexpected counterattack has on a tactical leader. If direct involvement in labor disputes could be anticipated because of strained relations or labor contracts due to expire, then the estimate could be adjusted to allow for fluctuations. Less predictable are the indirect effects of strikes in supporting industries. While an Army depot commander might fairly accurately determine that his workers would be extremely unlikely to strike, he would be less able to predict the likelihood of a strike by supporting commercial truckline drivers, an event that could cripple his ability to ship supplies to the user or to replace items already shipped. Strikes by workers in other industries could cause shortages of items available for issue and cost increases when they became available.

Intelligence, whether related to the enemy, the vagaries of battlefield weather, the uncertainties of material costs, or the availability of services such as transportation, is one of the major concerns of all commanders and their staffs. Few headquarters are without the services of experts whose job is to identify and analyze factors which could cause total or partial mission failure. Identifying them is the lesser part of the job.

Just as the six blind men carefully reported their impressions of the elephant according to the part of the animal each chanced to encounter, each of the people who report to the intelligence officer may be absolutely accurate about the aspect of the subject he has investigated without having any sort of grasp of the whole picture. Their stories may seem confusing, meaningless, contradictory until analyzed and assimilated. The intelligence expert must sort, analyze, and evaluate the bits of information, weigh them against information already available, and attempt to piece together a complete, meaningful picture.

Intelligence officers are an integral part of the staff and can function effectively only in close cooperation with the other members of the commander's team. The entire staff must be vitally involved in every phase of intelligence gathering.

Certain information is obviously required and will automatically be sought by the proficient intelligence staff officer: enemy situation, terrain and weather data, etc. For each mission and each task included in the mission, the other staff elements must identify to the intelligence experts the special information requirements for their own areas of responsibility.

An engineer in charge of bridge and road construction would need more specific, detailed data—soil types along proposed roadways, river depths and currents at the crossing sites, depth of soil above bedrock, etc.—than the general terrain information available to the staff as a result of the intelligence officer's routine interest in that type of information. Personnel officers would be interested in the enemy, the weather, the terrain and other factors which could cause excessive casualties. Operations officers would want to know any enemy capabilities which could make the crossing difficult to construct and maintain and to use when completed.

The entire staff must make known to the intelligence officer their needs for information. He in turn must coordinate with all members of the staff to assure that his capabilities for gathering information are directed toward those elements of information essential to the mission.

Like the rest of the staff, intelligence staff officers exist only to help the commander complete his mission and must direct their total efforts to that end. Information must not be gathered just for the sake of gathering information. Intelligence capabilities are resources and must be channeled toward gathering information needed to complete the mission at hand.

Coordination is also essential in the analysis and evaluation of intelligence. Assuming that elephants were still items of military equipment when the six blind men made their conflicting but partly true reports, who could better put the reports together to estimate that the animal in question might be a standard-issue elephant than the logistician. He should be familiar with elephants and with their many parts and be able to eliminate from the list of possibilities all those animals with no appendages resembling spears, ropes, snakes, trees, etc.

The operator of those days, familiar with the use, capabilities and limitations of elephants, could contribute by considering where the animal was observed and evaluating the likelihood of there being an elephant in that vicinity. The operator could further contribute by assisting the intelligence expert in estimating the all important "why?" Why was an elephant (or more likely elephants) in the locality where it was observed? Why would the enemy need elephants, and to what operations would they be committed?

The intelligence staff serves two purposes: (1) it learns as much as possible about outside influences and their possible impact on the commander's mission and (2) it attempts to prevent the opposition from obtaining similar information about the commander's capabilities and plans. A typical intelligence staff organization is shown on 3-4.

Operations

As stressed previously, no single staff officer, or staff element is the most important. All must work together to accomplish the mission. Their combined efforts must produce unified staff actions with one, and only one, staff position.

If forced to choose, most commanders would probably select operations as the one staff element around which their success most frequently centers. This statement may seem to contradict the preceding paragraph. It is certain to raise skeptical eyebrows among more specialized officers. After all, personnel officers ensure that balanced forces of people are available, and commanders could not operate without these human resources. Logisticians would point out that even the people would be useless (perhaps a detriment) without supplies and equipment. Both equipment and personnel would be less than fully effective if commanders were forced to operate blindly—without intelligence.

**Chart 3.4
Typical Intelligence Office**

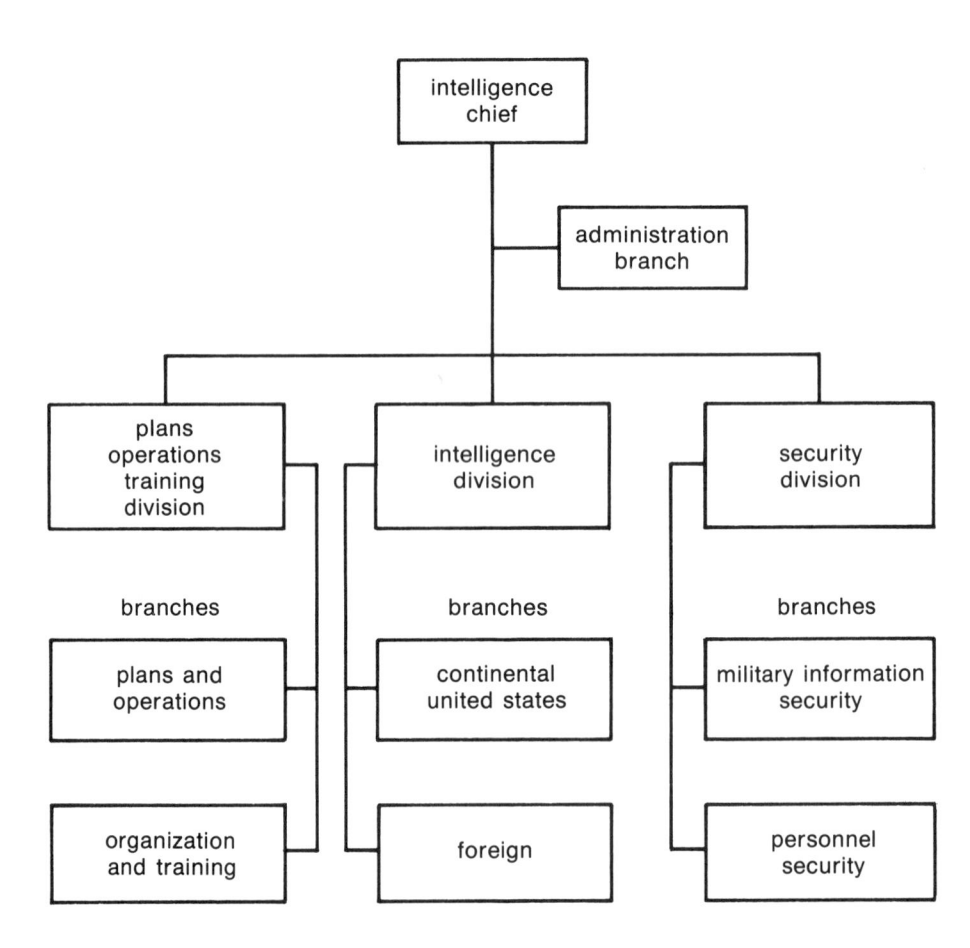

```
                    intelligence
                       chief
                         |
                         |—— administration
                              branch
         _____|_____
        |                |                |
      plans         intelligence       security
    operations        division         division
     training
     division

    branches         branches          branches

    plans and       continental      military information
    operations     united states         security

   organization       foreign            personnel
   and training                          security
```

Why then is the operator, who contributes no people, things, services or information, held in such high esteem? All staff elements have broad functional areas interfacing with and overlapping the functions of other elements. Personnel experts obtain, care for and replace the people who operate the equipment authorized to the command. Personnel staff efforts, therefore, are inseparable from those of the logisticians who provide the equipment to be operated. Because personnel welfare and motivation often are affected by such influencing factors as terrain, weather, enemy action, and so on, personnel and intelligence staff efforts are closely linked. The same close interrelation applies equally to the rest of the staff; often it is difficult to tell where one's interests stop and another's begin. No element of the staff functions in such broad, ill-defined areas as the operators. None depends so completely on the efforts of the other members of the staff.

To oversimplify, operators differ from the remainder of the staff in one important respect: they are generalists who assist and advise the commander on the overall mission and complete tasks rather than specializing in narrower fields of interest. The rest of the staff normally is organized around specific areas of expertise—people, intelligence, things.

In infantry divisions, for example, the operator (G-3) could be considered the tactical expert in the procedures and maneuvers that best apply available human and physical resources against the enemy with maximum chances of success. On the staff of a large supply depot, the operator would be the expert on overall depot operations, and would visualize the mission as a total operation, while others on the staff would be more inclined to view success or failure in the light of their specialized areas: supply, stockage, shipments, personnel, etc.

Operations officers and their assistants are the big-picture members of the staff, experts at piecing together the many little pieces that make the big picture. Operators bring together the efforts of the other staff elements and apply them to the whole mission.

To fully understand the function of operations staff elements, it is necessary to touch briefly on a facet of staff function that is dealt with more fully in a separate chapter: procedures and actions. Over the years, experience has proven that the intricacies of military operations require the discipline and controls of orderly, standardized problem-solving techniques. As they have evolved, these techniques fall into two categories: (1) the procedures used by commanders to bring to bear and control the full efforts of their staffs to solve major problems and (2) the separate actions taken by staffs within these procedures.

A commander's problem-solving procedures consist of the following steps: identifying the problem, analyzing available information, restating the problem to include all additional tasks, studying the problem to select the best solution, making a command decision, planning for implementation of the decision, issuing orders and supervising the execution of the orders. To accomplish these steps, the staff must complete equally standardized actions: estimates, studies, plans, and orders, to name but a few.

Each staff element, each staff member, contributes to each of these actions and assists the commanders with the final step, supervision. However, with the exception of extremely specialized actions falling into single areas of staff interest (logistics, personnel, etc.) the operational staff element is at the heart of each step in the commander's problem-solving procedures.

Identifying Problems. Missions are not always received as clear cut, detailed directives. They seldom come with a precise list of tasks to be performed, prescribe exact, specified criteria or pinpoint finite time frames for completion of each separate phase. Most are general, allowing maximum flexibility for selecting operating procedures. A commander must deduce from the general mission, and from situations as they develop, the tasks and projects to be undertaken as inherent functions of the general mission.

Logically, most commanders look to the operator (S-3, G-3, DCOPS J-3, Director of Operations, etc.) to supervise and coordinate those analyses because of the operator's overview of the mission, but every staff element becomes deeply involved. Often, seemingly simple missions have a multitude of included tasks identifiable only by the functional staff experts.

A mission to establish and operate a supply depot in support of a combat operation could have many unstated facets: storage areas and structures to be built, transportation to be arranged, personnel requirements to be identified and the people obtained, computers to be installed, items of authorized stockage to be determined and ordered, and operating procedures to be developed and implemented. Obviously, several elements of the commander's staff must identify and evaluate these and other tasks before the commander can begin to consider methods for establishing the depot.

Mission identification is a continuing function. For instance, if an armored or an air cavalry division were introduced into the example depot's area of responsibility, tanks and aircraft would be added to the equipment to be supported within the depot commander's mission. His staff must determine the scope of those requirements and their impact on personnel, storage areas and distribution workloads.

Although, the continuing analysis—like the initial one—is a task for the entire staff, operators (who must fit the new functions into overall operations) can best coordinate the efforts. This does not mean that other staff elements should not continue to identify the new tasks and functions in their own areas of interest which must be done to insure the success of the mission or to use resources more efficiently and economically.

Mission Restatement. Operations staff elements also assist the commander in restating the mission to include its key functions and tasks and their relative priorities. In a previous example we discussed the engineer commander whose mission, as received, was merely to construct a bridge over a certain river near a specified location to be used by an armored unit at a given time. After analysis, he restated his mission to include building an access road and an exit road.

It would be normal to expect that as the job progressed, additional tasks might be identified either by the commander or by his staff. For example, equipment parks or assembly areas might be required to facilitate both construction and use of the crossing. The restatement of the mission, initially and because of developing situations, helps generate the essential information needed by the commander to decide upon best courses of action.

Studying the Problems. In the study phase, also referred to as the *estimating phase*, again each staff element plays a part. Personnel elements consider the people-situations relating to the mission. Intelligence officers study outside influences—favorable or adverse. Logisticians evaluate available physical assets versus requirements, as well as services required to get these resources to the users. Operators then use this input from the specialists (1) to estimate the ability of the command to complete the operation and (2) to select the course of action most likely to succeed.

It is logical that operators should have staff supervision over this step of the process. With their broader areas of interest they are best able to see that all facets of the problem are considered, that each staff element uses the information developed by the others and that all practical courses of action are identified and studied in detail and the advantages and disadvantages of each, carefully weighed.

The Commander's Decision. If satisfied with the staff's recommendations, the commander makes his decision selecting the courses of action recommended or substituting his own. After selecting a course of action, the commander provides the staff with a general idea of how the operation should be conducted. Actually, this concept is an elaboration of the course of action decided upon and should be a part of the recommendation presented to the commander.

This highlights an important characteristic of good staff work, applicable to every staff member but particularly vital to operators—completeness. Recommendations to the commander should fully explain *where, what, when, why, how,* and *by whom,* the recommended action would be accomplished. Only with this information can the commander comprehend the full meaning of the recommendations and the rationale upon which the staff has based them. Also, plans that are complete in detail can be used for implementing directives.

Planning. Like all staff work, planning is continuous and involves the entire staff. Since plans are the basis and guidance for the many coordinated actions necessary to mission accomplishment, most commanders consider their operators best suited to coordinate and consolidate the many parts of the plans contributed by each staff element. Military plans could be compared to blueprints. They are designs to be followed by each element, working together as a team to accomplish one overall objective. It is up to the operator to see that all parts are compatible, and that nothing has been overlooked.

Orders. When the plans are approved by the commander the operator must complete one more purely paper job to get the operation under way. He must assist in issuing orders to subordinates. In large operations, most commanders prefer two separate orders, or at least two separate parts to operation orders: an operations portion describing how the job is to be done from the operational viewpoint and an administrative and logistical portion, governing the use of resources to support the operation.

Administrative and logistical orders, or those portions of operations orders, normally are prepared under the supervision of logisticians assisted by such personnel and other staff elements as are needed. This does not relieve the operator of his overall supervisory role. The plan and the order must represent a single integrated staff effort and must be compatible in every sense. The operator must ensure that the administrative and logistical portions of the plan and the directives do support the operation and agree with the commander's conception of it.

Staff Supervision. Having issued orders, the commander is responsible and must assure the implementation of the orders by his subordinate commanders, who translate them into actions leading to mission accomplishment. The entire staff must assist with this supervision, each member working in his own area of interest. Operators, as generalists, should know better than other staff elements the rationale behind and the intent of the complete plans and implementing orders and should be more familiar with the commander's concepts of operation.

Operators have several functions. They supervise and coordinate the efforts of the rest of the staff throughout the procedures used to analyze the mission, study alternatives and initiate operations; and they coordinate staff efforts to help the commander supervise the planning and implementation of his directives by subordinates.

Additional Functions. In some headquarters the commander combines other functions with those of the operator. A commander who has little need for pure intelligence and a great need for information directly relating to operational factors may combine intelligence and operations into one staff element.

Planning has already been mentioned as a normal operational function. Because planners should be looking ahead at all times, operations is often divided into two sub-elements, one for supervising on-going operations, one for planning. This division makes assignment of staff responsibilities easier and helps action officers from other staff elements identify their counterparts for the purposes of coordination and liaison.

In actual practice, planning and operations are so closely related that dividing lines between their functions are difficult to distinguish. To do their jobs operators must be intimately familiar with the plans and by the same reasoning planners could hardly plan ahead without knowing exactly what is happening currently.

The Major Staff Elements 49

Training. Because mission success so hinges on the training of the organization and of the individual, operators often supervise that important function. Training programs must be balanced to assure that a commander's entire force is trained, individually and in small units, to work together with other individuals and units to form teams. This function requires close coordination among all staff elements, particularly in training specialists and support units, but operators can best visualize the end objectives.

Organization. Some commanders prefer to have their operators advise and assist them in determining the best methods for organizing their force to achieve optimum mixtures of personnel skills and equipment to accomplish the mission. Since resources seldom meet the desires of the commander, this is an important element. Its position in the staff depends on the commander's preference. It may be a part of several elements, or it may be a separate staff section operating directly under the chief of staff. Organization is included in the operations element here only because most commanders seem to prefer that organizational arrangement. A typical operations staff element in a large headquarters could consist of the subelements shown on Chart 3.5.

Logistics

The last of the four original general staff elements common to most headquarters is logistics. Other elements are considered primary to some staffs because of the peculiarities of the mission or because of the commander's preference. Those will be discussed later. The logistician, by one name or another, will be found on the staff of virtually every commander.

Even organizations that receive their logistical support from others, such as the Army Health Services Command and the US Army Recruiting Command both of which are supported by other Army activities, require that the staff have some expertise in logistics to be able to help the commander with planning and to cooperate with supporting activities for adequate logistical support.

Of all the areas of interest that require a commander to have assistants and advisors, logistics in one of the most complex and includes more separate functions. Logistics is the true culprit behind the staff expansion of recent years which had led to the greater numbers and greatly increased size of the headquarters now needed to manage the United States Army. The burgeoning inventory of equipment available to the soldier has affected every area of the commander's job and has required increases in all staff elements.

According to the 1923 infantry division tables of organization and equipment (appended), the division was authorized only those major items of equipment providing the capabilities to maneuver, shoot and communicate.

**Chart 3.5
Typical Operations Office**

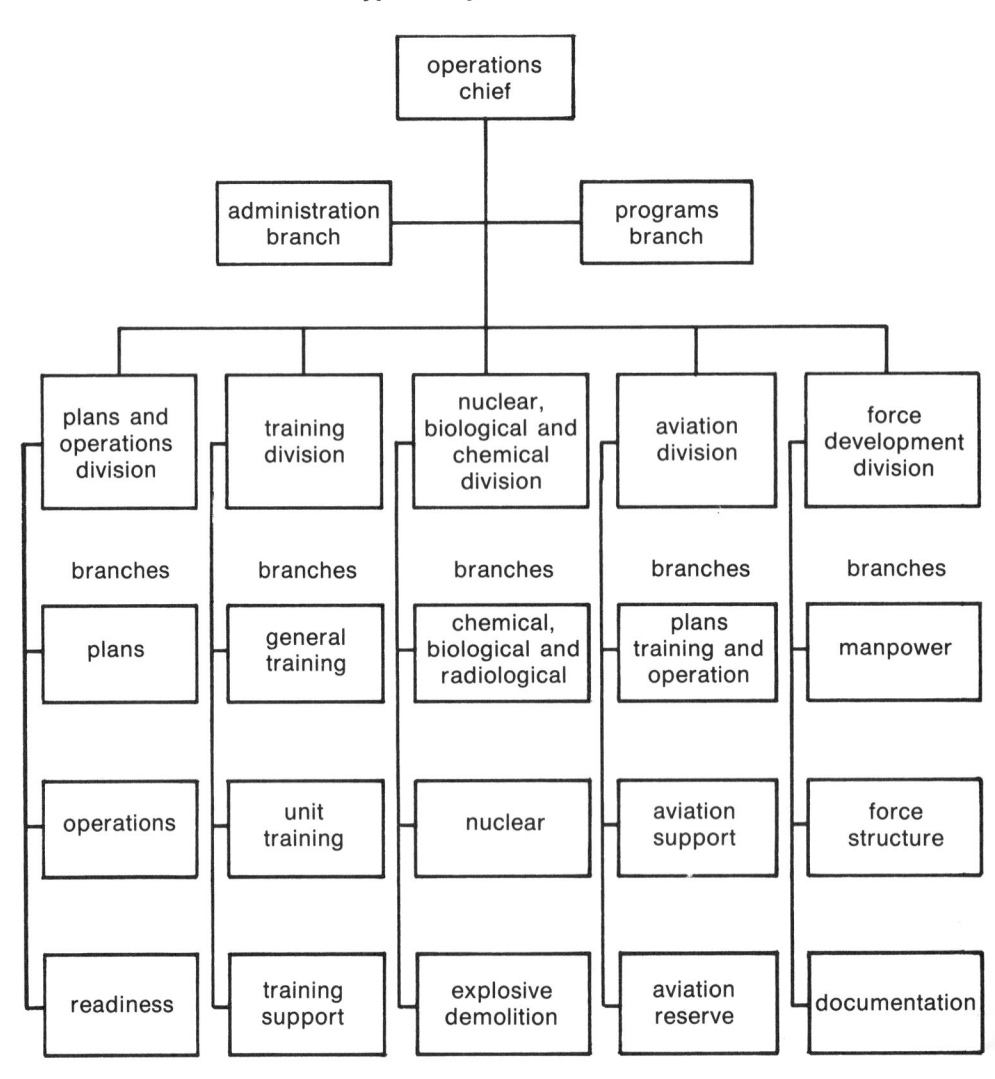

```
                         operations
                           chief
         ┌─────────────────┼─────────────────┐
  administration                          programs
     branch                                branch

┌──────────┬──────────┬──────────┬──────────┬──────────┐
plans and   training   nuclear,   aviation   force
operations  division   biological division  development
division              and chemical          division
                      division
```

plans and operations division	training division	nuclear, biological and chemical division	aviation division	force development division
branches	**branches**	**branches**	**branches**	**branches**
plans	general training	chemical, biological and radiological	plans training and operation	manpower
operations	unit training	nuclear	aviation support	force structure
readiness	training support	explosive demolition	aviation reserve	documentation

The proliferation of equipment during the fifty years and three wars since 1923 is dramatically demonstrated when the equipment of the 1973 infantry division is compared to the 22 lines of items from 1923. It is true that some of the equipment now included was available to the division in 1923 in its supporting units, *e.g.* 105 and 155mm artillery. However, supporting artillery units also still exist in addition to the fire-power of the infantry division itself.

Furthermore, equipment authorizations for today's divisions vary with the number and mix of maneuver battalions.

The appended chart lists major items from the consolidated equipment list of the infantry division tables of organization and equipment in use in the early 1970's. Equipment is listed for a division made up of six mechanized infantry battalions, four tank battalions and the division base.

The comparison demonstrates the modern commander's increased dependence on equipment and on its operators and repairmen. Less obvious is the staff explosion caused by the increased technology. Commanders must have the benefit of professional advice on the capabilities and limitations of each item and its best use, operator qualifications and maintenance requirements. Estimates, studies, choices of courses of action and planning, all require the advice and assistance of experts familiar with the gadgetry of the modern Army. Logisticians must be assisted by virtual hordes of experts.

Supply. Each Army organization and activity is authorized specified amounts and types of equipment, usually listed in tables of organization and equipment for tactical units, and in tables of distribution and authorizations for functional commands. Separate tables of allowances list certain items of personal clothing and equipment authorized for issue directly to the individual soldier or civilian employee. These authorizations are the upper limits of the equipment and supplies which a commander may have available for his normal mission. Unless restricted by specific directives, the authorized items must be on hand.

The first consideration of the logistician and his assistants is that measures be taken by all command elements to obtain all authorized items. A large portion of the logistics staff element will be devoted to establishing and supervising programs to assure that each subordinate element of the command has requisitioned each authorized item. It will also see to it that each unit has a plan, as well as management tools such as suspense files, for following up requisitions with queries when an item is not received within a reasonable time.

This is a major area of concern to the commander and a significant factor in initial staff estimates. Initial estimates and more complete follow-on analyses of physical resources consider not only the number of items authorized and those actually on hand, but also the probabilities of obtaining missing items, shortages, before the operation actually gets underway.

The effect of the shortage is a major factor in determining the commander's course of action. If extreme, it could force him to choose a less than desirable course. In some instances estimates reveal that, even if all authorized equipment were on hand, some items would be insufficient to accomplish the mission. When this is the case, the commander must ask for increased authorizations.

Receiving, storing and issuing equipment and supplies also occupy much of the supply expert's time. They are key steps in the economical use of resources. These functions have proved extremely troublesome in past wars, and they become more difficult to manage as the numbers and types of equipment proliferate. The logisitician must see that the items received are the ones authorized and requested, that the receipt is recorded to prevent duplication, and that items are properly stored to prevent damage so that they can be identified, located and issued.

Maintenance. Supply and maintenance are closely related. Some commanders combine these elements of logistics into a single supply and maintenance element. Maintenance experts on the staff establish and carefully supervise programs to minimize equipment breakdown through preventive measures (lubricating, tightening, adjusting, replacing faulty parts, cleaning, etc.). They also make sure that maintenance shops are properly organized to function efficiently and return equipment to use as rapidly as possible.

Good maintenance, depends upon the supply of repair parts and replacement components. Despite automation this is probably the most complex and difficult aspect of supply in today's equipment-oriented Army. Although such major items as tanks, heavy trucks, self-propelled artillery, and bulldozers are large, expensive and vital to mission success, they also are relatively easy to account for, and they seldom require replacement.

Repair parts for these monsters are quite another matter. At division level the maintenance battalion stocks some 5,000 different types of repair parts. Selection for stockage is based primarily on demand. The supply system is counted on for delivery of those items not carried in stock.

The supply activity at an installation which houses a division normally carries between 10,000 and 15,000 back-up repair parts. In the field, the division would look to its supporting maintenance and supply units for similar service.

It is the job of the supply systems to back up the back-up units. Obviously then, supply of repair parts is one of the logistician's major concerns, not only as a function of supply but also as one of the controlling factors in his ability to keep equipment operating.

Obtaining, storing, issuing, accounting for and repairing supplies and equipment are considered by many to be the heart of logistics. Perhaps they are. They are, however, only a part of the function of the logistics staff and are themselves dependent on the effectiveness of other facets of logistics, such as construction and the allied functions of facilities repairs and maintenance.

Construction. The physical facilities necessary for supply and maintenance must be included in the analysis, study, estimates and plans for support of an operation. In the modern Army the receipt, storage and issue of supplies and equipment are problems of complexity and great magnitude. Many of the sophisticated items used by the modern soldier are most sensitive to natural and artificial environments. Warehousing requirements range from relatively simple structures designed only to keep out the weather to completely environmentally controlled storage facilities for items that cannot resist extremes of temperature, dust, humidity or the shocks of natural or man-made disturbances.

Some of this equipment can only be used in similarly controlled environments, further increasing the variations in standard construction criteria. Building these special structures is a major effort. Maintaining and repairing them to assure that they continue to perform their design purposes are also major undertakings. It would do little good to assure an adequate supply of equipment that is sensitive to shock, such as computers, or supplies that are sensitive to moisture, such as maps, without simultaneously assuring the adequacy of structures for storing, issuing and using the items.

Construction, particularly in theaters of operation and on large military installations, is also inseparable from the movement of supplies and equipment. As with storage and maintenance, the ability to get the items to the hands of the user is dependent on transportation, which in turn must depend on construction and maintenance of roads, railroads, ports, airfields and other transportation related structures.

Even though the staff engineer may not be part of the logistical element, in some headquarters functioning as a special staff officer directly supervised by the chief of staff, his expertise is an important part of the logistics. Much of his work is directly associated with other logistical functions and must be closely coordinated with the other logistics experts on the staff. Obviously, much of his function is more directly involved with people and with the personnel staff than with the logistician.

As stated earlier, all commanders are vitally concerned with the comfort and welfare of the troops under their command. Physical facilities are major contributing factors to that welfare. Barracks, dining facilities, recreational and welfare facilities and hospitals and clinics are good examples of the troop-oriented construction which rests almost entirely in the area of interest of the personnel element of the staff. Headquarters and administrative buildings to house the commander and his staff involve all members of the staff.

A wide range of technical and professional skills is required of the engineers in all but the smallest commands with the simplest missions. Construction alone requires the entire scope of engineering disciplines to assure that plans include all of the essential electrical, mechanical and structural features necessary for their execution.

Similar skills are needed to plan for and supervise the routine maintenance of the completed structures and the repairs and modifications of buildings damaged or remodeled for other than their original use. The engineering staff must also have most of the skills required to manage and operate cities and other civilian communities: Knowledge of utilities such as water, electricity, gas, sewage, and fire protection, as well as long range master planning to assure maximum usage from all resources expended for real property.

Transportation. Closely allied with the logistician's supply and maintenance functions is transportation. The adequacy of supplies and equipment cannot be evaluated without also considering the availability of transportation. Like construction, transportation is closely related to personnel. For this reason, some commanders prefer to separate the transportation staff element from logistics and to treat it as a special staff element. Whatever their place in the staff, transportation experts must cooperate closely with both logistics and personnel.

As important as it is to have sufficient transportation for supplies and equipment, it is equally important to have soldiers in the proper place to apply them to the mission. Transporting units and individuals in the command area so that they can perform the mission is a major logistics effort, as is the transportation of units and individuals into the command and away from the command when their tour is completed.

An idea of the magnitude that this task can reach was demonstrated during the fighting in South Korea. At the peak of US involvement, about 270,000 Army personnel were stationed in that country for approximately twelve-month tours of duty. About one-twelfth of the force departed and was replaced each month of the year—an average of 750 persons arriving daily and a similar number departing. Managing that flow of traffic was an immense job. Because morale and troop welfare hinged heavily on timely departures from the unpleasantness of the combat area, transportation became a sensitive activity not only to local commanders but to leaders, both civilian and military, at the national level.

Food Service. Because of its dependence on supply, construction and transportation, food service, including supervision of the methods of preparation and serving, is normally considered a logistics function even though its effect is almost entirely on the morale, welfare and comfort of the personnel. Perhaps no other single factor has such direct and severe impact as the quantity, and more importantly, the quality of food.

Long gone are the days of Army "chow" and its well deserved reputation for, at best, mediocrity. In our more affluent society, soldiers have become accustomed to more and better food in their homes and rightly believe that they should receive equal quality in the military service, at least when situations permit. This applies not only to sufficient quantities of good foods properly prepared and attractively served, but also to varieties of foods, particularly those popular in certain areas of the country and those appealing to certain ethnic groups. Food service can be expected to be of highest interest to the commander and one which demands qualified and dedicated staff officers.

Property Disposal. Disposal of items which have served their purposes and are no longer needed, and those that have become uneconomical to repair because of age, accident or wear, could be considered the last step in the supply process. Earlier we stressed the importance of accounting for the supplies and equipment received, on hand and on requisition so that commanders could know their exact requirements compared to physical resources. An obvious adjunct of this requirement is the final accounting to show that items have been legitimately removed from the status of available resources. This is the function of the property disposal experts on the staff. They must develop and supervise programs to assure that items no longer usable or no longer needed are disposed of through controlled activities. They must see that every effort be made to either continue each item in use by some federal agency, sell it for its full remaining value, or convert it to salvage and dispose of it for maximum return to the taxpayer.

Miscellaneous Logistics Services. Several other logistical services found in most headquarters are mortuary services, household goods shipment, unaccompanied dependent travel and procurement. While these functions usually require fewer staff members to advise and assist the commander, they are important.

The miscellaneous services of mortuary assistance, household goods, unaccompanied travel, and so on, are primarily personnel services that directly effect the morale and welfare of the people who comprise the command. Their connection with logistics is their dependence on resources supervised by the logistics staff in most headquarters: supplies, transportation, maintenance, etc. These functions are extremely important to the commander because of their adverse effect on morale if they are not properly planned and executed.

Logistics includes all functions which control and provide the physical resources needed by the commander. Like most military functions, logistics is so closely related with many other functions that the interface is difficult to define. This difficulty is reflected in the many methods chosen by commanders to organize and use the logistics portions of their staffs.

Frequently, the engineer and the transportation officers are considered separate special staff elements answering directly to the chief of staff. In many other headquarters organizations one or both function under the supervision of the staff logistician.

Most commanders now designate their surgeons as special staff officers or in some cases as personal staff officers reporting directly to the commander. In either case, this removes medical supply and maintenance, evacuation of patients and hospitalization from the supervision of the staff logistician. Because these functions are in many ways inseparable from other supply, maintenance, construction and transportation functions, the need for close coordination and cooperation remains.

It is not the purpose of this work to comment on the desirability of any particular staff organization or the propriety of any particular method of staff employment selected by a commander. One will work as well as any other if the staff officers are professionally competent and dedicated to making their particular organization an effective one. In the area of logistics, however, as elements are removed and given special or personal staff status, it becomes more and more incumbent on all members of the staff to observe the requirement for close cooperation to assure maximum returns from all physical resources available to the command. Chart 3.6 illustrates the internal organization of the logistics staff of one Army headquarters early in 1973.

Civil Affairs (G-5)

In war the US Army's mission is normally twofold: first, to defeat enemy forces in land warfare; second, to gain enough control over the enemy population to permit conclusion of the conflict on terms compatible with United States interests.

For the most part, commanders and their staffs are trained in the skills for and are oriented toward the first objective: defeat of the enemy military force. Experience indicates that in combat, military victory becomes such an overriding consideration that commanders and their normal staff organizations must devote most of their time to that objective.

Despite its importance, the mission of gaining control of the land and its people unavoidably becomes second in priority to those members of the staff whose primary interest is winning the war. To offset this natural tendency, civil affairs experts have been added to the staffs of tactical commanders when their missions included dealing with indigenous populations.

The civil affairs staff officer has primary staff responsibility for all relationships between military forces and operations and the civilian environment. Their responsibilities include psychological operations aimed at creating in the civilian community such emotions, attitudes and behavior patterns as support command objectives.

Civil affairs operations become important under widely varying conditions. Their nature may vary from relatively static situations involving only liaison, advice and assistance to local governments, to complete military occupation, exercising executive, legislative and judicial power over the occupied area. These operations most often occur during and after military operations. Sometimes, as a result of treaties and international agreement, they can occur in areas where there have been no combat operations.

The civil affairs staff element is usually a small organization consisting only of the experts who advise and assist the commander in promulgating and supervising his operations as they relate to the civilian community. It does not include the full range of staff expertise required to plan, implement and

Chart 3.6
Typical Logistics Office

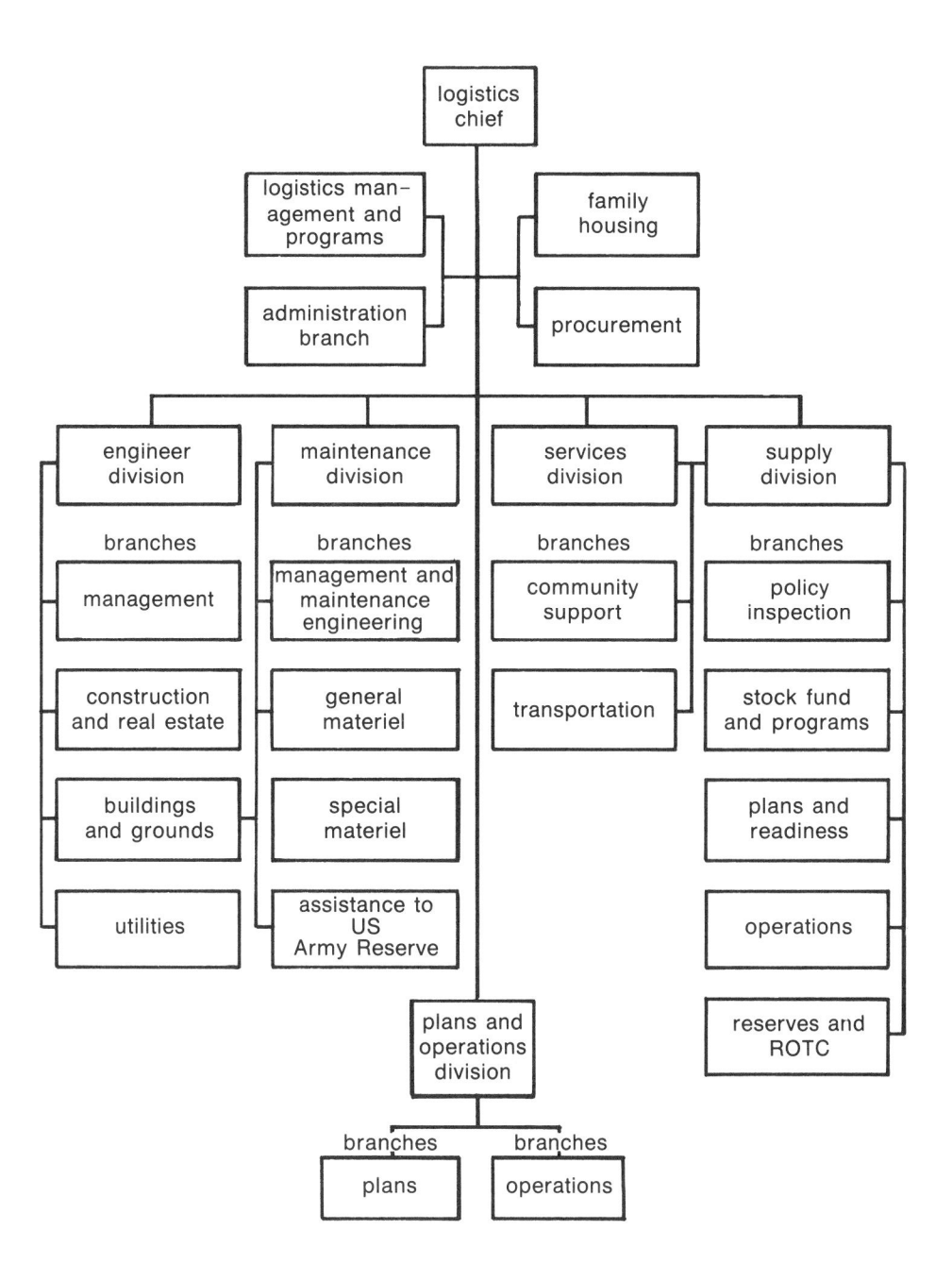

```
                            logistics chief
                                  |
    logistics management          |         family housing
    and programs                  |
                                  |
    administration branch         |         procurement
                                  |
    ┌────────────┬────────────────┼────────────────┬────────────┐
  engineer    maintenance      services          supply
  division    division         division          division

  branches    branches         branches          branches
  management  management and   community         policy
              maintenance      support           inspection
              engineering
  construction general         transportation    stock fund
  and real    materiel                           and programs
  estate
  buildings   special                            plans and
  and grounds materiel                           readiness

  utilities   assistance to                      operations
              US Army Reserve
                                                 reserves and
                                                 ROTC
                            |
                    plans and operations
                    division
                       ┌──────┴──────┐
                    branches      branches
                    plans         operations
```

supervise civil affairs operations—personnel, intelligence, logistics, law enforcement, legal and judicial experts, etc. In those areas, the civil affairs staff officer coordinates the efforts of the other staff elements. In the field, actual operations are performed by civil affairs organizations that include specialists in most fields of community activities—displaced persons, refugees and evacuees, public health, public safety, language, civil defense, and logistics. The civil affairs staff officers assist their commanders in supervising the activities of those organizations.

Comptroller

In recent years two trends have increased the requirements of many commanders for some very specialized advice and assistance. One of these has been the decentralization of fiscal responsibilities; the other, increased emphasis on modern management techniques. Both have added unique technical facets to command responsibilities, some of which are quite alien to normal military backgrounds. As a consequence, comptrollers (money and management experts) have risen to prominence. In most large headquarters, comptrollers now have major staff element status.

The comptroller is the commander's manager. He is responsible for advising and assisting in the overall management of resources to assure not only economy of operations, but also maximum effectiveness in the use of all resources. It cannot be overemphasized, that the comptroller's overall responsibility does not relieve other staff elements from their management responsibilities. Management of resources is not a fad. It is here to stay and will undoubtedly become a more dominant factor in command and staff success as the austerity of peacetime and even wartime military operations increases. Every staff officer should now—and must in the future—appreciate, understand and apply sound management practices. Generally speaking, the comptroller's management function is divided into two areas: money and management.

Fiscal Management. Commanders responsible for public funds must require constant control over every facet of the funding cycle: programming (estimating requirements), budgeting (allotting funds received to accomplish the mission), funding (distributing funds), accounting (keeping tabs on expenditures) and analysis (evaluating the effectiveness of fiscal resources expended). The comptroller supervises and coordinates those activities in most areas of the command. Again, each staff element chief supervises the same fiscal matters in his own area of interest.

The military budgeting and funding system is extremely complicated. Its details are far beyond the scope of this book and the needs of the average staff officer. It is important, however, that all staff officers understand the general procedures well enough to appreciate the funding implications in their respective areas of interest.

Like all US Government activities, the Army gets its money from Congress. Every year, each major element of the Army tells the headquarters of the Department of the Army its estimated requirements for operating funds for the following fiscal year. These estimates are based on guidance regarding missions, limitations, anticipated operations and priorities.

The requirements from the field are modified as necessary and are presented by Department of Defense to the Commander in Chief (the President) for inclusion in the national budget which is then presented to the Congress. This is, in effect, a formal request for funds.

As a separate action, all Army commanders responsible for funds submit and justify their estimates for funds for the coming year based on the Army's total request to DOD, as modified and presented to the Congress. This is the programming, or requesting, phase of the cycle.

As all newspaper readers and television viewers know, Congress often approves and allocates amounts somewhat different from those requested. The next phase of management is the critical process of managing those lesser amounts of money with minimum effect on missions. This requires stringent controls to assure that funds are applied to the highest priority requirements, and continuous supervision to be certain that the controls are working. These measures are necessary to assure that the money for the year lasts the full twelve months. All staff elements are involved in each of these steps.

The Army's funds are divided into appropriations, some of which have little interest to the average staff officer. Most frequently encountered by almost all staff officers is the one for Operations and Maintenance, Army (OMA). A cursory examination of that program reveals the staff's total involvement. OMA funds are divided into primary programs according to the type activities they support: Primary Program 1, strategic forces; Primary Program 2, general forces; etc. Each staff officer should know which primary program applies to each facet of his area of interest. OMA funds also are divided into mission funds and funds for base operations.

Mission funds are intended for those expenditures directly identifiable with the mission of the Army or an organization of it. Units in training would use mission funds for their supplies, transportation, personnel expenses other than pay, etc. Base operations funds would be used to operate and maintain the installation on which the units live and to provide certain support service. Normally, operations staff elements supervise and coordinate mission funds; all elements become involved with managing base operations funds.

Base operations funds are subdivided to support the major activities normally found on military bases: administration, personnel, maintenance, supply, medical services, and maintenance and repair of facilities. These are the subdivisions that bring staff elements into the funding business. While the comptroller is the overall money expert, and probably has some management expertise in the functional areas, he cannot replace the detailed knowledge of the specialists.

Most major staff elements have their own fiscal management experts who specialize in the funding cycle as it applies to their areas of interest. This organizational element relieves individual staff officers of the necessity of becoming financial experts; it does not relieve them of the necessity of understanding the funding process or of being aware of the availability of funds and the limitations and restrictions on their use.

Management Specialists. Many elements of a large staff organization are deeply involved in management of resources: people, things, services, time and money. Each manager is inclined to place primary emphasis on the resource for which he is personally responsible. Understandably, each staff officer believes that his special area of interest merits a larger share of resources than do other activities. This is not a sign of weakness. A staff officer could hardly support, assist and advise his commander energetically unless he believed completely that his specialty was important.

Unless controlled, however, this natural competitiveness could cause mass confusion within a headquarters. The management specialists who assist the comptroller provide that control by supervising distribution and use of resources. Chart 3.7 shows a typical organization for a comptroller's office in a large headquarters.

Communications and Electronics

In no other areas have recent technological advances been as revolutionary as in the fields of communications and electronics. Communications have always been a primary area of command concern. Many military men rate the ability to communicate along with fire power and maneuverability as the three essential elements for combat success. The first two probably have the most direct impact on the enemy, but they would be relatively ineffective if they were not coordinated with the entire military effort and directed by command. Communications provide that control.

To be effective, a commander must be able to find out what is happening in all areas of the command, transmit guidance and directives to all subordinate commands, receive information and directives from and report to superiors, and pass and receive information with other commanders. At one time the method was relatively simple—messengers darted about the battlefields carrying oral and written messages. Today commanders have at their disposal such arrays of electronic communications devices that technical experts

Chart 3.7
Typical Comptroller Office

```
                          comptroller
                              |
          administration------|
          branch              |
       _____|_____|_____
      |           |           |           |
   program    management   accounting  finance and
   budget     engineering  internal    accounts
   division   division     review      division
      |                    division        |
  branches                    |            |
      |                       |            |
  programs              accounting     finance
  analysis              policy and     services
      |                 procedures         |
  estimates             internal       operating
  and funding           review         accounts
```

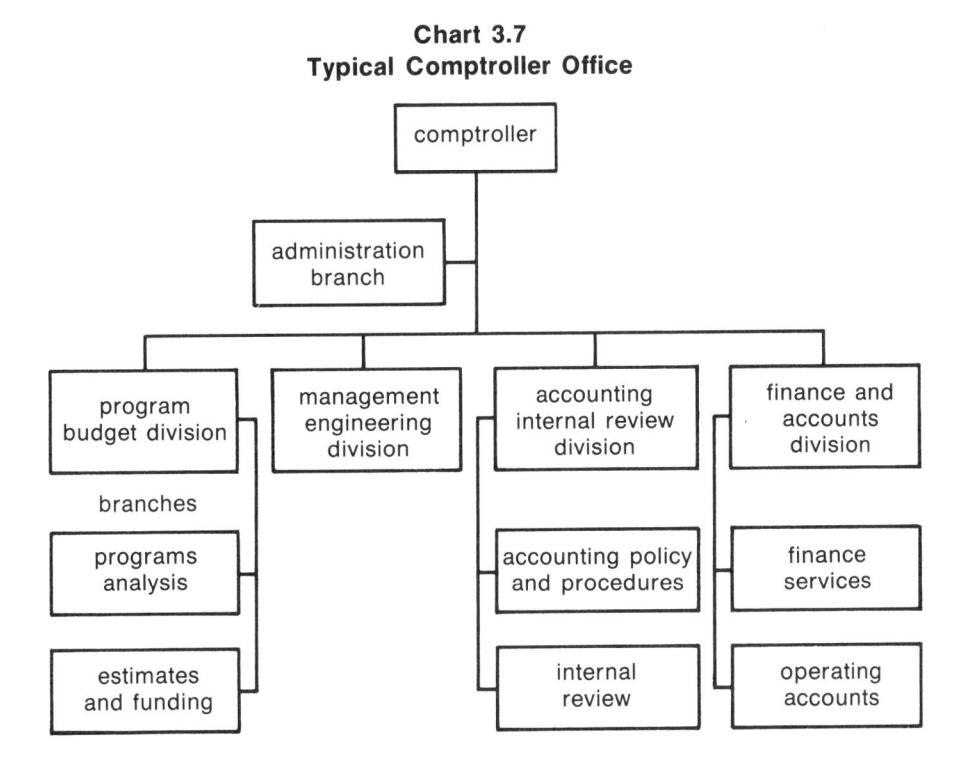

are required to advise them on using the equipment and to supervise its maintenance and operations.

The appended list of duties summarized from the operations and functions manual of a large headquarters demonstrates the magnitude and scope of the communications and electronics field.

Organization. Chart 3.8 demonstrates the size and complexity of a typical communications-electronics staff element in a large headquarters.

The Special Staff

As implied by the designation, the special staff is tailored to meet each commander's requirement for highly qualified professional and technical experts to advise and assist him in specialized areas of his mission responsibilities. The composition of the special staff varies from headquarters to headquarters, depending on the size and complexity of the mission. Also some staff elements organized as special staff offices in some headquarters are parts of major staff elements in others, e.g., engineer, and transportation.

Chart 3.8
Typical Communications Electronics Office

```
                    communications
                      electronics
                        office
                           │
                           ├──── MARS radio division
                           │
        ┌──────────────┬───┴────────┬──────────────┐
   telecommunications  audio visual   plans         telecommunications
   systems division    division       operations    center
                                      division
      branches          branches       branches       branches
   ┌──────────────┐  ┌──────────┐  ┌──────────┐  ┌──────────────┐
   │ electronics  │  │ support  │  │ plans and│  │communications│
   │ engineering  │  │ center   │  │ training │  │   center     │
   └──────────────┘  └──────────┘  └──────────┘  └──────────────┘
   ┌──────────────┐  ┌──────────┐  ┌──────────┐  ┌──────────────┐
   │    wire      │  │  photo   │  │          │  │   message    │
   │ engineering  │  │ facility │  │operations│  │   center     │
   └──────────────┘  └──────────┘  └──────────┘  └──────────────┘
   ┌──────────────┐
   │ control and  │
   │  services    │
   └──────────────┘
   ┌──────────────┐
   │telecommunica-│
   │tions         │
   │installation  │
   └──────────────┘
   ┌──────────────┐
   │  drafting    │
   └──────────────┘
```

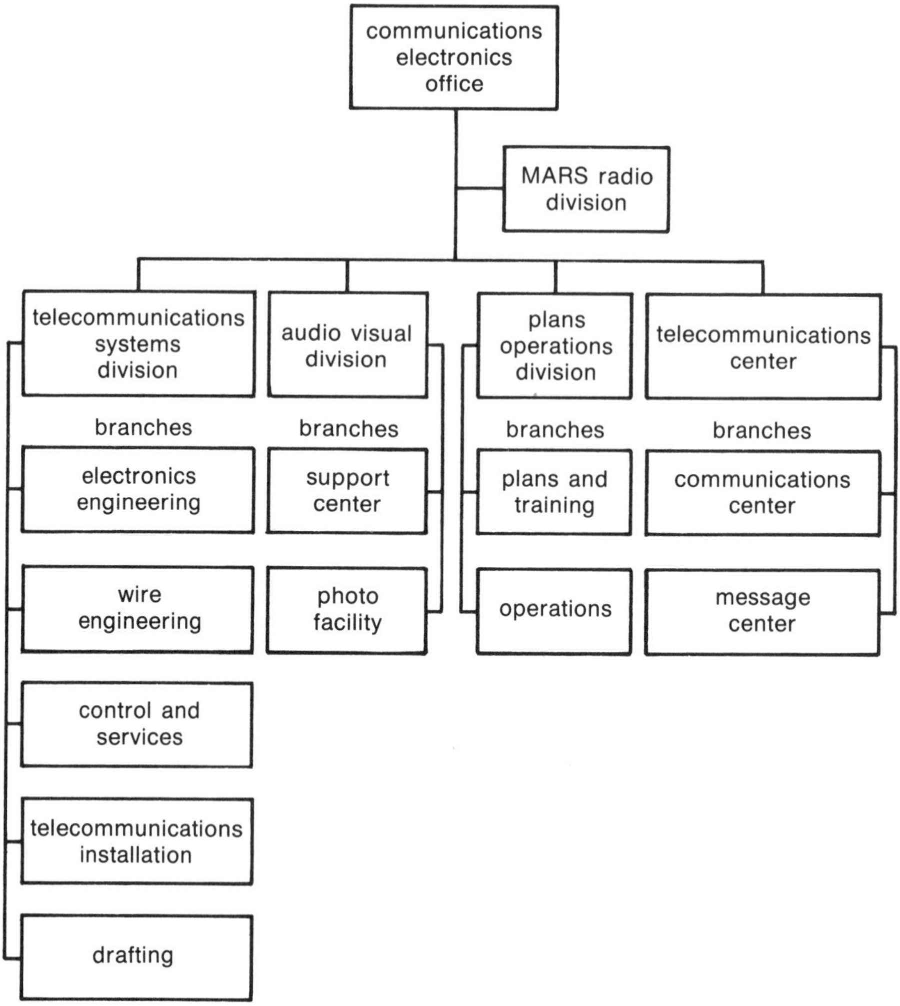

For this reason it is not possible to present a completely standard special staff organization which can be used as an index of what to expect when joining a new command. The order in which special staff elements are discussed is not intended to suggest their relative importance.

Headquarters Commandant

Like their primary (major staff) counterparts, special staff elements are organized and manned to best assist and advise their commanders on matters bearing on operational missions and mission related problems. However, major headquarters, like other large groups, generate their own internal support requirements—feeding, housing, transportation, security, supplies, equipment, housekeeping, administration, etc. Commanders and staff members cannot entirely divorce themselves from the efforts required to obtain, distribute and manage the resources that provide that support, but neither can they allow routine internal operations to distract them from their primary reason for existence: accomplishment of the assigned mission.

To free staffs as much as possible from mundane support activities, all headquarters have staff elements that specialize in operating the headquarters physical plant. In smaller organizations and a few larger tactical commands this "landlord" may be the headquarters company commander or the commander of separate support activities. In most major headquarters, the headquarters commandant supervises, controls and manages headquarters support functions.

The many types of internal support required by staff are appended in detail to show inexperienced staff members what kind of support they will need, what is available and what are their responsibilities to assist in providing and managing that support. To appreciate the complete staff organization, it is necessary to understand the major functions of the headquarters commandant. This can best be done by examining the appended pertinent extracts from the operations and functions assigned to the headquarters commandant of one large US Army headquarters.

Adjutant General

Unlike the headquarters commandant, the adjutant general is primarily mission-oriented. This key staff officer advises and assists the commander in controlling and managing the military's most precious resource, people. He is also the administrative expert, and in this role he becomes heavily involved in internal headquarters operations.

Probably the most revolutionary changes in military procedures incident to technological advances have been in administrative areas. Modern communications equipment and faster transportation of correspondence and publications have made it possible for commanders to greatly increase the volume of written material passed to their subordinate organizations—and the volume of replies demanded. At the same time, the increased sophistication of military weaponry, equipment and operational capabilities has vastly increased the need for rapid and detailed direction and guidance. As a result, all headquarters, even the smaller ones, are virtually inundated with torrents of written material: messages, letters, directives, orders, plans, studies, manuals, bulletins, pamphlets, circulars, regulations, books, magazines and other publications too numerous to list.

Many if not most incoming documents trigger actions within headquarters, creating paper rivers flowing outward and at least equalling the incoming flood. Add to the ebb and flow of massive incoming and outgoing paper tides the constantly circulating eddies of internal written actions (memoranda, disposition forms, studies, estimates, information papers, etc.) and the administrative effort of managing paper work within a headquarters begins to take shape.

To better understand the full magnitude of administrative efforts and their importance several other factors must be considered. Within the staff of a senior commander such as a lieutenant general, fifteen or more staff elements would not be unusual. Each element could be divided into as many as five major divisions, which could be further divided into several smaller subelements (branches, sections, etc.). Working within each subelement are many action officers with specialized areas of interest. The flow of incoming material must be channeled to the proper areas of interest. Each incoming item must find its way to the proper major staff element, progress to the proper subelement and finally reach the interested action officer. The flow of outgoing material follows even more tortuous channels before eventually finding its way into the proper exiting stream. Staff elements, subelements and staff officers are responsible for the flow within their areas of operation.

A second factor to be considered is the relative importance of the many individual papers that constitute the incoming and outgoing floods. Obviously, messages from superior commanders directing immediate actions and requesting replies within short time periods cannot be treated with the same precedence given to periodicals extolling the virtues of the Army's logistical system. Nor can a congressional inquiry be equated to bulletins which pass along routine personnel data. Each headquarters must have systems for retrieving the items requiring urgent action or containing critically needed information from the mass of arriving material.

Possibly most important, the flow of material must be controlled to assure that the incoming material gets to the proper person, and gets there in order of importance, and is acted upon within a reasonable (or unreasonable if demanded by higher authority) time.

Within the headquarters, this control of administration is the function of the adjutant general. Each staff element chief, his subordinate supervisors, and each action officer must do his part in making the administrative system work. The AG must develop the system, supervise its operation, and advise and assist the commander and the rest of the staff and subordinate commands on all matters relating to administration.

The adjutant general's interests are much broader than just the flow of papers. He advises and assists the commander on administrative matters throughout the command and oversees those functions in the subordinate organizations and activities.

The adjutant general's areas of interest are command wide. They encompass all aspects of correspondence management, records and forms management, postal service, reference libraries, printing and publication and personnel administration.

Military Personnel Administration. The adjutant general is also responsible for most administrative functions related to the management of military personnel. In this area of his function, the interface with the personnel staff officer's area of interest is extremely close. The line is difficult to distinguish and is a source of some confusion for even seasoned staff officers. To add to the confusion, commanders differ somewhat in their use of personnel staff officers and adjutants general. In principal, however, the dividing line between the two officers' personnel areas normally lies between broad supervisory responsibilities on the part of the personnel officer and the more functional, records-keeping actions and detailed management by adjutant generals. The organizations and functions manual for one large Army headquarters assigns the following responsibility to its deputy chief of staff, personnel:

... as the commander's principal staff officer with respect to the administration of military and civilian personnel, renders advice and assistance and with appropriate delegation of authority, acts for the commander in the direction, supervision and coordination of plans, policies and procedures pertaining to personnel administration, procurement, distribution and management . . . .

In the same manual, the adjutant general's personnel functions were described in part as follows:

... supervises the implementation of policies and procedures pertaining to the administration and management of military personnel. Exercises operational control over the personnel accounting activity. Exercises command-wide operational and administrative responsibility for Active Army and Reserve Components personnel administration . . . .

In that headquarters the relationship between the personnel officer's duties and those of the adjutant general was extremely close. The differences in their functions exemplifies the basic difference between the general and special staff elements. The duties of the deputy chief of staff, personnel, as those of a general staff officer, revolved around advising and assisting the commander in the broad area of personnel management while the adjutant general was the specialist in the nuts-and-bolts management functions: record keeping, requisitioning, distribution, accounting, etc.

To accomplish these tasks a typical adjutant general's staff section might be organized into four divisions and subactivities, as shown on Chart 3-9. In this example the adjutant general is an independent special staff element reporting directly to the chief of staff. Because of the personnel aspects of his function, some commanders place the adjutant general under the supervision of the personnel staff element.

The appended summary of the major duties of the adjutant general of one large US Army headquarters indicates the wide range of administrative functions in the modern army.

Chart 3.9
Typical Adjutant General Office

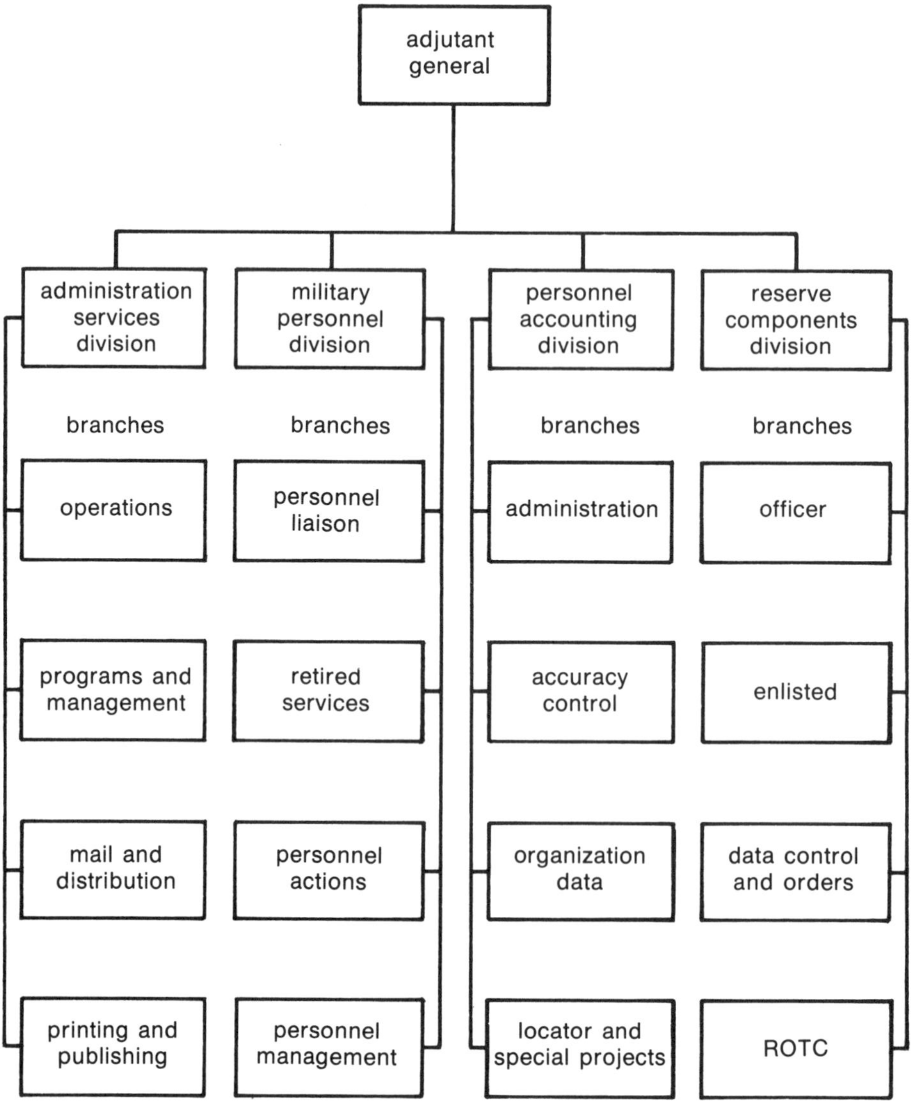

```
                        adjutant
                        general
     ┌─────────────┬────────────┴──┬──────────────┐
administration   military      personnel        reserve
  services      personnel     accounting      components
  division      division       division         division

   branches     branches       branches        branches

  operations   personnel    administration     officer
                liaison

  programs and   retired      accuracy         enlisted
  management    services      control

  mail and     personnel     organization    data control
  distribution  actions        data          and orders

  printing and  personnel    locator and       ROTC
  publishing    management   special projects
```

Provost Marshal

Like their civilian counterparts, military communities must have law enforcement to protect the community members, their property, and public property belonging to the taxpayers. Provost marshals are the staff experts in this important facet of caring for and conserving resources.

The provost marshal's areas of interest are not limited to law enforcement. His assistance to the commander is much broader. He advises and assists, not only in matters pertaining to enforcing laws and regulations that govern military operations and the conduct of its members, but also in several separate but allied functional areas: population and resource control; police intelligence nets; special investigations; operations of military confinement facilities; rehabilitation training centers for military prisoners; collection, evacuation and detainment of prisoners of war; aid to civilian authorities during civil disturbances; and controlling traffic flow in combat areas.

To military commanders these functions, while similar to those performed by civilian police forces, have deeper and more meaningful importance. Crime is regrettable and wasteful under any circumstance. In the military it is doubly costly. Soldiers convicted of criminal activities become burdens in the military as do their counterparts in the civilian community. In the military, however, they also represent losses of personnel resources needed to complete important missions. Stolen and damaged equipment or funds not only are unjustifiable losses to the public but also deplete badly needed physical resources. Therefore, the provost marshal's law enforcement function takes on additional importance to logistics and personnel in that it is intended to conserve human and material resources.

In his other staff functions of assisting the civilian community, handling prisoners of war, directing combat traffic and rehabilitating offenders, the provost marshal becomes a major staff member making direct, significant contributions to the whole command mission. A typical provost marshal's office organization is shown in Chart 3-10. Some of its functions are reflected in the appended sample duties summarized from the organizations and functions manual of a large army headquarters.

Surgeon

The functions of the military surgeon, like those of the provost marshal, closely parallel those of his civilian counterparts. Also like those of the provost marshal, medical responsibilities have a double importance to the military commander. The health of command personnel is of personal interest to all commanders from a purely humane viewpoint and a sincere concern for the troops under their command. But personnel losses from unnecessary illnesses or untimely and inadequate treatment, like losses from crime, are unnecessary and nonproductive expenditures of the most valuable resource, people. Surgeons are important advisors and assistants.

In recent years, increasing numbers of medical activities such as hospitals, dispensaries and clinics have been placed under the direct control of the Surgeon General, Department of the Army, in Washington, D.C. This arrangement has relieved many commanders of all responsibilities for actually operating medical facilities and for the treatment and care of patients.

The health and welfare of personnel remain command functions, however, and require the assistance and advice of professional medical staff officers, including specialists in several fields. Surgeons will continue to be members of most staff organizations.

Chart 3.10
Typical Provost Marshal Office

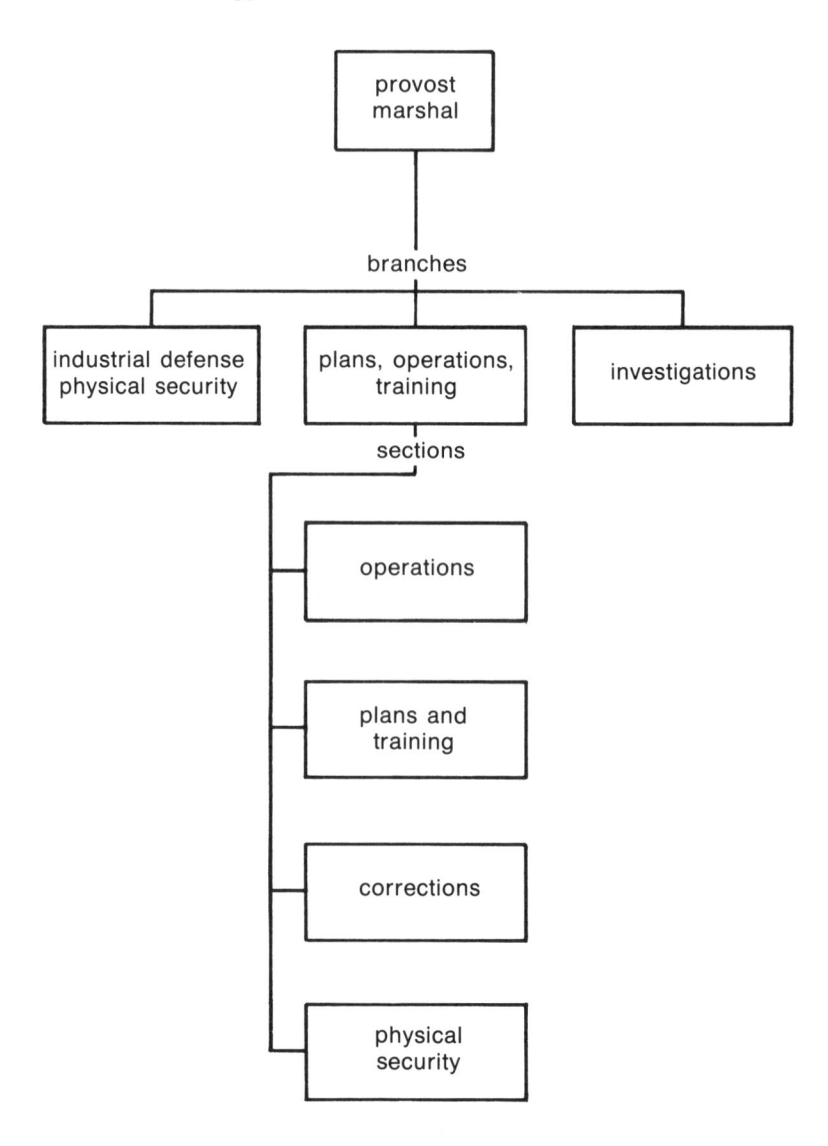

```
                    ┌──────────────────┐
                    │ provost marshal  │
                    └────────┬─────────┘
                             │
                          branches
        ┌────────────────────┼────────────────────┐
┌───────────────────┐ ┌──────────────────┐ ┌──────────────────┐
│ industrial defense│ │ plans, operations,│ │  investigations  │
│ physical security │ │     training     │ │                  │
└───────────────────┘ └────────┬─────────┘ └──────────────────┘
                            sections
                     ┌─────────┤
                     │  ┌──────────────────┐
                     ├──│    operations    │
                     │  └──────────────────┘
                     │  ┌──────────────────┐
                     ├──│ plans and training│
                     │  └──────────────────┘
                     │  ┌──────────────────┐
                     ├──│    corrections   │
                     │  └──────────────────┘
                     │  ┌──────────────────┐
                     └──│ physical security│
                        └──────────────────┘
```

The Major Staff Elements 69

While treatment of the ill, wounded and injured is a major concern to surgeons and commanders, prevention of disease and injuries is of equal concern. Preventive medicine encompasses application of established, practical measures for the prevention of disease and injury, including preventing the spread of communicable diseases, environmental health engineering, sanitation control, entomology and occupational health programs. Like all staff actions, the surgeon's operation must be coordinated and carried out in conjunction with other military activities and with civilian communities. Surgeons must work closely with outside agencies and other elements of the staff.

The duties appended are among those of the surgeon in a large, US Army headquarters. Chart 3-11 shows a typical organization.

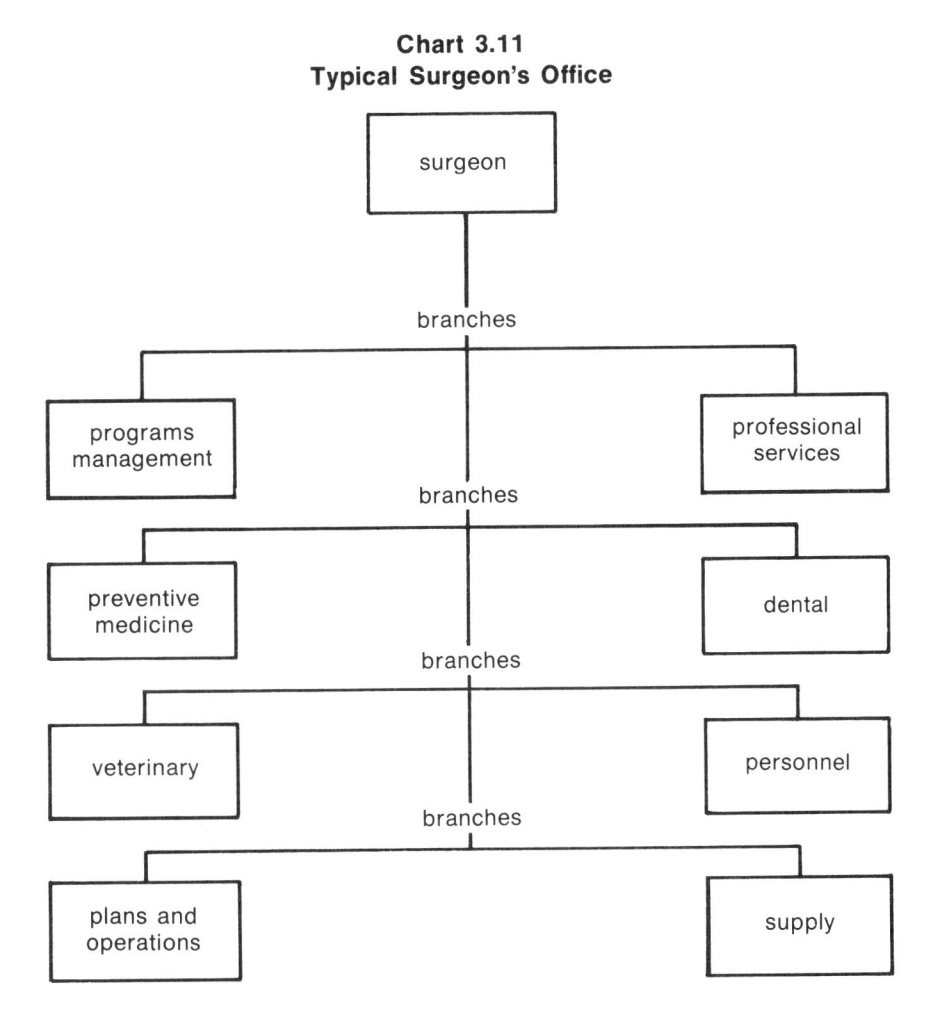

Chart 3.11
Typical Surgeon's Office

```
                    surgeon
                       |
                    branches
    _____|_____
   |                                       |
programs                              professional
management                              services
                    branches
    _____|_____
   |                                       |
preventive                               dental
medicine
                    branches
    _____|_____
   |                                       |
veterinary                             personnel
                    branches
    _____|_____
   |                                       |
plans and                              supply
operations
```

Chaplain

The commander's concern for personnel welfare is second only to his dedication to accomplishing the assigned mission. This concern has two origins: genuine feeling for the fellow human beings for whom he is responsible and the realization that the human resource, like physical equipment, functions best when well cared for. Soldiers who know that their superiors, particularly the commander, are concerned and are making every effort to make their lives as comfortable and pleasant as possible produce more than those who lack this assurance. Possibly no single factor has greater influence on this assurance than religion, even though the average soldier may seldom express this interest and may seldom participate in religious activities.

In most communities religion and the religious organization are important factors. Young people who find themselves far from home in the strange and sometimes seemingly unsympathetic military environment may particularly miss the religious aspect of their lives. Chaplains and their assistants constitute a familiar link between the new environment and the family and community life the soldiers have left behind.

The chaplain's responsibility consists not only of religious services for military personnel and their families, but also of religious education and counseling, advice and assistance for those who have problems that are difficult to discuss with their military leaders. Few commanders fail to recognize the importance of the religious welfare of their personnel and the value of the services rendered by the chaplain. Chaplain staff officers advise the commander on all matters relating to the morality and the morale of the personnel as affected by religion and assist in establishing and supervising active and effective religious programs throughout the command.

Like other staff officers, they cooperate with and advise other members of the staff to help them realize the religious aspects of all proposed actions and to assure that planned religious actions do not interfere with or adversely affect other activities essential to the command mission. Because many religious activities require resources also needed for mission accomplishment, such as transportation, supplies, construction, manpower and (above all) the time of the personnel participating in the activities, the chaplain does not work in a vacuum. He must coordinate with the whole staff.

The appended sample list of duties would be typical for a chaplain of the staff of a senior commander. Chart 3-12 shows a sample organization.

Management Information Systems Office

Management information systems officers are a commander's principal advisors on automation and automated information and data systems. This position is fairly new to the Army and is a good example of recent evolutionary staff changes. The army has used electric accounting machines

**Chart 3.12
Typical Chaplain's Office**

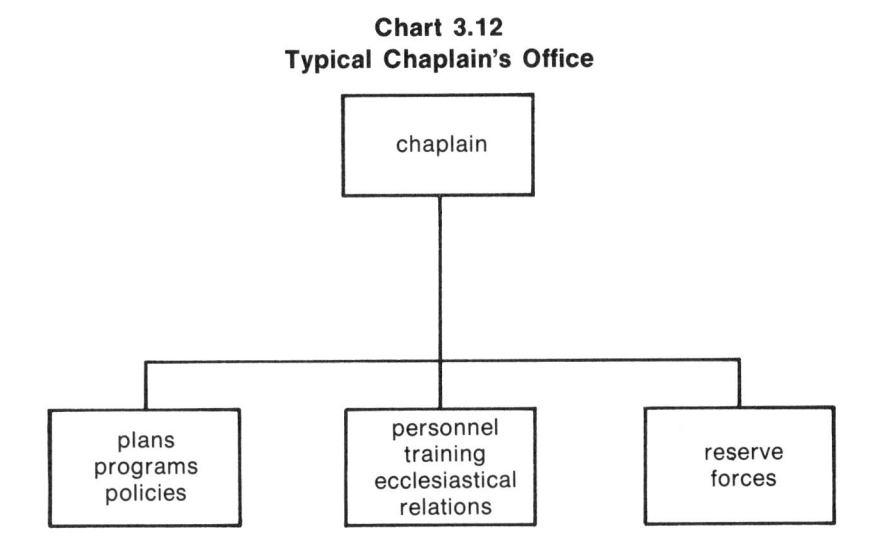

```
                    ┌──────────┐
                    │ chaplain │
                    └────┬─────┘
         ┌───────────────┼───────────────┐
┌────────┴────────┐ ┌────┴──────┐ ┌──────┴──┐
│     plans       │ │ personnel │ │         │
│   programs      │ │ training  │ │ reserve │
│   policies      │ │ecclesiast.│ │ forces  │
│                 │ │ relations │ │         │
└─────────────────┘ └───────────┘ └─────────┘
```

and automatic data processing equipment since those items first became available. In the early years, however, automatic data processing was developed and employed pretty much on a functional basis. Overall coordination and control was lacking. As computer use expanded experimentally the need for centralized direction was met in most large headquarters by establishing the staff position of management information systems officer.

Automated systems have now been developed to simplify and speed day-to-day operations in almost every functional field: personnel, finance, medicine, supply, maintenance, and facilities upkeep and utilization. Special systems are even being developed for use by the Army tactical and support units operating in the field. Divisions will have mobile automatic data processing centers linked automatically to subordinate units and, by teleprocessing ties, to corps and higher headquarters. Critical aspects of division operations such as fire control and logistics will be automated. In fact, the day may be approaching when our success on the battlefield could be determined by the extent and quality of automation.

All major installations in the continental United States and many overseas activities are serviced by computer centers linked by telecommunications with other centers in the chain of command. These systems are designed, installed and managed by functional experts. Most headquarters from division and installation level to Headquarters, Department of the Army, now include systems analysts and technicians in most of their staff elements as well as in the Management Information Systems Office. Although computer operations are controlled and supervised centrally, the real users are in the functional fields. Functional managers evaluate and use the numerous management reports generated and the data stored by automated systems.

In the Army, as in the business world, the use of electric accounting and automatic data processing continues to grow; and prospects for the future reflect the same trend. In fact, the situation has developed to such a point that computer resources are now available to support only those systems with the highest pay-off. Because present operations and future expansion must be tightly controlled, management information systems officers are command managers, establishing policies and determining priorities in the names of their commanders. Their offices are the clearing houses for computer use through which all requirements for new or replacement equipment and new or modified systems must be screened. Sometimes management information systems officers supervise actual data processing operations in the headquarters to which they are assigned, serving not only as staff officers involved with policy and management but as operators as well. Typical MISO organization is shown in Chart 3.13.

Weather Officer

Of all of the many influencing factors which commanders cannot control but which significantly influence mission accomplishment, none is more significant or less predictable than weather. Other factors, such as enemy capabilities, terrain, politics, sociological environments, and so on, often affect only limited aspects of current and planned operations. It is difficult to imagine any action, no matter how specialized, that could not to some extent be adversely affected by climatic extremes. Also, weather is the least subject to control of all influencing factors. Enemy capabilities can be altered by airstrikes, artillery preparations, etc. Construction can master the most forbidding terrain features. Civil affairs experts are trained to deal with and influence extreme political and sociological conditions.

At some future date weather may also succumb to technological advances. At present, and for the foreseeable future, weather continues to be in the hands of a Greater Technician. This being the case, the commander must plan actions and adjust operations around it. To make these plans and adjustments, the commander must have the assistance of a professional weather officer. Often, this valuable professional staff member will be a member of the US Air Force detailed to the Army headquarters.

Because his function is to gather, analyze and disseminate information about factors that influence command missions, the weather officer is sometimes a vital part of the intelligence staff. In other headquarters, he is a special staff element reporting directly to the chief of staff or working through the staff intelligence officer. Commanders have been known to assign their weather officers to their personal staff to eliminate all delays in receiving first hand, expert weather information. The appended sample

(Text continued on page 74)

Chart 3.13
Typical Management Information Systems Office

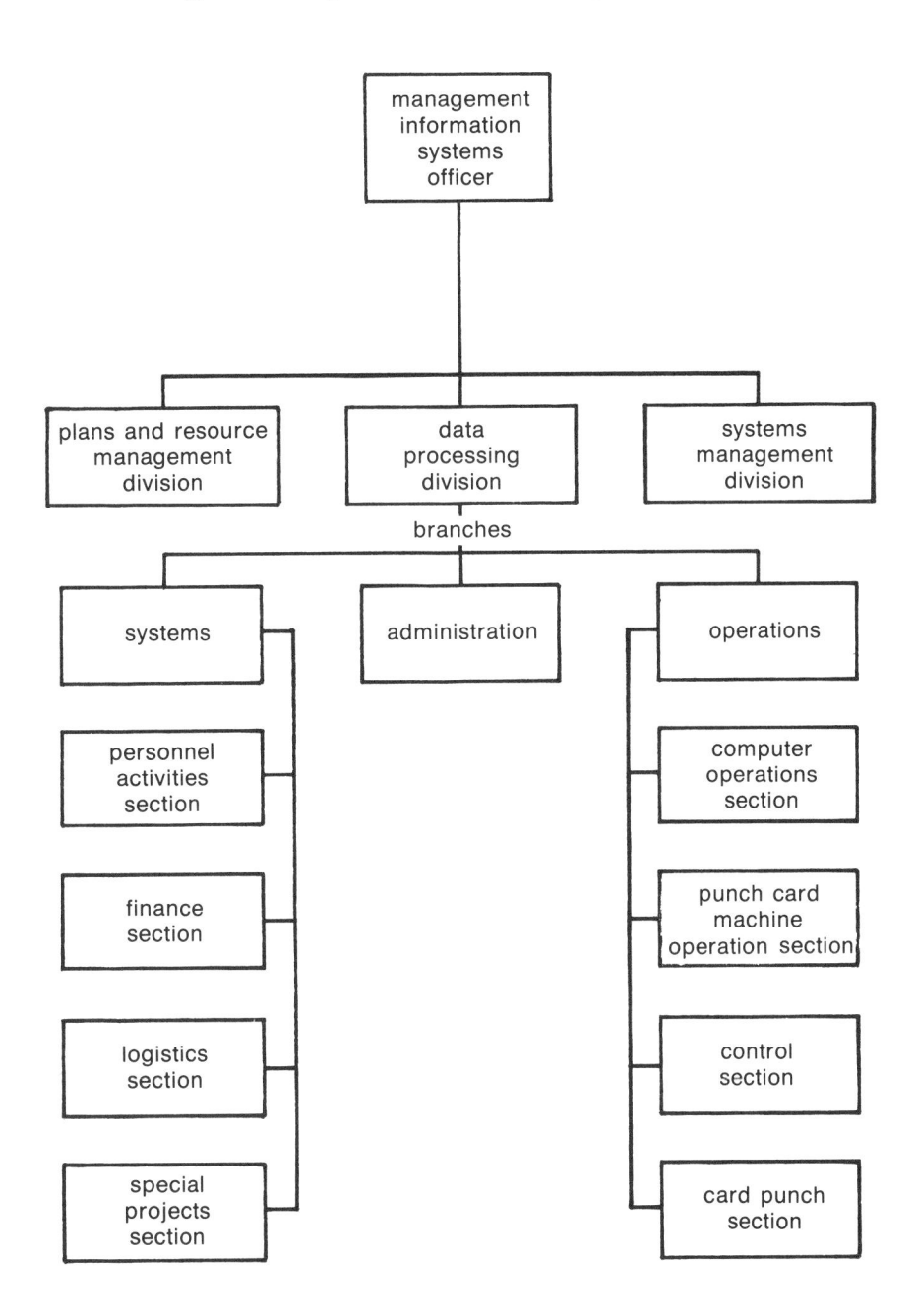

```
                    management
                    information
                      systems
                      officer
                         |
     ┌───────────────────┼───────────────────┐
plans and resource      data             systems
  management          processing        management
    division           division          division
                          |
                       branches
        ┌─────────────────┼─────────────────┐
     systems         administration      operations
        |                                    |
   personnel                            computer
   activities                          operations
    section                              section
        |                                    |
    finance                             punch card
    section                              machine
                                     operation section
        |                                    |
    logistics                            control
    section                              section
        |                                    |
    special                             card punch
    projects                             section
    section
```

weather officer duties were extracted from those assigned in one large headquarters where the weather officer was a special staff element reporting through the intelligence staff.

The Personal Staff

Most commanders rely on their chiefs of staff to supervise the efforts of the general and special staff elements. However, certain aspects of command responsibilities are so sensitive that virtually all commanders designate the staff officers who work in those areas as personal staff officers. Normally, these personal assistants report directly to the commander, at least on certain matters, skipping the chief of staff and other members of the command group. The areas in which sensitive matters most frequently arise are the inspector general's investigatory activities, legal affairs, and dealings with the public, particularly through the news media.

Inspector General

Most staff officers strive for objectivity and make every effort to view all military matters in a purely impersonal light. Commanders have discovered, however, that such objectivity is frequently beyond the reach of people when their own motives, effectiveness and professionalism could be in question. This situation frequently exists in three types of actions: certain investigations, inspections to determine effectiveness and propriety of subordinate operations, and complaints from individuals that their rights have been violated.

Since functional staff elements supervise personnel, intelligence, logistical and operational activities in subordinate commands, investigation into the propriety of those activities implies some criticism of that supervision. Similarly, detailed inspections are to some degree inspections of staff effectiveness, and individual complaints often center around policies related to certain areas of staff interest.

Inspectors general have no functional responsibilities. Therefore, they are able to represent their commanders with complete objectivity. Their status as personal staff officers enables them to work with greater freedom and to enjoy greater confidence from subordinate commanders and their staffs. Despite their somewhat independent status, inspectors general work closely with other staff elements and depend on them for advice and assistance, particularly in the inspection facet of their function.

In most headquarters, the inspector general prepares for an inspection by asking each staff element to submit suggested activities or situations that should be examined and to identify known or suspected problem areas in the organization to be inspected. Experts from the staff elements will often accompany the inspector general's team to assist with the inspection. After the inspection has been completed, the inspector general usually circulates a report of the findings to all staff elements and asks for comments about deficiencies or situations noted. After the inspected commanders report on their corrective action, the staff evaluates and comments to the inspector general on the adequacy of the corrections.

Some complaints require assistance from functional specialists on the staff. Other complaints center around purely human relationships (discrimination, prejudice, insufficient leave, etc.). In those instances, the facts are usually self-evident, and determinations can be made by the inspectors with little assistance from other staff experts.

Frequently, however, complaints center around functional support areas (food, mail, pay, housing, transportation, etc.). These require experts to determine exactly what the individual's entitlements are, to identify assets, and to evaluate the procedures that led to the complaint. The complaint facet of the inspector general's function is an extremely important one which can favorably influence morale and motivation. Most complainants associate their real or imagined mistreatment with actions that their own local chain of command has taken or failed to take. They are inclined to believe that little redress is to be gained from those who caused the problems.

The inspector general provides a healthy alternate channel through which frustrations can be released, even though his reaction to the problem may be identical to that of the complainants' supervisors. The person who feels that his rights were enfringed upon should be convinced that he has had a fair and impartial hearing.

Investigations may or may not involve functional areas of operation requiring expert assistance. Many are associated with circumstances surrounding complaints and are intimately associated with one or more functional areas. Others may involve allegations of improper procedures of a more general nature, requiring no assistance.

In all of their functions, inspectors general frequently must deal with extremely sensitive matters that could have unwarranted ill effects on the Army and on individual members. The personal staff status of the inspector general permits him to keep his commander informed without confiding in other staff members and risking premature release of information on alleged or suspected improprieties that could prove to be groundless. Chart 3.14 shows a typical organization for an inspector general's office.

Staff Judge Advocate

Military commanders have always had legal responsibilities not shared by civilian leaders in industry or government. In our country the three equal and independent branches of government (legislative, executive and judicial) were meant to guarantee that those who make laws, those who enforce laws and those who judge the violators be separate individuals, each answering to different lines of authority. Military commanders, however, are responsible for all three areas: making the local rules, enforcing them and judging those who disobey.

Yet meeting responsibilities, commanders are governed by the same complex statutes, codes and precedents that assure justice in the civilian community, plus the Uniform Code of Military Justice and many regulations and directives imposed by higher echelons of command.

The military equivalent of legislative procedures (issuing orders, regulations, directives, etc.) must conform to all provisions of federal law and the restrictions imposed by the military establishment. Law enforcement practices must remain within accepted standards, maintain discipline, protect people and property, and protect individual and group rights. As in the civilian community, judicial proceedings are subject to reviews and appeals.

A commander could not hope to become an expert in these highly specialized areas; yet both justice and career success often hinge on these important command functions. Small wonder then that most commanders prefer to have a legal advisor, the staff judge advocate, on their personal staffs.

Legal assistance is another staff judge advocate function. Military forces are comprised of normal people. Like everyone else, soldiers often encounter problems that require professional legal assistance. In the United States

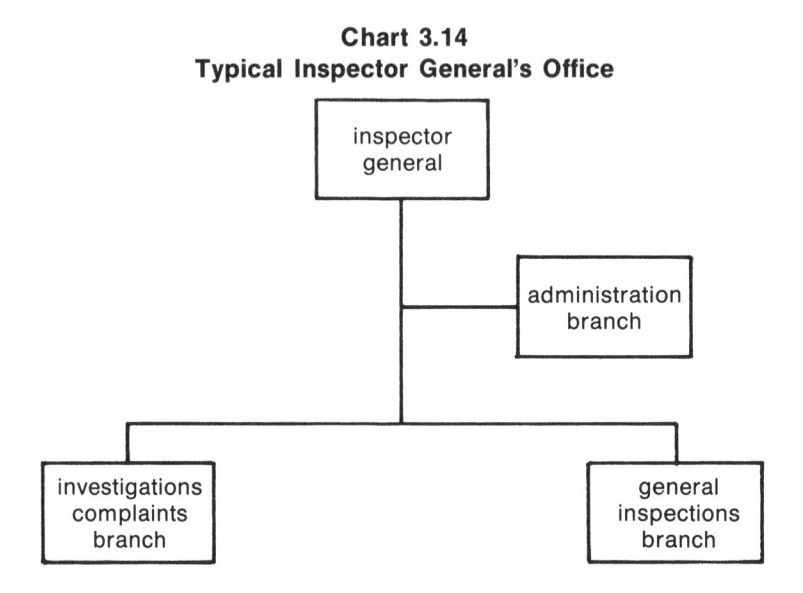

Chart 3.14
Typical Inspector General's Office

```
            inspector
            general
               |
               |----------------administration
               |                 branch
               |
   ------------|------------
   |                       |
investigations          general
complaints             inspections
branch                 branch
```

military men can and often do obtain the services of local civilian counselors, but in overseas areas civilian lawyers are often unavailable. Even in the United States, military personnel sometimes face situations beyond the normal scope of local laws. The availability of legal assistance oriented toward the military environment is a major, positive morale factor.

Another complex and vital legal aspect of command responsibility involves the laws which commanders themselves must obey in carrying out their operations. As stated earlier, all facets of military operations are subject to and must abide by the same federal laws that govern the civilian population. In addition, some military functions, particularly those involving large amounts of public funds, are covered by special legislation. Examples include construction; maintenance of real property; contracting; procurement of supplies, equipment and services from civilian sources; and many facets of employing, using and terminating employment of civilian employees. Commanders must be familiar with all such statutes; but only professionals can fully interpret them and keep abreast of the constant changes both in the letter of the law and in judicial interpretations.

Another consideration, besides dependence on legal advice, influences most commanders to place the staff judge advocate on the personal staff. Command lawyers, like inspectors general, often must handle extremely sensitive incidents and situations which are of no official interest to the functional staff. Chart 3.15 shows a typical organization for staff judge advocate's office.

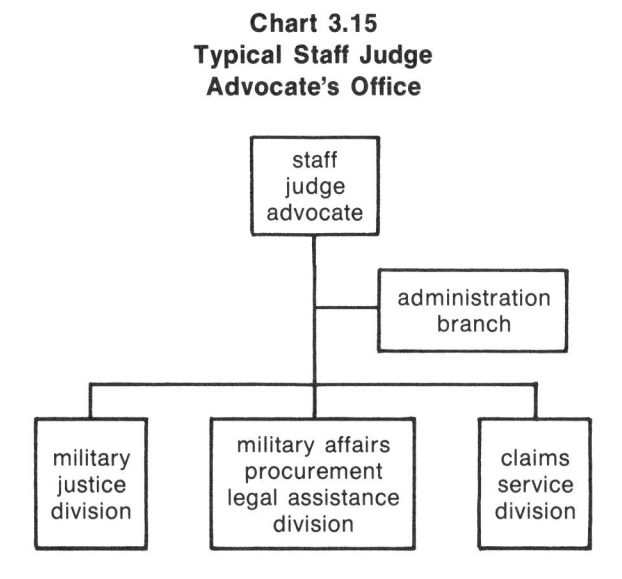

**Chart 3.15
Typical Staff Judge
Advocate's Office**

```
                    staff
                    judge
                   advocate
                      |
                      |────────────administration
                      |                branch
         ┌────────────┼────────────┐
     military     military affairs   claims
     justice      procurement       service
     division     legal assistance  division
                  division
```

Information Officer

The public is interested in the military establishment for several legitimate reasons. For one thing, national defense is expensive and American taxpayers are keenly aware that large portions of their incomes are used to support military activities. Also, many people have relatives and friends serving in one of the military services. On the local level, large military installations and activities have tremendous economic and social impact. The news media reflect public interest and so are anxious to report on military activities. Commanders welcome this interest, but few have the time or the training to personally handle the many details of public relations activities. The information officer provides this essential professional expertise.

Besides helping the commander keep the civilian community informed of military activities, the information officer develops and supervises programs to keep the military informed of significant developments—military and civilian. This is an important function. Its scope depends on the availability of external news sources and the level of command. Commanders at all levels recognize the importance of keeping the troops informed. Unit and installation newspapers are the most common means of accomplishing this program. In isolated areas Armed Forces radio and television networks serve the military communities. Chart 3.16 shows a typical information office organization.

Miscellaneous Staff Specialists

In this chapter we have discussed the staff organizations most commonly used by large US Army organizations, pointing out the primary function of each element. In conclusion, certain specialists who normally work within other staff elements should be mentioned.

Aviation Officer

Army aviation has become a major activity. Fixed-wing and rotary-wing planes provide combat mobility, heavy-lift construction and logistics transport, and fast command-supervision vehicles. These are expensive and sophisticated machines, and the people who operate and maintain them are highly trained experts. The operations staff elements of most Army organizations include an aviation officer who manages aircraft assets and advises the commander and the staff on their use.

Nuclear Weapons Officer

The advent of nuclear weapons with varying amounts of destructive power, diverse uses and multiple methods of employment has placed yet another re-

**Chart 3.16
Typical Information Office**

```
                    information
                     officer
          ┌─────────────┼─────────────┐
    community        public         command
    relations      information    information
     section         section         section
```

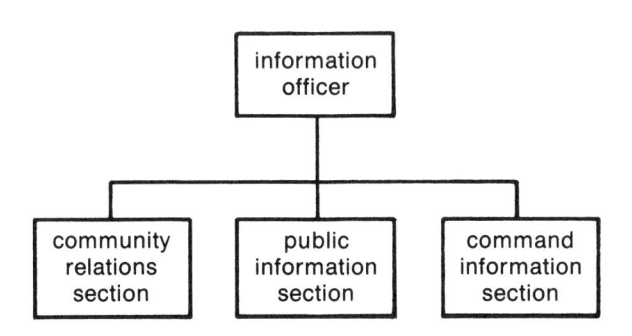

quirement for professional knowledge on commanders and their staffs. All military men must now understand and appreciate the capabilities of these new weapons. Their complexity and the wide range of effects that can be created by their use requires the analysis and evaluation of specially trained experts.

The operations element of most tactical headquarters has nuclear weapons specialists to advise and assist with planning the possible use of nuclear weapons. In the same headquarters, the intelligence staff office probably has similarly trained experts to assist and advise on the possible effects of enemy use of nuclear weapons. Other staff elements of tactical organizations, combat support activities and area commands would have nuclear weaponry specialists to analyze and evaluate the effects of nuclear strikes on their respective operations.

Emergency Operations Centers

Staffs are organized and manned to meet everyday requirements. They function best in their normal configuration, with references handy and coworkers in their accustomed places so that the full staff can focus on problems that arise.

Unfortunately, military activities are often far from routine. Situations arise that would be most difficult for normal staff configurations to handle. These emergencies are often so critical that staff work and command decisions must be almost instantaneous. To meet such unusual requirements many headquarters maintain emergency operations centers, normally operated by the operations staff element and manned, when activated, by highly qualified personnel from the major staff elements and such special staff representatives as are needed.

Appendix to Chapter 3

Engineer Battalion Skills
(extracted from TOE 5-155H, dtd. 30 November 1970)

Combat engineer senior sergeant
Combat engineer
Combat engineer tracked-vehicle crewman
Pioneer
Atomic demolition munitions specialist
Bridge specialist
Construction surveyor
Rodman and tapeman
Soils analyst
Construction draftsman
General draftsman
General construction machine supervisor
General construction machine operator
Crane operator
Crawler tractor operator
Grader operator
Rough-terrain forklift operator
Recovery specialist
Engineer equipment repairman
Track-vehicle mechanic
Wheel-vehicle mechanic
Machinist
Welder
Tank-turret repairman
Mechanical-maintenance helper
Equipment-maintenance clerk
Powerman
Power-generation-equipment operator/mechanic
Water-supply specialist
Tactical communications chief

Field radio mechanic
Avionics mechanic
Supplyman
Armored-unit supply specialist
Clerk typist
Legal clerk
Chaplains assistant
Medical specialist
Clinical specialist
Food service specialist

Motivational Activities

Social Activities

lounges
dayrooms
service clubs
non-commissioned officers clubs
officers clubs
hobby groups
teen clubs

Athletic Activities

gymnasiums
golf courses
bowling alleys
rod and gun clubs
team sports
tennis courts

Religious Activities

church services (chapels)
religious education
counseling
retreats
literature

Educational Activities

military occupational courses (MOS Improvement)
high school equivalent general educational development (GED)
civilian university courses
correspondence courses (military and civilian)

Community Recreational Facilities

libraries
theaters
plays (little theater groups)

parks
recreation centers
beaches
swimming pools

Personal Assistance

Army Emergency Relief
Red Cross
survivor assistance
insurance advisors
retirement assistance
voting assistance and information

Infantry Division Equipment, 1923
(selected items)

Weapons

9,734	pistols
8,349	rifles
648	rifles with grenade dischargers
792	rifles, automatic
207	machine guns (4 types)
12	mortars, 3-inch
48	guns, 75mm
22	guns, 37mm

Mobility

25	tanks (24 fighting, light, one signal–light)
13	airplanes
406	trucks (all types)
191	motorcycles (26 with sidecars)
4	reconnaissance cars
53	passenger cars
190	bicycles
40	motor ambulances
20	animal-drawn ambulances
513	wagons
459	carts
6,944	horses and mules

Communications

3	radio trucks (includes 1 repair truck)
6	radio trailers

Infantry Division Equipment, Early 1970's
(selected items)

Weapons

2,645	pistols, .45 caliber
235	revolvers .38 caliber

13,459	rifles, 5.56mm
528	sub-machine guns, .45 caliber
610	machine guns, 7.62mm
568	machine guns, .50 caliber
1,135	rifle grenade launchers
38	aircraft rocket launchers, 2.75-inch
117	recoilless rifles, 90mm
48	recoilless rifles, 106mm
54	mortars 81mm
49	mortars 4.2-inch
24	antiaircraft guns, 20mm
24	antiaircraft missile systems
54	howitzers, 105mm
18	howitzers, 155mm
4	howitzers, 8-inch
4	rocket launchers, 7.62mm

Mobility

27	armored reconnaissance assault vehicles
18	assault boats, 15-man
28	reconnaissance boats, 3-man
4	bridge launchers, M60 tank chassis
3	tank-mounted bulldozers
10	tractor-mounted bulldozers
4	cargo carriers, tracked
176	command and reconnaissance carriers
78	command-post carriers
346	personnel carriers, full-tracked
49	107mm mortar carriers
3	combat engineer vehicles
7	truck-mounted cranes
4	graders
15	attack helicopters
34	observation helicopters
39	utility helicopters
80	recovery vehicles
216	tanks, 105mm gun
3,008	trucks, all types
1,961	trailers, all types

Communications

50	radar sets
3,162	radio sets
57	radio teletypewriters
267	telephone switchboards
2,582	telephones, all types
13	teletypewriters
34	public address sets
3	motion picture camera sets
14	still picture camera sets

Communications and Electronics
(sample duties)

1. Advise the commander and his staff on tactical communications-electronics facilities, including headquarters locations communications electronics activities used for deception.
2. Monitor planning, installation, operations, maintenance and inspection of all tactical telecommunications systems, equipment and services throughout the command.
3. Monitor development of requirements for communications-electronics support and for signal units.
4. Monitor matters pertaining to activation, inactivation, organization, reorganization, establishment, movement, attachments, change of status, equipping, and personnel staffing of all TOE and TDA Army signal units and activities.
5. Recommend priorities for issue or allocation of communications electronics equipment and supplies to meet operational and training requirements.
6. Monitor tactical facilities and equipment excess reports and recommend redistribution of communications-electronics assets to insure that all supplies and equipment are fully and properly used.
7. Coordinate and monitor initial issue of cryptographic material and the establishment of cryptographic accounts.
8. Conduct technical inspections to evaluate the use, handling, safeguarding, storing and maintenance of communications-electronics equipment and material, including cryptographic equipment, by tactical units.
9. Exercise staff supervision over communications security and implements security policies and doctrine with the headquarters and subordinate commands.
10. Conduct cryptographic inspections, correcting minor irregularities on the spot and reporting major deficiencies in writing to subordinate commanders subsequent to inspections.
11. Review reports of inspection by other agencies and see that deficiencies are corrected.
12. Establish and operate the communications and electronics portion of emergency operations center, as required.
13. Exercise staff supervision over operation of the common user (AUTODIN) communications center facilities at subordinate activities and the headquarters communications center.
14. Coordinate joint use of communication center facilities with other government agencies.
15. Implement policies and directives, disseminate technical information to field communications centers and conduct staff visits and inspections to insure that prescribed standards are met.
16. Cooperate with appropriate activities to make available data transceiving computer programs to provide the necessary systems for the headquarters and subordinate communications centers.

17. Conduct periodic studies and recommend changes to the computer programs to meet changes in requirements.
18. Collect and analyze digital status reports from subordinate activities and recommend appropriate changes in personnel and equipment requirements and in internal procedural requirements.
19. Manage the command's authorized electromagnetic spectrum resources.
20. Coordinate frequencies with other federal agencies.
21. Maintain frequency assignment and usage records needed for frequency management and provide the information and data required for national electromagnetic spectrum management to higher headquarters.
22. Issue instructions to subordinate activities for collecting data for the Department of Defense electromagnetic compatibility program and review data submitted by those activities before forwarding to the electromagnetic compatibility analysis center.
23. Prepare and distribute standing signal instructions (SSI) and signal operations instructions (SOI).
24. Advise on matters pertaining to electromagnetic radiation environments and source produced radio frequencies and coordinate measures to reduce their effects.
25. Act as
    A. liaison officer to the headquarters maneuver director during exercises,

    B. communications-electronics representative during operational phases of maneuvers and field exercises,

    C. project officer for the Department of Defense electromagnetic compatibility program,

    D. representative at technical training inspections, as

    E. Army frequency manager for the command area, and

    F. electromagnetic compatibility control officer.
26. Prepare communications-electronics aspects of plans in coordination with other staff elements.
27. Supervise communications-electronic activities when plans are implemented.
28. Review appropriate parts of plans of subordinate and supporting commands.
29. Monitor the training readiness of assigned and attached signal units.
30. Monitor requirements for new equipment introductory teams (signal) and new equipment training teams to provide on-site instruction.
31. Monitor quota requirements for training schools operated by the Army or by the communications-electronics industry.
32. Coordinate installation, operation and maintenance of the record communications systems such as AUTODIN provided by higher headquarters and other agencies for common user service.

33. Analyze requirements for and initiate actions to obtain new telecommunications center computers and changes in existing facilities, equipment, supplies, personnel, operating spaces, etc.

34. Insure proper reproduction and distribution of incoming electrically transmitted messages and operate the headquarters telecommunications center.

35. Supervise and coordinate audiovisual activities including all photographic facility operations and the distribution of equipment, training films and allied materials through the audiovisual support center system.

36. Recommend establishing, discontinuing, or reclassifying audiovisual facilities.

37. Reallocate audiovisual equipment within the command area to satisfy local requirements.

38. Loan films, film strips, transparencies and audiovisual equipment to all authorized users within the designated support area. Perform organizational maintenance on equipment and films.

39. Provide photographic service to troop units and other authorized activities including color film supplies, color film processing and printing, and motion picture and still photographic teams.

40. Design and prepare detailed specifications and drawings for installation and construction of minor communications facilities.

41. Communications systems include but are not limited to:

   A. telephone plants consisting of dial, manual and magneto systems, wire carrier terminal equipment, control switchboards and consoles, and complex key telephone systems.

   B. high frequency radio systems, including single-sideband voice, teletype, and data transmission systems.

   C. on-line automatic encryption systems for voice, teletype, and data transmission.

   D. range instrumentation, consisting of microwave and carrier systems for transmission of the complex information required for surveillance and tracking radar, multiple synchronized timing pulses, telemetry data for computers, and video signals for closed circuit television displays.

   E. closed circuit television systems, including studio cameras, tape recording equipment, switching and control systems, video transmission systems and complete van-mounted mobile pickup facilities.

   F. air navigational aids such as ground approach landing systems, beacons, air-to-ground radio and tower control systems.

   G. mobile radio for fire, guard, taxi, and utility dispatch systems including fixed stations and remote control equipment.

   H. complex high fidelity auditorium and theater-type public address systems, including post-wide intercommunicating systems, hospital program distribution systems, and command and control systems.

Headquarters Commandant
(typical duties)

1. Furnish housekeeping personnel and facilities for very important visitors.
2. Supervise service of visitors' quarters including scheduling of suites.
3. Coordinate military aircraft and sedan use.
4. Review temporary duty requests to determine the most economical method of travel.
5. Inspect and supervise maintenance of special troops administrative records.
6. Supervise, monitor, and prepare correspondence pertaining to military personnel assigned to special troops units.
7. Maintain the strength rosters for the special troops.
8. Maintain the records used in promotions and reductions of special troops enlisted personnel.
9. Coordinate and schedule use of the headquarters conference rooms.
10. Plan, schedule and supervise the training of headquarters military personnel in general military subjects.
11. Plan and coordinate honor guards and ceremonies.
12. Prepare the headquarters commandant portion of all headquarters operations orders.
13. Prepare quarterly, monthly, and weekly training schedules.
14. Schedule inspections of the special troops training program and inspect training records.
15. Prepare and maintain charts, project boards, and records for headquarters commandant activities.
16. Review and process requests for facilities repairs, maintenance and modifications submitted by staff offices and headquarters support units.
17. Supervise the records management and forms management programs.
18. Review, process and coordinate military justice actions.
19. Control parking decals issued by the headquarters commandant's office.
20. Requisition, receive, store, issue, and account for supplies and equipment required by the headquarters.
21. Inspect and supervise organizational maintenance for headquarters equipment.
22. Maintain supply records.
23. Supervise fire protection program for headquarters facilities.

24. Supervise the following additional functions:
    a. maintenance of grounds.
    b. flag setups for various ceremonies.
    c. blood donor program.
    d. athletic and recreation programs.
    e. coordinating security policies and enforcement with the host installation.

Adjutant General
(typical duties)

1. Supervise administrative services for all elements of the command and provide internal administrative services for the headquarters.
2. Supervise command-wide records management programs, including alternate files and communications with and service to the public.
3. Supervise correspondence management, mail management, files maintenance and disposition procedures, and use of office copiers and filing equipment in the staff and subordinate headquarters.
4. Conduct annual administration surveys of subordinate activities to evaluate the administrative services functions of the adjutant general.
5. Conduct biennial records surveys in headquarters staff offices and at subordinate commands.
6. Develop procedures and directives necessary for the effective control of documents for alternate files programs designed to meet requirements of emergency and contingency plans.
7. Supervise office copying equipment and nonstandard filing equipment procurement throughout the command.
8. Coordinate, supervise, and assist in preparing adjutant general portions of command operating programs and command operating budgets.
9. Continually review and analyze program execution and resource utilization to attain programmed objectives.
10. Supervise command-wide postal service.
11. Supervise administrative functions associated with the receipt, distribution, dispatch and specialized processing-monitoring, as appropriate, of all command correspondence.
12. Provide the headquarters with unclassified messenger and postal services, breakdown and distribution of bulk mail, identification and specialized processing of command group and congressional communications, and final review and distribution of outgoing correspondence and printed matter.
13. Provide classified messenger and command courier service.
14. Maintain top secret and registered communication control points.
15. Maintain reference library of classified and unclassified publications.
16. Supervise command-wide publications stockrooms and provide command-wide publications support.

Appendix to Chapter 3   89

17. Supervise command-wide printing controls and provide command-wide printing and reproduction support.
18. Provide publications, blank forms, printing and reproduction support services to headqquarters staff.
19. Make initial distribution and resupply of Department of the Army and other publications and blank forms to headquarters staff.
20. Coordinate heraldic and military awards functions of the command and process awards and decorations actions for the headquarters.
21. Provide editorial and preparation services for administrative directives and orders issued by the headquarters.
22. Provide command-wide technical assistance for publications media.
23. Provide illustrator services for headquarters.
24. Review for administrative standards all publications and directives submitted in final form for reproduction, including proofreading.
25. Edit and prepare administrative orders.
26. Supervise military personnel administration and management.
27. Administer line-of-duty actions, appointment of RA officers, pay, and officer efficiency reports, including those for officers who are assigned outside the headquarters but rated, endorsed or reviewed by headquarters personnel.
28. Administer personnel management actions pertaining to distribution and utilization of the active-duty military personnel of the command, including requisition, classification, assignment, reassignment, and promotion. Assure proper utilization of personnel according to MOS and grade. Administer enlisted evaluation program. Monitor actions relating to levies. Process applications for school training and monitor school quotas.
29. Control requisitioning, distribution, reporting, assignment, reassignment, allocation of enlisted promotion quotas. Process operational deferment requests for enlisted personnel.
30. Maintain statistical records of personnel assets and evaluate personnel readiness reports.
31. Monitor and control enlisted permanent party TDY or permanent change of station requirements.
32. Process applications for compassionate, permissive and exchange reassignments and for compassionate deferments from foreign service.
33. Monitor enlisted evaluations within command.
34. Review military occupational specialty reclassification actions and supervise the Military Occupational Data Bank Questionnaires administration.
35. Control requisitioning, distribution, assignment and reassignment of officers below the grade of colonel.
36. Fill temporary duty requirements for officers below the grade of colonel.
37. Maintain statistical data concerning current and anticipated officer strengths.
38. Allocate and control use of Army school quotas.

39. Administratively process military and civilian employee requests, applications, and nominations to attend Army schools.
40. Prepare and disseminate command directives and other information relating to attendance at Army schools.
41. Administer personnel actions relating to retired personnel, nonbattle casualty reporting and the uniformed services identification card program.
42. Inspect military personnel files at all levels of command, including classification, utilization and assignment of personnel; records maintenance; personnel accounting; data reporting; enlisted evaluation; proficiency pay; promotions; personnel actions; and personnel readiness files. Conduct unannounced reinspection of unsatisfactory units within 60 days.
43. Provide unit personnel administration for all assigned and attached headquarters military personnel.

Provost Marshal
(sample duties)

1. Advise commander and staff on military police affairs, including policy and the training, equipping and employing of military police personnel and units.
2. Supervise command police operations to maintain order and discipline, including criminal investigations, physical security, and crime prevention.
3. Maintain liaison with civil police agencies, Federal Bureau of Investigation, Secret Service, Federal Bureau of Narcotics and other law enforcement agencies.
4. Prepare provost marshal portion of contingency plans.
5. Develop, coordinate and supervise portions of operating programs pertaining to Army provost marshal's activities.
6. Receive, review and process serious incident reports and forward to higher headquarters those which qualify. Insure, where appropriate, that supplemental and terminal reports are submitted.
7. In coordination with personnel staff, review and recommend action on applications for commissions in the Military Police Corps Reserve.
8. Monitor and advise subordinate commanders on motor vehicle traffic supervision and administration.
9. Help appropriate staff elements prepare agreements pertaining to preservation of order with other armed services, federal and local law enforcement agencies.
10. Analyze statistical data reports on provost marshal and military police activities to determine trends; identify problem areas where applicable; recommend corrective action.
11. Coordinate military convoy movements with civil authorities when required.
12. Supervise command participation in the National Crime Information Center system.
13. Supervise the Absentee Apprehension Programs to include monitoring reports pertaining to personnel who are absent without leave (AWOL).
14. Monitor Armed Forces Disciplinary Control Board actions.

15. In coordination with the personnel, operations and training, and logistics staff representatives, plan for provost marshal and military police participation in field exercises.
16. Recommend allocation and distribution of military police units and equipment.
17. In coordination with operations and training, observe and evaluate Army training tests of military police units.
18. Supervise the custody and rehabilitation of military prisoners.
19. Supervise and coordinate criminal investigations, crime prevention surveys, character investigations and other investigative tasks as assigned.
20. Conduct on-site industrial defense surveys of industrial facilities and advise management on suggested corrective measures for deficiencies noted during surveys.
21. Advise and assist management in developing industrial defense plans and mutual aid programs.
22. Supervise programs for safeguarding small arms and ammunitions. Review, evaluate and maintain records of weapons and ammunition lost and recovered.

Army Surgeon
(sample duties)

1. Advise the commander and staff on the medical aspects of operations.
2. Supervise medical department facilities and activities of the command, including medical, dental, veterinary, nursing, and ancillary medical functions.
3. Advise on medical, operational, planning, training and medical supply and maintenance services.
4. Supervise individual and unit medical training throughout the command.
5. Manage medical personnel use and provide technical assistance and recommendations on medical personnel actions to include requirements, procurement, appointments, assignments, classification and transfers.
6. Supervise medical laboratory operations.
7. Exercise operational control over veterinary food inspection units.
8. Serve on the Program Budget Advisory Committee as program director for operating program medical activities.
9. Assisted by the chief nurse, advise and assist on all matters pertaining to nursing services, the Army Nurse Corps and nursing service personnel.
10. Inspect nursing activities to insure high professional standards.

Chaplain
(sample duties)

1. Advise the commander and his staff on all matters pertaining to religion, spiritual and moral welfare, and the morale of military personnel, their dependents, and civilian employees within the command area.

2. Provide guidance, policies, and procedures for comprehensive programs of chaplain activities to include group and individual worship services, individual religious ministrations, religious education, pastoral care and character guidance.
3. Interpret and implement policies and directives and disseminate technical information pertaining to chaplain activities.
4. Supervise and coordinate technical training of the chaplain and chaplain assistants, including branch training.
5. Represent the commander to civilian religious communities and promote the cooperation of the general public, civilian churches and religious organizations in chaplain activities.
6. Supervise planning, programming and funding for chapel construction, chaplain and chapel equipment, religious activities, and civilian personnel employees.
7. Advise subordinate command chaplains on purchase of nonstandard items of supplies and equipment.
8. Coordinate personnel actions affecting chaplains, staff specialists, chaplain assistants and auxiliary chaplains.
9. Conduct religious services and provide counseling to individuals.
10. Conduct staff visits and technical inspections and participate in command inspections.
11. Maintain liaison with staff chaplains of other headquarters and other services.
12. Insure that chaplain activities are integrated with the overall program of the command.

Weather Officer
(sample duties)

1. Advise and assist the commander and his staff on all matters pertaining to weather.
2. Inform the commander and his staff about Air Weather Service capabilities, limitations, plans and activities which may affect weather support to the command.
3. Advise Air Weather Service of command requirements for climatological information, weather forecasts, reports of current weather, weather summaries and weather advice.
4. Recommend to Air Weather Service new doctrine, developments, procedures and equipment needed to provide weather service to the command.
5. Monitor the service actually provided to units and activities subordinate to the commander by USAF Air Weather Service units compared to actual requirements, and recommend improvement as appropriate.
6. Evaluate weather factors in connection with investigations concerning Army aircraft accidents or incidents in which weather or weather service are actual or suspected causes.
7. Interpret weather information; brief and advise the commander and his staff.

4. Procedures

Ever since commanders first began using advisors and assistants to help with the planning and execution of military missions, they have recognized the advantages of standardized organizational structures to help these advisors and assistants function effectively. They have also realized that formalized procedures are necessary for maximum productivity. Although staff organization changes because of technological advances and changes in strategy and tactics, staffs are relatively standardized by the common interest of commanders in the four basic considerations: people, resources, information, and planning and supervision. Standardized procedures for eliciting valid, coordinated and mutually agreed upon advice and assistance from a staff have developed slowly.

Even at the major staff element level, conflicting interests make agreements difficult to reach. Personnel experts wish to spare human resources; logisticians are dedicated to conserving physical assets. Intelligence specialists tend to view all problems through the eyes of an enemy and with an eye to adverse outside influences. The operator wishes only to succeed at any cost.

Obviously, these conflicting interests are unlikely to reach immediate concensus on even the simplest problem. At lower organizational levels the divergence becomes more marked, making agreement difficult even within the major staff elements.

Personnel officers are responsible for maintaining an adequate force of qualified and motivated people, a seemingly clear-cut, well defined responsibility. Within this broad area of interest, however, are many subareas. Each is important, and each is supervised by experts inclined to think their own functions are the most important to mission success. Before the personnel expert, for instance, can take a stand in favor of the solution most compatible with his responsibilities, he must settle many differences within his own shop.

The logistician's house is similarly divided. It is difficult to imagine a problem, solution or course of action that would meet the unanimous approval of supply, transportation, maintenance, engineering and other support experts. The problem is magnified in logistics by the fact that resources are seldom sufficient to meet all the requirements of the many missions, tasks and projects that the commander would like to accomplish. Every expert in the logisticians office, therefore, is extremely conscious of the need to conserve the resource for which he is responsible. Unfortunately, conservation of one resource usually means greater expenditure of another. Like the personnel officer, the logistician must resolve his in-house controversies before he can take a position.

The intelligence staff probably encounters the fewest areas of internal disagreement on most problems. Even there, of course, it is likely that specialists will feel strongly that their own areas deserve greater consideration. Adverse weather could be argued to outweigh difficult terrain or certain possible enemy reactions. Those who study terrain factors or enemy capabilities and probable actions would disagree.

Even the operator, with his clear-cut function of getting the job done, may find wide divergences of opinion within his organization. Opinions and preferences for operating methods are apt to be highly colored by individual experience and training. On a tactical staff armored, infantry, airborne, airmobile, and special forces backgrounds are certain to produce many recommended courses of action. On technical staffs supply, maintenance, engineering, transportation, and other backgrounds would cause diverse opinions on the conduct of support operations.

Without controls and standardized procedures, problem-solving would be next to impossible. Even the simplest of routine problems would become mired in controversy. Major actions involving mission accomplishment would be completely stymied. Military scholars, military educational institutions and individual commanders and their staffs have tried to develop procedures to produce optimum results from staff organizations without inhibiting the initiative of individual members. Many methods have been tried. Unfortunately, the perfect system has not been discovered. Controlling and managing human thought processes is much more difficult than standardizing headquarters organizations, but most commanders recognize the need for orderly, standardized procedures for attacking problems.

Commanders differ in many respects—character, mental capacity, reasoning processes, temperament—virtually every human characteristic. These differences are reflected in their individual approaches to problem-solving and their methods for managing their staffs. Procedures for solving problems vary from headquarters to headquarters. When they are analyzed, however, striking similarities become apparent. Despite differences in approach, most commanders recognize the same important management techniques and stress the same critical aspects of staff operations: speed, coordination, thorough consideration of all factors, evaluation of all possible solutions, clarity and completeness of directives, and supervision to ascertain that those directives are being followed.

Although commanders may achieve essentially the same results from their staffs by somewhat different methods and varying orders of precedence, certain identifiable steps are common to all of them and constitute a more or less standard problem-solving procedure.

Standard Procedures

General Approach

Presenting any discussion or explanation step by step has one critical weakness common to the cookbooks with which this method is often associated. The difficulty is in avoiding the impression that each step is a completely separate function to be finished before beginning the next. In practice neither the good cook nor the effective staff officer can afford to ignore future steps in the process as he strives to complete an attractive, edible product. Presented with a complex recipe to be prepared in a limited time, the expert cook recognizes many tasks that can be started immediately even though they are well down in the procedure. Some of them must be started long before they are to be used. The experienced staff officer does not wait until his input to the problem-solving process is due before he starts to get it ready. Like the good cook, he returns often to the recipe to be certain that no essential step is slighted and no ingredient omitted.

The generally accepted procedure by which the commander and his staff solve military problems consists of eight distinguishable steps. For clarity these steps are first summarized in the following outline. They are then discussed separately to explain the logic and importance of each and how each fits into the overall process.

Staff Procedures Outline

1. *Identify problem.* Commander and staff analyze mission, task or problem to determine scope and magnitude and to identify included tasks.

2. *Consider available information.* Staff informs commander of aspects of current situation bearing on mission or task to be undertaken or problem to be solved.

3. *Commander's initial guidance.* Commander informs staff of his interpretation of mission, task or problem and issues instructions, states policies and provides guidance for use by staff in choosing solution or course of action.

4. *Study problem.* Staff studies mission, task or problem in light of all identifiable influencing factors, prepares estimates or studies and recommends course of action or problem solution.

5. *Decision.* Based on studies or estimates, commander chooses course of action or solution to be undertaken.
6. *Planning.* Staff develops detailed, time-phased plans for implementing commander's decision.
7. *Orders.* Commander orders subordinate commanders to implement plans developed by staff and approved by him.
8. *Supervision.* Commander, assisted by staff, supervises subordinate commanders and their staffs to assure that orders are carried out.

Procedures. Each of the steps summarized in the outline is essential to the development of sound, supportable recommendations by the staff and workable decisions by the commander. Further, the detailed consideration of all possible courses of action and solutions to problems provides alternatives which can be applied if the situation changes. To fully understand these advantages it is necessary to examine each step in order.

Step 1—Identifying the Problem

Military missions, tasks and problems spring from many sources. They may be directed by superiors or identified as inherent to broader, overall responsibilities. They may arise from unforeseen changes in situations or influencing factors or be recommended or proposed by subordinate commanders. They may be correlaries to actions contemplated by other commands and agencies. Regardless of the sources, military problems are seldom simple. Military commanders, like cooks, must first determine what is to be produced and when it is to be completed before they can begin. Unlike cooks, military commanders are seldom presented with both the problem and the detailed instructions for its solution at the same time. Neither are they handed a complete list of all the ingredients (included tasks) necessary to accomplish the mission or solve the problem. If this were possible, the level of command receiving such explicit instructions could probably be eliminated with little loss to the nation's defense.

Upon receiving or identifying a mission, task or problem, the commander's first consideration is to determine exactly what is expected of him, when it must be accomplished and, to the extent necessary, why. This may appear to be so obvious that it requires no discussion. Yet one of the greatest weaknesses of all problem solvers (not only in the military) is a tendency to plunge headlong into the solution before understanding the problem.

Few military leaders pass the platoon level without at some time presenting their troops in perfect formation, properly equipped, faultlessly instructed, and on time—at the wrong place. The senior leader cannot afford the penalties of undue haste. He must be certain that both he and his staff understand the problem to be solved—*before* they solve it.

While the first step truly belongs to the commander, the staff is not excused from advising and assisting him. Often, perhaps usually, the staff becomes aware of new missions and tasks or identifies problems before the commander is aware that they exist. Only a most ineffective (and unwise) staff would present the problem to the commander without first using expertise and experience to determine the full extent of the matter. Although the commander may delete some of the factors identified, add some of his own, even completely revise the staff's interpretation, it is still the duty of the staff to try to help him with every facet of his responsibilities.

Step 2—Considering Available Information

The difficulty of new missions, tasks and problems is relative to the particular situation of those who must deal with them. A river-crossing project would present little challenge to an engineering organization newly arrived in the area with equipment in good condition and not yet committed to other projects. It could be an ulcer-builder for the commander and staff of an engineering unit already heavily committed to essential work, particularly if men and equipment had begun to feel and show the strain of being overextended. Orders to initiate an offensive might be just routine for a well trained, fully equipped tactical unit not committed to any other missions but near impossibility for one that is barely holding its own in a hotly contested battle area. These are extreme examples of the type of information considered by commanders and staffs in the second stage of the problem-solving process—evaluation of the current situation, the position of the command, and the peculiarities of new requirements or problems.

This is an *initial* analysis of the situation. It may serve as a point of departure for the much more detailed study and analyses that follow later in the procedure, but to the alert staff this step is far more than a cursory examination of obvious considerations. Each staff member must be at all times well informed on the details of the ongoing operations affecting his area of interest, as well as the weaknesses and strengths of the resources for which he is responsible and their effects on all facets of the situation. A well informed staff should be able to discuss the effects of current conditions on missions almost as soon as they are received and on problems as they arise. Very often the staff is called upon without warning to do just that.

A common method for initial analysis of existing information is by commander and staff conferences in which key members and individual experts contribute as much as the others may need to know about the situations in their areas of interest. In more complex problems, the commander may need formal written studies and analyses to get a thorough understanding of current commitments, the status of resources, and the priorities and relative importance of his present assignments.

Steps 1 and 2 may seem so closely related as to constitute a single step unworthy of division. They are closely related and must of necessity overlap in actual practice, but it is important to recognize that the weighing of the problem against the current situation and available information is a process that can only be undertaken after the problem is fully understood. The interrelationship between the first steps will be discussed in more detail after the next preliminary step in the staff problem-solving procedure.

Step 3—Issuing Initial Guidance

Having identified the full scope of the matter under consideration and weighed it against all available information, the commander issues his initial guidance for seeking a workable course of action or appropriate solution to the problem. A commander normally keeps this initial guidance as general as the situation permits to allow his staff maximum flexibility in applying their knowledge and experience to the solution.

Unless dictated by higher authority or indicated by information available only to the commander, initial guidance seldom indicates a preferred course of action or solution. To avoid unnecessary work commanders may at this point either eliminate unacceptable courses of action to prevent their being considered by the staff during the next phase of the procedure or include specific instructions for the use of special resources, or other personal preferences or policies that will help the staff find a solution compatible with the commander's desires.

A commander faced with a tactical problem might specify that he would not consider any solution that placed major requirements on one or more units weakened by recent engagements. He might also direct that any solution recommended have artillery moved well forward before the attack, but leave the staff free to recommend the appropriate composition and exact locations of the supporting artillery. The purpose of this initial guidance step is to start the entire staff at the same point of departure in the active problem-solving effort.

The first three steps can easily be recognized as preliminary measures only. They may even seem a waste of time. In practice, however, an experienced staff would be working several steps ahead. Having faced many similar problems in the past, experienced staff officers anticipate much of the commander's guidance. Certainly they would have identified the problem much as the commander did and have started weighing its impact within the framework of available information, particularly in their own areas. The headquarters is not in a state of complete paralysis waiting for the completion of the initial three steps. Even if it were, the wait would be short.

It is difficult to discuss the three preliminary steps without giving an impression of tedious deliberations and extended time lag. The process is not broken into three separate relays—commander-to-staff, staff-to-commander, commander-to-staff. More often than not the staff will be the first to know about the mission, task or problem. Normally, the operations staff element assumes responsibility for coordinating preliminary actions. If the task is of a special nature primarily affecting another staff area, that element may assume the task of coordination.

The staff could well complete its portion of the first three steps before going to the commander. Unless the situation is so urgent that it must be brought to the commander's attention immediately, the staff can identify the problem, weigh it against all available information and develop recommended command guidance. This method saves time and offers the commander maximum advice and assistance at the outset of the problem-solving process. He is given not just a statement of the mission, or problem but also an analysis of the problem, an evaluation of the available pertinent information, and a recommended version of the initial guidance to be issued so that problem-solving can begin in earnest.

This is not a lengthy process. Few commanders tolerate delays in being informed of missions, tasks or problems for which they are responsible. Often the entire matter can be accomplished by a single conference of interested staff officers. They must be sure that all aspects of the problem are identified, all information studied and such guidance outlined as each believes applicable in his area of interest. The results of this conference can then be passed to the commander either in writing or in a briefing.

The first three steps, which consume little time but are of overriding importance, form the basis for unity of staff effort and set the stage for logical, orderly and objective problem-solving. As the commander and the staff start the actual problem-solving, they agree on three important factors: (1) exactly what the problem is, (2) how it is affected by existing information, (3) the limitations and restrictions that govern methods of solving it. The staff is now ready to undertake the actions that will lead to a recommended solution and thus accomplish the mission.

Step 4—Studying the Problem

Some military references and many commanders and staff officers refer to this phase of the problem-solving procedure as the staff-estimate phase. This seems an unduly restrictive designation, because many other valuable problem-solving techniques are available. If a formal staff estimate is used, this is the place for it, but other techniques such as staff studies, special studies, or application of standard operating procedures are often more useful.

It is during this step that the staff and the commander really begin to tear at the meat of the problem. Typical staff actions and techniques used in this step will be discussed in detail later. Here is the reasoning process used to give full consideration to all areas of staff interest in the light of all possible influencing factors:

1. Identify, study and evaluate all facts and assumptions which could have a bearing on the problem in this situation.
2. Identify all possible solutions or courses of action which seem feasible.
3. Weigh each possible solution against each factor, situation and influence to test its feasibility and to determine the advantages and disadvantages. At this point, impossible or infeasible solutions are discarded.
4. Compare the advantages and disadvantages of each retained solution as analyzed.

To emphasize the importance of a unified staff position, the estimates or studies produced during this phase have been referred to in the singular. Obviously, this single staff estimate is not easily achieved. To arrive at it each interested staff element and its appropriate subelements must complete an independent estimate, weighing the possible solutions from a specialist's viewpoint.

First estimates by all the elements are seldom completely compatible. Standardized procedures provide a vehicle for objective resolution of these differences. Each staff element started from the common understanding of the problem; each evaluated existing information; each had the benefit of identical command guidance. Although there are differences, they are less severe than they would have been had each staff element tackled the problem in its own way, using its own formula.

Supporting estimates and studies prepared by the staff elements identify, besides their own preferred courses of action, all other solutions supportable by their fields of specialization and those which for some valid reason could not be supported. It is therefore possible to bring together these supporting positions in a single staff opinion, eliminating all the infeasible solutions and retaining only the viable ones. The field narrows. Because each supporting estimate or study includes a discussion of each solution and the factors against which it was weighed, it is relatively simple to identify the best solution in light of all considerations. Final staff estimates or studies should include the significant factors, introduced by the supporting elements, that influenced the recommendation. Extreme shortages of critical resources reported by the logistician or an absence of critical skills reported by the personnel expert might be listed in the final estimate as important factors bearing on the recommended solution. It should also be noted that the course of action or solution chosen will seldom be the one preferred by each member of the staff. However, this process should produce a solution that all agree to be the best course of action available.

Step 5—The Commander's Decision

When the commander has assured himself that the staff has exhausted all possible considerations, has identified and properly evaluated all possible solutions to the problem and has recommended the one most likely to succeed, he adopts the staff's recommendation as his own. The recommendation becomes the commander's decision and establishes the solution to the problem, the course of action to be followed.

The decision may not include detailed procedures, timing, supporting actions, assignment of missions to subordinate commanders and other details, but the commander has decided what is to be done. The staff must now return to the drawing board to determine how it is to be done. Many officers think the commander's decision ends the problem-solving procedure for commander and staff. In an academic environment the problem could be considered solved. In actual practice, much remains to be done.

The solution to a military problem can only be proven by application. If it works, it was a good one. If it fails, it was incorrect. Military problem-solving can only be considered complete when the solution has been proven. To assure this, three additional steps must be taken: planning, issuing orders and supervising the application of the solution to the problem.

Step 6—Planning

For clarity, planning is introduced here as though the planners remained entirely aloof from the process until the commander reached his decision. For the moment we are interested only in the planning activity that follows the decision.

The course of action recommended by the staff and accepted by the commander should include considerable detail: what is to be done, where and when, who is to take the actions and how they are to proceed; and some explanation of why. Plans must now be developed that expand these points into a complete, time-phased, coordinated scenario. Resources must be allocated and support procedures established, administrative instructions added, controls imposed, and responsibilities fixed.

The plan should stand alone as a complete script suitable for use by all subordinates in preparing more detailed supporting plans. It should also be detailed enough to present a complete picture of the planned action to senior commanders and their staffs.

Step 7—Orders

Just as estimates form the basis for the commander's decision, plans form the basis for the commander's orders and directives. To save time and to assure that actions are performed exactly as the commander intended, planning formats are identical with those of standard orders. When a commander approves plans and directs that they be implemented, the staff has only to change the titles from *Plans* to *Orders* to turn them into directives for actions by subordinate commanders.

This dual (plan/order) format has another advantage. Often plans are developed to meet contingencies for future actions and are approved by the commander long before implementation. It is convenient to issue these to subordinate commanders for preparation of supporting plans, to higher headquarters for approval, and to other interested organizations and activities for information and coordination. When the time arrives for execution, these completed plans become orders to be implemented without additional directives.

Not all plans, orders or directives are formally issued as standardized field orders. Many informal directives are issued by letters, messages, conversations, telephone calls or other means. These are not usually based on the full working of the formal, step-by-step processes outlined in this chapter.

Regardless of the speed or informality of the staff work preceding directives, or the routine nature of the action, good staff officers present their plans complete and ready to be implemented. Even such minor efforts as agendas for conferences, briefing schedules or plans for hosting and entertaining important visitors should be prepared in such detail that they can be issued to all participants as directives after approval.

Step 8—Supervision

In a letter of instruction to his subordinate commanders, a very famous World War II general cautioned that only 10% of command responsibility involved the processes of reaching decisions and issuing orders. The remaining 90% involved personal supervision by commanders and their staffs to assure that these directives were vigorously executed. The general's exact percentages might be challenged; his emphasis on the importance of supervision and personal leadership cannot be.

Unlike the student, the military commander must do more than just arrive at a valid solution supported by facts and reasonable assumptions. He must effectively and completely solve the problem. Consider the classic problem of determining the meeting point of two vehicles traveling in opposite directions at given speeds along the same route. The student is finished with a perfect score when he has calculated the meeting point correctly. The military commander has only started. He must be certain the vehicles are in good shape and that each is capable of maintaining its speed over the prescribed distance. He must be certain that each driver is skilled and familiar with both his vehicle and the route. Above all he must supervise the operation to be certain that both vehicles start on time, that both maintain the prescribed speed and that neither stops or is diverted from the prescribed route. The military commander succeeds not only by selecting the proper solution, but by making it work. He must see that the vehicles meet at the spot selected whether or not things go well.

The commander who would trust his mission, the welfare of his troops, national security, and his professional reputation to the vagaries of chance after having issued his directives would be naive indeed. As in the decision-making process, a commander cannot personally supervise all aspects of the action. The staff must provide personal observation and supervision to see that the commander's decisions are being efficiently executed in each area of specialization.

The steps outlined and discussed in this chapter may be difficult to distinguish in practice. The pressure of time, the burden of massive workloads and many other factors may lend an air of perpetual panic to large headquarters. Everyone seems to be going in several directions on diverse actions simultaneously. It may seem to the untrained observer that all reasoning, formal or informal, has been abandoned in favor of snap judgements. To the trained eyes of experienced staff officers and commanders, the hustle and bustle consists of the rapid but orderly movements of many experts, each engaged in several, possibly unrelated, actions, with each action at a different stage of the problem-solving process.

It would not be unusual for the staff of a senior commander, a lieutenant general, for example, to be studying several completely new missions and task assignments and several newly identified problems on a typical morning. At the same time, available information would be gathered by the staff to study the effects of equal numbers of yesterday's actions while also concentrating on the commander's guidance for still others.

Estimates and studies would be underway to determine courses of action and solutions for still other newly assigned missions and tasks and to find solutions for unsolved problems. Planners would be busily developing details for implementing decisions reached by the commander and, along with this hodgepodge of activity, all actions underway would be supervised and tomorrow's tasks, missions and problems, anticipated.

If the commander and his staff are to succeed under these (normal) conditions, order and standardized procedures are essential. Although it may not be immediately apparent, each problem is probably receiving the full treatment: detailed analysis, evaluation of all available information, issuance of guidance, study and analysis of possible solutions, decision making, plan development, issuance of orders and supervision of actions.

5.

Typical Major Staff Actions

Standardized procedures make it possible for commander and staff to deal in an orderly, objective manner with all the duties and problems they face each day. Such procedures also assure that each action receives full, logical evaluation and analysis in all areas of staff specialization. To achieve such overall order and effectiveness requires fast, reliable methods for controlling the major staff actions.

The importance of understanding the mechanics and purposes of individual staff action cannot be overstated. Senior staff members (element chiefs and their top assistants) become deeply involved in procedures. They spend much of their time with other senior staff members analyzing problems; evaluating conditions; establishing priorities; informing, advising and assisting their commander with decisions; and supervising their counterparts on subordinate staffs. Junior supervisors such as division chiefs, branch chiefs, section chiefs, and so on, guide their subordinates in developing and coordinating the staff actions that make the element chiefs' efforts possible.

Below these junior supervisors, action officers usually find themselves involved with highly specialized, detailed efforts to produce minute fragments of the completed staff action. Like a chain, the most complex staff estimate, study, plan, order or other action is only as sound as its weakest link. The action officer developing even a small bit of the supporting data for a larger action must understand the nature of that larger action and the many tests it must undergo for validity, completeness, objectivity and feasibility. His contribution, no matter how seemingly insignificant, must undergo the same tests.

Although it would be impossible to anticipate every action that could be encountered by a staff officer in the course of a career, certain actions are common and most staff officers will encounter them. More important, they demonstrate the disciplined, orderly thought processes that produce the very best results by a group or by an individual.

These mental processes are equally useful for missions of national importance or the most trivial daily endeavor. A senior general officer planning a major action such as the World War II invasion of Europe must test his solution against the same criteria as the young staff officer preparing his first memorandum for his branch chief.

1. Does it address the complete problem with all of its included and inherent aspects?

2. Have all influencing factors been identified and their possible effects analyzed?

3. Were all possible solutions objectively considered and weighed against all advantages and disadvantages?

4. Is the chosen solution the best possible solution?

The major actions most frequently encountered are:

1. Staff estimates

2. Staff studies

3. Special studies

4. Analysis of the area of operation

5. Standing operating procedure

6. Plans

7. Orders

8. Reports

Estimates

Probably the most important phase of the staff procedure is the completely detailed study of the influencing factors and alternate solutions to problems. It is the key to effective staff work and sound command decisions.

Estimates are a favorite way to accomplish these studies. In the military, the word *estimate* refers to something more precise and substantial than the usual meaning. In military problem-solving, the guesses, surmises, conjectures, predictions (estimates) made by senior, experienced staff officers are seldom only guesses.

Although even the guesser may not always realize it, rather detailed and orderly reasoning based on knowlege and facts probably has occurred before the guess is made. This is true in any field. The farmer who guesses the weather, the commercial fisherman who predicts a good or bad catch, the bridge expert who guesses that a finesse to his left is more likely to succeed than one to his right, all base their guesses on carefully weighed facts garnered over years of experience.

Similarly, the military man who guesses the point of weakest enemy resistance has probably, and perhaps subconsciously, weighed many factors before making his guess. He has projected himself mentally into the enemy commander's position, and from that vantage point envisioned the most logical concentration of strength.

The problem with these educated guesses is that they are difficult to evaluate or to defend. The farmer will have to do much better than state an unbacked confidence in the weather to convince bankers to lend money for seed or new equipment. The commercial fisherman will have trouble selling in advance a catch that exists only as a "feeling in his bones". The bridge player had better have more than a hunch to explain to his partner a finesse to the left when apparent facts indicate one to the right. The military guesser is in a far more serious position.

The farmer and fisherman are risking only money and business success on their conjectures about weather and the dietary customs of fish; and the bridge player, the loss of a game and the fury of a frustrated partner. The military officer who operates on guesswork risks his professional reputation—and often, the lives of people and the defense of his country. The military officer like the farmer, fisherman and bridge player, seldom has at his disposal all the facts needed to reduce his problems to a mathematical formula. In view of the gravity of military decisions, they must come as close to mathematical certainty as possible. The estimate removes as many unknowns as possible and provides a standard format for analysis of the data and factors upon which conclusions, recommendations and decisions are based. It also reveals the estimator's rationale.

While still part guess, part surmise, and part prediction, the military estimate results from examination and evaluation of facts and assumptions, and the forming of conclusions, recommendations and decisions based on an orderly reasoning process. The estimate is a complete, formalized action designed to eliminate unknowns to the maximum extent possible and to deal with or allow for those which cannot be eliminated.

The Estimate discussed here is the full scale process usually reserved for major problems such as selecting the best method for performing an entire mission or for those major tasks in a mission which are the key to its success. The thought processes and controls used to try to eliminate errors in judgement are sound and can be modified to suit even the most routine daily action.

Military references divide estimates into several categories on the basis of their purposes. Staff officers prepare different types of estimates—the commanders' estimate of the situation, staff estimates, intelligence estimates and various support estimates. Actually the support estimates only serve to reinforce the overall staff estimate that becomes the commander's estimate of the situation and the basis for command decisions after it is approved. The staff estimate is the completely coordinated position of a whole staff.

Preparing Estimates

The steps by which estimates evolve are not completely distinct and time-separated. As in other staff work, they often overlap, but each is important and must be taken. The relationship of the steps to each other and to the whole estimating process must be thoroughly understood.

Mission Statement

To the beginner the first paragraph on estimates may seem redundant. The mission or problem has been analyzed and identified or the estimate could not be started. So why restate it as a part of the estimate? There are good reasons. A formal approach to military problem-solving assures uniformity, speeds and simplifies internal and external coordination and makes presentation to the commander easier. What could contribute more to those purposes than for all to be working on exactly the same problem?

Like advanced mathematical problems, military situations important enough to justify a complete staff estimate are complicated and include many functions. The commander and all members of his staff must interpret the problem identically to work together on a totally satisfactory solution. A restatement of the problem is not a verbatim repeat of the mission as received. It is the commander's restatement, and it incorporates the major included tasks in the mission. There is always the possibility (or probability) that all members of the staff receiving the same guidance may not interpret it identically. Quite possibly, without the mission restatement in the estimate and supporting estimates, individual elements of the staff and individual officers in the elements might be solving slightly different problems.

The importance of the mission restatement is even more apparent when the techniques of staff estimating are better understood. The whole staff works concurrently to produce the estimate, each element developing its part independently but in constant coordination with the other elements. Such coordination is expedited by the assurance of mutual understanding of the problem established by the statement of the mission at the outset. As in all reasoning processes, the first step must be to understand the problem.

Situation

Identifying the facts, assumptions and situations that may bear on the problem and its solution is also a valuable step that combats a major human weakness, the tendency to jump to conclusions. When presented with a problem, large or small, most people are inclined to speculate on the spot. This shoot-from-the-hip method of problem-solving has one significant fault. It implants answers in the mind that are most difficult to erase or correct later when additional information is considered, making objectivity unattainable. To counteract the tendency toward preconception, military problem-solvers follow formats that resist their urge to deduce easy, immediate answers by forcing them first to list, analyze and evalute the factors that could influence the mission or problem solution.

The flexibility of this part of the estimate allows staff members to consider the significant influences at their level of the staff and according to the specific interests of the action officers preparing the estimate.

Terrain, for example, can be looked at in many ways. To the staff of a theater commander it is a broad, general topographical condition, favorable or unfavorable to the type of theater-wide actions contemplated. Local geography is much more significant to the division commander's staff considering attack routes and avenues of approach. The smaller areas of operation and limited choices of maneuver methods of battalion commanders can make even a single terrain feature an overriding factor.

Staff elements and individual staff officers must identify and weigh factors of interest in their areas that might be insignificant to other staff members. By letting their imaginations run free, staff officers working on an estimate can virtually eliminate the chances of overlooking significant factors.

Certain established factors cannot be ignored at the discretion of the staff; they so obviously influence most actions that the estimate format dictates that they be included until discounted by valid data. It would be difficult to envision a mission, task or problem in a combat situation that would not be influenced in some way by enemy capabilities, intentions and probable actions. Few major actions, combat or otherwise, are unaffected by weather and terrain. Special missions and problems can be so sensitive to other factors as to make their consideration mandatory—at least until proven inapplicable.

To the mission of establishing and operating industrial facilities such as a depot maintenance shop or a procurement activity, labor, transportation and communications are significant factors. Some of the influencing factors initially identified could later be discarded if it is determined that they applied equally to all possible courses of action. In the beginning, however, to get the problem-solving process underway, *all* possible factors should be identified.

The purpose of the situation paragraph is not merely to identify and to list the factors involved. Each factor must be studied, evaluated and weighed and the possible influences on it identified. Negative influences, difficulties or limitations are most significant. Sound solutions are often those which suffer least from such difficulties. Favorable factors are also important and should be studied. Sometimes the best solutions are those which benefit most from favorable factors. Two types of factors—facts and assumptions—must be considered.

Facts. Conditions, events or situations that are known (and can be proven) to exist are facts. Facts are extremely rare. A river that confronts an entire division is a fact. It can be seen, and the chances of its going away of its own accord are nil. It constitutes a firm, factual military factor. But how much of a factor? Rivers change. Floods make them larger, swifter, muddier, more difficult to cross and easier to defend. Rivers also decrease in volume, sometimes suddenly, making them less effective as obstacles to offensive actions and less effective as defensive barriers. Be extremely slow to accept any factor as a *fact*. When the forward elements of a division confront such a physical feature, a river's existence is a fact and an important influence to be considered in the estimate. If it is a sizable river, its influence as an obstacle would be a fact. That it will remain the same volume may or may not be.

Assumptions. The other category of factors considered by estimators also must be approached with caution. Assumptions are as essential to military problem solvers as they are to everyone else. Seldom are enough facts available to substantiate sound decisions, so the truth of certain conditions, situations, and factors must be assumed. Because assumptions are inferior to facts, they should be used only after careful testing to assure their validity.

Dictionaries define *assumption* as "taking for granted." The military commander and his staff may only take for granted things which merit such confidence. Assumptions should be used only as absolutely necessary to complete the estimate, but they should not be avoided when they are necessary.

Necessity should be the first test of each assumption. Unnecessary assumptions should be discarded. Take the assumption that friendly operations over which the commander has no control will succeed. If the mission, task or problem being considered will only be undertaken if the other operation succeeds, then an assumption of success would be valid. If, on the other hand, the local action must proceed regardless of the success or failure of the other operation, the assumption is invalid. Instead, the commander and his staff must seek courses of action with good probabilities of success regardless of the outcome of the other operation. The wise staff would weigh its possible solutions against the possible failure of the other action, rather than assuming its success.

The second and more difficult test is logic. Can the assumption be supported with positive data? Assumptions must be supported by more than urgent need. An engineer commander charged with the mission of constructing a bridge cannot properly assume that the river will not rise just because the course of action he has selected depends on its remaining at low ebb.

Flood data, weather conditions, etc., must support the assumption that flooding is unlikely to occur within the time frame of the solution he has selected. The only exception would be a situation in which limited bridge supplies, time limits, or other unavoidable conditions absolutely prohibited constructing a bridge of any type if flooding should occur. In such a situation, an assumption that water levels would remain stable would be valid and necessary. However, the weakness of the assumption and the recommended solution should be explained.

By now, the problem has been thoroughly analyzed. All of its parts have been identified; all aspects and conditions of the situation that could affect the solution have been analyzed and their adverse or favorable aspects identified. It is time to look for solutions.

Every possible solution should be identified and listed. Again, the staff should allow the imagination free rein. No solution should be considered too far out for listing. At this point no course of action should be ignored because it appears to conflict with command policy.

Some of the reasons for such completeness are obvious; others, less clear. First and most important is the requirement for complete staff work. If each staff officer lists only the solutions he believes have some chance of success, most likely the staff will all proceed in different directions in search of the best solution.

Then, too, listing all possible solutions simplifies coordination within the staff and with the staffs of other headquarters. Papers are presented for coordination in order to reach an agreement on a solution or course of action. The persons trying to reach an agreement can evaluate each proposal much better if they can see that all other possible solutions have been identified and considered.

The overall staff estimate presented to the commander must include a single recommended course of action or problem solution. This will be much easier to sell if the commander can see that all possible solutions, even the far out ones, were analyzed and only discarded for valid reasons. Although commanders may prohibit certain courses of action in their initial planning guidance, even these solutions should be listed although they need not be analyzed to determine other reasons for discarding them.

There is another value to all this effort. It is good mental discipline, particularly for inexperienced officers. It demands broad thinking and thorough analysis. To the impatient, it may seem that the estimate is a slow-starting problem-solving process. It has only laid the foundation by the preparatory steps of identifying the problem, the factors bearing on it, and all possible solutions. Now let's solve the problem.

Analysis of Courses of Action

In Paragraph 3 of the Staff Estimate Format the actual problem-solving begins by weighing each possible solution against each of the difficulties anticipated as a result of the factors listed in Paragraph 2. As a preliminary step, this is the point in the procedure for purifying the list of influencing factors. Two types of factors may now be stricken from the list, those which bear equally on all possible courses of action and those which bear on none.

Suppose that a commander is charged with establishing a large depot in one of three cities. Severe labor shortages would certainly be an influencing factor to be identified. However, when all possible solutions were developed, it might become apparent that all solutions are equally affected by the labor factor.

Absence of water transportation might be identified initially as an influencing factor, but should it develop that no items are to be shipped to or from the proposed depot by water, the lack would no longer be an influencing factor and could be stricken from the list.

When the list of influences has been revised, each course of action must be objectively analyzed in the light of each remaining factor and the strengths and weaknesses of each solution stated positively and completely. The logical pattern of the military problem solving process begins to emerge. Not only is the best solution taking shape, so is the sound, defendable reasoning on which the final recommendation and command decision can be based with minimal chance of error. At this point the problem-solving process becomes self-checking.

As the various possible courses of action are checked against the factors previously identified, deficiencies in the list of factors may become apparent. The list was made before the courses of action were identified; it included only such factors as seemed significant to mission or problem. When courses of action are added to the analysis, the list of influences may have to be expanded to include situations not previously identified.

Considering the initial list of possible solutions in the light of influencing factors may bring to mind possible solutions overlooked in the first effort. The most common example of this is the combination of two or more of the initial courses to form a new course. Still another self-correcting action during this phase is that one or more of the possible solutions may be revealed to be impossible after all.

The free thinking which identified and included these impossible solutions was not wasted and may later be very valuable and save much time and staff effort. A favorite question raised by commanders asked to accept a recommendation and by staff officers asked to concur with a position is, "Did you consider this or that alternate solution or course of action?" Lucky indeed is the staff officer who can answer, "Yes, Sir, I considered that alternative but discarded it. It could not be undertaken because...."

When each possible solution has been weighed against each difficulty and the weaknesses and strengths of each have been duly listed, it is time to move to another step in the analysis.

Comparison of Courses of Action

The comparison of courses of action is actually only a continuation of the evaluation of possible solutions started in the previous paragraph. In this step, however, each possible solution is stated and discussed in terms of advantages and disadvantages as they compare to the advantages and disadvantages of the other possible solutions. This analysis should indicate the course of action or solution most likely to succeed.

Some officers prefer to reduce this step to table form, particularly for complex problems with many influencing factors to be considered and several feasible courses of action to be compared. Tabled comparisons can take either of the two forms shown in Table 5.1 which considers a problem with three possible courses of action and only three influencing factors.

Table 5.1a
Comparison of Courses of Action

Considerations	Course of Action		
	A	B	C
Weather	3	2	1
Terrain	1	2	3
Enemy	3	2	1
Summary	7	6	5

Table 5.1b
Comparison of Courses of Action

Course of Action	Considerations			
	Weather	Terrain	Enemy	Summary
A	3	1	3	7
B	2	2	2	6
C	1	3	1	5

In Table 5.1a each consideration is applied to each possible solution in turn. Its advantages and disadvantages are analyzed, and a conclusion is reached as to which course of action is favored from the viewpoint of that single consideration. In Table 5.1b the same results are obtained by applying each of the three solutions to each consideration. This shows how each solution fairs in the light of all considerations. If the reasoning is valid, the results should be identical.

Obviously, either method is acceptable; obviously, neither can be used as a strict formula to replace mature judgement. Consider the solutions arrived at in the two sample tables. In very few situations would the three considerations be likely to have equal weight overall or to apply equally to each solution.

Suppose the problem demonstrated on the tables were the attack of an enemy position and the three solutions were (A) tank attack, (B) airmobile attack or (C) infantry attack. The first two considerations, terrain and weather, certainly could weigh more heavily against certain solutions. In extreme cases, weather could completely eliminate an airmobile attack as a possibility and could severely limit armored operations. If the weather is expected to be only moderately poor, air and tank operations might be only slightly affected, their flexibility limited but their use not completely negated. Enemy capabilities could range from "suicidal for infantry attack" to only "some probability of slightly higher casualties" versus "some anticipated delay in capturing the objective for an armored attack but with lower casualties." Finally, speed and surprise might favor airmobile operations. The staff must weigh the relative value of speed against lower casualties and the conservation of human assets. Pure bookkeeping cannot replace human judgement.

In the two examples given, course of action *A* is the apparent favorite. It scored a total of seven points compared to six points for course of action *B* and only five for course of action *C*. It appears to be an excellent choice, having lost only two points from a possible nine. Sound judgement might show this to be an entirely false picture. If solution *A* were an armored attack over terrain that might severely limit the maneuverability of tanks and turn the operation into a prolonged agony of inching forward, building roads and bridges, removing obstacles and barricades, then inching forward again and repeating the operations, terrain would be a major consideration that might more than outweigh the favorable weather and enemy considerations. Weather considerations might be relatively minor, influencing only troop comfort, with little adverse impact on the probable success of courses of action *B* and *C*. In such a situation the extreme disadvantages of terrain would greatly outweigh the advantages of weather and enemy.

The point is clear: problem-solving cannot be entirely reduced to a standardized process format that automatically cranks out the best solution without human mental effort. Before reducing the solution to summmarized table form, the staff officer must do some extremely detailed and difficult mental exercises. This introduces a difficult subject to discuss. One facet of professionalism that cannot be developed by the advice presented here (or any other mode of instruction) is human judgement.

Judgement. Dictionaries define *judgement* as "comparing, understanding and coming to an opinion." Military references add to this the ability to weigh facts and ideas and to identify those to be discarded as irrelevant and those to be retained.

There are no formulas for developing judgement. However, certain personal characteristics that must become second nature to all successful staff officers can at least minimize the chances of exercising poor judgement. For the moment they can be summarized as those characteristics such as caution, thoroughness and, above all, curiosity which assure complete staff work. Although proven good judgement, the hallmark of the successful staff officer, comes with years of experience and requires an alert, active mind and some degree of mental aptitude, most incidents of really poor judgement result from a careless, lazy approach to the responsibilities of the staff and its members.

The beginning staff officer must remain conscious of his lack of experience and professional background and must be particularly cautious about spur-of-the-moment conclusions reached without deliberating all possible alternatives. This applies not only to the missions and major problems to which complete formal estimates are applied but also to the routine daily actions that occupy so much of every staff officer's time. In fact, the inclination to exercise snap judgement is probably stronger in the rush of everyday business than during the serious crisis atmosphere requiring complete estimates.

Recommendations

The final step in the estimate is the payoff, the conclusion or recommendation arrived at after complete consideration of all factors and influences on each possible course of action. The staff must now recommend to the commander the course of action that he should adopt. It is at this point that the true value of the standardized estimate becomes apparent.

Seldom will the first staff effort result in a unanimous opinion. Even though all staff element chiefs may be equal in education, experience and training, and all have an identical understanding of the problem and the commander's guidance, their initial recommendations are likely to vary widely. This reflects the different interests of the different staff elements rather than inferior staff work or faulty judgement.

Nevertheless, differences must be resolved so that the commander may have the benefits of a complete, coordinated recommendation representing the best efforts of the staff. The resolution of differences is greatly expedited by the fact that each member has followed the same reasoning process and can present his position in a format familiar to the other members. This allows objective and orderly discussion and simplifies the process. Without standardization, it is doubtful that unanimity could be achieved without great confusion and lengthy, heated discussion.

Consider some possible areas of disagreement based on the example problem previously discussed. We have shown that the overall staff evaluation concluded that course of action A was superior to course of action B, which in turn was better than course of action C. Let us examine some of the possible, initial conclusions of some of the more specialized staff elements.

The logistician may have selected course of action C as the easiest to support, deciding that B was possible but more difficult with some chances of delay in delivery of critical supplies and that A would be extremely difficult with a high probability that many facets of logistics (supply, maintenance, construction) would be extremely difficult. The communications expert may have found B easiest to support and C possible, agreeing with the logistician that A would be most difficult with good chances that contact might be lost during the operation. Quite likely, the personnel expert, the surgeon, the provost marshal, and others would have equally diverse opinions.

These are all valid professional positions resulting from detailed analysis of influencing factors and all reflecting significant strengths and weaknesses of the possible solutions. Here again judgement is the deciding factor. These considerations do not have equal significance, and they bear unequally on the chances of mission success. The relative importance of the factors is made apparent by standard procedures. The staff can then decide, based on all considerations, which course has the best chance of success.

The second advantage of a standard format becomes apparent when the estimate-recommendation is presented to the commander. Not only can he see the reasoning that led to the recommendation and the advantages and disadvantages of the recommended course of action presented in a logical order with which he is familiar, he can also, in the same logical order, see the courses of action that were considered but not recommended—and their advantages and disadvantages.

He can examine the problem, as understood by the staff, to determine whether it agrees with his interpretation. He can check the factors considered significant by the staff for completeness. He can weigh the judgement of the staff in evaluating those factors and arriving at its recommendation and he can examine the recommendation itself to be sure that it is a complete course of action including the necessary elements of *what, where, when, who, how* and *why*.

If the commander accepts the recommendation, the staff estimate becomes the commander's estimate of the situation and the recommendation becomes the commander's decision. That decision then becomes the basis for staff planning and the eventual issuance of orders implementing the commander's decision.

Other Estimates

So far we have discussed the completed staff estimate which, when accepted, becomes the commanders estimate. It includes the commander's decision on the course of action to be undertaken, but it is actually a coordinated compilation of the results of independent estimates prepared by several staff elements. These supporting estimates merit some brief discussion.

Intelligence Estimates

In a tactical situation, the intelligence estimate plays a major role in the staff estimate and a key role, often a deciding role, in determining the course of action most likely to succeed. It is the main tool for identifying, analyzing and evaluating those outside influences over which the command exercises little control but which could significantly influence the mission, task or problem.

In preparing his estimate, the intelligence officer follows a format compatible with the overall staff estimate format. However, when his part is complete, it can easily be recognized as being only a single part of the estimate. Properly prepared, the intelligence estimate can be used, as it is, to form a paragraph of the estimate, as the appended sample intelligence estimate format demonstrates.

Support Estimates

Other staff elements may contribute supporting estimates to the complete staff estimates upon which the commander bases his decision. Although the wide range of technical considerations make strict adherence to detailed formats difficult when preparing supporting estimates. Completeness and objective analysis are essential. The summarized format in the appendix can be used to accomplish those purposes, but local considerations may require modification for special requirements.

Two aspects of staff estimates must be reemphasized. First, military operations seldom remain static; situations change constantly and rapidly. Estimating the situation is a continuing action involving updating and changing influencing factors and modifying recommendations and decisions. Second, although estimates normally are best suited for large problems such as entire tactical problems, the general concepts of mental discipline can be applied to great advantage in approaching simple problems or in organizing and managing daily personal workloads.

Staff Studies

Staff studies and estimates are similar, but the staff study format lends itself more easily to the solution of specific problems than to consideration of the wide ranges of possible courses of actions to accomplish entire tactical missions. Some military manuals oversimplify the distinction between studies and estimates by relegating staff studies to technical and administrative problems and reserving staff estimates for the resolution of tactical or operational problems. This probably is true in the vast majority of instances, but it is unduly restrictive and limits the full advantages of both the estimate and the study.

In many instances staff studies could be ideal vehicles for solving tactical operational problems, and the more complex estimate format could apply well to completely technical situations with no tactical implications. For example, technical commands such as depot complexes, maintenance activities, or theater support organizations might well find estimates necessary to expose fully the many considerations and influencing factors confronting the commander and to weigh all possible methods of accomplishing their missions. Conversely, combat commanders faced with simple choices between a limited number of solutions, such as whether or not to attack, could well use the less sophisticated staff study to examine the problem.

Generally, the study format lends itself to the solution of more direct problems involving a limited choice of options—to move or not to move, to build or to repair the old, to buy or to lease, to relocate or to commute, to approve or to disapprove. Admittedly, these types of problems are most often found in technical, logistical and administrative areas. Again, the choice of problem-solving technique should be governed by the scope, magnitude and complexity of the problem, not by whether it is tactical or technical.

Staff studies and staff estimates serve identical purposes: they both assure complete and orderly consideration of all facets of problems before solutions or recommendations are developed. Like the estimate, the study assures common understanding of the problem, identification of all factors bearing on the problem, full analysis and evaluation of these factors, complete statements of all advantages and disadvantages of opposing solutions or courses of action, and recommendations or conclusions supported by logical data and rationale. Also like estimates, the standardized and formatted study simplifies coordination and presentation of the results.

Staff Study Procedures

The most perfunctory examination of the staff study format in the appendix reveals its similarity to the estimate format. The problem is stated; influencing factors (facts and assumptions) are identified; alternate solutions are weighed against the influences; conclusions are drawn; and actions are recommended. The difference is in the complexity of the problem to be solved and in the resultant necessity for detailed controls to insure that all possible factors have been identified and properly considered.

The appropriate method is usually apparent to experienced commanders and staffs when they are presented a problem. The choice may be difficult for the less experienced, and some borderline problems could challenge even the most experienced staff members. Some discussion of each paragraph as it differs from its counterpart could prove helpful.

Problem

Although military publications and many commanders and experienced staff officers infer significant differences in the two paragraph titles (*Mission,* for estimates; *Problem,* for studies), similarities far outweigh differences. In both instances the purpose of beginning a solution by stating the mission to be accomplished or the problem to be solved is to assure understanding and community of action toward the common goal. The important consideration is not the paragraph title but the completeness of its presentation, no matter what it is called.

Complete problem statement is equally important to large, nationally significant missions such as the World War II invasion of Normandy and to such a routine procedural problem as when to schedule morning coffee call. If the assignment is "Determine whether coffee call should be at 0930 hours or at 1030 hours," the problem must be stated in exactly that manner. If it is stated only as "Determine the best time for coffee call," solutions will range from 0800 hours to 1200 hours. If it is stated "Determine whether 0930 hours (or 1030 hours) would be an appropriate time for coffee call," solutions will be limited to yes or no. Properly stated the mission of the estimate or the problem of the study restricts the staff's efforts to the limits of the problem parameters and assures that the entire problem will be solved. Consider that a saving of even five minutes of lost coffee call time for a headquarters with 1000 people could save as much as $100,000 annually. This example should demonstrate that *all* problems deserve serious, objective and thorough staff consideration. The foundation for that consideration is complete and accurate identification of the mission or problem.

Facts and Assumptions

A decisive consideration for choosing between full-scale estimates and staff studies lies with the numbers and complexities of the influencing factors to be considered. The choice is simple in both extremes. Obviously, in major military missions, influenced by every detail of the physical and sociological environment of an area, all possible information concerning potential military opposition and multiple courses of action should be controlled and disciplined by the infinite detail of the estimate format. At the other extreme, simple, routine problems would only be delayed and complicated by the estimate format. In the more common middle ground the choice is much more difficult but still governed largely by the applicability of the estimate to the influencing facts and assumptions and by the numbers of possible solutions to be analyzed and evaluated in the light of these influencing factors.

Discussion

In studies the discussion replaces the analysis and comparison paragraph in the format for estimates, removing the rigidly controlled procedures of formatted, step-by-step analyses followed by highly repetitive comparison of courses of action. Relief from the rigidity of format of the estimate does not mean abandoning requirements for thorough analysis and comparison. Staff studies must completely analyze each problem solution or course of action in the light of each fact and assumption and compare the advantages and disadvantages of each in the discussion paragraph. The flexibility of the study is advantageous when few solutions are available; it is often preferable even for more complex problems with many possible solutions if the problems are technical ones requiring specialized application of rather unique influencing factors.

The discussion paragraph of the study lacks one other control imposed by the estimate format: limits on verbosity. The very word *discussion* tends to invite lengthy, philosophical harangues which may range far afield of the problem, facts, assumptions and possible solutions. As in all staff work, brevity is absolutely necessary in staff studies. Discussion which stretches into interminable diatribe makes coordination difficult and presentation to the commander virtually impossible. Yet thorough discussion is essential, and lengthiness is often unavoidable. In such instances a summary in the body of the study, with full discussion hidden mercifully away in an annex, makes the study much easier to coordinate with other staff officers and much more palatable to busy commanders.

Conclusions

The rigidity of the estimate format is such that the logical solution and the rationale by which it was reached become apparent during the analysis and comparison of the possible solutions. Because the free-wheeling study discussion may not result in this kind of clarity of expression, the conclusion compensates for the possible weakness. Conclusions provide an opportunity to explain briefly why certain solutions were adopted, others were considered feasible but not desirable, and still others were discarded. If unnecessary, the conclusion paragraph should be omitted. Redundant prestatements of the recommendation only waste time and lengthen the study.

Recommendation

Recommendations must meet the same tests whether presented as the results of studies or of estimates. They must include the *who, what, where, when, how,* and *why* in enough detail to solve the problem, be compatible with conclusions, and consider all facts and assumptions; but they must confine themselves to the mission or problems being studied.

Special Studies

Both the staff estimate and the staff study formats and procedures were developed to meet the requirements of normal military operations. Unfortunately, the military business is far from routine. Commanders often find themselves confronted by special problems having little resemblance to the assigned mission. Staff study and estimate formats often fail to meet the requirements for a full and objective consideration of these unusual problems. Then special formats must be developed and formalized before the problem-solving process begins.

Some special problems occur with such frequency that the Department of the Army, the Department of Defense and other agencies have developed formats to be sure that all important features of the problems or proposed actions are properly evaluated and presented uniformly. One example of such a recurring special problem is the development of data to support closure, inactivation or reduction in the size of military bases or other actions that would significantly decrease the civilian workforce at one or more military bases.

Major changes in the scope of military operations nationwide or in a single locality can affect many factors in the communities where they occur: labor, community income, housing, schools, recreational facilities, law and order, public transportation, and almost all other aspects of community affairs. Quite naturally, residents of these affected communities take considerable interest in such actions. The news media and the local, state and national elected officials of the area reflect this interest.

Defense Department officials have discovered that major changes in military activities evoke valid, detailed and searching questions from individuals, government representatives and the news media. To make sure that data will be available to answer these queries and that proposals will be for valid actions justifiable on economic and operational grounds, standardized case study and justification formats have been developed and are completed for each such action. Because these formats change frequently and must be adjusted to meet the requirements of many specialized situations, they will not be discussed in detail here. They are extremely detailed, covering the history of the affected installation or activity, the missions, the scope of its activities, the impact on the community, the economic factors (savings and costs), and a host of other considerations.

When completed, these studies are often the size of the annual catalogues published by major mail order firms. Included as addendums to these case studies and to almost all significant actions proposed by the military and the civilian communities is another special format that has come into prominence during the last few years, the environmental analysis.

In recent years, people have become much more interested in their physical surroundings and aware that these surroundings must be preserved if future generations are to enjoy the beauties and pleasures of living that have been an American heritage. Such interest is immediately translated into official interest by government representatives. Congress has become more and more interested in finding out what impact military activities may have on environmental conditions before it provides the money to finance them. Virtually all proposals must now be accompanied by written proof that the environment will not be adversely affected. Without such proof proposals must be absolutely essential to the national defense, and ecological effects must be overridden by that military necessity.

To adequately analyze and evaluate these considerations, two formalized study formats have been developed. One is an ecological analysis to determine whether or not any adverse environmental effects will result from the proposed action. The other is an ecological impact study to determine the exact extent of these effects if the results are affirmative.

Environmental studies and case studies for major changes in the scope of military operations are but samples of the many standardized, special studies that may face the staff officer. Many more situations arise in which neither estimates nor staff studies apply and no standard procedure has been developed. In these instances commanders and staffs must develop their own procedure and design formats to assure complete, objective and logical analysis of all factors and all possible solutions.

Analysis of Area of Operation

These staff actions are included because of their usefulness as background and reference material. They are not typical actions frequently encountered by average staff officers. In fact, they are seldom required by most commanders and their staffs. However, when they are required, they are very important and should be understood.

Area analysis may be undertaken for a specific mission or as pure intelligence information in anticipation of future military operations. A sample format for area analysis is included in the appendix.

Standing Operating Procedures (SOP)

The heavy emphasis on problem-solving techniques, estimates, studies and analyses may imply that each day a staff officer encounters completely new problems with no precedents upon which to base solutions. Of course, this is far from true. Each mission, task or problem solved and each action undertaken establishes precedents useful in solving other problems as they arise. Through its long history the military profession has established with reasonable certainty that some strategies and tactics generally work better than others and that certain principles of war apply to most military situations. Each commander can, therefore, develop certain policies, rules and philosophies that can be automatically applied to standard operations, to individual steps in staff proceedings and to staff actions.

Most commanders have the most important and most used of these commonly applicable practices formalized as standing operating procedures (SOP) and published as directives for use by their staffs. In turn, major staff elements and subelements develop supporting SOP applicable to their areas of interest. These SOP, or rules of the road for solving standard recurring problems and for internal headquarters operations, change frequently. Each new commander, chief of staff, staff element chief, division chief, branch chief, and section chief has his own preferred techniques and methods requiring SOP changes. Consequently, staff officers find themselves often involved in developing, updating and revising SOP. Unfortunately, each new supervisor probably also has strong preferences for SOP format and content. Writing completely new SOP is not an uncommon staff project.

Because of the wide divergence of preferences in SOP, a standard format tends to be whatever the local commander or individual staff supervisor directs. To demonstrate the flexibility of SOP format and its wide applicability for simplifying procedures and establishing methods for handling recurring actions, two extremely different sample SOP formats are listed in the appendix. The first is typical of what might be used in the headquarters of a combat division; the other is a summary of one actually used by one of the smaller, more specialized, offices within the logistical staff element of a Continental Army Headquarters in peacetime.

Summary of Major Problem Solving Actions

To this point we have discussed those major staff actions which provide the analysis and study upon which commanders base their decisions and from which they select problem solutions. Before moving on to those typical actions that follow command decisions, the basic, logical progression of military problem-solving techniques merits final reemphasis:

1. Identify mission, task or problem.
2. Identify all influencing factors.
3. Categorize factors, facts, or assumptions.
4. Identify *all* possible courses of action.
5. Weigh each course of action against each factor.
6. Compare the advantages and disadvantages of each course of action.
7. Select the best course of action.

Appendix to Chapter 5

Staff Estimate Format

1. Mission statement: restatement of the mission by the commander, including tasks identified or implied in the mission, task or problem.
2. Situation: facts, assumptions and probable situations which could influence mission accomplishment, and all possible courses of action or solutions that could accomplish the mission or solve the problem.
3. Analysis of courses of action: analysis of each possible problem solution or course of action in the light of the facts, assumptions and situations identified in Step 2.
4. Comparison of courses of actions: comparison and evaluation of the advantages and disadvantages of various courses of action or solutions.
5. Recommendations: the who, what, where, when and, as appropriate, how and why of the preferred solution or course of action.

**Intelligence Estimate
(sample format)**

1. Mission: the mission as restated by the commander.
2. Area of operations: a discussion of the influencing factors inherent to the area of operation, based on an analysis of the area of operations, if one has been prepared.
   A. Weather
      (1) existing situation
      (2) effects on enemy
      (3) effects on friendly forces
   B. Terrain
      (1) existing situation
      (2) effect on enemy
      (3) effect on friendly forces
   C. Other characteristics: Add subparagraphs in same format as 2.a. and 2.b. to present other significant features of the area, such as sociological factors, economy, ecology, etc.

3. Enemy situations (if appropriate):
   A. Disposition
   B. Composition
   C. Strength
      (1) committed forces, (those not available for reinforcement)
      (2) reinforcements
      (3) air power
      (4) nuclear, biological, chemical capabilities
   D. Significant activities
   E. Peculiarities and weaknesses
      (1) personnel weakness (if appropriate)
      (2) intelligence capabilities and weaknesses
      (3) operational effectiveness
      (4) support capabilities
      (5) civil affairs
      (6) personalities (strengths, weaknesses, peculiarites)
4. Enemy capabilities:
   A. List each possible enemy action as subparagraph; include strength, what, where and when, for each capability
   B. Analyze each capability in a separate subparagraph to determine probable enemy actions
5. Conclusion:
   A. Effects of area on friendly courses of action
   B. Probable enemy actions in order of likelihood
   C. Enemy vulnerability

Annexes: (Formatted estimate should be brief and concise, with supporting material annexed as necessary.)

Support Estimate

1. Mission: as restated by the commander.
2. Situation and Considerations:
   A. Intelligence situation (If available and suitable, an intelligence estimate can be annexed with a brief summary in this paragraph of the factors influencing support; if not, complete the format as applicable to the area of interest of the estimate: personnel, logistics, civil affairs, etc.)
      (1) characteristics of area
      (2) enemy strengths and dispositions
      (3) enemy capabilities as they affect:
         (a) tactical operations
         (b) support (personnel, logistics, civil affairs) activities
   B. Tactical situation
      (1) present tactical force disposition
      (2) possible courses of action (from staff estimate)
      (3) projected operations affecting support area
   C. Personnel situation (to be used by all except personnel)
      (1) disposition, and other data relative to personnel assets as they apply to support area under study
      (2) projected personnel developments
   D. Logistics situation (to be used by all except logistics)
      (1) dispostion and other pertinent data
      (2) projected logistics development

E. Civil affairs situation (to be used by all except civil affairs)
   (1) disposition and other pertinent data
   (2) projected developments
F. Personnel, logistics, civil affairs and other situations use subparagraphs to present all aspects of the current situation, or summarize and include details as annexes
G. Assumptions (Everything up to this point should be factual unless clearly marked otherwise)
3. Analysis: Use subparagraphs to list and analyze each possible course of action; discuss all support factors, indicating problems and deficiencies.
4. Comparison:
   A. General deficiencies of the support area under study
   B. Advantages and disadvantages. Use a subparagraph for each course of action
5. Conclusions:
   A. Adequacy of support for the overall mission
   B. Preferred course of action from support standpoint
   C. Disadvantages of other courses of action
   D. Significant support deficiencies, problems or situations that merit command attention
Annexes: Support estimates should be as concise as possible, with supporting data annexed.

Staff Studies
(sample format)

1. Problem: (stated as the mission – what must be accomplished).
2. Assumptions: (only those necessary to solve problem).
3. Facts: (only those necessary to solve problem.)
4. Discussion: (analysis of possible solutions weighed against facts and assumptions. Should be brief. If necessary, summarize and include detailed discussion as annex.)
5. Conclusions: (results of analysis discussed in Paragraph 4).
6. Recommendation: (must be consonant with conclusion and compatible with discussion: allow for the effects of facts and assumptions; and contain the who, what, where, when, how, and why, in sufficient detail to satisfy all facets of problem.)
Annexes: (studies should be brief with supporting material included as annexes.)

Analysis of Area of Operations
(sample format)

1. Purpose And Limiting Considerations:
   A. Purpose or reason for analysis of the specified area
   B. Limiting considerations, missions or operational restrictions; time-phased requirements which may limit, restrict or expand the analysis
2. General Description of the Area: (a complete listing of pertinent data, not limited to the following subparagraphs)
   A. Climatic or weather conditions
      (1) precipitation

Appendix to Chapter 5

      (2) fog
      (3) clouds
      (4) temperatures
      (5) relative humidity
      (6) light data
      (7) magnetic phenomena
   B. Terrain (preferably by color-coded maps)
      (1) relief and drainage systems
      (2) vegetation
      (3) surface materials (soils and subsoils)
      (4) manmade features
         (a) roads
         (b) railroads
         (c) bridges
         (d) tunnels
         (e) mines
         (f) towns
         (g) industrial areas
         (h) fortifications
   C. Additional considerations
      (1) sociology
      (2) politics
      (3) economics
      (4) religion
      (5) materials
      (6) transportation
      (7) manpower
      (8) hydrography
3. Military Aspects of the Area: (analysis of characteristics listed in Paragraph 2 as they pertain to military operations.)
   A. Tactical aspects
      (1) observation and fire
      (2) cover and concealment
      (3) obstacles
      (4) key terrain features
      (5) avenues of approach
   B. Support aspects (the influence of characteristics on:)
      (1) personnel
      (2) logistics
      (3) civil affairs
      (4) others as appropriate
4. Effects of Characteristics of Area: Contains conclusions in form of affects on general courses of action; e.g. attack, defend, withdraw.
   A. Effects on enemy actions
      (1) weather
      (2) terrain
      (3) others as appropriate
   B. Effects on friendly actions
      (1) weather
      (2) terrain
      (3) others as appropriate

Standing Operating Procedures
(sample format for a combat division)

1. Purpose:
   A. Purpose (general coverage, uses and applicability)
   B. Conformity (instructions to subordinates re. conforming)
2. Command and Control:
   A. Organization (normal task organizations)
   B. Command posts
      (1) composition, movement, controls, alternates, etc.
      (2) C.P. Reporting requirements and procedures
   C. Liaison and coordination
   D. Communications
   E. Order, reports, distribution (instructions common to all)
3. Coordinating Combat and Combat Support Operations:
   A. Intelligence
      (1) reconnaissance and surveillance (acquisition and processing information obtained)
      (2) prisoners of war (levels of interrogation)
      (3) captured documents (handling instructions)
      (4) technical intelligence (items needed and processing)
      (5) maps and substitutes (availability, requisitioning, use, etc.)
      (6) weather (source, dissemination, etc.)
      (7) counterintelligence (standard counter measures)
      (8) fallout (radiological monitoring)
      (9) intelligence units
   B. Operations
      (1) fire support coordination
      (2) security (coordination and responsbilities)
      (3) developing situations (contact, reconnaissance, etc.)
      (4) tactical air support
      (5) nuclear weapon employment
      (6) air defense operations
      (7) Army aviation
      (8) chemical biological (if appropriate)
      (9) engineer operations
      (10) communcations operations
      (11) barrier and denial operations
      (12) tactical cover and deception
      (13) electronic operations
      (14) unconventional operations
      (15) psychological operations
   C. Techniques (operations orders and reports)
   D. Special considerations
      (1) mobility (instructions for movements)
      (2) night operations
      (3) airspace regulation and coordination
      (4) actions to reduce enemy CBR effects
      (5) rear area security
4. Coordinating Combat Service Support Operations:
   A. General (normal support task organization)

B. Techniques (orders and reports re. service support)
C. Detailed procedures
   (1) combat service support
      (a) coordination
      (b) materiel
         1.) supply
         2.) maintenance
      (c) services
   (2) personnel
      (a) strength
         1.) records and reports
         2.) replacements
      (b) personnel management
         1.) procedures (policies and activities)
         2.) civilian personnel (if applicable)
            a. emergency modifications to procedures
            b. administration (standard and emergency)
      (c) maintaining morale
         1.) morale and personnel services (passes, leaves, recreation, etc.)
         2.) graves registration services
      (d) health services
      (e) discipline, law and order
      (f) headquarters management
      (g) miscellaneous
   (3) civil affairs
   (4) miscellaneous support matters
      (a) location of rear boundaries
      (b) designation of service areas
   (5) damage control
   (6) public information and community relations
Annexes: (the body of SOP should be brief with detailed supporting SOP as annex.)

Standing Operating Procedures
(sample format for a logistical office subelement)

1. Purpose: (to establish standard procedures for normal operations.)
2. Control:
   A. Matters for division chief's attention
   B. Organization (Interrelationship between branches for certain tasks)
   C. Reading Files (content and use)
3. Coordination:
   A. Intra-division (general and by specific assigned functions)
   B. Inter-division (general and by specific assigned function)
   C. External (general and by specific assigned function)
4. Administration:
   A. General (standards, speed, suspenses, etc.)
   B. Correspondence/mail management
      (1) Distribution of incoming
      (2) Processing outgoing
   C. Security of classified documents

D. Files
   E. Briefing procedures
5. Personnel:
   A. Personnel rosters
   B. Leaves and passes
   C. Civilian personnel roster
   D. Emergency notification procedures
Annexes: administration, security, emergency notification.

6.

Plans, Orders and Reports

Planning

Staff procedures do not consist of a series of independent, clearly defined steps toward completed actions. Procedural actions meld together into barely distinguishable phases and steps. From the time missions and tasks are assigned or identified, often before commanders are aware the problems exist, staff members should be busy on the solutions. Intelligence, personnel, logistics, and other supporting staff members should be identifying factors and situations affecting the problems and solutions. At the same time, technical experts should start evaluating and operators should be thinking of possible solutions to the problem.

To the uninitiated, the orderly military problem-solving processes may be difficult to detect, even for single missions, tasks or problems. In a large headquarters, literally hundreds of actions may be underway simultaneously, each in a different phase, each requiring staff action, and in many cases all placing demands on the same resources. It is this characteristic of staff work more than any other that challenges the staff officer, demands his maximum in effort, dedication and mental flexibility, and confuses the beginner. This, also, is the main reason why controlled, formatted problem-solving techniques and procedures are necessary.

Planning has been discussed as a separate and distinct phase of the commander's problem-solving procedures. After he decides the course of action to be taken, the plan is the detailed methodology for accomplishing that particular course of action. In actual practice, a good staff would have been at work from the receipt or identification of the mission, task or problem. Good planners often anticipate contingencies and do preliminary planning long before the problems arise. When the commander accepts the staff's estimate and makes a decision, preparation of plans should actually be well underway.

Planning sequences are intermingled with the problem-solving procedures. In the following outline of those procedures, many of the steps are taken concurrently with or form part of the other steps taken by the commander and his staff.

Planning Sequences

Step One—Forecast to Determine Probable Commitments

Just as the commander and the staff begin evaluating the impact of new missions, problems, or tasks by examining the influencing facts and assumptions, the planners must begin to look into the future to examine other commitments, missions and tasks, known or assumed, that could affect or be affected. These are closely allied considerations, but there are subtle differences. The commander's initial analysis of available information deals primarily with the new missions, problems or tasks to be undertaken. Planners must take a broader and longer range view, considering all the missions which must be completed by the command before, during and after the new missions and forecasting the likely impacts of these developments. Of particular interest during this initial planning phase are anticipated requirements for human and physical resources. What will be the impact of other commitments on the people and things required to complete new missions, and what impact will the new actions have on the resources needed for the other commitments, current and anticipated.

The forecasting phase, better than any other, demonstrates that planning is not a single, one-time action. Instead, planning is a continuing process that starts when requirements for an action are recognized and ends only when that action has been completed. Since forecasting deals with factors and situations as they will exist days, months or even years later when the plan is executed, unknowns and assumptions far outnumber firm facts. Unavoidably, initial forecasts must rely heavily on the crystal ball and are liberally seasoned with probabilities. Constant updating and revision is necessary to remove all possible uncertainties before the plan is executed and even while the planned action is being carried out.

As time passes, decisions from higher headquarters, changes in available information, and new developments alter these probabilities. Each changed forecast causes a domino reaction of changes in every phase of the planning process and in the plan itself. The most outstanding characteristic of planning and plans is their tendency to change during all phases of the planning process, during the interval between plan completion and implementation, and during execution of planned actions.

Perhaps more initial forecast changes occur during implementation than at any time. Few plans are based on perfect clairvoyance. Some anticipated commitments never develop and some not contemplated are certain to arise as the action unfolds.

Forecast developments do not always occur. Often they have unanticipated effects. Sometimes conditions develop that could not have been anticipated. A small change could affect all parts of the plan.

Since staff planning slots seem to be particularly frequent assignments for younger, less experienced officers, a word of advice is appropriate. One of the most frequent, and most costly mistakes made by inexperienced (or lazy) planners is to complete plans, file them away and forget them until time for implementation. This often results in plans which are excellently suited to the situation for which they were developed but inapplicable to the situation which has evolved. Invariably, the fault can be traced to failure to update initial forecasts. Planners must keep in constant contact with the entire staff, stay informed on all developments, be aware of new commitments, know of all changes in resource availability, and above all apply that information to plans.

These requirements for constant coordination, research and review lead to another related bit of advice for new staff officers: planners who state or demonstrate that they have little to do are to be avoided as though they (and professionally they may) have the plague. Either they are completely ignorant of their duties and responsibilities to their commander, or they have chosen to ignore them. In either case they will be of little assistance.

The forecast is the foundation of the entire plan, but it is not a one-time step. Forecasting and modifying forecasts are continuing actions that must be constantly in process as the plan is prepared, coordinated, and implemented.

Step Two—Examine Probable Commitments and Developments and Establish Planning Priorities

After all probable commitments have been identified and analyzed to determine their impact on the new mission and the impact of the new mission on other commitments, relative priorities must be determined. This includes relative importance and time-phasing priorities. These priorities are imporant. Relative importance dictates the priorities of assigning resources to the many commitments. Time-phasing priorities dictate the order in which the events must occur; this, in turn, establishes the planners' schedule for completing plans to meet each commitment.

It must be emphasized that these priorities do not replace judgement. That commitment *A* is absolutely vital to mission accomplishment does not mean that commitment *B*, a lesser task, can be ignored and depleted of resources essential to its completion. It could mean, however, that higher risks of failure could be accepted for the minor task than could be considered for mission-essential commitments.

A commitment which must start or be completed before another can begin need not necessarily be planned first. The planning of major actions of great magnitude and complexity may require much more time and effort than more simple actions preceding them. Plans for the larger action sometimes must begin before plans for the simpler, earlier action.

Examination of priorities is essential. It reveals to staff planners the order of precedence that their workload must follow. Like forecasts, however, priorities change from day to day—sometimes from hour to hour or minute to minute.

Step Three—Study the Implications of Commitments to Determine the Scope of the Mission

The planning procedure coincides with the commander's overall problem-solving sequence, but with slight differences in nature and scope. At this early problem-solving step, the commander's primary interest is in examining the newly assigned mission, task, or problem, somewhat as though it were his only commitment, to determine its scope and extent. Planners must have much broader interests. During this step the planners continue their efforts toward identifying the entire scope of commitments: all missions and tasks assigned to the command, and their attendant problems, priorities as they can be defined at that point, and how to fit the new operation or problem into that pattern. While the commander is beginning his procedure for identifying the best problem solution or course of action, the planner is examining all possible solutions and beginning to form ideas as to the actions that will be necessary if one of the less desirable courses must be implemented. While the rest of the staff is concentrating on the new problem and seeking its best solution, planners must be examining the entire spectrum of the commander's commitments and all possible courses of action that may become necessary. Planners must protect the commander against every conceivable eventuality.

Step Four—Analyze the Mission to Determine All Included Tasks

Although planning procedures and the overall command problem-solving process are syncronized, the commaner's interests at this early point are largely confined to tasks included in the mission at his level of concern. Planners must also identify the smaller tasks included in those larger ones which concern the commander. This particularly is true for planners working with human and physical resources.

Step Five—Determine Command Guidance

In the commander's procedure for considering individual problems, initial guidance often pertains only to the problem, mission or task being considered. This guidance is an important part of planning. The commander's expressed desires and policies as they pertain to the particular problem are essential and must be strictly followed. Planners must use additional guidance available from many sources:

Discussions and Comments. Most commanders have reached their positions through many varied assignments and have garnered experience and professional knowledge exceeding their staff's. Senior officers have found that, as a rule, some things will work most of the time, others seldom succeed. They may also have discovered that they personally are better equipped to direct certain types of operations and that they exercise leadership more effectively through certain techniques. The benefits of their experience and knowledge and insights into their individual preferences often are revealed through comments at briefings, conferences, casual conversations, or in their approvals and disapprovals of certain recommendations and proposals. These gems of wisdom are invaluable to all staff officers and subordinate commanders and their staffs. They are indispensable to successful planners.

Policy Statements by the Commander. Many commanders issue formal policy statements soon after arriving at a new job and periodically after that to keep the staff and subordinate commanders informed of their concepts and desires. These can range from broad statements of guidance concerning intrastaff and interheadquarters relationships to the fine details of the preparation of papers and correspondence. These formal official guidance documents should become planners' bibles.

Standing Operating Procedures, (SOP). Most headquarters and many of the staff elements and their subordinate offices have standing operating procedures for recurring or routine actions. These directives apply to many aspects of operations and planning, particularly some of the more detailed mechanics of preparing the plan: format, coordination, approval, numbers of copies, distribution, etc. These SOP's also often delineate planning responsibilities within the staff, including the differences between planning functions and normal mission assignments.

Directives and Orders from Higher Headquarters. Most senior headquarters publish large numbers of directives, orders and instructions covering almost every type of activity, operation or incident that could conceivably occur. Most staff officers can concentrate their efforts on those applying specifically to their rather narrow areas of interest. Planners, however, must be aware of all these directives, the guidance from their bosses' bosses.

Step Six—Preparing Planning Studies

Here, the planning process and the commander's problem-solving process converge at a single point: preparing estimates, staff studies, or special studies to select feasible courses of action that could lead to success. As these studies reach the analysis stage, planners again begin to take slightly different views from those charged with recommending only a single, best solution.

Step Seven—Selecting the Courses of Action

Commanders expect from estimates and studies, clear-cut recommendations for a single course of action that can be acceptable as a command decision. The experienced planner learns from bitter experience that a course of action and a commander's decision that are valid one day may become less desirable with later developments. He must be most interested in the courses of action which appear to have possibilities of success, even though they may seem extremely undesirable at the moment.

Changes in plans come from many sources: a senior commander may disapprove a previously selected course of action, other commitments may arise requiring the resources necessary for the preferred course of action, influences beyond the control of the commander (weather, enemy capabilities) may change, or additional information may become available dictating a change in method of operations. Wise planners place first priority on the recommended course of action but do not ignore other possible courses which might be successful. During the estimating or study phase, while the rest of the staff concentrates on finding *best* solutions, planners prepare outline plans for each course of action. These outlines serve several purposes. They act as quality control tests, establishing the feasibility of actually putting into practice the various available courses of action or problem solutions. They provide a further basis for additional detailed planning at later dates.

Step Eight—Preparing Complete Plans

The planner is now on his own. The commander has completed the problem-solving procedures and decided on the course of action or problem solution. The staff estimate has become the commander's estimate of the situation, and its recommendation has become his decision. That decision, together with any additional guidance he may see fit to issue, becomes the basis for preparing the complete, time-phased plan for implementation. Like the other staff members, the planner considers time a precious resource and seldom has enough to do the many things that need to be done. Time requires expert management. Experienced planners accomplish this by strict scheduling.

Plans, Orders and Reports   137

Step Nine—Developing Planning Programs

Planning programs are management devices used to assure that all available time is used to maximum effectiveness. Programs also serve as checklists to assure that nothing has been overlooked during the planning. Many experienced staff officers use the backward planning method to develop planning schedules, starting their schedule with the date when the last planning action must be completed. In an attack situation in combat, for example, this could be the exact time of the attack.

From this point the planner begins to think and to schedule backward. Units initiating the attack should have some rehearsal not later than the day before. So subtract one day for unit rehearsals. Before they can rehearse, units must have completed their own detailed plans, so a reasonable time must be subtracted for that planning.

Table 6.1a

Typical Backward Scheduling

Planning Action	Date Started	Date Completed
1. Planned action begins	1 August	1 August
2. Rehearsals	30 July	31 July
3. Unit level planning	25 July	29 July
4. Distribution of division plans	23 July	24 July
5. Division level planning	18 July	22 July
6. Distribution of Army plans	16 July	17 July
7. Army plan completed	16 July	14 July
8. Final modifications and administration	13 July	14 July
9. Command approval	13 July	13 July
10. Post coordination modifications	11 July	12 July
11. Coordination	9 July	10 July
12. Administration (typing, copies, etc.)	8 July	8 July
13. Finalizing plan	6 July	7 July
14. Staff input received	6 July	6 July
15. Staff input developed	2 July	5 July
16. Staff input requested	2 July	2 July
17. Planning guidance studied and planning program developed	1 July	2 July

Table 6.1b
Planning Program

Planning Action	Date Started	Date Completed
1. Planning directive received	1 July	1 July
2. Staff input requested	2 July	2 July
3. Staff elements develop input	2 July	5 July
4. Basic draft plan developed	2 July	5 July
5. Staff input received	6 July	6 July
6. Plan completed	6 July	7 July
7. Administrative time (typing, copies, etc.)	8 July	8 July
8. Coordination	9 July	10 July
9. Modifications	11 July	12 July
10. Present to commander	13 July	13 July
11. Final modifications	13 July	14 July
12. Distribute plan (or orders)	15 July	

The units planning can only start after the plans and directives from higher headquarters have been received and studied. Subtract the time necessary for all intermediate headquarters to complete and distribute their plans. Backward planning now arrives at the time available for completing plans, coordinating them, securing command approval, and distributing them to the field.

In continuing the reverse thought process, experienced planners should have some idea of the time required for approval, publication and distribution of the plan. The time available for actually preparing plans should now be apparent, but the planning program is not yet complete. The planner's efforts must now be fitted into the remaining time so that he meets the deadline he has established for delivery of the plan to the administrative experts who will put it in final form. Times for final coordination, for receiving input from other staff elements, for requesting that input, for briefing contributors and for administrative processing must be subtracted.

The appended sample backward scheduling table and resultant planning program are included as examples only. In actual practice, time requirements seldom permit such leisurely approaches to planning.

Plans

The somewhat wordy discussion of planning as a prelude to this fairly brief discussion of the end product may corroborate the old adage "Planning is everything; plans are nothing." Far from it. It does, however, reflect a conviction that thorough, objective planning must result in good usable plans. Inferior plans do not result from weaknesses in format or the vagaries of chance. Inferior plans result from faulty planning or failure to continue planning after the initial product has been sold to the commander, packaged and distributed to the users.

Plans, like other staff actions, follow set formats for certain standard, recurring actions, such as operations plans for combat situations and the administrative and logistics plans that support them. As in estimates and studies, however, many situations arise that do not fit the strict formats prescribed for tactical plans. Examination of those formats should point up the importance of certain key features that all good plans must contain, regardless of format.

To save time and to reduce the chances for misunderstanding and error military plans normally are prepared in such a manner that after approval and the order for implementation the plans themselves can become orders. Unlike the estimate, the plan is not intended solely for the internal use of the commander and his staff. It should contain only information and data suitable for release to subordinate commanders and their staffs as basis for planning. Plans should be positive and written in the language of military orders. Suggestions such as "Commanders *should* not lose contact with adjoining units" or "Use of ammunition *should* be strictly controlled" are not directives and are not appropriate for military orders or plans. If they are important to the success of the planned operation, positive wording should be used. "Commanders *will* maintain contact with their adjoining units", and "Commanders *will* institute and enforce strict controls to conserve ammunition". Throughout the planning process the planners should bear in mind that what they are writing will be distributed to many people at many levels and that it must be amenable to translation into directives by scratching out the title *Plan* and substituting *Order, Directive, Instructions,* or similar titles.

This dual-purpose aspect of planning formats is applicable to some extent in even the most minor planning actions affecting routine everyday occurrences. For example, simple plans for the entertainment of an important visitor or for sending groups of staff officers to conferences at a distant city should be prepared in formats that, when approved, could become directives. As an even simpler example, plans for a briefing schedule or an agenda for a conference should be in sufficient detail and appropriate format for issuing as directives to establish procedures and order of precedence. Failure to do this can often cause considerable additional work for the unfortunate staff officer who failed to put forth the slight amount of additional effort needed to create a completed piece of staff work. Regardless of format, a good plan should meet the requirements of the following test.

1. Does it accomplish the mission?
2. Is it based on facts and valid assumptions?
3. Does it make use of existing resources?
4. Does it clearly establish command relations and fix responsibilities?
5. Does it provide continuity?
6. Does it decentralize controls?
7. Does it authorize direct contact?
8. Is it simple?
9. Is it flexible?
10. Does it establish sufficient controls?
11. Has it been thoroughly coordinated?

Formats

Military references quite properly focus on those facets of military activities directly associated with the military establishment's primary reason for existing, combat. Consequently, planning formats discussed in these references are best suited for plans for combat missions: strategic plans, campaign plans, operation plans, contingency plans, allied supporting plans.

In actual practice, staff officers are involved in many planning activities with little relationship to combat operations. Even during periods of open hostilities, commanders and their staffs often operate in situations most difficult to identify directly with the Army's combat mission. Yet their missions are important and often include many separate complex and difficult tasks. Obviously, these missions and tasks can be performed effectively only with considerable planning and with plans of many types.

During 1972, one Continental Army headquarters with no mission directly associated with operations in South Vietnam or for direct participation in possible future involvment in combat operations maintained more than forty separate plans. Some related to supporting tactical organizations during possible future military operations, primarily from the viewpoint of providing resources to support those operations. Other plans covered a wide range of subjects from assisting civilian communities in the event of natural disaster to training military and civilian personnel, to managing funds to meet objectives to conducting national level ceremonies of state, etc. Many of these could not follow the standard operations plan format. In general, however, the operation plan format provides a basis, or starting point, for developing formats compatible with any operation. A detailed operations plan sample format is included in the appendix.

Orders

Formal, full-scale operation orders and their supporting administrative orders require little discussion or further explanation. With only minor modifications, operation and administrative plans can be issued by commanders as implementing, operations and administrative orders. Formats are identical and both plans and orders must meet the tests of completeness and clarity. Many situations, however, do not require complete operations orders to convey commanders' desires. These require different techniques that merit discussion.

Warning Orders

Sometimes commanders become aware of situations that appear likely to require military operations by their subordinate commanders. To allow those subordinates to start preparations and planning, commanders often issue warning orders alerting them to the known or anticipated operations. Warning orders are issued at the earliest possible time, usually before estimates have been prepared or detailed planning started. Because these warnings could cover many diverse situations and could contain either a great deal or very little information, formats are not appropriate. Under all circumstances, however, the warning should contain one vital ingredient that the recipients will be most anxious to know: when additional guidance will be available.

Fragmentary Orders

As operations proceed, changing situations often require modification of the operations order but are not of sufficient magnitude to justify rewriting the entire order. A minor change to the order may be issued by message or letter. When these changes are in vital portions of the order and directly affect mission accomplishment, they normally are issued as *fragmentary orders*. As with warning orders, the diverse contents and uses of this order modifying device preclude standardized format.

Letters of Instruction (LOI)

Unlike operation orders, fragmentary orders and warning orders, letters of instruction normally are used by very senior commanders to issue broad quidance to subordinate commanders for general conduct of operations of larger units for extended periods of time. They may, however, contain specific instructions, policies or guidance for control, coordination and command relationships for special operational situations that last only a few days. The appendix includes a sample outline summarized from a letter of instructions issued by a senior commander in Europe during World War II, demonstrating that the LOI can be used to issue relatively detailed guidance.

Miscellaneous Directives. In addition to formal orders and letters of instruction, commanders pass along instructions, direction and guidance by many less formalized methods: messages, oral instructions, letters, phone calls, briefings, conferences, various publications such as bulletins, pamphlets, regulations, circulars, and by approving and disapproving recommendations and proposals. Different commanders prefer different methods of issuing directives. Staff officers must therefore remain flexible, not assuming that just because previous commanders and some military reference documents prescribe formal orders for certain type operations that this is sacred law from on high. Each commander must choose the format and method of preparation that best serve to impart his directives in clear, concise language.

Reports

Reports are key instruments in the supervisory stage of commanders' problem-solving procedures and are indispensable tools for assuring effective resource management. Staff officers must understand the value of reports. They must not, however, be deceived by the Army's apparent fanaticism with reports into believing that reports replace personal, face-to-face coordination, on-the-ground supervision of operations or sound human judgement.

Reports are management tools intended to facilitate supervision for commanders, managers and their staffs. Unfortunately, some staff officers become so obsessed with reports and reporting that they lose sight of the purposes of these devices, and become slaves to rather than masters of potentially valuable management tools. These—fortunately few—report fanatics mistake the mechanics of gathering, organizing, storing and passing along pure, unanalyzed data with management. Young, inexperienced staff members may find this a tempting retreat from their actual purpose for existing, which is to use all available information to help commanders accomplish their missions. Providing that assistance requires hard mental and physical work.

Information and data must be evaluated to separate the meaningful and useful material from the insignificant. The useful must be analyzed and its impacts determined, and positive actions recommended. Raw data are meaningless. Reports such as "Installation A is underfinanced $1 million for base operations," "B Division is short 500 rifles," or "An enemy division is moving along Highway X," are interesting but useless until they are analyzed and their meanings interpreted. First, are they factual? Can they be substantiated by other information? Second, if they are true, what are the impacts?

If Installation A is an extremely large installation, the $1 million fund shortage could be a small percentage of its annual budget, indicating that only low priority activities would suffer. If, on the other hand, the shortage represented one-fourth of the annual fund requirement of a small installation, the impact could be disastrous. Similarly, a shortage of rifles matched by an equal shortage of riflemen would be significant but not urgent in itself; and an enemy division on the move is only important to the extent that the meaning of the move can be determined.

Reports are management and supervisory tools. They take many forms, from simple notes passed from one staff element to another to voluminous tomes of data processed automatically by huge, multimillion-dollar computers. Like all tools, however, they are inanimate and serve no purpose until put to use by human intelligence capable of applying them to their intended purposes.

Before discussing some of the types of reports used by the Army, some precautionary words are appropriate to those who prepare reports. The importance of reports as tools to managers and supervisors has been emphasized; now, a word to the toolmaker. Although a manufacturer of precision tools for automotive repairs need not be a mechanic, he must have a thorough knowledge of the tools required to repair an automobile. Similarly, persons who prepare reports must be selective about what is forwarded to the user.

Indiscriminately flooding higher headquarters, commanders, and staff supervisors with every minute bit of information and data available is a poor solution and only swamps the recipient with useless material. Reporting only exactly what has been requested is even more dangerous. Information cannot be requested if no one knows it exists. Striking the balance between excessive and insufficient reporting is difficult and requires years of experience in varieties of assignments, plus the kind of sound, mature military judgement seldom available to the junior staff officers faced with deciding whether to report or not to report. Army leaders at all levels, including those in Headquarters, Department of the Army, are aware of this problem and have long attempted to control both extremes by inhibiting excessive reporting—either voluntary or through unnecessary requirements imposed by the report fanatics who lurk in every headquarters—and by insuring through standardization and format that no useful bit of data escapes notice.

Reports Control System

Reporting is expensive and time-consuming. If it is not controlled, disproportionate amounts of command and staff time, especially at lower levels of command, will be taken up by reporting, with little time left for planning and supervising operations or managing resources.

To control the tendency toward overreporting, Army regulations require Headquarters, Department of the Army, and subordinate headquarters to establish and maintain a reports control system. Basically, reports control systems are intended to control reports by insisting that requests for new reports from subordinates, recommended changes to existing reports and proposed report discontinuation be completely justified. Each commander must see that every report meets the following criteria.

1. Report is not being used as a substitute for more effective, direct and active management or supervisory procedures.
2. Information requested is actually needed for effective management of resources, or supervision of operations.
3. Report is the most effective and economical method of obtaining required information.
4. Information requested by report is adequate.
5. Excess information is not requested.
6. Report format and reporting procedures will actually serve stated purpose of report.

As an enforcement device and a reports management tool, each approved report, whether recurring or one-time, is assigned a report control symbol. This method of recording all reports required by a headquarters facilitates reviews of the program. Additionally, it presents a rapid picture of the reporting load placed on subordinate commanders and their staffs. Regulations recognize that sometimes information is needed that, for cogent reasons, should be exempted from complete reports controls. This does not remove the demands that the report meet the requirements of validity and necessity.

In theory, requests for reports containing neither a report control symbol nor a statement of exemption from report controls could be ignored by the recipient. In practice, however, refusing to comply with requests from commanders on such technicalities would be ill advised. A much more prudent procedure would be to set about packaging the requested information. To be sure that the requirement is valid it would be appropriate to request that a reports control symbol or statement of exemption be provided.

Reporting Formats

Supervising the far-flung Army operations of today and managing its complex and sophisticated resources require literally thousands of standard, recurring reports. Special situations arise that require similar numbers of one-time reports. Discussion of formats for these standard one-time and recurring reports would be impossible and unnecessary. Requests for reports usually include explicit format instructions. If not, the details of the information required should indicate an appropriate format for logical presentation.

In most headquarters, formats are prescribed for even the most routine reports—trip reports, conference reports, committee meeting reports, progress reports, etc. When no format has been provided, most experienced staff officers fashion their reports around the logical order of presentation provided by the staff study format, modified as necessary. The appendix provides an example for one suggested format.

Appendix to Chapter 6

**Operation Plan
(sample format)**

References: maps, SOP's, other plans, letters of instruction, miscellaneous information such as time zones, etc.

Task Organization: Usually refers to Annex A. (includes assigned and attached units that will accomplish operation)

1. Situation:
   A. Enemy forces (usually annexed, includes factual information on enemy, sometimes extracted from intelligence estimate).
   B. Friendly forces (higher, adjacent, supporting, reinforcing units other than those in task organization. Limit to significant units.)
   C. Attachments and detachments (lists with effective dates and times)
   D. Assumptions (list assumptions critical to the success of the plan).
   E. Effective date (time, date, condition or event that would cause the plan to be implemented).

2. Mission:
   Complete statement of mission and included task to be performed, stated in terms of command level preparing plan. Must contain: what, where, when, who, and to the extent necessary, why. How, to the extent required, should be part of paragraph 3 a. Concept of Operation.

3. Execution:
   A. Concept of operation (statement of commanders general tactical concepts, visualizes conduct of operation and clarification of purposes and objectives. Concepts may be divided into subparagraphs as necessary for clear presentation.)
   B. Specific task assignments (describe in as much detail as necessary the exact tasks to be accomplished by each unit assigned and attached. State all priorities and time sequences essential to the plan. Use additional lettered subparagraphs as needed.)
   C. Coordinating instruction (paragraph letter will depend on numbers of preceding paragraphs). Details of coordination and control measures applicable to more than one element of the command.

4. Administration and Logistics:
This paragraph may be accomplished by several techniques. Simple plans, requiring little support, could include all details in the paragraph. More complex operations could summarize critical administrative and logistical functions in the paragraph with details in supporting annexes; or a separate administration plan could be prepared. In any situation, all plans must include or be supported by detailed plans for administrative and logistical support.
5. Command and Signal:
Details of command and operations of communications equipment.
Annexes: (basic plan should be brief as possible with supporting details annexed).

Administrative Plan
(sample format)

References, maps, charts, standing operating procedures, miscellaneous information such as time zones, etc.
1. General
Outline general plan for supporting operation, including general information not suited to other paragraphs.
2. Materiel and Services:
A. Supply (use numbers and paragraphs to prescribe supply procedures, give locations of supply activities and establish requirements, limitations and controls.)
   (1) Class I
   (2) Class II
   (3) Class IV
   (4) Class V
   (5) Class VI
   (6) Class VII
   (7) Class VIII
   (8) Class IX
   (9) maps
   (10) water
   (11) excesses
   (12) salvage
   (13) captured materials
   (14) additional subparagraphs as needed
B. Transportation
C. Services
   (1) maintenance
   (2) construction
   (3) other services (use subparagraphs as needed)
      (a) laundry
      (b) bath
      (c) clothing repair and exchange
      (d) added subparagraphs as needed
   (4) health services
      (a) medical
      (b) dental
      (c) veterinary

        (d) add subparagraphs as needed
    (5) installation services
        (a) real estate
        (b) utilities
        (c) repair of facilities
        (d) sewage
        (e) add subparagraphs as needed
    (6) Other, as required
  D. Labor (use of civilians, prisoners of War, including restrictions).
3. Medical Evacuation and Hospitalization:
  A. Evacuation (list facilities and establish procedures)
  B. Hospitalization (list facilites and establish procedures)
4. Personnel:
  A. Maintenance of strength
    (1) strength reports
    (2) replacements
  B. Personnel management
  C. Discipline, law and order
  D. Headquarters management
  E. Miscellaneous
5. Civil Affairs (if appropriate)
6. Miscellaneous:
  A. Boundaries
  B. Headquarters (locations)
  C. Protection
  D. Special reports
  E. Added subparagraphs as needed
Annexes: (Basic plan should be as brief as possible with supporting details annexed.)
Distribution: (List of organizations, activities and individuals who are to receive plan, and number of copies for each recipient)

Letter of Instruction
(sample format)

Subject: Letter of Instruction
To: All Commanders
1. General (Purpose and scope)
2. Command:
  A. Leadership
    (1) personal leadership by commanders (be seen)
    (2) visits to front (frequent)
  B. Execution (importance of supervision)
  C. Staff Conferences (frequency)
  D. Rest periods (essential to operations)
  E. Location of command posts (well forward)
3. Combat procedures:
  A. Maps (importance)
  B. Plans (keep simple)
  C. Reconnaissance (constant requirement)

D. Orders
   (1) formal
   (2) fragmentary (use to change formal orders)
   (3) warning orders (must be early)
E. Keep troops informed
4. Administration:
   A. Supply (user must anticipate needs)
   B. Replacements (vital)
   C. Hospitals (near front)
   D. Decorations (important to morale)
   E. Discipline (must be perfect)
   F. Rumors (must be stopped)
5. Physical Condition (key factor – enforce)

Report Format
(sample)

1. Purpose: complete statement of the reason for the report.
   Example. To report the results of a maintenance inspection of armored equipment conducted by Colonal Mat. Readiness, office DCSLOG, at Fort Rust, on 13 May 1972. Inspection complied with commanding general's directive of 1 May 1972 (CG's memo at Incl. 1).
2. Background: data or information required to update commander or supervisor on subject being reported.
   Example. During last four months, deadline rates for armored equipment at Fort Rust have increased steadily. Instructions and guidance provided by five letters (Incl. 1 through 5) and four informal visits (trip reports Incl. 6 through 9) have proven ineffective. On 1 May 1972, the Commanding General directed that a formal inspection be conducted at the earliest possible date (Incl. 1).
3. Discussion: present information to be reported.
   Example. Fifty-five tanks and twenty-four personnel carriers inspected. Conditions generally poor. (See detailed report Incl. 10) Many indications of faulty preventive maintenance. Reviewed maintenance records; discovered many errors, omissions and incomplete entries. Discussed maintenance management with installation maintenance officer suggested several changes. Maintenance officer not experienced. Little sign of active command supervision.
4. Conclusions: summarize the principle points of information reported.
   Example.
   A. That armored vehicle maintenance at Fort Rust is unsatisfactory
   B. That Fort Rust needs an experienced maintenance officer
   C. That increased command interest in maintenance will be necessary to improve the Fort Rust maintenance program
   D. That urgent, immediate corrective actions be initiated by this headquarters to correct current unsatisfactory conditions
5. Recommendations: (if appropriate)
   Example.
   A. That the commanding general sign a letter to higher headquarters requesting that an experienced maintenance officer be assigned Fort Rust as early as possible (proposed letter at Incl. 11)

B. That commanding general sign a letter to the commander, Fort Rust, urging personal command emphasis on maintenance and close supervision of the maintenance program (proposed letter at Incl. 12)

C. That two maintenance management experts be placed on temporary duty to Fort Rust effective 25 May 1972 for two weeks to assist in establishing sound maintenance program (proposed order at Incl. 14)

7.

Other Typical Staff Actions

The actions described so far relate to the command problem-solving, decision-making and directives by which the staff assists the commander in analyzing missions, making decisions and supervising execution. These are the major, complex actions bearing directly on the mission. They are used most frequently by tactical headquarters in tactical situations, but they could also be used by a hospital commander or a depot commander in a fixed installation. In fact, they may be used in any headquarters at any time. For this reason every staff officer must be able to participate in them even though he may not see an estimate or a letter of instruction from one year to the next. Staff officers in most headquarters spend most of their time on routine daily actions that solve small problems before they become big problems. These routine actions cover every facet of the commander's responsibilities and consume most of the staff's efforts.

Major actions have been described here in detail because they are fundamental. The approach to routine actions is less complicated; but since it is what most staff officers do most of the time, it deserves attention. The new staff officer can expect to be completely immersed in correspondence, phone conversations, conferences and briefings. If he is lucky, he may get to make a field trip from time to time. The following paragraphs discuss some of the more common activities.

Correspondence

Each day, every large headquarters receives hundreds of electrically transmitted messages, letters, and telephone calls which require replies and generate equally impressive quantities of outgoing correspondence. Most headquarters issue detailed instructions on procedures for handling and responding to incoming correspondence and even more detailed guidance for preparing outgoing material.

Incoming Correspondence

Staff officers are in constant danger of being completely inundated with paperwork. As each day progresses, *in*boxes pile up and the individual action officer can easily develop a strong aversion to each added letter and message and avoid the telephone as though it were a mortal enemy. Natural as this tendency may be, it must be fought. The staff officer must bear in mind that somewhere, at a similarly paper-laden desk, a fellow staff officer has written the letter or placed the call because he or his boss thinks the subject matter important. His work, even his professional reputation, may hinge on the results of his correspondence in the form of action or of information. Each paper and each call must therefore receive serious, objective consideration and, when appropriate, a reply.

Experienced staff officers, with their wealth of background knowledge, may appear to wade through stacks of correspondence rapidly and effortlessly and to satisfy phone inquiries and requests with equal ease. The less experienced officer must discipline his actions to more orderly mental processes. What is the purpose of each item of correspondence? What other information is available on the same matter? What actions are possible? What is the best action to take? Very often the best action for the *very* new staff officer is to consult with supervisors or more experienced fellow action officers.

Outgoing Correspondence

As staff officers prepare messages and letters or pick up phones to place calls, they would do well to envision the paper-clogged desks where their correspondence or calls will be received. This should cause them to consider their work carefully. Obviously, the best results will come from making the correspondence palatable to the harassed action officer on the other end. That recipient's biggest problem will likely be time. So, compose letters, messages and telepone calls with that in mind. For technical guidance in the preparation of letters, refer to Army Regulation 340-15; for messages, to Army Regulation 105-31. For local guidance seek out the applicable headquarters directive, and for office style review a sample of the sections files. There are a few basic guidelines for all outgoing correspondence.

1. *Be brief.* Commanders and staff officers like short letters and messages and are particularly fond of brief telephone calls. When desks are piled high with stacks of voluminous, ominous-looking documents, a one-page

letter or message is refreshing. One page may not always be enough but all excess should be cut away, leaving just the matter to be discussed.
2. *Be brief but not cryptic; state the matter clearly.*
3. *Be coherent.* Present your thoughts in a logical order with understandable transition between thoughts.
4. *Cover the subject completely* whether issuing directives, requesting assistance, passing information or responding to requests or directives. Don't make some busy officer fill in the blanks.
5. *Stick with the subject.* Resist the temptation to digress.

Internal Correspondence

Several portions of this book have stressed staff unity of purpose and the importance of preserving it. Equal emphasis has been placed on the many conflicting interests within the staff and the close interrelationship necessary between the elements to assure community of effort. This interrelationship can only be accomplished by close and frequent contacts at all levels. Much (perhaps too much) of this contact in large headquarters is written and telephoned.

The Army has developed several standard formats for this intraheadquarters correspondence: memoranda, disposition forms, etc. Almost every major headquarters supplements these with locally produced standard forms. Staff officers seldom have problems determining appropriate formats for corresponding between staff elements. Most headquarters go even further in their guidance, often prescribing exact paragraphing for every conceivable type of action. Within these guidelines, however, staff officers must impose on themselves the same disciplines essential to incoming and outgoing external correspondence: responsiveness, accuracy, brevity, clarity, unity, coherence and completeness.

Because every staff officer spends a great deal of time and effort on these internal communications, some additional discussion is warranted. Although formats are prescribed, it should be of interest just to examine their variety.

Memoranda. The most commonly used medium of correspondence among staff officers is the memorandum, an informal paper used to convey any sort of topic, discussion or message. When there is not time for personal contact, the memorandum is the next best choice. As in a letter, the subject matter should be limited to one topic. Army regulation 340-15 prescribes memorandum format with illustrations.

A special *disposition form* has been printed for memoranda between staff offices. A memorandum on this form may be routed through several staff offices where comments may be added. It is a convenient, time-saving form which can be used as a single memorandum or to collect multiple comments.

Other special memoranda forms have been printed to record telephone and face-to-face conversations for convenience and efficiency. This type of memorandum is retained as a record rather than passed between offices as a communication.

Summary Sheets (Abbreviated Staff Studies). Communications for the command group are always of special interest. They can be divided into two categories: those designed to seek a decision or those intended to inform.

The point has been made earlier that although not all staff officers work on each plan, estimate, or formal study, most staff officers prepare input for the command group. Many face this challenge daily. Any paper going to the command group commands the attention of all the chiefs in the chain—from the section chief to the chief of staff. Most headquarters demand near perfection in these communications. The format and content of the several hundred papers produced by the staff and handled by the command group of a large headquarters in a single day must be rigidly controlled to save time by eliminating excess material.

The most common vehicle for moving a decision paper up the chain is an abbreviated staff study, used for routine actions where a formal staff study would be inappropriate. The format and titles may vary slightly from headquarters to headquarters, but they are essentially the same. A typical format follows.

SUBJECT:

THROUGH: FROM:

TO:

  1. Purpose
  2. Discussion
  3. Recommendation
  4. Coordination
     Authority line

                                                  Signature

In Paragraph 1, the word *purpose* may be replaced by *problem*. It is the action that needs resolution and for which approval is sought. It is no different from the problem of a formal staff study. The discussion paragraph should summarize the action as briefly as possible, preferably in only one page. Some headquarters may permit two pages or even more, but that is the exception rather than the rule. Despite its brevity the discussion must fully support the recommendation and answer the essential questions of what, who, when, where, how and why. If a lengthy discussion is needed, it should be summarized in Paragraph 2 and annexed.

The recommendation is the proposed action or solution. The chief of staff or commander need only indicate approval or disapproval.

The abbreviated staff study or summary sheet, as it is sometimes called, often is used to seek approval of intrastaff actions. It is also used to gain approval of an outgoing action such as a response to a higher headquarters or a directive to a subordinate command. In the case of the outgoing action the proposed letter, message, directive or order should be attached at the first tab. Supporting material should also be included in the file at successive tabs. The entire package should be able to stand up in court so to speak.

Abbreviated staff studies are normally addressed to the chief of staff. If the commanders' approval is sought, this should be indicated in the recommendation. If the action is to be coordinated before reaching the chief of staff, the addressees should be listed under *through*, and their coordination, recorded in Paragraph 4. In the normal line of authority these would be the chiefs of the staff offices, such as "For the Deputy Chief of Staff Personnel" or "For the Provost Marshal." The signature would be that of the office chief or whoever is authorized to sign for him.

Outgoing actions requiring command group approval are often under tight suspense. In such an air of tension and drama the new staff officer wrestling with one of his first actions of this type would do well to seek help. At the least he would have his product reviewed in draft within his office. With a twenty-four-hour suspense there is not much time for rewrite. The problem is compounded when outside coordination is required.

When the package reaches the chief of staff, he has several options; only one of them is good from the action officer's viewpoint. If the action is complex or controversial, the chief of staff or the commander may request a briefing on the proposal. The action officer should have this in mind while working on the action, because he may have to make the presentation.

Items of Command Interest. One of the staff's primary responsibilities is to keep the commander informed. A popular way to accomplish this is a written communication called in most headquarters an *item of interest*. Typically it would be addressed to the chief of staff even though it is intended for the commander. The subject should be stated as a heading; the text should be straight, factual reporting. Because items of interest are informative they normally need no coordination. Copies should be furnished to other interested staff offices. They should be coordinated if the reported information infers criticism of other staff elements or implies poor performance in their areas of interest. As with all reporting, the big question is what to report. Guidelines will usually be established, but they are certain to leave room for interpretation. The best approach is to err on the heavy side, if at all. When in doubt, report.

Fact Sheets and Talking Papers. Several other types of informational papers may be called for in a particular headquarters. Two of these are the fact sheet and the talking paper, which serve the same purpose—to provide information on current matters to supervisors, briefers, fellow action officers and members of the command group. These are especially useful to a commander when he travels outside headquarters.

When the command group announces the commander's planned visit to a subordinate command or his participation in an upcoming conference, fact sheets or talking papers are often called for. Each staff element then reviews the current situation in its area of interest and attempts to anticipate key questions or problems that could come up for discussion during the visit or conference. When these have been identified, fact sheets or talking papers are prepared.

Formats may or may not be standardized. The information should be presented in straight, factual language. The three main points to be addressed are background, current status and future outlook, particularly for actions underway or planned. Because the papers are for instant reference, they must be brief. Ideally, all of the information should be presented on a single page.

Some commanders maintain a permanent file of fact sheets pertaining to elements of their command and the status of major actions. Often these may be slanted toward statistical information and performance data more than toward general problem areas. In any case, the staff must keep the files current. This can be a major effort and is frequently assigned to the most junior staff members.

Other special purpose formats may be used in other headquarters. It is up to the new action officer to learn the requirements and comply. All are designed to facilitate the staff's support of the commander.

Conferences

Major actions often involve many staff elements, and sometimes several subactivities within each element. By making sure that everyone approaches the problem from the same departure point, conferences can save time and repetitious correspondence, liaison and phone calls among staff members. Conferences are particularly valuable when wide disagreement is anticipated. At the conference table, controversies can surface, be debated objectively face to face and resolved before they inhibit staff production.

Conferences are also ideal vehicles for disseminating information and guidance, for seeking assistance from the rest of the staff at the beginning of actions and for collecting staff input as actions reach decision points. They are in themselves a form of communication and should receive the same care and preparation as written material. Staff officers designated to represent their own element or subelement at a conference should prepare to present their supervisors' positions as succinctly as if they were stating those views in letters, messages or official phone calls. Positions and recommendations should be supported by valid, applicable data and information. Presentation should be based on the same criteria as other correspondence: brevity, clarity, completeness, cohesion, etc.

Briefings

The frequency with which large, formal briefings occur varies greatly among headquarters, reflecting the preferences and operating procedures of various commanders. By its very nature, however, staff work creates many briefing requirements. Productive staff officers complete few work days without participating in at least one briefing (more probably several) as presenter, as observer or as briefee.

Unfortunately, most briefings pass unrecognized and consequently receive less than adequate attention. Briefings range from elaborate presentations featuring expensive animated cartoon slides to the simple verbal exchange of information between two junior staff officers. For the spectaculars, guidance generally is more than adequate. Everything—words, gestures, position, facial expressions of the briefer, the timing of each chart—is prescribed and rehearsed. However, even simply passing along bits of information to fellow action officers, instructing a secretary or making a progress report to a supervisor is a briefing and merits some degree of planning, organization and rehearsal.

As the name implies and the practice seldom achieves, briefings are intended to be quick procedures for passing along information. Brevity is not achieved without prior consideration of the material to be presented. Briefing techniques are discussed elsewhere in this book; however, one point must be reemphasized here. *All professional skills are important and are the ultimate determiners of success.*

Briefing abilities (with writing a close second) are those most visible to supervisors and fellow staff officers. Written documents can be edited, even virtually rewritten, and still bear the originator's name, disguising to some extent his lack of writing ability. But when an action officer must pass along information verbally, he must rely on his own skills. Often the commander, senior staff supervisors and other members of the staff will remember an action officer from his briefings only. It is imperative, therefore, that particular care be exercised in preparing and presenting all briefing, whether a staged spectacular or the simple interchange of information.

Research

To most people, the word *research* conjures up visions of men in white coats bent over microscopes, or of scholarly types in academic robes searching through dust-covered volumes among the stacks of some great library. Dictionaries define research as "diligent, protracted investigation." In military staff work it is the quest for the relevant information which must be considered in arriving at a valid course of action. In the military the term *research* is commonly applied to all investigations into background material, no matter how simple. At the same time, it is used to cover the most extensive searches for new, pertinent facts. Under this broad usage it is easy to understand that research is a vital part of staff work. Research is the initial step in every action undertaken by the effective staff officer. The extent of that research varies with the problem.

Writing even a single-paragraph letter calls for some review of previous correspondence and other actions on the matter. At the very least, good staff officers search their memories and their personal working files before starting to write. Perhaps in the dictionary sense the term *research* is inappropriate here. To staff officers, however, this is research. In a full scale staff study it would be insufficient just to review background material. It would be necessary to uncover and consider all available information bearing on the problem. This is real research. Special studies on complex matters can involve research of the highest order.

Consider, for example, investigation by the staff preparing an environmental impact statement for an off-post, corps-size maneuver. Factors requiring assessment would include: climate, topography, hydrology, soil trafficability, communications net, agricultural development, industrial development, municipal development and on and on. For the letter, the research was informal; in major studies it would be formal.

Formal means *organized* research. A detailed plan of the information and data requirements should be developed and matched against a similarly detailed list of potential sources. Then a schedule should be prepared that insures examination of all sources within the time available. As in all staff work, time will almost always be tight. Seldom will an action officer finish his research efforts without feeling that more time should have been taken. The time squeeze requires that sources be attacked in order of priority, examining first the ones which promise the biggest pay off. Here are a few of the many sources available to action officers.

1. Personal project files
2. Section files
3. Office files

4. Headquarters files
5. Staff associates
6. Staff experts
7. Reference libraries
8. Public libraries
9. Experts in other headquarters and agencies

If information and data requirements have been logically organized, then the data itself should be logically organized. Many approaches could be used. The data could be keyed to subdivisions of the study: assumptions, facts, discussion and so on. It could be approached topically. In the environmental impact statement, information could be compiled under each heading—climate, topography, hydrology and so on.

Most important is that the data or information be arranged in logical, usable order. Data should be weighed for applicability and accuracy as a test of usefulness. At the end of the research effort all questions must be answered. Data and information must provide a sufficient basis for sound conclusions and recommendations.

Staff Supervision

Staff supervision is a mysterious realm to most newcomers to staff work. First, the term *supervision* implies that the staff members actually direct subordinate commands, but it has been shown that only commanders direct. Staff supervision differs from command supervision in that it merely assists the commander by informing, interpreting, observing and guiding.

Another puzzle may result from the wide dispersal of most major commands. Subordinate units are often far removed from their parent headquarters. How does the staff supervise them? Instant communications and rapid transportation have helped solve this problem. The staff keeps in touch, and the staff gets out.

The typical sequence of staff actions has been spelled out in great detail. In summary, the staff recommends, the commander approves or disapproves and orders are issued. The rest of the action is command and staff supervision as the command embarks upon accomplishing the mission. The commander's mission is also the staff's mission. The staff is committed to doing everything within its power to make the mission successful, including helping the commander supervise. Some of those things are done as soon as the mission becomes known and before any orders are issued.

First, the subordinate commands are alerted to the upcoming requirement at the earliest possible moment by whatever means best suit the purpose—a telephone conversation, a message, a liaison officer, a letter. In any large headquarters literally hundreds of different actions are in progress simultaneously involving many different fields of interest. New missions or requirements are not necessarily major changes in direction but include common actions that are a part of everyday staff life. Activation of new armored divisions is rare, but levies for personnel are common and are major actions at the level where the losses occur. Even a small levy such as one for ten radar repairmen can be serious and, while the staff digests this requirement, the losing commands should be warned that it is coming. In most cases adequate advance notice makes for a smoother operation; in some, it could be the difference between success and failure. Advance notice could be called both the first step in staff supervision and the initial staff coordination effort. In this situation it is difficult to distinguish between the two.

Many new requirements and missions are initiated by the commander and his staff. It is the staff's job to insure that each requirement is completely identified and clearly defined regardless of its origin. The phrase *staff's job* could be misleading. Most requirements will be left to an action officer for the actual analysis and clarification. When his efforts have been processed, coordinated and cleared with his superiors, the results could be called a staff product. Most routine requirements are approved for implementation at division or office chief level. Only the nonroutine go through the command group.

In spite of the staff's best efforts to make requirements clear, questions about requirements sometimes arise in the field. As part of staff supervision it is up to the staff (action officer) to answer those questions. If further clarification or interpretation is needed, the staff should provide it. No means should be spared in getting the answers. If a requirement has come down from higher headquarters, the staff of that headquarters may have to assist. If the questions cannot be answered, then perhaps some new direction is needed.

Despite questions, subordinate commands initiate action to comply with new requirements to the best of their ability. In so doing, it is possible that some completely unforeseen circumstance may be uncovered. In the case of the levy for radar repairmen, eight of the twelve shown in official record as assigned to a unit could have been discharged under the Early-Out Program too recently for records to reflect the losses. The problem is now passed back to the staff (action officer). New sources must now be found.

In other instances, new missions highlight resource deficiencies, some of which must be corrected before the mission can be accomplished. An armored infantry battalion, for example, could hardly participate in a test of new tactics if it were short one-third of its armored personnel carriers. If it did participate, the validity of the test results would be questionable. In this situation the local commander would take whatever remedial actions were available to add carriers by expedited maintenance, emergency requisitions, etc. If carriers still were short, the problem would be passed back up the chain to the commander who assigned the mission.

Along the way, each intermediate headquarters staff would try to solve the problem with its own resources before passing it along. At each level several staff elements and many action officers may be involved. Operators deal with questions concerning priorities; comptrollers worry about money; logisticians, often with command support, attempt to shake the needed items out of the supply system. As the problem progresses from level to level, subordinate commanders should be kept informed of all significant developments. In practice, this situation would probably be handled by many telephone calls between action officers.

Once a mission has been set in motion, the staff monitors its progress. Staff supervision can take many forms, from daily conversations or periodic visits to monthly or bimonthly reports. The degree of contact should depend upon how critical the action is and the speed at which it should move. Too much goes on for all actions and missions to receive equal attention.

The staff must be continuously aware of the commander's interests and desires. It should concentrate its attention and effort on meeting his demands and carrying out his programs. Actions of command interest must receive top level attention. Staff supervision of lesser, routine actions may of necessity approach the management-by-exception concept, "If an action is proceeding smoothly, leave it alone." This does not mean that routine or lower priority actions may be ignored. Time may dictate, however, that they be checked only as much as necessary to be sure that they are on track.

How do junior staff officers check on the progress of actions in their areas of interest? Several channels are open. Certainly the telephone is the most used by action officers for close coordination with their counterparts and for receiving progress reports.

Although the telephone is the easiest means of contact, it cannot equal on-the-ground observation. Staff visits provide the opportunity for a firsthand look. By going to the scene, a staff officer can meet those he deals with and personally observe the status of the action. Nothing can substitute for personal contact.

On-the-spot observation facilitates understanding to an extent impossible to achieve in any other way. However, meaningful observation is a skill in itself, and one that each staff officer must master. It could be relatively easy when physical actions like river-crossing exercises or maintenance shop operations are involved. It becomes more difficult when the areas to be observed are less visible, such as procurement procedures or personnel records administration.

In these latter areas observation may consist primarily of discussions with the responsible people and a judicious sampling of the files. Although inexperienced junior staff officers seldom go alone on official staff visits, it can happen; and when it does, the visitor should be primed for the occasion. He should know precisely why he is going, what positions he can represent, and what to expect when he arrives.

It is sound practice to coordinate staff visits in advance. Most headquarters have firm procedures for handling visitors. These rules should be studied before the visit and then followed. When no guidance is available, a safe procedure is to work closely with one's counterparts in the visited headquarters.

For example, a visiting staff officer interested in maintenance of personnel records would be well advised to coordinate in advance and start his visit with administrators in the adjutant general's office to make them aware of the purpose of his visit. Upon his arrival the administration officers could be expected to pass him down, probably through a division chief, to the section and action officers he wished to visit. He should restate the purpose of his visit at each level of supervision and to the action officers with whom he is to work.

At the conclusion of his visit, unless told otherwise, he should check out in reverse order and pay courtesy calls to other supervisors as appropriate. The division chief might even ask him in to discuss his conclusions with the adjutant general or his assistant. If the results were startling, he could well conclude his visit at the local commander's office. If the findings are dull, he might go no higher than a branch chief.

When the visitor gets back to his own headquarters, he should report his findings. In most headquarters local procedures require some sort of formal trip report. Whether required or not, however, the results should be reported at least to the intermediate supervisor. Most important, the returning visitor must not consider the episode closed until he has completed all follow-up actions on matters brought to light by his visit.

The fledgling staff officer is more likely to find himself going on staff visits as a group member, part of a team. Staff visits have many purposes. The most common are gathering information and rendering assistance. Others are required by regulations. The area of interest of a staff visit may be limited or may cover several fields. The size and composition of visiting groups reflect this fact. Groups are usually headed by senior staff officers such as division chiefs or staff office chiefs.

Visits are arranged and fully coordinated in advance, including transportation, living accommodations and possible itineraries. When a group arrives at the organization to be visited, the team chief, selected team members, or even the entire team should report to the local command group unless other contacts have been prearranged. The purpose of the visit should be explained in detail; methods of conducting the visit should be proposed and required assistance should be made known.

If a visit is being made in response to a request for assistance, the opening scene will be somewhat different. The hosts explain their problem and offer such local assistance as is available. In either case, individual team members would probably be paired with their counterparts to work in their respective areas of interest. The team chief might collect his team from time to time to discuss progress and any problems which may develop.

One of the team's principal missions in such a situation is to help solve problems and provide guidance. When answers cannot be provided on the spot, team members should get in touch with their home office and start them on the trail of responsive information. In rendering guidance, team members interpret command policy as they understand it. If this understanding is inadequate, they must obtain additional guidance. Problems not solved during the visit become homework.

Like individual visitors, teams check out with their counterparts before leaving visited organizations. Before a team departs, the team chief usually calls on the commander or his representative to convey team findings, both good and bad. This exit report must be tactful but straightforward. Nothing destroys trust more quickly than a formal report loaded with unpleasant surprises that arrives after a visiting team has departed.

Inspections

Although inspections are generally more formal than staff visits, there are similarities in approach. Inspections are specifically designed to measure performance and uncover deficiencies. While some staff visits have similar goals, for the most part they are organized to assist or instruct. Inspections and staff visits give staffs the opportunity to observe how well actions and missions are carried out and to synchronize coordination.

Inspections and staff visits also turn up instances of less than satisfactory performance. When this happens, the staff must take action on the problem with the objective of improving performance. Two fundamental considerations pertain. First, the headquarters or unit involved can be pointed in the right direction, but it must correct its own deficiencies. Second, deficiencies should be corrected at the lowest possible level. Only those who are necessary to solve a problem should be brought into it.

The staff may also be confronted with instances of flagrant noncompliance with or disregard of orders. This is a more serious situation. The first question to be answered is *why*? If the dereliction is willful, this is a matter for immediate command attention. If the failure resulted from honest oversight, corrective action should be taken at the lowest possible level and should include provisions to preclude future failures.

The question no doubt will arise as to how much commanders should be told about deficiencies, failures and instances of noncompliance. No set rules could cover all situations. A few simple guidelines can be quoted that apply in most situations. They cannot replace good judgement and common sense. In general, commanders should be informed of all deficiencies or failures affecting or potentially affecting the mission, any willful acts of noncompliance by subordinate commanders (because this normally involves senior officers), serious wrongdoing or illegal acts within the command, and any other situations which could cause adverse publicity. The staff keeps the commander informed on all matters vital to his mission.

Meeting with Representatives from Subordinate Commands.
Although staff supervision through staff visits, inspections and other on-the-spot methods is preferred, when the staff cannot get out, it sometimes pays to bring in selected staff members from subordinate commands. If a multidivision maneuver were being planned by a field Army headquarters, standard procedure would be to call in staff representatives from the participating corps and divisions to discuss problems and participate in planning. The Army commander would direct the actual conference, but his staff would manage the project. Individual staff officers and groups of staff officers from subordinate commands are continually visiting headquarters for all sorts of purposes. These visits also provide excellent opportunities for meetings and conferences to exchange information, clarify positions and discuss other matters normal to staff supervision.

Liaison. Under some circumstances, commands may maintain one or more liaison officers at higher headquarters. The liaison officer is a convenient contact for members of the higher staff and second only to direct personal exchanges from staff to staff. Liaison officers are at least theoretically, commanders' representatives—not staff representatives. Their function is to assure closer contact, faster exchange of information, and responsive interaction between commanders—not between headquarters.

Because the liaison officer must work with the staff of the commander to whom he is attached as well as with his own commander's staff, he can also serve as an invaluable interface between staffs. Properly used, he can greatly assist in staff supervision. His home headquarters can relay questions, problems and requests for assistance. He can pass back suggestions for improvement, clarification of directives, delineation of priorities, and policy guidance to his own commander and his staff.

Every staff officer should become familiar with and make use of the services of all liaison officers in the headquarters. Seldom is this done. Too frequently liaison officers find themselves grossly underemployed, mostly ignored by both the commanders and staffs with whom they should work, and forgotten by their own headquarters. Sometimes this is entirely the fault of the individual liaison officer who prefers the peace and quiet of remaining uninvolved. More often the underuse is caused by lack of understanding by all involved—the liaison officer not understanding the importance of his role and his potential for contributing to the mission; the staffs at both headquarters being equally uninformed; and both commanders being too busy to teach the value of the liaison officer.

Wise liaison officers and experienced staff officers do not tolerate this sort of waste. Liaison officers represent their commanders. Their actions and productivity reflect on their commanders' professionalism and good officers recognize that coffee drinking, magazine reading and napping are poor representation. They recognize even more keenly that those activities, no matter how well performed, make poor reading on efficiency reports. Effective, professional staff officers use every tool available to reduce expenditures of effort and time and to increase productivity. They would never overlook the value of frequent contact with and assistance from subordinate commanders' direct representatives.

Supervision by Correspondence. Besides personal contacts, telephone exchanges and liaison officers, the written word is always available. It is used extensively for staff business and staff supervision. Much interpretation and guidance goes out in letters and messages, and much performance data comes back in reports. The staff's job is to see that reported data covering critical operations are promptly analyzed and evaluated. Good performance should be recognized; bad performance should be investigated and immediate corrective actions initiated.

Reacting to Supervision. Supervision is a two-way street. While a staff is supervising operations, it is being supervised by the staffs of higher commanders. It must react to supervision from above as it expects staffs of subordinate commands to react to its supervision. The mission of its commander is also the higher commander's mission. Their common goal calls for united effort and harmonious relations at all levels. Staff supervision is more subtle than command supervision, but it is an essential extension of the commander's capability. Its success contributes heavily to his success.

Coordination

General

One of the staff officer's typical activities is coordination. Unlike the other activities discussed, coordination is not a separate but an integral part of *all* staff actions. Coordination is so important to good staff work and, when properly done, consumes such large amounts of staff time that it must be included in any discussion of typical staff actions.

Despite its importance, coordination is one of the most difficult aspects of staff work for new staff officers to appreciate and apply. In fact, many not-so-new staff officers find it difficult. The need for coordination springs from the singular nature of the staff and its community of purpose—to advise and assist the commander. All advice and recommendations presented to a commander should be presented as a unified position from the staff—not from individual staff officers or offices. Actions taken by a staff in its commander's name must also represent a unified position. The effort to maintain such unity makes all staff actions (with possible minor and isolated exceptions) of interest to more than one staff office and therefore in need of coordination. Exceptions are so rare that it is safe to say that if an action does not need coordination, it probably does not need doing.

Intrastaff Coordination

For a new staff officer the most difficult part of coordination is knowing with whom to coordinate. Not uncommonly, fledgling staff officers become so wrapped up in their projects that they completely overlook any outside interest. Engrossed to mental capacity, they fail to realize that matters which seem entirely within their areas could be of interest to anyone but their bosses. This attitude is to be expected of someone with limited experience, but several approaches can help to overcome it.

The first is knowing and understanding the local organization and functions manual from cover to cover. It spells out staff responsibilities in detail down through branch level. With that knowledge an action officer can almost certainly identify some interests common to other staff elements in any project.

The organizational half of the organization and functions manual also can be a most helpful guide to those with whom actions should be coordinated. Action officers should study their headquarters organization until they are familiar with every last block. When they have finished that, they should try to become familiar with those who occupy the positions and to understand the personalities of at least the key staff officers and those who are potential personal contacts. It is just good business for a staff member to know the other players on his team.

Another indispensable tool is knowledge of the organization and missions of subordinate commands. If an action officer is aware of the effects of an action on subordinate units, he also knows which other staff activities may be affected. If an action officer in supply contemplates proposing a ration on certain types of ammunition, it should not take much reflection to lead him to the operations and training people.

Coordination is not only important between staff elements. Action officers should also look well within their own offices. In large staff offices, even though functions are normally decentralized, most actions are of interest in several areas and should be coordinated there before going outside to other elements.

The discussion to this point has centered on identifying the subject matter to be coordinated and the persons with whom to coordinate. What follows will be concerned primarily with coordination methods: the procedures for getting official concurrences from other staff elements or staff officers. This involves both formal and informal coordination: direct conversations, telephone discussions, meetings, conferences, briefings, and written memos and notes.

Formal Coordination

The most vexing question for the novice faced with formal coordination requirements is the level of participation required. After determining which divisions and offices have interests in the subject matter, he still must determine at what level to initiate coordination. Most headquarters issue some specific rules for coordination as part of their policy guidance or standing operating procedures.

For example, most commanders, deputy commanders and chiefs of staff insist that actions coming to their attention be coordinated among staff element chiefs. Element chiefs usually supplement headquarters guidance with further instructions to their suboffice chiefs, who add their own guidance before passing the instructions along. At the action level this process leads to fairly complete, detailed direction.

In the absence of local guidance, common sense should strongly indicate appropriate coordination levels. As a rule, coordination should be at the level at which the action is to be approved and released. Not all actions require the attention of staff element chiefs. Only those actions which go to the commander or his close representative or those which might be of interest to the command group need office chief clearance. Other actions can be released by the division chief in whose area of interest they fall. It is up to the releasing division chief to keep his boss informed on critical matters.

In most headquarters, release authority for certain types of routine actions is delegated to branch chiefs, section chiefs and even selected action officers. In such headquarters it is possible that actions could be approved at many levels: the commander, his close representatives, staff element chiefs, division chiefs, branch chiefs, section chiefs and action officers. Unless local guidance indicates otherwise, formal coordination levels should be compatible. Actions to be released by the command group and by chiefs of major staff elements should be brought to the attention of staff element chiefs and should be coordinated at that level. Actions to be released by subelement chiefs or action officers should receive the blessing of equivalent level personnel in other staff elements. Similar rules could be applied for coordination within an office.

Coordination Protocol. For some unknown reason the term *chop* has been applied to the initialing of a paper to signify agreement, coordination or concurrence. The precedence for chopping is a sensitive matter. An action officer's immediate boss may or may not want to see an action before it is coordinated internally with other action officers. He probably will insist, however, on seeing all actions before they are coordinated formally with his equals or move upward for approval.

Except for actions to be approved at the command group level, custom demands that the releasing authority approve the action before asking his counterparts to concur. That is, if the paper is to be coordinated with other staff office chiefs, it should first be approved by the home office chief. Violations of this custom only waste time. Many office chiefs refuse to consider coordination action without such approval. An action officer seeking the coordination of a division chief in a neighboring staff office should first get his own division chief's approval.

Where to Start. When coordination in several outside offices is needed, it is best to start with the toughest one, the one least likely to agree totally. This technique involves much more than just getting the bad medicine down in a hurry. Coordination consists of give and take. Its purpose implies exchange of views and compromise solutions. It is wise, therefore, to coordinate first with those who may demand some give. If the action must be modified, the changes should be made early in the coordination process to prevent repeat efforts.

Informal Coordination

The procedures just cited refer to formal coordination. The dissenting staff office will be particularly tough if it has not previously heard of the case. Through informal coordination (telephone calls, memos, visits, etc.) action officers should have been working in advance with their counterparts to smooth the way in the dissenting office. Such informal coordination uncovers divergent views and permits adjustments while the action is being developed, before it becomes a crisis. If a common position could not be found, both office chiefs should have known about it in advance.

There is no substitute for informal coordination. It is essential to smooth staff work. When an action officer takes his paper to an outside staff office for coordination, he should always work through his counterparts, who have been working with him. They should be in a position to help him sell his paper or even to sell it for him, whether to the division chief or to the office chief.

This leads to another crucial point. If possible, action officers should hand carry actions for coordination. As indicated, they may have to sell or defend their proposals. Nothing beats face-to-face, eye-to-eye contact. An exception to this rule might be an instance in which the advance work has been done so well that counterparts guaranteed coordination without the action officer's personal appearance.

Timing. Action officers would do well to understand early just how long it takes to coordinate an action. Each case will be different, but patterns exist. Even when an officer hand carries an action, he can spend considerable time cooling his heels in some chief's outer office. He may in some cases have to make a second or even a third trip back to make the right contacts. Experience should teach him to make allowances for these delays when planning deadlines. In emergencies, when time is critical and the action is noncontroversial, coordination may be obtained by telephone. This technique is more likely to succeed when used by division chiefs or office chiefs seeking the nod from their counterparts. When agreement has been reached, the caller should so note on the action paper. Junior action officers should resort to this approach only in dire emergencies and should be certain that no other course is available before tying up an outside division chief or office chief with this type of coordination.

Coordination by Conference. Another time-saving technique that can be used when circumstances permit is a conference or a briefing on the matter to be coordinated. If the position is accepted and if the participants are authorized to chop for their respective offices, much time can be saved. Here again, a junior action officer will probably need help. The conference may be his idea, and he will probably present the material and control the meeting, but he will still need the support and sponsorship of bosses at least to division level. In some extreme and infrequent circumstances there is no time for coordination. Then the officer approving the action and the action officer must, at the earliest possible moment, bring the matter to the attention of all supervisors and action officers who would normally have been involved in coordination.

Coordinating Others' Actions

Many papers come into each office for coordination. This is the other side of the coin. Action officers bring their papers seeking chops. Whether or not there has been the usual prior informal coordination, action officers should place the highest priority on helping their counterparts by taking them up the office chain as far as necessary to get concurrence. Sometimes section, branch or division chiefs may prefer to take the action officer on to the higher levels, but the action officer should always be prepared to go all the way if necessary.

Nonconcurrences

As mentioned earlier, 100% agreement is not always possible between staff offices coordinating positions. One or several offices may nonconcur. This is to some extent a staff failure in that the staff's job is to arrive at single, unified, coordinated positions. When it cannot do that, the commander is still faced with the problem, but without the benefit of a staff recommendation.

Even in its moment of failure, the staff must help as much as possible by analyzing or considering the nonconcurrence. When an action officer and his supervisors believe strongly that an action is necessary and another staff element chief feels just as strongly that the proposed action should not be taken or should be taken differently, the difference must be passed to the commander in logical format.

Usually, the nonconcurrence is attached to the action, presenting orderly, logical rationale for the disagreement. The initiator of the action then prepares and attaches a *consideration of the nonconcurrence*. This must be complete and objective, covering each point raised in the nonconcurrence. If the staff cannot do its job, at least it should give the commander sufficient information so that he can act as his own staff.

In practice these disagreements seldom go beyond the chief of staff before they are settled. In fact, on effective staffs they seldom go to the chief of staff. Good staff officers dislike failures and spare no effort to arrive at mutually acceptable positions. Those who seem constantly to be opposed to others' ideas, argumentative and against every proposal, have little chance of success in staff positions.

External Coordination

Higher headquarters and outside agencies must be approached with some caution, with complete understanding of the chain of command and command policies. If overdone, external coordination can, in effect, transfer a commander's decision-making responsibilities to others: his boss, his subordinates or his equals. If underdone, decisions can be embarrassingly unworkable because of unknown situations in higher, subordinate or outside activities. Experienced staff officers become quite expert at walking the thin line between too much and too little.

Staffs must work in close harmony with other staffs to assure a continuous flow of essential information. Each staff member must know and talk with his counterparts in higher, subordinate and adjacent headquarters. This unofficial, informal communication serves several purposes. It broadens the perspectives of all involved, allowing staff work to encompass a much broader spectrum of facts and assumptions so that recommendations can be based on a better view of the overall situation. It prevents the surprise of unanticipated missions and tasks, unexpected disapprovals and unexpected criticism and adverse comments. Constant interstaff contact builds mutual respect and confidence at all levels, smoothing the operation of the massive military machine. The problem for new staff officers is to understand the nature of interstaff cooperation and to grasp the ethical limits to which it may be carried.

The best guide is the loyalty of each staff to its commander and the common loyalty of all military men to their common cause—national defense. Coordination must never be confused with trickery or shrewd manipulation of opinion in order to circumvent a commander's decision or to shortcut the chain of command. Its purpose is only to help commanders perform their missions by providing better advice and assistance based on more complete knowledge and understanding.

Coordination with staff counterparts at higher headquarters must be handled with particular care. Few commanders want their problems relayed back to their bosses (or their bosses' staffs) for resolution. Staff officers must ensure that their informal coordination with counterparts at higher headquarters never, directly or by inference, places those counterparts in the position of having to solve problems belonging to the lower level. This could handcuff the local commander by creating a prepositioned decision at the higher command level.

For example, in a major command faced with a severe funding shortage many courses of action would probably be available to alleviate the adverse effects of the shortage. Maintenance could be deferred; civilian work forces could be reduced; travel, curtailed; facilities, closed; and many other similar economy measures, considered. If, however, the commander's staff places the problem (or any part of it) with their higher level counterparts for resolution, the commander's flexibility in choosing his best course of action is seriously compromised.

When his proposed action reaches the higher commander, it is certain to be referred to the staff for consideration and comment. If the staff has decided in advance on a course of action other than the one proposed, there is certain to be some natural reluctance to change positions. On the other hand, failure to coordinate at all could lead to equal disadvantages. Staff officers at all levels like to be informed on all matters in their areas of interest. Some discussion of the problem with members of the senior staff and a warning that proposed corrective actions are on the way probably would greatly enhance interstaff relationships.

Properly warned, the senior commander's staff could do its homework and be prepared for the action when it arrived. Another advantage of advance coordination on the funding problem would be learning from one step up just how universal the funding shortage might be, possible availability of additional funds, and any contemplated actions that could affect the shortage.

With lower staff counterparts the sensitivity of coordination is less marked but still must remain within the bounds of certain proprieties. The primary guidelines are in command relationships. In the military, commanders normally do not ask their subordinates whether they would like to assume additional missions, lose some of their reponsibilities, correct deficiencies, improve performance or decrease expenditures. Unless directed otherwise in exceptional cases, staffs should take the same approach. Lower level staffs should not be invited to concur or nonconcur with proposed actions.

This does not preclude some very valuable interstaff coordination. While commanders do not ask their subordinates' concurrence before passing along orders, they do insist on knowing the exact impact those orders may have on the receiving commanders, their missions and their resources. In large commands the full extent of those effects are often known only at the lower levels where the actions must be taken. Coordination can bring those effects to light. Informal telephone calls or visits are often sufficient. Major, complex actions may require more formal coordination, especially when wide-ranging, long-term plans of action are under consideration.

The authors participated in the development of an area support plan which covered off-post support to the Army Reserves and ROTC as well as miscellaneous activities in fourteen midwestern states. The support was to be provided by thirteen Army installations in the area, each with diverse missions and capabilities. The task was highly complex. Most of one continental Army commander's staff was involved in the planning. Months were needed to hammer out a solution.

Because of the far-reaching and possible unknown effects the plan might have on the installations and the supported activities, it was circulated to the installations and to the supported activities for comment prior to implementation. As a result, numerous points were uncovered that the staff could not have foreseen. In this case, input from the field went a long way toward improving the quality and workability of the plan. Unique requirements for coordination called for special treatment. However, even in this major undertaking, only comments and impact statements were solicited—not concurrence or nonconcurrence.

Coordination with lateral command and with agencies not in the same chain of command is usually a matter of exchanging information and providing opportunities for comment if the proposed actions might have unknown impacts in the areas of interest of other commands. This facet of coordination generally requires only common sense and a sound understanding of the missions and functions of other military activities.

One type of action requires complete formal coordination. Any proposal that would affect either the missions or the resources of outside agencies should be coordinated with those agencies for concurrence. Nonconcurrences should be treated much the same as intrastaff nonconcurrences. If possible, they should be resolved.

Very often separate chains of Army command meet only at Headquarters, Department of the Army. If the nonconcurring agency is from another service, the meeting place would be at Headquarters, Department of Defense. If the nonconcurrence arises in another branch of government, the difference might have to be resolved at cabinet level. The disadvantages of recourse to those levels should be apparent.

The procedures for effective coordination may seem relatively simple, but effectively carrying them out demands great skill. Beginners would do well to observe closely some experienced hands as they go through the coordinating exercises and to discuss with bosses and experienced coworkers the coordination procedures and problems that arise during the first several actions. Most officers will be eager to advise and assist, and their help will be invaluable. No amount of advice and assistance, or salesmanship can substitute for a good product. Good actions are easy to coordinate, and it only takes a few successes to build self-confidence.

8.

Command Policy

Like most civilian institutions, the Army operates within a framework of formal, written rules and policies supplemented by less formal but equally binding ground rules reflecting the policies of individual commanders and supervisors. The formal parts of this framework are published as regulations, bulletins, circulars, manuals, pamphlets and correspondence from commanders to their subordinates. Less formal local rules take many formats. Commanders may issue their policies in writing as memoranda to their staffs or orally as addresses and presentations. Some commanders may choose not to publish their policies. In the latter instance, the staff must glean the commander's policies and preferred methods of operation from the reactions to their various efforts, from casual remarks and from approvals and disapprovals of proposed staff actions. A truly effective staff works in rapport with the commander, reacting to each project and to each new task in much the same manner as he would. This happens only if each member of the staff is thoroughly familiar with the commander's policies.

Command policy is a vital force in military operations. Without it each headquarters would be a carbon copy of all other headquarters at the same level. Worse, all military operations would proceed mechanically. All problems would be solved identically throughout the Army, and all decisions would be the same regardless of who the commander might be. The commanders' personalities, characteristics and idiosyncracies in the decision-making and supervisory processes make the difference between mediocre and outstanding organizations—often, between successful and unsuccessful military operations.

Command policy reflects important personal traits, and commanders should not have to battle to have their preferences followed. Every staff officer should try to approach each problem from the vantage point of his commander, viewing it through his commander's eyes and applying the commander's thought processes and policies to the solution. To do this successfully, staff officers must study their commander and analyze his policies.

Commanders differ. Some run tight organizations. Others give wide latitude to their subordinates. Some commanders emphasize administrative perfection, while others concentrate on operational matters.

Despite individual differences, the fundamental relationship between the commander and his staff has been fixed. It cannot be altered. The commander alone is responsible for mission success or failure. The staff is but an extension of the commander's capabilities. The staff must, therefore, mirror the commander's approach to military affairs. Only in this way can the staff properly protect the commander's interests in conducting official business.

To insure conformance with their personal methods, most commanders establish policies as frameworks for performing internal staff functions and as general procedures which clarify the staff's relationship with its commander. Since the commander's position and the commander-staff relationship are unchanging, this internal operational policy is more or less standard. Although the details vary with the commander's style, a common core can be identified.

Keeping the Commander Informed

The higher the command and the larger the headquarters, the less the commander can be directly involved in and personally informed on all detailed operations. Spans of control have practical limits. Yet every commander must be informed on certain important matters needing command attention. Only commanders can decide the appropriate course of action on many key actions, particularly those bearing directly on mission accomplishment.

Often it is difficult for staff officers to judge what papers the commander should see and what information he should have, what he should hear and what decisions should be left to his personal discretion. For this reason most commanders, even those who publish no other policies, issue written, clear-cut policies concerning information of command interest, listing certain types of actions to be brought to the commander's attention. These insure that the commander receives the right information in time. When a commander has published no such policies, the staff must use its own judgement until experience reveals the commander's preferences. During that learning phase no hard-and-fast rules apply; however, the following generalizations are sound guides.

Report the Bad as well as the Good. No one challenges the idea that commanders need information. But there is a natural tendency to report only good news, omitting or suppressing the bad. It is much more pleasant to make a commander happy with favorable reports than to risk spoiling his disposition by pointing out operational failures or passing along unfavorable reports concerning shortcomings within his command or staff. Experienced staff officers know, and beginners soon learn, that the bearers of ill tidings are seldom welcomed with open arms.

The ancient custom of putting to the sword messengers bringing bad reports has not been entirely eliminated—only modified. Experienced staff officers, therefore, attempt to leaven bad news with at least a modicum of progress toward improving adverse situations. No matter how unpleasant, the bad must be reported along with the good. Commanders can only solve problems if they know about them, and know about them quickly.

Suppose, for example, that an infantry brigade staff hesitated to inform the brigade commander that one of his battalions seemed likely to fail to take its objective. The results could be disastrous. If informed, he could adjust his plans, request additional support, realign priorities and take other remedial action. If unaware of the situation, the brigade commander and the battle could be lost.

Little imagination is needed to apply the old "for want of a nail" idea to this example and visualize far-reaching and disastrous effects at division, corps, army, theater and even national level. Even less imagination is needed to visualize the disastrous effects on the staff officers who failed to keep their commander informed. Not all information is so decisive, but one of the staff's most important and most difficult functions is recognizing and passing along items of interest to the commander.

Commanders should not be surprised or embarrassed. Information that could keep a commander from being surprised or embarrassed might not win battles. To staff officers, however, it is almost that critical. Failure to pass on such information usually comes home to roost. Most leaders in any field do not like to be caught short. Military commanders are particularly sensitive to such failures by staffs whose job it is to keep them informed.

The commander should be informed of official adverse comments. He should be informed of criticism leveled by any meaningful source against any element of his command, including staffs and subordinate activities. Criticism in this category reflects directly against the commander's effectiveness and professional qualifications. It is particularly acute when it comes from higher commanders or their staffs. The message, literally translated, is that somewhere along the line the commander is not doing his job. He must be aware of this type of charge immediately so that he can investigate and take corrective actions or correct his critics misapprehensions if necessary.

General guidance could be helpful but cannot replace formal, written guidance issued by the commander. The following directive setting forth policies regarding items for command attention is a good example, and was actually published by a general officer whose responsibilities include a large geographical area, one Army corps, several divisions and more than ten major installations.

Matters to be Brought to the Attention
of the Commanding General

"The following will be brought to the attention of the Commanding General, through the Chief of Staff, WITHOUT DELAY.
1. Subjects of importance requiring prompt attention which are not covered by existing policies and instruction.
2. Correspondence signed by the Commander, Deputy Commander or Chief of Staff of a higher headquarters; The Adjutant General, Department of the Army; General Officers of subordinate commands; and General Officers of other organizations.
3. Proposed visits by personnel from higher headquarters.
4. Errors, deficiencies or irregularities alleged by higher authority, other than routine personnel actions.
5. Requests and recommendations to be made to higher headquarters that directly affect the mission of this command.
6. Disapprovals from higher headquarters that directly affect the mission of this command.
7. Communications from higher headquarters that establish new missions or responsibilities.
8. Communications that allege neglect or dereliction on the part of commissioned personnel.
9. Appeals of subordinate commands, or attached units of decisions made at this headquarters.
10. Disapproval of any requests from subordinate commanders.
11. All matters pertaining to complaints, criticism, or derogatory information critical of the operation of this command or its subordinate commands.
12. Serious accidents or incidents involving personnel of this command.
13. Reports of financial and property irregularities.
14. Correspondence with civil authorities in high positions.
15. Correspondence concerning emergency plans.
16. Communications of exceptional information.

All of the above matters are mandatory; however, after staff analysis, many other matters will be of immediate command interest and will be referred to the commander through Chief of Staff as determined by the staff office chief.

A copy of these instructions will be kept in a conspicuous position upon the desk of each staff officer of this headquarters."

It is important to note that this directive not only informs the staff of the type of actions of personal interest to the commander, but also establishes the commander's method of using his chief of staff by directing that the listed matters be brought to his attention "through the Chief of Staff." The directive also brings to light another important point. Even with the most explicit instructions, matters will arise that have not been covered but which are of urgent command interest and must be recognized.

To beginners this may well be the most difficult facet of staff work, especially on large staffs. At battalion level, actions and reactions are fairly visible and commanders' needs and desires well known. At the level of the Department of the Army and other large intermediate headquarters new staff officers are conversant only with their immediate areas of concern and have direct contact with one, two or possibly three levels of supervisors. Commanders are far removed from them, insulated by several more unseen layers of supervision.

The fledglings' best defense is solid understanding of the commanders' missions. With this they can test information against the policies of mission accomplishment, surprise or embarrassment, and criticism. Judgement should improve with experience. When in doubt, inform.

In large headquarters, information started in the commander's direction by action officers is screened several times as it moves up the chain. Beginners should not hesitate, therefore, through reluctance to overinform. Information unworthy of the commander's attention will never reach him, significant information started on its way by even the most junior staff officer will reach the commander.

The problem is in knowing what to start on the way. To assist action officers in making these decisions many experienced supervisors supplement the commander's guidance with their own instructions concerning matters which they wish to see or to take personal action on. The following is an extract from such instructions issued by the logistician on the staff of the general who published the directive quoted previously.

"Correspondence addressed to or concerning the following will be routed through the Deputy Chief of Staff, Logistics for final release:
1. Higher headquarters.
2. Commanders not under the jurisdiction of this headquarters.
3. Congressmen and similar civilian officials.
4. The command group.
5. The Chief (by name) of any coordinating or special staff office.
6. Any general officer.
7. Disapproval of requests from subordinate commanders.
8. General Accounting Office, Army Audit Agency, Annual General Inspections and similar reports.
9. Unsatisfactory inspection reports.
10. Matters that pertain to, or will result in, substantial expenditures of funds ($5,000 or more).
11. Any communication involving commendation, censure, pecuniary liability of any officer or key civilian employee.
12. Any policy or precedent directive.
13. Directives submitted to the Adjutant General for publication."

To this point our discussion has concerned information flowing from the staff to the commander. Commanders also have policies concerning the flow of their guidance to their staffs.

With rare exception, the commander is the most experienced and most senior person in the headquarters. In all instances, he is responsible for all headquarters' actions, and he is in command. Most commanders take both their official responsibilities and their obligation to pass along the benefit of their experience quite seriously. In fact, most items that interest the commander do so because they are the types of actions on which the commander desires to guide the staff's approach.

In the previous illustration the commander specified that any communication establishing new missions or responsibilities be brought to his attention. This was not idle curiosity. Commanders want to know about new assignments so that they can personally influence actions to carry out the new jobs, issuing guidance to their staffs and, as early as is appropriate, to subordinate commanders. Unfortunately, commanders, like other people, express themselves with varying degrees of clarity. The initial guidance may or may not be clear to all staff members, whose abilities to comprehend also vary.

It is incumbent on the staff as a whole and as individuals to be certain that the guidance is understood and is sufficient before embarking on the actions. The commander's policy for passing guidance to the staff must be observed. If a commander has directed that all matters be brought to his attention through his chief of staff, then questions and requests for additional guidance should follow the same channel—through the chief of staff. If you don't understand, ask questions.

To the inexperienced staff officer this advice may seem to violate the longstanding rule that one does not ask the commander for solutions, that solutions are worked out by the staff and presented to the commander for approval. Far from it. However, only those staff members who understand the commander's guidance will reap the benefits. Those who do not understand are likely to reap a far different harvest.

Command guidance should be sought only when needed. It is usually needed only for problems and action requiring ultimate command decisions. Routine action made known to the staff through reports, inspections, personal contacts and various other sources can normally be handled by the staff without bothering the commander unless it falls into the no surprises category. When command guidance is needed, it is needed quickly, needs to be understood and needs to be followed.

Although the commander likes to have first crack at tough problems that could affect his mission, guidance seldom includes detailed solutions; it only indicates general approaches and the broad directions in which to proceed. It is up to the staff to develop plans and work out details. This sequence makes the commander aware of problems and saves valuable time and effort by preventing false starts.

The importance of bringing bad news to the commander's attention cannot be overstressed. Sometimes (hopefully seldom) a commander's guidance is unworkable. As the staff plans and prepares it sometimes becomes apparent that the commander's approach is faulty or that another method of operation would offer a higher probability of success. This falls under the heading of bad news. Depending on a commander's character and disposition, casting doubts on his judgement could even be classified as catastrophic news, but integrity demands that staff officers give their very best professional advice.

Staff work is not a popularity contest, and any member who attempts to tailor his judgement to suit those around him is dead weight, contributing nothing. Loyalty, also, demands that the staff attempt to protect the commander from mistakes, even if the potential mistakes relate to faulty command judgement. The commander must be advised when other lines of action seem better than those indicated by command guidance. Obviously, integrity and loyalty do not preclude the judicious use of diplomacy.

Decision Policies

Guidance is one of a commander's prerogatives. Decision-making is another. It follows logically that if the commander alone is to be responsible for the results, he alone must make the decisions. There are practical limits, however. Large staffs would be paralyzed if commanders had to make each single decision regardless of how minor or routine. Many decisions are actually made and directives issued by staff officers without specific command approval. These staff actions are based on guidance laid down by the commander and are taken in the commander's name.

When available guidance does not fit, or when no guidance has been issued, a decision must be sought. This is the prime purpose for publishing policies regarding actions to be brought to the commander's attention. Commanders cannot possibly anticipate every action that could arise. Each day in a large headquarters brings its own surprises. New problems arise. Yesterday's minor action turns into today's panic. Yesterday's panic recedes into the routine. The commander's officially published policy is only a starting point. Establishing policy is a continuing function of command. One Continental Army commander issued this continuing guidance by handwritten notes in the margins of incoming letters and messages: "All action on this through me"; "Chief, you handle"; "I will take action, etc."

Most commanders are liberal with guidance but retain decision-making authority in many critical and sensitive areas. Each commander has personal views regarding these critical areas, and most publish extremely clear guidance, but sometimes action officers still have trouble identifying items that should be decided by their commander. Although there are no hard and fast rules, there are a few areas that almost all commanders reserve for their personal decisions. No attempt has been made to organize these discussions into priorities, if indeed any precedence could be established. Each is important in its own way and at its own time.

Changes in Missions

Most commanders want the final word on any major changes in direction, policy, procedure or method of operation that could have an impact on their command responsibilities. Commanders take their responsibilities very seriously. They are keenly aware of their official and moral obligations to accomplish each mission and every task as thoroughly and as economically as possible. This is their primary and overriding concern.

Keeping up with those responsibilities is no easy matter. Senior commanders have extremely diverse and complex missions that include literally thousands of individual tasks in constant states of flux. New responsibilities are added. Old ones are cancelled. Priorities are rearranged. If a commander is to do his job, he must know what that job is. Not what it was yesterday or last week, what it is this day, hour and minute. An action officer developing any staff action that would even slightly alter, modify or realign those responsibilities would seldom be wrong to refer the proposed actions to the commander for a final decision.

Negative Replies

Another policy shared by most commanders is that only commanders make negative replies to anyone, including all requests made of the command, regardless of their source. Some commanders modify this to requests from specific sources.

A commander might permit his staff to refuse certain types of requests except those submitted personally by a subordinate commander. Few commanders authorize their staffs to reply negatively to requests or directives from higher headquarters. It would be rare indeed for a commander to permit unrestricted negative replies. Staff officers should be well versed on local policy; if no policy has been issued, they should be cautious with negative actions.

The line of authority between commanders is direct—commander-to-commander. A subordinate commander may, as a matter of courtesy, place his requests through his superior's staff. Often, these requests may come to a very junior staff officer for action. The subordinate commander is *not* asking for approval or disapproval (particularly disapproval) from a junior staff officer.

This applies even more firmly to requests or directives from higher commands. Although a request for supply data could reach a very junior logistical staff officer, the superior commander would be less than happy if that officer decided that the requested data could not be provided. The local commander would be even less happy; the senior logistician, very unhappy; and, eventually, the ill-advised junior member would be miserable indeed. It cannot be overemphasized that the correctness and logic of the negative reply is completely immaterial. The junior logistician's commander might well agree that the request for supply data was unreasonable or even impossible to meet, but few commanders would authorize their staffs to refuse to comply with directives from superior commanders.

As a special case under the negative reply policy, most commanders also make the necessary decisions to resolve conflicts between subordinate commanders or between principal staff members when these cannot be worked out by the chief of staff or, at lower level commands, the executive officer.

Changes in Resources

Closely allied to commanders' concern with their mission responsibilities are their interests in the human and physical assets entrusted to them. Most commanders are keenly aware of their moral and official obligations to care for and wisely use those assets. They are even more keenly aware of their dependency on those people and things to get the job done. For these reasons, programs for the use of resources are carefully set up, and few commanders will tolerate changes in such programs without their personal approval.

This emphasizes the importance of every staff officer's understanding at least the general concepts of management. In today's economy-oriented military establishment, few actions do not affect resources of some sort, whether people, money, physical assets, services or time. Resource management has become a major facet of the military profession. The staff officer who ignores this facet of his professional development is certain to be at a disadvantage.

Changes in Organization

Military organizations have been developed and standardized over periods of many years and through much study, trial and error, and experience. For the most part they are arranged for maximum efficiency and economy. This does not mean they cannot be improved, but commanders are aware that most possible arrangements have been tried at some time and, for valid reasons discarded. For this reason most commanders prefer to approve all proposed organizational changes, even minor ones.

Other decision areas may also be staked out as the exclusive preserve of the commander. These vary with individual desires and change with time and circumstances. The central point is that the commander alone will make the decisions in areas he considers critical to his success.

Creative Thinking. Although they seldom spell it out in writing, most commanders demand original thinking from their staffs. Command guidance may fix the general approach to be followed in solving a problem, but infinite numbers of contributing factors must be identified, evaluated and combined into the best solution. Even the most thorough analysis of these factors could lead to a choice of several solutions.

The payoff is for those who choose the best solution. This calls for the best thinking available throughout the staff. New ideas should always be, and usually are, welcomed and considered, whether they come from a fledgling or an old-timer. Rank has no monopoly on creative thought. In fact, the less experienced officer may have some advantage in the area of original thinking.

Too often the old-timer's thinking is somewhat inhibited by overfamiliarity, leading to what might be called the We've-always-done-it-this-way syndrome. To the younger officers each action is a new challenge and can be attacked from many vantage points. This freshness of thought by younger staff officers can contribute greatly to staff effectiveness.

If ideas came only from senior staff officers, a headquarters would be dead from the neck down. New staff officers should accept the challenge and contribute their most imaginative thinking. Lack of experience can be offset by originality. A policy of encouraging and accepting original thinking is fundamental to a forward-looking, dynamic headquarters.

Interheadquarters Relations

Many policies firmly entrenched and widely practiced relate to the relationships of commanders and their staffs with other headquarters. The policy on negative replies mentioned earlier falls in this category, as do policies relating to command decisions. As might be expected, most of these policies cover relationships with higher and subordinate headquarters. Relationships with other headquarters usually can be managed within the general policy framework without need for special provisions.

The positions of commanders in relation to the headquarters of their immediate supervisors are usually similar in several respects and easily understood. All want to be responsive but self-sufficient. They want to accept willingly and accomplish all missions to the best of their abilities, turning in consistently superior performances. These common objectives are natural and must become staff objectives. Detailed policy on methods of working with higher headquarters to achieve these goals varies, and each staff must determine its commander's desires.

Some commanders encourage close, personal but informal, liaison and coordination between members of their staffs and counterparts in higher headquarters. Others prefer more formal and official relationships between their staffs and the staffs of their commanders and discourage excessive informal contacts. Some practices are basic, proven procedures and can be assumed to be the policy of virtually all commanders. First among these is a universal reluctance to yell for help.

Although help should be sought if it is necessary, military commanders realize that missions and tasks assigned to them are assigned to be accomplished. Running back to the boss with problems and troubles is hardly responsive. Ideally, when a mission is assigned to a subordinate commander, it can be forgotten and assumed to be accomplished. In the Turkish Army, subordinates acknowledge orders with a phrase which means "It is now on my head."—or in the modern American vernacular, "Consider it done."

Problems do arise which require assistance from higher headquarters. Situations change. New considerations arise. Resources dwindle. Unexpected outside factors arise. No commander would hesitate to ask his superior for help when these or other reasons dictate. Most commanders insist that one basic condition be met before asking for help: all available means must first be exhausted and every attempt made to solve the problem locally before higher headquarters are asked to assist. This applies to every member of the staff.

Junior staff officers often come up against seemingly blank walls in their efforts to complete a complex action and are tempted to seek help from obvious sources: counterparts in higher headquarters. Similar thoughts also cross the minds of more senior staff officers in tight situations, and they have even more influential counterparts. Commanders, however, prefer to be as independent and responsive as possible. Going back to the higher headquarters that assigned the task creating the problem is not being responsive.

In requesting authority from higher headquarters to pursue a particular course of action, most commanders prefer to decide on the best course of action and inform higher headquarters of their decision. If the senior commander objects, he can so advise. Many commanders feel that requesting permission indicates overdependence and to some extent passes the buck back to their bosses.

Chain of Command

Most commanders are sensitive about lines of authority—and for good reasons. These lines are fundamental to the exercise of military authority, even though occasions arise when staff members are tempted to circumvent the next higher commander and his staff. Sometimes a commander and his staff become aware that the headquarters two links up the chain shares a local view. By going directly to that headquarters and receiving a favorable hearing, they could tie the hands of the commander one step up and force him to go along. This is what the policy is all about. Intermediate headquarters will not be bypassed. To do so violates the chain of command—not to mention causing consternation, friction and ill will.

Commanders will not tolerate this tactic either by their own staff or by subordinate commanders. Commanders insist that the next higher headquarters be informed of significant developments on important actions. This is common policy for all successful commanders. Division commanders must know what their brigades are doing; brigade commanders must know what the battalions are doing, etc. Of course, information going to the higher commanders and their staffs must be screened to insure that it meets the requirements of command-wide interest or mission significance.

Suspense Dates. Another area of relationship with higher headquarters to which most commanders are extremely sensitive is responding within the specified time limits. When assigning missions and tasks or even requesting information or establishing reports, commanders usually set time-frames or "no-later-than" dates for the actions to be completed. In the military, doing the job within the assigned time-frame is an indispensable part of mission accomplishment. Commanders are extremely reluctant to miss suspenses and consider tardiness a degree of failure. Most commanders also consider requesting extensions to suspenses a form of asking for help and apply the same rules as for other requests for assistance. First, make every effort to solve the problem and meet the time requirements.

Frequently, commanders several levels up the chain generate requirements based upon inaccurate, inadequate or outdated information. A commander might be directed to transfer to another organization a specified number of medical technicians to serve on an emergency team on temporary duty in an overseas area. Loss of that number, even on temporary duty, could cripple essential medical services in the command or in extreme cases even exceed the total number assigned. Here is a clear-cut case in which higher headquarters must be informed of the facts in the matter.

The requirement cannot be rejected if it can be met, but its full impact must be clearly stated. Even in such extreme cases, commanders dislike failing to comply with directives or seeming to argue with their superiors by presenting adverse impact statements. The policy of most commanders in such situations will be the same as toward requests for help. Along with the statement of adverse impacts, they will insist that a complete analysis be made of all possible actions to be taken to offset those impacts.

In the example given, after explaining the shortage of medical personnel remaining to support the command, it might be appropriate to outline the measures that would be taken to maximize the effectiveness of those remaining, such as centralized treatment facilities. The scarcity of funds and equipment today is probably the most frequent causes of situations in which directives from above can only be followed at some sacrifice to other essential facets of the mission.

Commanders are likely to be most impatient with impact statements that only list the many adverse effects without outlining the management steps to be taken to make maximum use of the resources available. When directives cannot be followed, or can only be followed at serious cost to the mission, the next higher headquarters must be informed. The information must be given with the assumption that the directive was not issued in complete ignorance, and that some adverse effects were anticipated. Command policy will invariably call for a statement of those impacts along with a positive plan for continuing to function and continuing to accomplish the assigned missions.

Support to Subordinate Activities

Because it is with subordinate units and activities that commanders accomplish their missions, they are dedicated to providing all possible support to those subordinates to enhance their performance and insure mission accomplishment. Within this philosophy most commanders like to consider subordinate commanders to be right until proven otherwise. The staff must share this philosophy.

Just as it is important to keep higher headquarters informed, it is also important to keep subordinate headquarters informed, especially of actions that could impact on those subordinates in the future. Commanders issue warning orders to give maximum advance notice of upcoming operations. The staff should keep the staffs of subordinate commanders informed, with as much lead-time as possible in advance of assigning actions of major significance that will require extensive effort or quick response. This should include staff projects as well as actions involving new or changed missions. The quality of the performance is often proportional to the preparation time available.

Contributing to Actions

Many staff officers are unable to resist the temptation to become highly paid message center operators or postal clerks. Neither the taxpayers nor higher commanders can afford the luxury of intermediate commanders with expensive staffs that contribute little to the success of the Army's mission. A common fault among staff officers is the habit of passing actions from higher headquarters directly to the next subordinate activity for action, adding no additional guidance or assistance except a shortened suspense date and passing back to the next higher headquarters untouched actions taken by the subordinates. The only contribution made by this type of operation is the negative one of additional delay.

Young staff officers may find no written prohibition against this practice and may even find fellow workers and a few lower level supervisors who favor the procedure. Common sense should dictate, however, that the commander probably feels his role in life to be greater than that of relay-point operator. Each staff officer must share this conviction and must make every effort to contribute something to each action.

The staff must analyze each requirement destined for subordinate commands to ensure that it is absolutely clear and should provide clarification if it is not. This may be accomplished through local interpretation or, if necessary, by questions to the next higher headquarters. The requirement should also be examined to determine how much of the answer can be provided locally, passing to the subordinates only those actions that cannot be met otherwise.

When requirements are passed, they should not be subject to interpretation, and all possible guidance must be provided. Responses from the field must be analyzed by the staffs of intermediate commanders to ensure that the answers are clear and that the requirements have been fully met. If not, the staff must either satisfy these conditions or refer them to the subordinate headquarters for completion. The staff must insure that all responses meet their deadline to higher headquarters.

Supervision

Before leaving command policy and its importance to the staff, one more aspect of that policy should be examined. Advising and assisting the commander within the headquarters are only small portions of a staff's job. The major portion of any commander's responsibility lies in supervising the activities of his subordinate commanders. It follows then that the major staff functions relate to assisting with that supervision. Assisting, directing and guiding subordinate commanders' staffs contribute to command supervision. To do these things with maximum effectiveness, the staff must be familiar with another aspect of the commander's policies, those concerning methods of operations, procedures and standards expected from subordinate commanders.

Commanders are often much more explicit in their policies for the conduct of business by subordinates than for operations within their own staffs. This is probably a natural reaction as the success of the mission is so directly related to the activities of the subordinate commanders and their organizations. One of the most famous combat commanders of World War II was particularly well known for providing his subordinate commanders with detailed and unmistakably clear guidance. The following policy statements, summarized from some of that commander's letters of instruction to his subordinates, illustrate the point that his staff would have had to be familiar with these policies in order to be helpful.

1. Plans: "Plans must be simple and flexible. Actually they are only datum plans from which you build as necessity dictates or opportunity offers. Plans must be made by the people who are going to execute them."
2. Supply: "The onus of supply rests equally on the giver and the taker. Forward units must anticipate needs and ask for supplies in time. They must stand ready to use all their means to move supplies."

3. Maintenance: "Preventive maintenance will be enforced. Particular attention will be given to tire pressure, lubrication, battery, water in radiators. Vehicles will be serviced and made ready before the crew rests."
4. Execution: "In carrying out the mission, the promulgation of the order represents not over 10% of your responsibility. The remaining 90% consists in assuring, by means of personal supervision on the ground, by yourself and your staff, proper and vigorous execution."
5. Decorations: "Decorations are for the purpose of raising the fighting value of troops; therefore, they must be awarded promptly."

These are only a few of the many instructions and policy statements issued by that general to his subordinates. They are sufficient to demonstrate the point that his staff could only assist him and the staffs of subordinate commanders by fully understanding these and all other command policies relating to his concepts of operations.

The importance of command policy cannot be overemphasized. Each staff officer should make a habit of studying each action and each statement by the commander to ascertain in as much detail as possible that commander's philosophies, concepts and policies on all types of actions with which the staff might become involved. This study of policy should include more detail than just the major items discussed in this chapter. It should include such minute matters as words preferred or disliked by the commander (and, for that matter, all supervisors).

What must be done is determined largely by laws, regulations and directives from higher headquarters. How it is done is a matter of command policy and, after all, that is the staff's primary concern. The commander knows what must be done. It is the staff's job to assist and advise him in determining how it is to be done. To do this effectively, the staff must think like the commander. His policies must be its policies.

Staff Services and Internal Support

The staff exists for one purpose: to assist the commander in accomplishing his missions. The staff does this by advising and assisting in a wide range of technical specialties and professional disciplines. Previous chapters have dealt primarily with that purpose and with the organizations, procedures, and actions which accomplish it. These are the facets of staff work that relate directly to mission accomplishment and consume at least ninety-five percent of a staff's time and efforts. They are the aspects of headquarters activities that all staff officers must master. Staffs accomplish these output-oriented functions in the headquarters in order to produce positive results in the field. Although not directly applied to problem-solving, the other five percent of the staff effort must be understood and appreciated. That five percent is devoted to functions that staffs perform to sustain themselves, or which they supervise when outside agencies support internal headquarters operations.

As staffs have increased in size, and their operations have become more complicated, they have created massive headquarters with their own peculiar support problems. In order for the staff to bring its administrative, personnel, intelligence, operational and logistical expertise to bear on the commander's missions, they must be supported internally with much the same services.

Transportation experts who ponder the intricacies of transporting the people and things essential to operations in the field must themselves be transported around the headquarters, to and from higher and adjacent headquarters, and to and from the field as they supervise transportation operations. Supply experts wrestling with the ever-present problems of operational requirements versus paucity of resources must themselves have desks, chairs, paper, pencils, and paper clips. Personnel experts find that their own military and civilian work force must be managed. Entire staffs find that the mountains of paper work constantly flowing in, out, and circulating within every headquarters require extensive management.

Some of these internal support functions can be accomplished by staff members, in addition to their primary duties. Others require support by special elements within the staff or from outside agencies and organizations. Some, like administration, require both specialized staff elements and the combined efforts of the entire staff and each of its members.

The number, type, and magnitude of the internal support and services required vary with the headquarters size and mission. Also, headquarters differ in their organizations to provide or obtain internal support. For example, in the continental United States, installations on which large headquarters are located are required by regulation to provide to the tenant headquarters certain standard support services: personnel management, transportation, supply, personnel services, bachelor and family housing, communications, etc.

Tactical headquarters in theaters of operation would provide these and other services from within their own headquarters organization and their assigned and attached support units. The purpose of this discussion is to highlight important internal support functions and to emphasize their importance more than to identify their sources.

Administration

Of all internal support services provided to and performed by the staff, administration is the most pervasive. It requires outside assistance, special staff elements, specialists in all staff elements and their smallest subelements, plus the efforts of every staff member. Administration is the lubricant that keeps the staff machinery moving. Like a defective lubricant, defective administration slows and hampers operations, eventually bringing the staff machine to a jarring halt.

Efficient administration, on the other hand, smoothes and eases headquarters operations by mitigating the friction of minor chores that can dissipate staff energy and prohibit full concentration of efforts on those tasks that contribute directly to mission accomplishment. In larger headquarters, Adjutant Generals are the administrative experts. In addition to planning, directing, and supervising administration throughout commands, Adjutant Generals also are the internal administrators of headquarters. Although all elements of the staff are deeply involved in administration, Adjutant Generals and their specialists perform certain administrative services for headquarters as a whole, such as in-and-out processing of all mail.

At the same time, a myriad of administrative services are performed throughout the staff. In addition to the Adjutant General's office force, each major staff office in a headquarters has administrative elements designated as divisions, branches or sections depending upon the organizational framework and the size of the element. Moving down the staff chain, subdivisions also have personnel responsible for administrative service. These may or may not be organized into formal units such as branches or sections. Even the smallest staff elements at the bottom of the chain have administration responsibilities, often visible only in the form of a single clerk.

All together, significant parts of every staff are directly engaged in providing administrative services, rather than in solving operational problems, planning military actions, or supervising mission-oriented operations. This administrative support is vital to the action side of the staff function.

In addition to these separate administrative specialists, action officers to some degree become involved in administration. Even though their primary tasks are to accomplish mission-related staff actions, they must be supported by administrative services and must, therefore, understand, employ to maximum effectiveness, and supervise these services to best advantage. As staff officers progress up the career ladder, they shoulder increasing responsibility for assuring effective administration. Early appreciation of administrative procedures can only work to the young staff officer's advantage.

Correspondence

In any headquarters, management of the torrents of paper flowing in and out, circulating among the many elements, and eddying within the elements and subelements is perhaps the most important of all internal support functions. It is certainly the most difficult. This paper flow deserves special discussion if for no other reason than to point up its mind-shattering volume. Even at the company level, commanders must insist on alert management or be buried beneath mounds of paper.

Few technological advances have affected today's Army more drastically than the vast improvements in equipment to produce, reproduce, and transmit the written word. The first printing press catalyzed the proliferation of the written-word. The advent of the typewriter set the torch to the final explosion. Teletypewriters and instant reproduction equipment have in their turn compounded the paper problem almost beyond control.

Headquarters paperwork stems from three sources: mountains of paper coming in from above, below, and all sides; equivalent mountains going out in every direction; and paper rivers circulating internally. The paper must flow without interruption to the proper recipient, where it will, hopefully, be read and if necessary, acted upon, and filed or otherwise disposed of. The sheer magnitude of this task in large headquarters is frightening.

The complexity of maintaining a fast, uninterrupted flow should be apparent. Papers coming in must pass through many hands on the way to the proper action officers. Papers created by action officers must pass through many hands on their journeys out of the originating headquarters. At the same time, the massive volume of internally generated and internally consumed paper must sift up, down, and laterally. In larger headquarters this total flow could amount to thousands of documents—with division level offices handling several hundred pieces of staff paper on any normal day. Staff members who make the paper flow are vital members of the team. One of their more complex functions is to determine to whom each paper should go.

Distribution

Some papers moving through headquarters are important to the commanders and to all staff members; others are important to many staff officers; others, to only a few. Still others may be of interest to only a single technical expert. Each is of interest to someone, but identifying that someone often can be difficult. A frequent but unsatisfactory solution is to give copies of everything to everyone. As a result, in headquarters where that practice is tolerated the entire staff virtually drowns in a stagnant sea of dead papers.

Staff members may be hard pressed to identify even the documents they need. New staff officers particularly are bound to be confused by the mass of paper, and to have difficulty in deciding which papers apply to their functions. Deciding which papers should be passed along to associates or bosses may be even more difficult. Even deciding what to keep and what to dispose of can cause problems.

Reading all of the material crossing their desks becomes a problem for staff officers, new and old, but read they must. Few staff officers escape the sting of having failed to read an important directive. The importance of reading as a staff technique is addressed in some detail elsewhere in this book. It is a challenge itself.

New staff officers may be inclined to look upon the task of moving the paper mountains as clerks' jobs. Admittedly, action officers should not have to be experts in the mechanics of internal distribution. This job belongs to the administrative specialists. Action officers should have a working knowledge of the distribution system, however, and know how to utilize it to best advantage, so that in crunch situations all shortcuts can be used to save time and to help meet deadlines. Staff work is complete only when in the hands of users, not when dropped in the *out* box.

When informed by counterparts in other headquarters that important correspondence relating to urgent projects which they are handling is en route, action officers can save time by alerting their local staff administrative people and those in their headquarters message center to be on the lookout. By arranging to pick up the urgent correspondence as it enters the headquarters instead of waiting until it has filtered down through several administration layers, valuable time could be saved.

The same process can work in reverse. Action officers should be fully cognizant of the administrative time required to move papers out by routine procedures through message centers. When an action needs coordination in several staff offices and is due the same day, it had better be hand carried. Routine travel through message centers could take several days. These shortcuts apply equally to internal and to incoming and outgoing correspondence. In the course of normal business, message centers move urgent papers along with the masses of routine internal paperwork that never leave the headquarters. This can be a slow process. Smart action officers soon learn to make allowances and to shortcut bottlenecks.

Incoming mail is normally received in the Adjutant General's mailroom. There it is screened to determine who should see and who should act on each item received. Based on these determinations, mail is then routed to the appropriate headquarters elements. Copies of particularly significant correspondence are furnished to the command group. Incoming electronically received messages are handled similarly, except that they may arrive at a separate communications message center.

Normally, Adjutant General's messengers deliver incoming correspondence and messages to the major staff offices and, at the same time, collect external and internal outgoing material. Administrative elements of the major staff offices further break down the incoming mail and messages for internal distribution to their major subelements, where the process is repeated down through the echelons until each paper winds up in the hands of the appropriate action officer.

The distribution process must have the help of all staff members if it is to succeed in getting all papers into the right hands. As stated previously, message centers usually determine which documents should go to the commander and to each staff element. Considering the magnitude of the correspondence handled and the diversity of subject matter, message center experts do an amazingly good job at this difficult task. However, they are not infallible.

Occasionally items of command interest are passed directly to staff elements. When this happens, the recipient must correct the oversight. Similarly, items sometimes arrive in the wrong staff element. Again, the receiver must correct the error and get the mail into the proper hands. If the paper will require considerable effort, the proper addressee can be expected to exhibit certain, finders-keepers reactions.

Outgoing correspondence originates in the staff's lowest levels with individual action officers and must proceed back up the chain to be approved at levels determined by the importance of the action. Once approved, the correspondence either enters the messenger service or is sent to the message center for dispatch.

Suspense Controls

Equally important, and just as difficult to administer as the machinery for sifting actions down to the staff's lower levels and working the responses back into the light of day, are controls to assure these responses emerge on schedule. These are *suspense* controls. Like so many facets of administration, they are the responsibility of both the administrative elements and the staff members.

Each document or message entering a headquarters is scanned at the message center to determine whether a response or action is required within a specified time limit. If so, the message center assigns an appropriate suspense date, the date the reply or action must be back in the message center if it is to reach its destination on time. This is only the beginning. Many more, ever shorter suspenses often are added.

Commanders may impose suspenses to their offices well in advance of the original suspense, thereby forcing staff element chiefs to establish even earlier deadlines. This progressive tightening of the schedule often leaves the unfortunate action officers little time to complete their work. In fact, action officers may occasionally find that certain suspenses are impossible to meet, or can only be met with hasty, incomplete and unreliable staff work.

In these instances, every effort should be made to obtain the additional time needed to produce good work. This requires working in reverse order through the supervisory chain that established the suspenses. In a large headquarters considerable additional working time might be gained. For instance, if on a particular action the headquarters message center, the command group, staff element chief, division chief, branch chief, and section chief have each in their turn established suspenses with small safety factors, concessions of only one-half day by each could release three full days for use at the action level. When time shortages are extremely critical, the higher commands directing the actions could be asked for additional time to complete the work.

Even when they seem unreasonable, suspenses must be met unless extensions can be obtained. Extensions must be sought through the supervisory chain that imposed the suspense. Action officers who consider assigned suspenses unduly tight must work through their direct supervisors in their attempts to obtain relief.

Filing

Moving paper is a vital function. Storing paper is equally important, so filing is another vital administrative chore. Although it often rates little attention, inadequate, sloppy filing can cause gross consternation and embarrassment when needed documents are lost. Action officers are not file clerks, but as with distribution, they must have more than a passing interest in the proper storing and recording of information. In their own sections, at least, they should know where to find filed material when administration experts are not there to help.

Normally, copies of all outgoing correspondence are retained in the files of the originating staff subelements, as are copies of the incoming documents that triggered the actions. Record copies are filed at the level where approval for dispatch was given or at central headquarters repositories. In addition, experienced action officers maintain their own working files of all projects.

While projects are active, these working files are instant sources of all material pertaining to each action: letters, messages, memoranda of conferences, phone conversations, discussion notes, appropriate backup data, etc. Project files should be retained after the project is completed until no chance remains that the same or similar project may again become active.

Action officers must be absolutely certain that classified materials are not included in working files unless those files are properly protected and secured in approved, classified repositories when not in use. Even so, a hazard with working files that contain classified material is their complete informality. Action officers who set them up usually are the only ones to handle and maintain them, and often store them in desks or ordinary filing cabinets. If classified material slips into a file, it could by force of habit be stored in an unprotected container. This could lead to big trouble.

Few things in the Army can cause instant difficulty more surely than mishandling of classified material. Receipt, storage, control, and disposition of classified material are administrative services. Unlike distribution and filing, however, these are services for which each staff member is fully responsible. He becomes fully responsible when classified material is turned over to him. He remains responsible until that material has been officially transferred from his control.

Provisions of Army regulations and local directives on the subject of safeguarding classified material must be virtually memorized and must be scrupulously observed. Looseness in this sensitive area could result in compromised national security as well as an untimely end to a promising career. These cautions apply equally to those action officers who seldom work with classified documents. They may at any time be detailed to additional duties of assisting with periodic inventories, witnessing document destruction, or for other reasons taking responsibility for classified material. They should be prepared to protect both the sensitive material and their careers.

Unclassified files are screened annually. Filed record material is segregated for retirement to the Army's central records center, destruction, or further retention based on content and regulations. Reference material may be retained as long as needed. Records management, as the process is called, is an administrative support service, but action officers usually are called upon to screen and recommend disposition of the filed material they have produced.

Typing

Numerous administrative services are available to and must be understood and supervised by action officers. Typing is one of the most obvious. Except in tactical headquarters, most Army typists are civilian employees, usually shared by several action officers. Unfortunately, the ratio of action officers to typists is quite high, causing problems and clamor. This valuable resource which provides the essential step of putting action officer efforts in the final format for transmittance to supervisors, commanders, and users, must be properly managed and conserved.

As a human resource, typing is difficult to measure by standard criteria. Yet criteria are established at national levels to determine the number of typists needed to support specific numbers of action officers. These criteria change from time to time, but usually provide for about one typist for four action officers, based on the assumption that the typist and the action officers have average technical and professional qualifications, average energies and average dedication, and that the office has an average workload. Unfortunately, averages, while excellent for Army-wide application, seldom seem to prevail at the office level.

Fortunate indeed are the average (or below average) action officers with average workloads, who are blessed with an above-average typist. The only management needed is to prevent the typist from becoming bored. Unfortunate are the above-average, productive action officers faced with overpowering workloads, who must share the services of an average or below average typist—this takes real management. Like other austere resources, typing must be husbanded and applied to the most urgent needs as their priorities relate to mission accomplishment. Alternate methods of communications must be substituted for lesser tasks: hand written notes, face-to-face discussions, telephone conversations, etc.

Reproduction

To satisfy demands for multiple distribution, to provide information to all interested organizations, agencies, and individuals, and to create copies for record, reference, and project files, modern headquarters have insatiable appetites for reproduced material. Headquarters meet their requirements through various procedures. In some, reproduction equipment is centralized and one activity services the entire headquarters. In others, all reproduction capabilities are decentralized, and each staff element has its own complete capability.

Most large headquarters choose a middle course. Large multipage documents and projects requiring large numbers of copies are centrally processed; smaller requirements are met by equipment within the staff elements. Whatever the local arrangement, reproduction is a job for experts, not action officers. Reproduction equipment is sophisticated, sensitive to abuse and, above all, expensive. Action officers' time is also expensive and can be used to better purpose than operating machines. They must, however, understand the reproduction equipment available and be aware of its capabilities and its limitations, particularly time limitations.

Audiovisual Aids

Briefings, presentations, displays, and other staff activities frequently require complex visual aids to clarify, emphasize, and supplement narrative presentations. This support requires the services of very talented specialists: draftsmen, artists, illustrators, photographers, etc. It also requires sophisticated and expensive equipment and supplies. This capability may be available within the headquarters, otherwise it must come from the supporting installation. Properly and sparingly used, this support can often greatly assist action officers in completing difficult projects. Its value is limited to the extent that action officers understand its uses and limitations.

Funds

In today's Army, management of the dollar has become an overridingly important facet of every commanders' responsibilities and consequently governs their staffs' every move. Control of the funds required to accomplish mission-related operations and support functions is discussed elsewhere. Internal headquarters operations also require money and money management. Supplies, equipment, and services must be purchased; facilities, leased and maintained; civilian employees salaries, paid; and travel expenses, reimbursed.

Staff comptrollers or supporting installations often manage these internal funds at the command level; however, staff element chiefs, subelement supervisors, and all staff members must do their part. Most commanders decentralize detailed control and management of internal funds to their staff element chiefs, who in turn decentralize to their subelements. In the end, almost every staff member becomes involved in estimating and justifying future requirements for funds, and in managing and accounting for money allocated for his activities.

Quite properly, American taxpayers, through the Congress, insist that most of the money appropriated for national defense be applied directly and visibly to operational forces, activities, and equipment which provide that defense. Paper, pencils, typewriters, desks, typists, administrators, and other headquarters accoutrements are difficult to classify in that priority. Headquarters funds, therefore, are always austere. It behooves every staff officer to become expert in management of and accounting for funds.

Duty Rosters and Additional, Non-mission-oriented Duties

Young officers, when assigned to large headquarters for the first time, may be surprised to find that a multitude of trifling but necessary extra jobs have preceded them. Such irritants as voting, incentive awards, bonds, army emergency relief programs, suggestions, cost reduction, zero defects, and escorts must be accomplished in the headquarters, as elsewhere. As much as possible, most commanders and staff supervisors use administrative support personnel to perform these duties; however, there are seldom enough administrative personnel to completely spare the action officers. Duty rosters are maintained at all staff levels, and additional duties continue to add to the experience and professional knowledge of young officers, albeit at some cost to their effectiveness in their primary assignments.

Routine Orders

Headquarters personnel, like their compatriots in the field, come and go permanently and temporarily. Processing orders for these permanent and temporary moves, and for other personnel actions (promotions, awards, duty changes, etc.), is a major effort in large headquarters. Normally, the only responsibility of staff officers in this endeavor is to insure that orders affecting them, their people, and their activities are issued promptly and accurately.

Visitors

Much like correspondence, visitors converge on large headquarters from every side. They consist of every possible military rank and civilian employee grade, representatives of local, state and federal agencies, members of the news media, and people from all conceivable community activities. All come for purposes important to them. This flow must be regulated, controlled, and managed for three reasons: first, to assist the visitors in accomplishing their purposes as rapidly and with as little effort as possible; second, to prevent every office in the headquarters from being disrupted by a constant stream of visitors; and third, to assure that each visitor is afforded appropriate courtesies and necessary support such as housing, transport, food, etc.

In very large headquarters, protocol officers on the commanders' personal staffs oversee these efforts as they relate to senior visitors or those whose purpose is of personal interest to the commanders. Protocol officers usually relegate lesser visitors to the staff elements that share the visitors' primary interests. Staff element chiefs and most staff members often find themselves in the role of host.

Personnel

Personnel administration is in some respects closely akin to paper work administration. Although specialists in the personnel sections manage most personnel actions, some functions, such as personnel accounting and maintenance of specified records, are performed at every staff level. Staff element administration experts perform most of these personnel tasks, just as they manage the paper flow. Some personnel functions, particularly those related to performance and pay, are responsibilities of supervisory staff members. This, of course, is in line with supervisors' overall responsibilities for administration.

Most headquarters break personnel administration into three categories: officer, enlisted, and civilian employees. Exceptions could be found in major tactical units where staffs are limited to military members. All military staffs include some military personnel, but some consist of as high as ninety-nine percent civilian members. These civilian-heavy military organizations are most common in specialized activities such as procurement, research and development, engineering, and manufacturing.

In more conventional headquarters, officers are assigned directly to the headquarters, enlisted members are assigned to headquarters companies, and civilians are employed (normally by the supporting installations) to work in the headquarters. Detailed officer-personnel administration may be accomplished by Officers Personnel Sections, normally elements of Adjutant Generals' offices. Adjutant Generals' enlisted personnel staff elements may administer enlisted personnel records.

An alternate method, favored where major headquarters are tenant activities on installations, consolidates personnel offices under the direction of the installations' Adjutants General. Supporting civilian personnel offices, either in the headquarters or in the staff of the supporting installation, administer civilian work forces. When major headquarters are tenants on installations, the installations' civilian personnel offices usually service the tenant headquarters.

Action officers are spared detailed involvement in most personnel matters. As already pointed out, these are tasks for supervisors and administrative specialists. At working levels, civilian clerks or enlisted specialists submit feeder data for the headquarters military morning report. These data are fed up the supervisory chain and are consolidated by administrative personnel at each successive echelon, finally reaching the respective officer and enlisted personnel sections where the reports are prepared and submitted.

Time and attendance data for civilian pay are submitted level to level up the administrative chain, finally coming to rest with the proper finance and accounting office. Supervisors reporting military and civilian personnel data are primarily concerned with accuracy and timeliness of submissions. Few military personnel records are maintained in working-level staff offices. If any such files exist, they normally would be for convenience only and could contain burned copies of officers forms 66, enlisted forms 20, orders applicable to current assignments, etc. Certain civilian personnel records are maintained at division, branch, or even section levels. These concern time and attendance, job description, and possibly information relating to performance.

Miscellaneous Personnel Functions

Supervisors play important roles in a number of personnel actions. One of the most critical is rating the performance of military personnel and civilian employees under their direction. The importance of these ratings cannot be overstated. With modern centralized management systems, military men and civilian employees find that many of the most important aspects of their careers are handled at centralized locations by boards, committees, and individuals who are total strangers.

Many factors are career determinants, and periodic efforts are made to decrease the influence of performance ratings. The fact remains, however, that how a person does his job is a most difficult factor to supplant. Each officer should approach his responsibilities for rating others with extreme care and honesty. An unduly harsh rating could easily do irreparable harm to a career. On the other hand, unjustifiably high ratings are hardly fair to those who actually produce outstanding results. Promotion, retention, favorable assignments, and awards are only a few of the career stepping stones influenced by performance ratings. With so much riding on them, ratings must be objective and honest.

Staff supervisors and action officers also become involved in preparing job descriptions and in hiring civilian personnel. When manpower surveys are called for, they can be up to their ears in developing production data to justify their work forces. After the surveys wipe out half of an element's personnel authorizations (which can happen), they may spend additional months preparing reclamas in attempts to reestablish the work forces. Even the small chores of managing leaves and passes and assigning details can be important.

All actions involving personal rights, privileges, and duties are significant and can have an impact on personnel effectiveness.

Communications

Staff officers are not expected to be communications experts, but they must know what communications capabilities are available and understand the advantages and limitations of each system. Much of the correspondence coming into and leaving most headquarters moves by ordinary mail. Significant percentages may also pass by electronic transmission, telephone, radio, computerized data, circuits, and other electronic means. This could be especially true for tactical headquarters. Additionally, some correspondence comes into and leaves all commands, particularly tactical headquarters, by couriers and messengers.

Postal and Messenger Services

Mail is handled internally by messengers and ultimately dispatched by the Adjutant General. It requires little special equipment or technical skill. This common method of communication was discussed under *Administration*.

Electronics

Message traffic also moves by messengers within the headquarters, but it is received and put on the wire by communications experts in communications and electronics staff elements. Complete message communication centers may be maintained by headquarters organizations, or the electrical communications services may be provided by host installations. In any case, electronic message services to most military addresses worldwide are available to action officers. If not overloaded, the service is prompt and efficient. To avoid overloading the system, messages should be used only when other means cannot meet the requirements.

Telephones

Telephones are among the most obvious, other means. If not overworked, the telephone service available to action officers should be able to contact any military party needed through the worldwide, Automatic Voice Network (AUTOVON) system which services installations of all military services and some other government agencies. Those located in the forty-eight contiguous states can be reached by direct dialing.

To prevent overloading, telephone control officers are designated at all headquarters and in each staff element to insure that traffic is limited to official business. The AUTOVON system is a real boon to those conducting staff business. Despite controls, circuits can become overloaded and delays can result.

Experienced staff officers avoid these irritants whenever possible by getting their calls through to particularly difficult terminals early in the morning before the rush starts or late in the evening after it stops. This sometimes requires prior agreement with staff counterparts on the other end of the line. Another time-saving device used by experienced staff officers is telephone call planning. Either in writing or mentally they decide exactly what each call should achieve, and they organize their conversations in advance to accomplish exactly those predetermined purposes, as quickly as possible.

Because AUTOVON circuits are not secure, telephone conversations must be limited to unclassified matters. When classified material must be discussed by phone, most headquarters have expensive pieces of equipment that electronically scramble speakers' voices at the sending end; similar pieces of equipment unscramble at the receiving end. Because of the expense, these items usually are not scattered through staff offices even in small numbers.

Most headquarters having this capability place it under the control of operations staff element representatives who manage its use. They clear all calls and assist in arranging them through the operators. The scrambler is a valuable tool when needed; but at the working level, telephone discussion of sensitive material can almost always be avoided. Although most action officers may never have occasion to employ this sophisticated item, every action officer should be familiar with it and know how to use it if necessary.

Data Transmission

AUTOVON has a companion system in AUTODIN, the Automatic Data Network. As the name implies, this system is used exclusively to transmit data. Like AUTOVON, it is servicewide and worldwide, and depends primarily on commercial telephone circuits leased for the purpose. AUTODIN is used for passing automated systems data up the Army's chain of command. It is put on the wire in communications centers. Anyone who is not a communications action officer or a computer expert would probably have little to do with AUTODIN, but all action officers should know of its existence and its function.

Radio

In the continental United States radio communications between fixed installations are nonexistent except for the quasiofficial Military Affiliated Radio System (MARS). This system can be extremely useful in situations such as civil defense emergencies. It is not used for day-to-day official traffic.

In some overseas commands, fixed installations are connected by radio networks which parallel nets of major tactical units.

To action officers, messages are messages. They should care little whether their work is transmitted by mail, wire, radio, telephone or messenger, or all means, as long as it reaches its destination in the expected time. How it travels is the communicator's job.

For the most part, communications support in today's Army is outstanding. The latest equipment is available and the most modern techniques are used, including communications satellites. If Army communicators do not have the wherewithall, it has yet to be invented. The same can be said for military efforts in the field of automation.

Data Processing

Today's Army takes full advantage of data processing. Standard programs have been developed and are operational in every functional field. By and large, data processing support is available for all justified new programs and projects. Data processing is supervised in most headquarters by management information systems officers, members of the special staffs. Their offices have expertise in all aspects of the technology. All major commands directly under the Department of the Army, and their subordinate elements, include management information systems staff offices. This organizational pattern extends to all installations in the continental United States. Major tactical organizations down to division level also possess data processing capability under centralized control.

In some headquarters such as installations, management information systems officers exercise staff supervision over all data processing resources within the command. In larger major commands their controls may be somewhat diminished and actual data processing operations may be performed by special detachments. At Department of the Army data systems of the different staff elements are processed under centralized control.

The important point for staff officers in any headquarters from division up is that data processing is available. Occasions arise when this capability can be put to good use. The possibilities are literally infinite. Staff officers do not have to be experts, but it would be helpful if they could recognize problems to which data processing could be applied to advantage.

A common tendency among novices is to consider computers for projects more suited to electric accounting machines. Typically, this includes situations that require only compilation or sorting of data. Computers should be used only for data which must be manipulated and processed. Computers can store data for future comparison as well as perform mathematical calculations. Anything less would be underutilization.

Staff officers who believe they have projects which could be run on computers should consult the experts. Most major staff elements have management information systems assistants who serve as points of contact with the headquarters management information systems office. On large staffs, management information systems assistants may even be designated at division and branch levels. It is with these local specialists in their own offices that the staff officers should start.

If a project is considered adaptable to automation, experts in the management information systems office will scrutinize it to determine whether automation is practical and can be justified on the basis of savings in resources or improved efficiency. Computer services can greatly enhance staff production. Individual staff officers should be alert for opportunities to employ them.

Counterintelligence (Internal Security)

Intelligence staff members also find that internal headquarters functions accompany their primary functions of identifying and analyzing external conditions, situations, and factors influencing their commanders' missions. An adjunct of the intelligence gathering function is countering enemy attempts to gather similar data concerning U.S. forces. Like other staff work, counterintelligence efforts concentrate largely on activities directly related to current and planned missions. In two areas, however, these preventive countermeasures must be applied to internal headquarters operations: personnel clearances, and security of classified material.

Most staff members will need security clearances to be able to handle classified security information. This applies to all grade levels: typists, file clerks, action officers, senior supervisors, and commanders. Without clearances their usefulness would be limited. Consequently clearance validation becomes one of the first steps in preparing new staff members for duty. Data concerning each new member's clearance is provided to the staff intelligence experts. They take it from there.

For persons with previous clearances, a check of national intelligence files usually is sufficient. For persons who have never been cleared, personal history statements must be prepared in great detail for use by intelligence experts. Depending on the level of clearance, required background investigations may be conducted by supporting counterintelligence organizations. Headquarters staff specialists monitor the progress of each security clearance and maintain local personnel security records.

Safeguarding military information is an individual responsibility shared by commanders and every member of their staffs. Specialists in the staff organizations of intelligence officers monitor those internal functions. They visit other staff offices, inspect security procedures and facilities, and provide technical guidance. Supporting counterintelligence organizations help with these functions and may also inspect and survey headquarters security measures to help prevent security violations. Security of classified information is governed by rigid rules that must be diligently followed. When problems develop, intelligence staff experts are on call.

Management Engineering

The term *management engineering* is symptomatic of a malady that affects many experts, an uncontrollable tendency to disguise basic, commonsense activities behind fancy but meaningless titles. Military personnel seem particularly susceptible to the ailment. Stated simply, this internal function is nothing more than management of human and physical resources to assure maximum effectiveness within economic limitations. In any organization, military or civilian, this management function is an important and continuous effort. In large military headquarters, it is vital.

Like other internal functions, resource management is the responsibility of commanders, staff element chiefs, supervisors and every action officer. Each must be constantly alert for possible organizational and procedural improvements at his level that could increase the effectiveness and economy of resources under his control. As with other specialized functions, staff officers are not expected to excel in the details of this complex area of expertise.

Most large headquarters staffs include management experts to study headquarters organizational structures, missions, operations, and resource utilization. Unfortunately, their effectiveness often is hampered by two factors. On the one hand, their time is consumed in supervising specific management programs (work measurement program, work simplification program, management improvement program, zero defects program, etc.) On the other hand, they often find few takers for the little time that is available for assisting the staff. Many supervisors hesitate to call in outside experts to do what they consider their job of organizing and running their own shop.

Supply

Large headquarters with hundreds or even thousands of members use vast quantities of equipment and supplies. Few staff officers appreciate the supply efforts required to support internal headquarters operations. However, a glance around their offices and surrounding ones would indicate the scope. Desks, chairs, typewriters, tables, filing cabinets, safes, bookcases, wall clocks, ash trays, pencil sharpeners, pictures, and desk lamps are standard for almost every office in all headquarters. Senior supervisors enjoy the added comforts of sofas, overstuffed easy chairs, coffee tables, rugs, etc. Special activities require additional equipment: drafting sets, art items, darkrooms, reproduction equipment, etc.

To these major items must be added the amazing number of smaller, expendable items found in or on almost every desk (needed or not): book ends, staplers, scissors, rulers, paper weights, paper clip holders, loose leaf binders, calenders and staple extracters—to name only a few. When a continental army headquarters was inactivated in the early 1970's, amazed and almost buried supply personnel assisting with the turn-in of equipment, estimated that each of the more than one thousand desks in the headquarters contained at least one of more than twenty separate items. Obtaining, maintaining and replacing this equipment is no mean task.

Supplies for a large headquarters are at least an equal task. The numbers and types of items needed probably exceed equipment items, and rates of consumption are much greater. Large headquarters consume tons of pencils, typewriter ribbons, scratch pads, pens, paper clips, typing and reproduction paper, staples, correction fluid, ink, erasers, and hundreds of other items.

Outside support agencies such as host installations are usually responsible for requisitioning, receiving and storing in bulk the equipment and supplies used by large headquarters. Internal distribution must be accomplished by headquarters personnel, usually supervised by the headquarters commandant. Some of the impact of the supply function reaches every staff level.

At the major staff element and major subactivities, administrative organizations consolidate requirements, submit requisitions and receive, store and issue equipment and supplies. Requirements must be determined and management of the resources must be at the level of use by staff officers and their enlisted and civilian administrative assistants.

Transportation

The discussion of supply and equipment indicates one aspect of headquarters internal transportation requirements: movement of things. The supply responsibilities of supporting activities normally end when the items arrive in the warehouses of those activities. Similarly, their responsibility for disposal of excess and damaged items begins only when the items reach their collection points. Transporting such items from and to support facilities is normally the responsibility of the headquarters even though transportation resources may be furnished by the support activities.

Transportation of people also becomes a major function in large headquarters. Staff members must move about within the headquarters, which may be scattered over large installations with several miles separating its elements. This requires local buses, taxi fleets and assigned automobiles (for those with more critical movement requirements).

As staffs perform their supervisory and external coordination functions, their members travel constantly to all areas of the command and to other distant destinations. Considerable staff and administrative effort is required to manage these transportation requirements. Most staff officers become involved in this function only to the extent necessary to plan and arrange transportation for their own travel.

Facilities

In most major headquarters, the headquarters commandant is the landlord. He must obtain, manage and arrange for maintenance and repair of the buildings and areas needed by the headquarters. Except for the fact that virtually every staff officer in the US Army is convinced that he needs more and better office space, action officers need to know little about this complex support function. It is a major effort, however, and its scope should be understood.

Despite repeated and sincere efforts from the highest national levels to decrease numbers of personnel assigned to headquarters, staffs habitually tend more to expansion than to reduction. Unfortunately, physical plants have little elasticity. Optimum management of office space, conference rooms, special facilities, parking areas and so on is mandatory. Meeting requirements takes hard work and considerable diplomacy.

Assuring proper maintenance and repair of buildings and grounds to the standards demanded by the occupants within limited budgets also requires firm but somewhat flexible management. Utilities such as sewage disposal, water, electricity, refuse collection, heating and cooling also must be provided to allow the staff the amenities and comforts conducive to efficient production.

Housekeeping, the constant headache, also must be accomplished. Interior and exterior public and work areas require cleaning. Few headquarters or their support activities have assigned personnel to accomplish these menial tasks. Budgets seldom permit adequate contract custodial services. Staff officers can expect that one of their most critical personnel management challenges may be convincing highly skilled technicians that dusting desks, sweeping floors, washing windows and so on are tasks compatible with their positions and dignity.

Summary

In summary, internal support functions are essential facets of headquarters operations. The principal ones have been discussed here, but all staff elements perform internal support tasks from time to time in their fields of interest. These would be of the nonrecurring type such as the chaplain's performing a wedding ceremony for a staff member or the staff engineer's assisting the headquarters commandant in preparing the technical documents for a headquarters renovation project.

When appropriate and consistent with mission requirements, headquarters skills are applied to sustain or support internal operations. Most headquarters organizations include staff specialists to provide the required recurring support and to control and supervise services provided by supporting activities. Internal support functions are designed to assist the staff and should function so that they cause the least possible distraction from the staff's primary goals. Staff members must participate actively in many support functions and must understand all of these services sufficiently to take full advantages of them. They must also appreciate the importance of the functions of support personnel and the difficulties encountered in performing them. They need and deserve every staff member's cooperation.

The message for new staff officers is simply "Do your part". This includes knowing and observing the ground rules. Even such mundane details as following correct administrative procedures, conserving supplies, using communications judiciously or employing administrative assistants effectively help, and individual efforts can soon add up to a significant contribution to the support effort. Be part of the solution, not one of the problems.

10.

Personal Skills and Techniques

To this point we have presented the origin of staffs and their evolution from a few messengers and advisors to massive modern headquarters, some typical staff organizations, staff procedures, command policies, typical staff actions, and the internal support required to keep a headquarters running. Hopefully, in developing this broad coverage of the staff as a whole we have presented a clear picture of the environment new staff officers can expect in their first headquarters assignment and have alerted them to some of the activities in which they can expect to be involved. We have dwelled at some length on the commander's dependence on the staff and the related necessity for staffs, their elements, and their individual members to produce high quality work. We come now to the real heart of the staff—the individual member. What personal skills must he possess, and what techniques must he master to produce the results discussed in previous chapters?

In attempting to answer this question, the authors have painstakingly searched the memories of their combined thirty years on various level staffs, reviewing the most common attributes of fellow officers who consistently produced fine work, earned the confidence of their supervisors and coworkers and, not surprisingly, rose to positions of great responsibility in their profession. At the same time, the weaknesses of some less fortunate acquaintances were studied in retrospect.

On the surface, some of those who produced and succeeded had seemingly overriding advantages. They were brilliant scholars or came from long lines of military ancestors (and where thus oriented to military thinking from childhood) or were handsome, masculine, and verile-looking (mirror images of fictional military officers) or possessed other natural attributes. Make no mistake—these are advantages. But they are not absolute guarantees of success. In fact, if leaned on too heavily, they can prove unsteady props indeed.

Every staff has a few members with all the natural qualifications who produce little or nothing, who enjoy no one's confidence and whose careers are stymied. In those same headquarters, less brilliant officers, quite ordinary in appearance and with no military ancestry, are producing outstanding work and building enviable professional reputations. With rare exceptions, however, those who have forged ahead shared certain common skills and practiced the same working techniques: they could communicate orally and in writing; they were avid researchers spurred on by unquenchable curiosity about all things salient to their profession; they accumulated vast quantities of usable information pertinent to their official duties; they were management conscious, aware of their responsibilities to conserve resources; they followed through on all actions (supervised); they were completeness addicts; and they were loyal. These are not natural, inherited characteristics. They can be acquired, but only by hard work, concentration and a strong desire to be an outstanding, respected member of a demanding, complex profession. They must be mastered by those who hope to succeed.

Communications

By definition, staff officers exist only to advise and assist their commanders. Advice and assistance are rendered as a team effort. This means many people work together to arrive at common recommendations and pool their individual knowledge and experience to help the commander. A team member unable to communicate with his fellow workers, his supervisors and his commander, contributes little to such efforts. He can neither receive information, directives and guidance from others nor share the benefits of his knowledge.

Military professionals are keenly aware that their productivity and their careers depend largely upon their ability to receive, understand, analyze and use information and to transmit information to others. Consequently, those who wish to produce effective work, and to be recognized for it, strive constantly to improve their communication skills. They also recognize that communications skills fall into two equally important categories: receiving and sending.

Receiving

Unfortunately, too many people concentrate their efforts to improve their communication skills only in the more active function—sending. In the military, the skills used to transmit information, directives and guidance to others are invaluable. The most dedicated and brilliant staff officers would be completely ineffective if they were unable to pass along the results of their efforts. To produce high quality outgoing written and oral material, staff officers must first be experts at receiving and understanding written and oral material. Military schools and reference material place far less emphasis on those skills than their importance merits.

Listening

This is not a medical book. The authors are not doctors, psychiatrists or psychologists. They are, in fact, completely uninformed about the barriers which seem to exist between many peoples' ears and brains. The authors do know that many staff officers' weakest points are their inabilities to listen and to understand what they have heard. They also know that rapid, thorough assimilation of the spoken word is indispensable to the success of staff officers, and they know that with effort, listening skills can be improved by all and perfected by some.

Commanders, staff supervisors and busy action officers have neither the time nor the inclination to reduce to writing, each bit of information, guidance or instruction they must exchange with fellow workers, subordinates, or counterparts at other headquarters. Consequently, the massive paper flow in most headquarters is more than matched by oral communications from all sides and all levels. These oral channels of communication are at least equal in importance to their formal, written counterparts—and often supersede them. Because of their informality and sometimes confidential nature, tidbits of background information not suitable for the written records but extremely helpful to the recipient can sometimes only be conveyed orally.

Unfortunately, unless electronically recorded, oral information is a one time affair. Unless the recipient takes dictation, there will be no verbatim document to be reread, studied and analyzed to determine exactly what was said. To be successful, a staff officer must learn to receive the oral word as well as the written, and to understand and remember it better.

Concentration. Probably the greatest distraction from listening is failure to concentrate on the speaker's message. It is impossible to understand either written or oral material when one's mind is on the golf course, at the beach, or hoisting the first one at an upcoming happy hour. To a certain few in every headquarters, those and similar thoughts are firmly entrenched and form barriers that the entire Corps of Engineers could not dislodge. This discussion is not for them. We leave them to their dreams of holes-in-one, bikinis and arid martinis. There are, however, other less overwhelming distractions that can and must be overcome. Chief among these is the press of other work.

Staff officers are always desperately behind schedule. The truly productive action officer seldom finds the hours of the day sufficient to comfortably complete the day's work. It is most difficult to concentrate on telephone calls, instructions from supervisors, or information from fellow action officers

Personal Skills and Techniques

when the *in* box is piling higher and higher with unfinished work. The thought of all that work and its suspenses is difficult to obliterate, even briefly. The ability to do so is a skill at which all good staff officers are adept. To receive, the channel must be clear. All other matters must be tuned out long enough to give full attention to the speaker's message.

The impatience caused by the urge to start sending is another bar to concentration. Most people prefer speaking to listening. The first few words striking the auditory system trigger frantic activity among the mental speech writers. As a result the persons who should be listening are often preparing their replies instead. These responses seldom address the entire subject matter presented, because the person who was supposed to be listening did not hear the full presentation.

This common tendency is more difficult to overcome than is the temptation to allow at least part of the mind to return to other pressing problems. Yet it must and can be overcome. Staff officers must discipline their minds to concentrate on every word spoken, cataloguing each bit of information recieved, relating it to information already on hand and filing it away in its appropriate mental niche. Then, if called upon, the data for logical, orderly and complete response are neatly organized and ready to use.

Preconception is closely allied to premature preparation of replies as a concentration killer. In some unfortunate persons this tendency reaches maddening proportions. Everyone has met people who finish each sentence for the speaker, preconceiving the full meaning, perhaps even before the speaker himself has decided what his position is to be. While most persons control this tendency at least enough to remain silent, few can completely overcome the temptation to get mentally ahead of the person attempting to convey an oral message.

This failing is extremely detrimental to good listening because, unless rigidly disciplined, human minds tend to hear what they want to hear. If the mind is allowed to roam ahead of the speaker, forming its own interpretations of the speaker's intentions before they are stated, it may hear exactly what it had decided to hear, regardless of the actual words. The military mind must be disciplined, held in check and forced to concentrate on the words as they are spoken—not allowed to race ahead, anticipating those not yet formed.

Lack of interest underlies most bad listening habits. Most people are able to concentrate completely on well-presented subjects in which they are keenly interested even when their *in* boxes are running over. Some spoken information reaching a staff officer may have little bearing on his immediate activities. Seldom will an entire presentation apply directly to each listener. Even less often, however, will the message be without any value to all. Someone has taken the trouble to pass along information; the mind must be forced to be interested.

Besides being an essential professional skill for every staff officer, good listening is a distinct personal asset that can make life in any headquarters immeasurably more pleasant. Everyone likes a good listener. Passing information is a difficult and demanding art. It becomes an intolerable task when those who should be receiving are tuned out. The vacant stares of those who have mentally returned to their offices, the moving lips of those preparing to get their two cents in and the nodding and shaking heads of those who have decided in advance what is to be said—all are excruciating burdens for those attempting to issue instructions, extend guidance or pass information. Conversely, the silent, attentive listener who appears to cling to each word with avid interest is a relaxing, comforting and ego-building influence.

Staff officers who are receptive and attentive to criticism, recommendations and nonconcurrances in coordinating their papers find all doors open. Their counterparts enjoy working with them and are anxious to assist them. Those who cannot or will not listen soon find themselves isolated. When someone is speaking, *Listen.*

Reading

Large headquarters are paper mills. An action officer might well have hundreds of pages of incoming, outgoing and circulating pages of written material crossing his desk on an average day. This could amount to thousands of words of daily reading. Additionally, most staff officers must consult references and files repeatedly to research problems and accumulate background data. Only fifty 200-word pages of this research could add to the daily reading requirement by as much as ten thousands words. Staggering? Yes! Probably few people realize just *how* staggering.

Reading Speed. Reading improvement classes are taught at many headquarters and in local colleges. Most commanders recognize the value of these classes and encourage all staff members to take that route to increased reading skills. It does not take dramatic results to ease office reading workloads although spectacular speeds in the thousands of words per minute could certainly be used to good advantage. Even student levels would drastically reduce the reading burden, and these should be well within each staff member's capabilities. Reading improvement experts believe that study and improved reading methods can increase reading speed at least fifty percent. Even this modest goal would greatly ease the reading problem. Staff officers should investigate the possibility of attending an approved reading improvement course. If none is available, reading skills still can be improved with effort.

Concentration and Comprehension. Slow readers often share another time-consuming weakness: poor reading comprehension. When slow reading is further hampered by the necessity to reread material several times before it is understood, staff officers are severely handicapped. It is not possible to maintain professional skills without constant study and research. Daily work requirements cannot be understood unless incoming distribution is read. The status of ongoing actions is revealed in outgoing and circulating documents. The data and background material on which actions must be based are buried in massive files.

Staff officers who read slowly face tremendous obstacles to their efforts to become effective members of the team. Those who must slowly reread must find ways of improving if they are to succeed. Educators have identified several causes for poor reading comprehension. Some problems require professional assistance; others disappear with increased reading speed. One major bar to comprehension is poor concentration, which can be largely alleviated by self-help.

Like listening, reading comprehension requires giving one's total attention to the material being presented. Staff officers must discipline their minds to tune out interference and focus entirely on the effort being undertaken. This is particularly important to effective reading. Concentration should eliminate double reading and might improve speed at the same time. Concentration is not easy amid the turmoil of office activities. Many staff officers must have a better environment for their heavy reading. To do this, they report to their offices well in advance of the work day or remain after coworkers have departed.

Reading the daily flow of material, studying professional material and doing research is much easier in quieter surroundings. Many outstanding staff officers who read rapidly with near perfect comprehension prefer to take advantage of the peace and quiet of the early morning and late afternoon to wade through the *in* box, undisturbed by ringing telephones, visitors, calls to the front office, etc.

Young and inexperienced officers may find this practice most beneficial. Their reading requirements should be much greater than their senior counterparts. Not only must they read the daily flow of paper and assist with project research, they should in addition be reading and studying every available reference document to increase their knowledge and improve their professional qualifications.

Outside, unofficial reading is a professional technique practiced by all good staff officers. As has been stressed, military operations have become extremely complex, requiring extensive knowledge of the strategies and tactics of modern armies and the other military services that support and fight with them as well as an appreciation of the military equipment and tactics of other countries. This includes at least general understanding of the myriad scientific and technical devices now available.

Advances, changes and modifications to the machinery of warfare are endless, and the effective staff officer must be qualified to inform his commander of the very latest developments in his field, their impacts and their capabilities and limitations. To keep professionally informed, military officers must read—and read avidly—military publications, trade magazines, books, technical material, etc. Effective reading is an absolute requirement for military personnel of all grades and in all positions. To the staff officer it is an indispensable ingredient of success.

Reading as a Professional Technique. Effective reading involves more than the reading skills needed to assimilate incoming and outgoing information related to current work requirements. In the military, as in all professions, one must read large amounts of material, much of which is only indirectly related to daily operations.

Observation

Last but not least of the receiving communications skills is the ability to observe. Like listening, this may seem a natural skill, unworthy of mention. Not so. Thorough, logical and orderly observation requires mental discipline equal to that required for good listening and reading.

A common story emphasizing most people's poor observation concerns the college professor who asked his class to follow his example in taste-testing a particularly vile chemical compound. Dipping a forefinger carefully into the compound the professor then ceremoniously placed a forefinger into his mouth, his expression mirroring his distaste. With equal ceremony and far greater distaste the entire class followed suit. None observed that the professor dipped the right forefinger but tasted the left.

Law enforcement agencies would find this example easy to believe. They are keenly aware that witnesses to accidents and crimes are seldom capable of describing what occurred and even less often, of agreeing among themselves on just what they saw. Staff officers must do better than that.

Perhaps as much as ninety percent of the responsibility of most commanders involves supervising the activities of subordinates. Assisting in this supervisory function also occupies considerable staff time. Although some supervision can be done at desks—reading reports, analyzing performance data, etc.—this cannot substitute for on-the-ground observation. It is here that the careful observer discovers what actually is happening, can see how well a mission is being accomplished, and can determine to what extent command directives are being followed. This personal, face-to-face supervision can pay big dividends: mistakes can be corrected, plans altered, priorities shifted and, if necessary, changes to commanders' policies and directives recommended. Like other communication skills, observation requires mental discipline and concentration. Its value depends on the observer's skill.

Official visits are not pleasure tours. The visiting staff officer must prepare as carefully as though he were presenting a briefing, writing a document or completing a study. He must determine the missions and major tasks of the units to be visited, identify any known problems and find out what is being done to help solve those problems. The official visitor should review *all* directives, policies and guidance previously provided the units to be visited, and he should do his professional homework.

Good professional observation is only possible if the observer is professionally qualified and knows in advance something about the activities to be observed. For example, a staff visit to an engineer unit building a bridge would be of little value unless the visitor knows something of the bridge being constructed. A nonengineer can hardly become an expert overnight, but he can peruse manuals and references and discuss the bridge project with staff engineers before his visit. Although still far from expert, he will then have some appreciation for the task being undertaken.

This type preparation is essential no matter what the visitor's specialty. All aspects of military activities result from and are governed by the mission. Conditions, situations and operations observed must therefore be analyzed, evaluated and reported in relation to missions.

Commanders cannot be everywhere and cannot see everything for which they are responsible. Staffs must serve as their commanders' eyes. Each staff officer must discipline himself to focus his entire attention on the activities surrounding him, analyzing all aspects of military operations and support functions in relation to his commanders' directives and guidance, weighing them professionally against accepted, proven practices and storing them away for future reference and reporting.

Sending

To the staff officer, the most important personal skills are those which enable him to transmit his professional knowledge and the results of his efforts to commanders, supervisors, fellow action officers, and staff members of other headquarters. Staff officers should be multi-skilled, dedicated and loyal, and willing to work long, demanding hours.

The absence of those qualities can be offset to some extent by close supervision. However, some production can be achieved by relatively inept, lazy staff officers whose concepts of integrity and loyalty are casual to say the least, if they can speak or write effectively. The most diligent and skillful staff officer is virtually worthless to fellow workers, supervisors and commanders if he cannot express himself. To be successful, staff officers must speak *and* write effectively. To survive professionally, they must speak *or* write effectively.

The criterion by which military writers and speakers are measured is effectiveness. Golden-throated oratory is not needed, nor is flowing literary grace. Admirable as those qualities may be in politicians, lecturers and novelists, they could handicap military staff officers. Eloquent rhetoric and glittering prose are most useful for entertaining listeners and readers or for selling propositions that cannot be or have not been substantiated with facts. To the professional audiences faced by military speakers, and the technical experts who critique military writers, oratory and literary genius have little to do with effectiveness.

Although this book will not cover either public speaking or English composition, their importance is critical. All staff officers should try to improve their speaking and writing abilities. Following are some generally applicable suggestions based on and garnered from thousands of oral and written presentations that sold and from at least equal numbers that fell on their faces.

Know the Subject. Staff officers are busy people, faced constantly with short deadlines and the urging of equally busy supervisors. Staff officers are also human, subject to physical and mental fatigue. As the day progresses, sifting through files, regulations, manuals and other references becomes increasingly onerous; consultation with other experts becomes nerve-jangling; even deep thinking becomes a burden. The temptation to speak or write "from the hip" often becomes almost overpowering. That temptation must be overcome.

Readers and listeners also are busy, tired, sometimes irritable, and almost always anxious to get on to other matters. They are always critical, usually in a positive way, but critical nevertheless, demanding that all hypotheses be substantiated by hard, cold data and supported by objective, logical rationale. The speaker or writer cannot expect that even the smallest omission of pertinent data will go undetected, or the smallest technical inaccuracy, unchallenged. There can be no shortcuts or bluffing in professionalism.

Staffs are professional teams, and their commanders are demanding managers, insisting that each player meet high professional standards. Beautiful footwork and graceful swings with the bat impress neither coaches nor fellow team members. They also are professionals and are impressed only with results. They expect professional presentations, whether written or oral and demand professional integrity. Considerable weakness in form can be forgiven if the speaker or writer has obvious command of the subject matter.

Organization. Most headquarters prescribe formats for many written documents, and some issue similar outlines to be used in formal oral presentations to the commander and his senior assistants. These are good practices. They simplify the work of writers and speakers and prepare readers and listeners by providing a program or order in which material will be presented. Where formats have not been prescribed, and for minor actions such as written memoranda or telephone conversations, staff officers should organize their material for maximum effectiveness. The commanding general may demand that written memoranda, information papers and reports to him stay within maximum lengths (usually short), that oral presentations confine themselves to specified time limits (usually brief), and that both oral and written material be organized for easy understanding. Unfortunately, fellow action officers and junior supervisors are less able to make such demands. The hapless souls on the receiving end of rambling, disjointed telephone calls are at the mercy of the speaker. Organization is the key to effectiveness.

The objective of organization is to present material in logical sequence so that the receiver (listener or reader) can assimilate it in the light of information already available to him, follow the presenter's rationale and, hopefully, share the presenter's conclusions. There is no magic formula for achieving this organization. Each reader or listener reacts to different stimuli. Each mind receives, sorts, evaluates and stores information differently. With each reader or listener, information falls on different levels of background data and different areas of staff interests.

In the absence of other guidance, the following general organizational structure can be tailored to fit almost any situation from the most informal phone call to formal briefings for very senior commanders, from notes to the action officer at the next desk to formal letters prepared for a commanding general's signature.

Introduction. Numerous words such as *purpose, problem, situation, subject, topic,* and so on, could be used to identify this portion of written and oral presentations. Each is appropriate in certain instances. No matter what it is called, the objective is always the same: to let the recipient know what is coming.

This is the alert signal, and it can work two ways. Readers and listeners should be able to deduce from this introduction the extent of their personal involvement and the possible effects in their areas of interest. This alert is even more important in lesser actions than in more significant papers and formal briefings. Those usually come after considerable discussion, coordination, and preliminary actions. Most interested persons will know in advance what to expect. The action officer who returns to his desk to find a handwritten note, the supervisor who receives an unexpected visitor, and the busy staff member who answers his phone do not share those advantages. Let them know immediately what is to be talked or written about.

Background. Just as the introduction alerts the receivers on the topic to be discussed, the background explains why it is to be discussed, reminding readers or listeners of the past actions, other written and oral material, and current situations bearing on the subject matter which make writing or speaking appropriate. It sets the stage.

Discussion. Having informed the reader or listener of what is to be discussed and why it is to be discussed, discuss it. This is the meat of the written or oral presentation. It should be organized for maximum effect. Organization of the discussion depends on the situation. The estimate and staff study analysis processes are offered as dependable examples which can be modified to fit most situations.

1. Analyze all factors that could influence the matter.
2. Identify all possible courses of action. Even the simplest subject deserving conversation or the briefest note usually has alternatives. If so, they deserve mention. Failure to identify all possible alternatives could cast doubt on the objectivity of the presentation and set readers' and listeners' minds off on independent tangents, their interest and concentration lost.
3. Weigh alternatives against influencing factors and discuss favorable and adverse impacts of each factor on each alternative. This is the time to discard infeasible actions.
4. Compare alternatives. Discuss each alternative in relation to the others, pointing out the advantages and disadvantages of each. Integrity demands objectivity here; however, speakers and writers should present their favored solutions in the best legitimate light. This often is best achieved by presenting the favorite last and discussing the advantages after the disadvantages. This in no way implies that any part of the discussion should be slanted, that the facts should be distorted, or that factors should be omitted to favor the presenter's position. But when a professional staff officer is convinced that one position above all others favors the commander's mission, integrity also demands that he use every honest means to sell that position.

Conclusions. This important portion of any presentation is subject to much abuse and misuse. A common failing is to conclude with, verbatim, the recommendations to be repeated in the next part of the presentation. Perhaps this could be avoided by considering this portion as a summary rather than a set of conclusions. Remember that this is not the recommendation. It is the presenter's opportunity to sum up, to lead the readers or listeners persuasively along the path of logical rationale that led the presenter to conclude that his position is better than all others.

Recommendation. This is the payoff and may not necessarily be a recommendation. It can be a request, a suggestion, the significance of the information being presented, or the status of actions underway. Whatever the purpose of this final punch line, well organized papers or oral presentations should lead directly and logically to it. If they do not, then something is wrong. This checklist is a handy tool for testing recommendations: 1. Does it meet the promises of the introduction completely? 2. Is it in line with the background? 3. Is it compatible with and supported by all facets of the discussion? 4. Is it consistent with the conclusions?

Vocabulary. Most commanders and staff officers are educated well above the national norm. They have and need large vocabularies because the military business has become a technical and scientific one. Staff officers who are weak in this department should initiate improvements immediately. The more words at one's command, the better one's chances of success as a staff officer. However, these verbal tools must be used with extreme caution, or they may prove counterproductive. For the most part, a large vocabulary is for receiving (reading and listening). Smaller, more familiar words requiring little thought are more effective—in speaking and in writing.

Speaking

At all command levels, considerable oral information is passed between staff members, to and from the commanders, and to and from higher and subordinate headquarters. These oral interchanges range from casual phone calls, chance meetings in corridors and coffee shops, and informal and formal reports and conferences to full-scale briefings with stage settings worthy of a Broadway production. The importance of learning to listen to and receive this type of communication has been emphasized.

No matter how simple or elaborate the presentation, the listener must discipline himself to hear it and to dig out whatever meat may be hidden in its depth. A skilled speaker can certainly make the listener's job easier, and a well prepared and logical presentation makes it much easier for the speaker to hold the listener's interest.

Official Conversations. Inept, rambling official conversations are possibly the greatest squanderers of a staff officer's most precious asset—time. Many staff members, tend to ramble on and on, talking all around the subject. This condition seems to be severely aggravated by telephones, and unfortunately, the more critically a person suffers from this condition, the greater seems to be his fascination with the telephone.

Many action officers who write the simplest memorandum in an organized manner, and who prepare for each formal oral presentation as though their careers depended on that one performance, do not hesitate to grab the phone, drop in, or collar coworkers in hallways to discuss important subjects with absolutely no preparation or forethought. Such a waste of time and effort is unforgivable. Before picking up the phone, stopping someone in the hallway, or dropping in on good old what's-his-name, *think.* Is there really something to say? Valid information to impart? Assistance to request? A supportable recommendation to be made? If not, forget it for the moment.

Approach official conversation with the same professionalism devoted to writing letters, messages, studies, estimates, or to delivering major briefings. Avoid those who do not. Productive staff officers can ill afford the luxury of long rambling conversations. They must learn to cut them off, inoffensively if possible, offensively if necessary.

Exceptions do arise. Situations develop in which conversation is necessary, and either time or circumstances prohibit complete preparation. Problems may arise which lie completely outside an individual officer's area of expertise. Obviously, preparation to discuss the details of this subject would be difficult. He must have help from the experts.

In such cases the best approach is to refine the problem at least to the point of stating its importance to and impact on other matters. Bridge engineering experts should not be forced into a long, pointless, technical discussion of stream-crossing methods with an action officer who only needs to know whether a bridge is available that can be erected within a certain time, span a certain gap, and meet specific traffic requirements. Similarly, operators should not be forced into philosophical harangues over the pros and cons of the techniques of an approaching operation with engineers whose only official concern may be the roads to be used.

Formal Oral Presentations (except briefings and conference presentations). The lines between military conversations and formal presentations are dim indeed. Inexperienced staff officers should be very slow to attempt the definition. The newcomer can expect that virtually everyone whom he will speak to, report to, brief, or consult with will be superior to him in knowledge if not in grade. He should regard the term "informal" with suspicion. He should not take too literally invitations to "drop in and discuss your progress with me" or "read this and let me know what you think." The informality is informality of bearing—not of presentation. Be prepared to talk professionally, convincingly and from a background of research and preparation.

In this discussion the term *formal presentation* encompasses virtually all oral exchange between action officers and their supervisors, particularly their commanders. This can include reports, orientation, and information exchanges with action officers and supervisors from other staff elements and other headquarters.

Most college level, public speaking courses require three hours of instruction each week through an entire semester. In addition to the many hours of platform instruction, the students have the benefit of textbooks averaging some five hundred pages. Though most staff officers have had the benefit of college level courses on the subject, university classroom instruction does not always prepare the student for some unique aspects of military speaking, chief among which is the nature of the audiences. Staff officers are occasionally called upon to speak about their specialties to to visitors with little background knowledge or to address local civilian groups with no military experience. Far more often the military speaker finds himself addressing the supervisors and commanders in whose hands rests his professional success or failure. Even when this is not the case, his listeners are invariably experts in the subject on which he must speak. Military listeners may be on the one hand reassuring and on the other intimidating: they are intently interested in and critically concerned with all things military, they demand factual support for opinion and they are impatient with inept performances. Thus, military speakers face some challenges not anticipated in the public speaking classroom, and techniques for meeting those challenges are worth discussing.

Emotional Control. Most people approach formal speaking with some trepidation and a feeling of inadequacy. When the listeners are senior members of the same profession, equal in technical expertise and far superior in experience, trepidation can turn to horror. Add to these, supervisors and commanders and his condition might well approach terrified panic. This is a natural, and for most, never completely conquered unpleasant adjunct to oral presentations. In fact, some apprehension is beneficial. It prompts more thorough preparation, makes the speaker more aware of his audience, and increases his sensitivity to the listeners' reactions. However, fear must be controlled so that it does not interfere with the presentation; preferably to the point that it is undetectable. Stuttering, stammering, quavering voices, trembling lips, and fluttering hands are very distracting to listeners. Even the slightest signs of nervousness and apprehension lessen the speaker's effectiveness. A calm, self-assured manner imparts an automatic confidence in the speaker which no spoken words can match.

For the military speaker, the best cure for stage fright is an objective analysis of his position. Why must he speak? The answer is obvious and reassuring—he has knowledge not available to or not understood by others. He is being asked (or directed) to share that knowledge so that others can use it to do their jobs. In other words, the speaker is an important person. For a moment, however brief, he will be the dominant figure in some segment of the staff. This realization should ease the panic and replace terror with more realistic apprehensions concerning abilities to transmit the information.

Interest also is an effective balm for nervous tensions. Once the speaker realizes that he has been selected because he alone is considered most qualified and best informed on the subject, his interest in getting the information across should block out other emotions. When he has developed a good, logical presentation, self confidence should have all but erased earlier anxieties. However, some disquietude may remain due to the nature of the audience.

Understanding the Listeners. Renowned speakers of history who have affected worldwide religious concepts, stirred nations to conquests or heroic defenses, or led international political movements have differed greatly in purity of motivation. However, they all shared one essential attribute: they knew their audiences. This understanding is even more essential to the military speaker because his entire presentation must be tailored to suit a single listener or group.

Consider for example the situation of a junior logistical expert who must talk on a serious supply shortage. Senior commanders' interests probably will be broad, limited to major effects on overall missions and welfare of the total force. Operational staff officers' interests will be more specific and related to specific actions planned or underway. Senior logisticians' concerns will be more detailed, encompassing other logistical functions that might be affected—transportation, construction, maintenance and services. Supply experts will want the "nuts and bolts" and minute technical details. Therefore, the speaker must know to whom he will speak—the commander, the operator, the senior staff logistician, or supply experts—it makes a difference.

The difference is equally important to the formal briefer and to the action officer who grabs the phone to advise a coworker. Take time to study and understand the potential listener, then prepare and present accordingly. Understanding the audience pays off in two ways: it reduces the speaker's alienation from the listener and, as a result, it increases effectiveness. The unknown usually is somewhat frightening but it is difficult to be excessively apprehensive of those situations, conditions or people that are familiar and understood.

Types of Speeches. Unless official conversations are considered as separate types of oral presentations, military speeches fall into the same categories taught in public speaking classrooms: written, memorized, impromptu, and extemporaneous.

Written Speeches (read by presenter). Almost every commander and staff supervisor has strong feelings for or against being read to. There are advantages:

1. Written speeches can be approved in advance, thus allowing supervisors and technical experts to assure absolute accuracy.

2. Written speeches can be coordinated, assuring that the presentation represents the view of the entire staff.

3. Written speeches can be rehearsed verbatim, allowing supervisors an advance look at the speaker and opportunities to offer advice and assistance in developing a more professional product.

4. Written speeches on sensitive or controversial matters become permanent records of the message delivered.

Disadvantages also exist:

1. Few people are accomplished oral readers and this often results in audiences' hearing a monotonous drone, more conducive to sleep than attention.
2. Most readers have difficulty maintaining eye contact with listeners, thus losing the advantage of audience reaction.
3. Interrupting questions can be disastrous if they delve into portions of the presentation yet to be delivered.
4. Most significantly, written speeches are written documents and as such, could be read silently, more quickly, and with better comprehension than listening usually affords.

Regardless of personal preferences, written speeches are unavoidable and every staff officer occasionally finds himself reading to a roomful of people.

For most, writing a paper to be delivered orally is an extremely difficult job, especially during the preparation stage. Few people write and speak in the same manner and even material written by the most accomplished writer tends to assume an abruptness and a somewhat stilted style of composition not used in speaking. Yet, written or not, these are oral presentations and must sound like them. Regardless of how often rehearsed, critiqued, rewritten, rerehearsed, etc., they must retain a sufficient appearance of spontaneity for the listener to believe he is receiving first hand, the views of the speaker in the speaker's words. A few staff officers can write excellent speeches on the first attempt, but most must labor. Possibly the best approach is to write with little regard for the manner of delivery, concentrating on subject matter and organization of the material. When satisfied with this, read the speech aloud and revise the wording to match normal diction. While doing this, most inexperienced staff officers will be surprised to discover that they use many words in writing which they never speak. This oral examination serves two purposes: it gets the material into acceptable condition for presentation, and it is a form of repeated rehearsal.

Memorized Speeches. Some staff officers who are either prohibited by local policy from delivering written speeches, or who wish to give an impression of spontaneity, choose to memorize the material to be delivered. Some succeed, but repeating memorized lines in a natural, believable manner requires theatrical skills which few staff officers possess. Unless directed by supervisors to do so, most speakers would be well advised to forego the memory method.

A young and inexperienced officer may find it a particularly treacherous route to speaking success, for when he finds himself addressing a group of austere looking superiors, no matter how reliable his memory, the pressure can tax it. Sometimes a speaker may go completely blank. This can leave him in an awkward position and will usually destroy the cogency of his speech. If, for some reason, a speech must be memorized, the best guarantee of success is repeated rehearsal and research. The rehearsals lessen the chances of going blank and the research prepares a fall-back position in the event that blankness should occur. By becoming thoroughly familiar with the subject matter, the speaker can convert to extemporaneous speaking.

Extemporaneous Speaking. Many experts consider an extemporaneous presentation the most effective form of official communication, and for good reasons.

The extemporaneous presentation creates an intimacy between speaker and listener not possible in any other form of communication. Readings, memorized speeches and written material can only attempt to gauge the listeners' levels of interest, their technical background, their preconceived ideas and their preferences. Without exception, these are prepared in advance and are received by the listener or reader in that form, appropriate or not. To a large extent the extemporaneous presentation is a combined effort created simultaneously by both speaker and listener.

Preparation differs from written and memorized speeches only in some details, not in thoroughness. Most staff officers, at least once, make the mistake of believing that preparation is unnecessary. Extemporaneous presentations by experts are deceptive; the inexperienced observer can easily be mislead into believing that the speaker is relying solely on his personal store of professional information and has not found research, preparation, or rehearsals necessary. The more relaxed, natural and easy the presentation, the stronger (and more deceptive) the impression becomes that the speech is impromptu and unprepared.

The extemporaneous speaker faces all the challenges of the reader and the memorizer and in addition he must be able to "think on his feet." He also must be able to read listener reaction, livening the speech up to alleviate signs of boredom, clarifying points to offset the lack of understanding reflected on wrinkled brows—he must keep in tune with the audience. Make no mistake, the good speaker is prepared.

The good extemporaneous speaker may, like the memorizer, write his entire speech and rehearse it several times or more, but he does not memorize it. Instead, after sufficient rehearsals, the expert extemporaneous speaker usually will rehearse many more times using outlines or notes from the prepared text, converting the script to his own words as he goes along. This approach affords the speaker maximum flexibility. He confronts his listeners convinced that he has something worthwhile to say, confident that he is prepared to say it. However, he is not tied to preordained words, tones and gestures which may, or may not, suit the audience. Being free from script, written or memorized, the speaker can respond to audience reaction. For the doubter, he can supply additional substantiating data; for the confused an example; for those anxious to get to the point, he can omit the extraneous; for those whose interests are aroused, he can supply more information. Experienced listeners will recognize and respond to an expert speaker at work and only the most naive beginner will believe that it was easy.

Impromptu Speeches. Staff officers exist to advise and assist. Supervisors, commanders and coworkers expect each staff member to provide that advice and assistance whenever asked. A few experts live up to those expectations most of the time; most experienced, productive staff officers meet the requirement much of the time; but the newcomer to staff work seldom has the answer (this will be understood). The "dud" is safe, he will not be asked. The point is that no one can be prepared for all possible questions all of the time. This brings us to the most difficult statement staff officers ever have to make, I don't know! When this is the only accurate response, make it. While not the most popular response from an expert, it ranks far above bluster and bluff.

Secondly, the staff beginner caught in the impromptu presentation must understand exactly what is required and confine his presentation to precisely that. If asked what time it will be in London when it is 0800 in New York, do not give an unsolicited briefing on the international time zone system. Just answer the question, consider it a successful encounter, and sit down.

Third, and most important, substitute extemporaneous presentations for impromptu responses wherever possible. How? By doing what the experts do—homework: Everyone admires the brilliant staff officer who, when asked a question, pops to his feet and discourses eloquently on the most mintue details of his area of interest as it relates to a most complex mission-oriented problem. Impromptu? Nonsense! Though the expert speaker has only a vague notion that a presentation will be required of him, he prepares and rehearses as carefully as if he had been scheduled to speak.

Throughout this book we have stressed the vital importance of every staff officer being constantly well informed not only in his area of interest but in the situations around him as well. *All* good staff officers adhere to this practice. However, knowledge is of no value unless it can be withdrawn and related properly to those who can use it. Consequently experienced staff officers not only gather information; they sort it, weigh it, evaluate it, classify it in relation to other information, and store it in a form that will be readily understood. The expert speaker recognizes possible delivery conditions and plans his presentation and as an additional safeguard against surprise, he reviews his information before exposing himself to possible questions, making certain that it is complete and thorough. When called upon to perform, the expert's presentation is far from impromptu.

Inexperienced staff officers must learn that official invitations to attend briefings, conferences, meetings, etc. do not reflect the invitee's popularity. He is not there to enjoy himself, he is there to contribute. If the newcomer doubts this, he has but to watch his more experienced coworkers head for the files and references when summoned for an "impromptu speech."

Mechanics of Good Speaking. To this point we have stressed preparation, discussed types of presentations, and offered a lot of general advice. Readers may be asking, When do I get the formula for instant success? The answer is simple, you don't! In fact most of us must face the fact that we shall never be golden throated orators but we can, and we must, develop sufficient capabilities for effective oral communication with our fellow professionals. With that in mind, here are some techniques which have proven helpful to many.

Language—Keep it simple. For unknown reasons, speakers often feel that their conversational vocabulary is inadequate or too drab for the speaker's platform. If your usual vocabulary is unsuitable for the platform, then it is unsuitable for conversation.

Affectation—Be yourself. It is impossible to manufacture a new personality for use on the military speaker's platform. Fellow staff officers become quite familiar with their coworkers' normal characteristics, and any differences at the rostrum sound false and disturb rather than impress listeners.

Gestures—Use with caution. Gestures are useful to the professional speaker, they lend emphasis and may tend to ease the tensions of public exposure; but to those who have not mastered them, gestures may be nothing more than a distraction. Gestures accent muscles already frozen by terror, and joints locked in place by stage fright never gesticulate easily.

Words and sentences—Let verbs and nouns retain their normal syntax. Verbs that are remodeled and converted into nouns become listless helpers and evoke little audience response. Nouns perform just as poorly when distorted into verbs. Verbs perform better when used to portray action, the more vigorous the better. Nouns, on the other hand, are used to represent people, places, things, conditions, and states of being, etc. The illegitimate pronouns are also culprits that can destroy listener concentration. Pronouns should clearly refer to the nouns they modify. Make listening easy.

Audience contact—Look at the listeners, do not ignore them. People maintain higher levels of interest if they believe that the speaker is speaking directly to them.

Humor—When in doubt, do not try it. Some experienced military speakers use jokes and anecdotes with some effectiveness (usually less than they imagine) in enlivening their presentations. To be effective, humor must meet several criteria: it must be used skillfully, applicable to the subject matter, and suited to the audience. Few people tell jokes well even in favorable circumstances and even fewer understand jokes well. Only the most skilled raconteur can insert humor into military presentations without weakening rather than strengthening audience empathy.

Unity—From introduction to final word, keep the subject in the forefront of the presentation. Do not digress into unrelated areas.

Accuracy—Get it right. Nothing destroys listener confidence more quickly than factual errors. Check, double check and recheck all factual data. If the slightest doubt remains, either alert the listener to the unverified nature of the data or do not use it at all.

Clarity—Keep it simple and direct. Interest dissipates when listeners must search for meanings among loosely connected or extraneous verbiage.

Coherence—Present material in a logical sequence. Organize the presentation and stick with that organization.

Objectivity—Tell it like it is. Americans, including military commanders and staffs, have a high resistance to salesmanship. Reactions to pitches are certain to be negative. Speakers must present *all* sides of their subjects, fairly weigh all alternatives, and fully state disadvantages of their positions as well as the advantages of conflicting positions.

Completeness—Tell the complete story; be concise, coherent, accurate, objective and, above all, thorough.

Writing

In previous chapters several references have been made to the massive paper flow into, within and out of every Army headquarters. Young staff officers should hardly be surprised to find that writing consumes large amounts of their time. It should be apparent that staff officers' productivity and professional success depend on their abilities to communicate in writing.

Except for speaking, writing represents the only means for converting staff efforts into usable, transferable information and for visibly demonstrating skills, energy, dedication and productivity. Effective writing is an essential skill for every staff officer and, as in speaking, *effectiveness* is the overriding criterion by which military writing is judged. This does not imply that basic rules of composition are unimportant, or that violation of those rules does not affect productivity and efficiency ratings. To the contrary, most commanders and their senior assistants are excellent grammarians and demand that written work meet high standards compatible with the elevated educational backgrounds of most staff members. Commanders demand high quality work because well written papers reflect professionalism and more importantly, they are less susceptible to misunderstanding and misinterpretation.

But literary perfection alone does not assure effectiveness. Most supervisors will tolerate some mistakes in spelling, punctuation and sentence structure if the subject matter is good and valid points are well made. Supervisors and commanders may even be willing to improve the composition themselves. Few supervisors will tolerate papers that fail to make their points, regardless of how beautifully they may be written.

Effectiveness. Compared to the speaker, the military writer works at a distinct disadvantage and with far greater demands for precision. Speakers deliver their material face-to-face with the listener and if they do not seem to be getting their points across, they can adjust their deliveries to correct the weakness. Even the telephone caller can detect the responsiveness of his listener and adjust as necessary. If, on his first attempt, the speaker fails to impart his information or make his point, he is available to answer questions, present additional data, strengthen rationale and expand explanations. Writers enjoy none of these second chances; their work must stand alone with its recipient. The writer seldom is present to defend, modify, strengthen or amplify his work. Therefore, staff officers must learn early in their careers that few tasks will be as demanding, as closely scrutinized by supervisors, or as difficult to complete successfully as written documents. If a staff officer is to succeed, he must learn to write *effectively*.

Writing Techniques. Military leaders recognize the importance of good writing and the necessity for improving those skills. Several excellent references offer sound advice and new guides are published frequently. Additionally, many large headquarters present frequent "military writing" classes. Every staff officer should take the time to study available reference publications and attend the classes. The following seven subparagraphs discuss the most important points contained in military references and emphasized in classes. These discussions are not substitutes for either the material or the classroom work; their intent is to whet the readers' appetites for additional research and study.

Clarity—Clarity of expression is the most important requirement for writing effectively. A paper cannot be effective if the reader has the slightest doubt about its meaning. Military writers must choose each word, construct each sentence and arrange each paragraph carefully to assure that their meanings are clear.

Words: Large vocabularies are for receiving, not sending. Words which the average person uses every day are less likely to be misunderstood than fancy, obscure words. Concrete words that deal with specific people, places and things and with descriptions that can be weighed or measured, paint clearer pictures than less specific, abstract words. Active words are more interesting than drab, passive words. Effective writing begins with effective words.

Sentences: Clear expression is not only a matter of using the proper words, it is also a matter of controlling those words in sentence construction. Like individual words, sentences must be structured for easy reading, precision and sufficient activity to grasp and hold the reader's interest. In constructing sentences and clauses, maintain a simple, logical order: subject, predicate, object, with adjectives preceding the words they modify. Basic as these reminders seem, they are keys to both easy reading and understanding. They are mentioned here because military writers often appear to approach them in reverse. Many military writers convert good, strong active verbs into nouns that make immobile sentence subjects, while they transform nouns into very weak verbs. Altered verbs and nouns make reading very difficult, and meaning very nebulous.

We do not suggest that military writing be reduced to preschool levels, we do suggest that standard sentence structures are easy to read and easy to understand, and that the parts of speech best play the positions for which they were designed.

Paragraphs: Words and sentences seem to be the real villians in military writing. Most people have little trouble assembling sentences into clear paragraphs. However, one or two reminders may be helpful.

In a sense, paragraphs are mini-compositions complete within themselves. The military writer uses them to express complete phases of his rationale. The completed paper can be no clearer than its component paragraphs. Therefore, writers must arrange the sentences within each paragraph in logical order to lead the reader into a particular thought, show him its validity, bring him out satisfied and, most importantly, agreeing with the writer. Paragraphs, like complete papers, must be arranged clearly. Clarity is the prime criterion of effective writing.

Brevity—Commanders and staff officers are busy people and have no time for verbosity, oral or written. With the rambling speaker, however, there are chances of getting him to the point by polite or, if necessary, impolite urging. When confronted by the same rambling on paper there is little recourse. Surprisingly, brevity seems to be the most difficult criterion for most young staff officers to meet. They seldom have problems finding enough to write; on the contrary, they have trouble finding a stopping place.

Another oddity related to lengthy writing seems to be an inverse ratio between knowledge and length. Surprisingly, it is the top logistician who can summarize a complex, theater wide supply situation in a one page memorandum. A young lieutenant newly assigned as third assistant S-4 in an infantry battalion probably would require more space to describe a toilet paper shortage. Thus the first rule for brevity is clear: know the subject.

Lack of knowledge invariably results in generalizations. Facts and logical assumptions lend themselves to short sentences that require little embellishment and no repetition. Generalizations, on the other hand, become verbose to disguise the weaknesses. Unfamiliar official matters are even more difficult to present briefly.

Another tip to those seeking brevity is to avoid meaningless adjectives and adverbs. The old truism that "words mean to the speaker (or writer) what he intends for them to mean, and to the listener (or reader) what he wants them to mean," applies to most adjectives and adverbs. A big, huge, tremendous, rapid, deep, etc. river has one meaning to a person from the arid Southwest, another to one from the banks of the Mississippi. This does not mean brevity should be achieved at the expense of all descriptive words. However, in the interest of brevity, seek out and destroy meaningless or indefinite descriptive words and passages. Regardless of its impressive sound, "the extremely significant, mission damaging, adverse impact" of an ammunition shortage says less than a simple statement of the number of days' supply remaining.

Accuracy—Next to loyalty, the most prevalent characteristic of successful staff officers is dependability. This attribute includes many factors such as punctuality, dedication, responsiveness, etc.; but the essential quality is absolute honesty which includes accuracy in all statements, written or oral. Passing along as fact, information and data which have not been positively verified is dishonest. No other shortcoming can destroy a staff officer's effectiveness, or his career, as quickly as a reputation for passing undependable information.

Accuracy is important in every phase of staff communications—coordination, informal liaison, telephone calls, casual conversations, and written material. It is most important to writers. Speakers have several opportunities to qualify their information as they present it, reveal their sources, recalculate, and even make on the spot changes if errors are discovered; but the writer has only one chance. Successful staff officers are keenly aware that any factual or mechanical error will destroy the effectiveness not only of the work containing it, but their future work as well.

Young staff officers should develop work habits that assure accuracy: research carefully, refer accurately, double check data, prove mathematical computations, and verify *all* information received from others. Above all, label all data and information which have even a small chance of inaccuracy or incompleteness. All good staff officers take these precautionary measures to assure accuracy, and outstanding officers repeat these steps; they check, recheck and double check their work. This approach pays off in the increased confidence of commanders, supervisors and fellow workers.

Coherence—If speakers wander from their subjects or present their material in haphazard order, listeners can ask questions and guide the conversation along logical avenues of reasoning. The reader faced with an illogical sequence of ideas on paper has no such advantages, although he does have choices: he can assume that such disorganized material must be worthless, and discard it; he can struggle through the paper, mentally rearrange the material, and laboriously dig out its meaning; or, and most probable, he can return it to the writer for rewrite. Along with any of these options, the reader will certainly take evasive action to avoid that writer's future efforts. Coherence can be considered an adjunct of clarity. Papers can never be clear if their information is not presented in logical order, with a readable transition between ideas.

Completeness—Completed staff work is discussed elsewhere, but one aspect of completeness is particularly important in effective military writing. When military documents culminate in a recommendation, suggestion, proposal, request, or a conclusion requiring action, the documents should contain all information and data needed to take that action. This applies to formal major staff efforts such as estimates, studies, and plans, and to the less glamorous, day-to-day actions.

For example, a memorandum to a supervisor or commander recommending that a letter be written to guide the efforts of subordinate commanders should have a proposed letter attached. Proposals for conferences or briefings should be complete with agendas, dates, participants, proposed presentations, and administrative details. Even a note to a fellow worker informing him of a call to be returned should include all information needed to make the call: caller's name and organization, assignment, subject to be discussed, urgency, when he will be available, and, by all means, the caller's phone number.

Military writers must check one other element of their writing to assure completeness—completeness of organization and compatibility of the parts of their presentation. This is discussed in more detail under organization of material, but it is worth repeating briefly:

1. Does the introduction (purpose, statement of the problem, etc.) completely cover the subject to be presented?
2. Is background information keyed and limited to the subject?
3. Does the discussion include all aspects of the subject—and nothing else?
4. Are conclusions complete; do they reflect the entire subject and all valid points of contention?
5. Do recommendations cover the entire problem?

Objectivity—Staff officers are, in a sense, salesmen. Having decided that one course of action is preferable to all others and is in the best interest of the country and the command mission, integrity and loyalty demand that every honest effort be made to have that course of action accepted. Unlike the used car salesman, staff officers' efforts to sell their product must include accurate and unbiased accounts of the advantages and disadvantages of competing courses of action, as well as the disadvantages of their own. Deception of any kind will probably be detected; military customers are experts in their markets.

Briefings

In the military, briefings have become a way of life. Briefings are special communications techniques, probably developed to save the time of very senior leaders by presenting information to them in the quickest, simplest and most expedient method possible. They are still used for that purpose, but their uses have been expanded to cover a wide variety of situations where information is passed to others quickly with little effort on the recipients' part. Briefings are particularly well suited to those occasions when several people must be informed on the same subject in a short time frame.

Purposes

Platoon leaders, non-commissioned officers and administrative assistants may find many occasions to brief their commanders on the status of projects in their area of interest, or subordinates and fellow workers on the intricacies of technical procedures. The Secretary of Defense may be called upon to brief Congressional Committees on defense requirements. Between those extremes almost every member of the Armed Forces becomes a briefer much more often than he would prefer. To staff officers, these are routine occurrences and they must be mastered and perfected as a means of communication.

One of the most common briefing situations to confront action officers relates to their normal, day-to-day functions. In many large headquarters it is customary for action officers to brief their proposed action papers through each level of supervision, including the commanders. This approach has several advantages. First, some preparation time may be saved by allowing the responsible staff officer to accompany his paper, explain its purpose and background, discuss the influencing factors considered, present his rationale and justify the conclusions and recommendations. To the experienced staff officer this should be simpler and less time-consuming than preparing equally convincing written explanations.

Very important senior visitors often are briefed on a commander's mission and the status of the actions for which the commander is responsible. The scope of this type briefing varies with the visitors' areas of interest. Senior commanders probably would receive a comprehensive but somewhat broad presentation on all significant activities, while a senior staff officer from a higher headquarters would receive more detailed information on activities in his area of interest. Regardless of scope, briefings for important visitors are apt to be quite theatrical. Newly assigned action officers probably are safe from roles as presenters in these superbriefings, but they can expect to participate in preparing briefing material to be incorporated into the overall presentation.

Briefings are also used to pass along information to other staff officers, with varying degrees of prescribed formality. This usually occurs when an action in one area of interest requires significant input and assistance from other parts of the staff. The staff officer who will coordinate the action and produce the final staff paper can often save time and avoid confusion by briefing other staff officers who will participate in the project. This face-to-face presentation brings the many advantages of oral communication into play.

Briefing purposes can be categorized according to their desired results. When presented to commanders, briefings usually either inform or recommend or both. When presented to others, briefing purposes cover a wider range. They may instruct; very often staff experts are called upon to brief other staff members on procedures or techniques peculiar to their expertise. Briefings also seek approval from supervisors, coordination from other staff officers, and comments from coworkers.

Format

Most commanders and their supervisors have very firm personal preferences for briefing formats when they are the recipients, and for those gala affairs presented for visitors. In the absence of other guidance, briefings can be effectively organized in the same manner as other oral or written presentations: first, begin with introductory remarks to let the briefee know what is coming; second, if appropriate, provide background information to tie the material being presented to available knowledge; third, discuss the subject or present information in logical sequence and conclude with a summary of the discussion; and finally, deliver the punch lines if appropriate (recommendations, requests for assistance, actions to be taken, etc.).

Briefing Techniques. Effective briefings involve the same skills and procedures necessary for the success of any oral presentation. There is one major difference—briefers almost always use visual aids, even when they are not needed. Properly used, they can save time and add to the clarity of the presentation. Aids can take many forms, the most common being hand drafted charts, view graph transparencies, thirty-five millimeter slides, maps, photographs, sample items, film clips, etc. Since briefings are supposed to be brief and to the point, most good briefers let visual aids tell the story to the maximum extent possible. This is a good practice but precautions must be taken: visual aids must be visible—they must be uncluttered and clear, legible to all viewers, and meaningful. When used to make comparisons, aids should have some baseline upon which to register; when used to illustrate performance, they should highlight trends. Most importantly, aids must relate to audience knowledge when used to introduce completely new material and should include some feature that ties back to information already known by those being briefed. It goes without saying, that the quality of the aids can make or break a briefing. Poor aids can become distracting, even irritating. Good aids can go a long way toward selling the presentation. At the same time the text is being written and coordinated, the audio-visual aids should be under construction. The briefer should decide on the type and design of the aids early in the preparation process. Even after making this decision he may have to adjust according to time and availability, but he should have all aids completed in time to meet the rehearsal schedule.

Audio-visual aids play an important part in putting the point over and deserve much attention, including rehearsals on their use. The first rehearsal usually is the briefer's first opportunity to coordinate his aids with his text. Regardless of how many times the briefer has rehearsed, he should check his charts when they are first displayed during the briefing. This is particularly true if they are projected on a screen; focus may need adjusting, or the chart may be upside down or backwards.

Some briefers have the bad habit of reading their aids to the audience—this should be avoided. Another common mistake is to allow too little time per chart. Briefers should watch the senior briefee. He will usually nod when he is finished or it will be apparent when he removes his eyes from the chart. The briefer should also be able to call back and display any chart in his presentation at any time. This requires a numbering system and coordination. Good briefers are never caught without some kind of pointer, and when considerable pointing is needed it can be effectively done by an assistant. It is often expeditious to use an assistant to change charts. Good chart handling in a briefing is almost as interesting to watch as good ball handling in any sport.

Rehearsals. As a fundamental rule, all formal briefings should be rehearsed. In fact, they should be rehearsed until they are near perfect because, in formal briefings, near perfection is expected. In the first three or four rehearsals something can always be improved. Rehearsals help perfect timing, diction, use of aids, as well as content and clarity, and build confidence as the briefing smooths into a professional presentation. Rehearsals also provide another advantage—those observing the rehearsal can pick the presentation apart for possible questions. The smart briefer will have a list of anticipated questions and ready answers in his hip pocket.

Conferences

Most that has been said about speaking, writing and briefings also applies to conferences. They are used extensively to accomplish staff business. On most staffs, conferences outnumber briefings and in a large headquarters dozens of conferences may occur in a single day. Like briefings, conferences take many forms, the most common being several officers gathered to discuss approaches to an action or solutions to a problem. From there up the possibilities are almost unlimited, with the annual worldwide senior commanders conference near the peak. Major conferences may involve a hundred or more conferees. The degree of formality depends on many factors and covers a broad range.

Conference Planning

Officers planning conferences must consider in detail the objectives, time available, participants, coordination, facilities, security, audio-visual aids, and follow up actions. Large conferences present numerous other considerations which might include travel to and from the conference site, living accommodations, local transportation, escorts, social activities, advance material, agenda, and reports on proceedings. Larger conferences are major productions. Planning groups often are needed to plan conferences of this scope.

Conferences, large or small, must be planned on an organized basis. Objectives must be fixed; they must be attainable within the time available and they must address only the problems at hand. For a formal conference, planned objectives should be controlled by a firm preannounced agenda. Objectives are also important for informal conferences and should be controlled by an agenda, but the leader can state them at the outset and as often thereafter as necessary. Conferences not proceeding toward their objectives are wasting time. Their objectives and agendas must be planned.

The conference planner should select conferees with great care and participation in a conference should be limited to those who have interests and something to contribute. The total present should be the least number needed to get the job done, and conference results can be coordinated with those who were left out.

The Staff Officers' Functions in Conferences

Action officers may serve several functions in conferences. They may be members of planning committees for major conferences, observers or spectators, or they may even be participants in a major conference. All staff members participate in numerous working level conferences and from time to time are in charge of, or chair, working conferences. It follows then that conference techniques are another area to master.

Staff officers must become expert or at least knowledgeable conferees and skillful chairmen. Productive conference participation calls for some skill and much preparation. The essential skill here is the staff officer's ability to represent his views. This becomes increasingly important when an action officer is heavily outnumbered by opposing views or is badly outranked. Theoretically, rank should not be a factor in a working conference, but it would be somewhat unrealistic to suppose rank would completely vanish at the conference room door—it will not. However, tact, salesmanship, courage, and sound professional rationale can more than offset that disadvantage. Preparation should be as thorough as time allows. Each conferee should know the background and current status of the problem or project to be discussed. Just as importantly, he must know the official position of his supervisors. If not, he must develop one and clear it with his chief who in turn may clear it all the way up through the staff element chief.

In addition to firm positions, broad guidance on the matters to be discussed also provides a comfortable base from which the action officer can operate as the conference develops. Conferences often take unexpected turns, and with broad guidance available the action officer has flexibility. If questions supersede his guidance he can either extrapolate or seek additional guidance. It also helps to know opposing positions in advance. Many times it is known prior to a conference that all parties are not in agreement. The conferee who knows what stand others will take can better prepare his own presentation. This, however, is not the same as two opposing attorneys preparing to go into court. Information on the different staff office positions should be available through informal coordination because, in the last analysis, they are working for the same commander and on the same mission.

Conference Leadership

Action officers acting as conference leaders assume many responsibilities: they arrange for the recording of minutes, arrange times, select facilities, notify participants, and coordinate results. The biggest job, of course, is chairing the conference. Even with small groups this requires skill; with larger groups it requires expertise. Many books have been written, and special courses offered, on the subject of conference leadership. We will not attempt to impart all the required skills and expertise, but some treatment of the basics is necessary.

The conference leader's first challenge is to define the conference objective in terms that will coalesce understanding and foster a spirit of cooperation. The objective should be finite and obtainable within the time allowed for the conference. If the overall objectives are too broad for one session they should be broken up and treated in a series of conferences. When this is done the leader must clarify the objective of each session.

If controversial matter is involved the conference leader's duty may well be some messenger work prior to the conference, making known the conference objective, background, and current status. In return, divergent positions can be identified and time spent on this effort proportionately reduces time spent at the conference table.

After the objectives are established, conference proceedings take many forms. Too many, in fact, to enumerate here. One typical approach, however, is for the conference leader to follow the statement of the objective with some opening remarks outlining the procedures to be used, the agenda and any rules of order he wishes observed. Next, the position of each conferee is solicited. This is then followed by controlled, orderly discussion. Hopefully, this will lead to a consensus.

Discussion is the substance of the conference. It is also the point at which conferences can get out of hand, and here conference leaders meet their biggest challenge. Each conferee must be allowed to present material pertinent to the matter under discussion. Most conferees are prepared to do this quietly, expertly, objectively and convincingly. Unfortunately, conferences attract a few with little to contribute and much to say. The conference leader must guide and control the discussion toward the objectives, and his most difficult task is keeping proceedings on track. It is easy to go astray and he must be attentive to any wandering, limiting the discussion to the objective with a deferential but firm hand. Both perseverance and tact are needed. When he feels the time is appropriate, the leader should summarize the results as agreed upon by the conferees and record those agreements, listing the parties involved.

At times no agreement can be achieved and further discussions without new considerations would be futile. The conference should be adjourned, and new direction and guidance sought. If there is no possibility of an agreement being reached, the objective or the course of action must either be abandoned or debated on a higher level.

Follow-up Actions. After conferences are completed, actions on the agreements can be as important as the conference itself—the results must be translated into some meaningful action. This responsibility normally belongs to the conference leader, but other conferees may be involved in the continuing action.

Conferences have many advantages as a business technique, but they also have some limitations and disadvantages. The wise staff officer will seek an early appreciation of these points and use them to best advantage.

Research

Formal research is a time-consuming staff activity required to assure completeness, accuracy and validity in formal staff actions. This type of required research is discussed in some detail in Chapter 7, "Other Typical Staff Actions." In discussing the professional techniques of successful staff officers, it would be misleading to omit their dedication to thorough research.

To the beginner watching more experienced action officers at work, their obsession with research may not be obvious—they may appear to approach new actions with a casual, *savoir faire* attitude and no apparent interest in, or need for, research. This may reflect the attitude of the few members on every staff who consistently produce unacceptable work, but it is certainly a false impression of the expert. Good staff officers approach even the simplest action carefully and are satisfied only with a complete, accurate and professional job—this demands research.

Some procedures are rudimentary to research on any staff action: all previous correspondence and actions must be reviewed to assure that the current action is compatible with existing policies; facts, assumptions, allegations, and rationale in the upcoming action must be verified; previously used information and data must be rechecked to determine their current validity; and related actions must be reviewed to determine possible ramifications. This kind of research is essential and cannot be overlooked.

Research is arduous, however, some forethought and preparation can make it a simpler, less time-consuming task. Experienced staff officers keep the most frequently used research material close at hand.

Maintaining Data

All headquarters maintain reference libraries containing regulations, circulars, pamphlets, manuals, directories and other publications that govern military activities. In larger headquarters, staff elements and subelements keep comprehensive libraries of reference material pertaining to their areas of interest. Therefore, staff officers have sufficient references available to guide them in almost any action they might undertake and we cannot overemphasize the importance of these references.

To do his job well, however, a staff officer must have available and must use much additional information pertaining to his commander's mission and the factors that influence current operations. Official references are of necessity broad in their application. They are intended for use over long periods of time by military men stationed in many parts of the world. To be useful, therefore, the general information contained in formal references must be supplemented with many bits of information more intimately related to specific actions. Each staff officer must gather and store as much pertinent data as is possible. This data can be maintained in several ways.

Memory

Few officers rise to positions of high command responsibility without developing exceptional memories, at least where official military matters are concerned. Young staff officers are continually amazed at senior supervisors and commanders who remember, in precise detail, facts and figures from previous conversations, papers and briefings. It seems axiomatic that the vast majority of those officers who achieve only limited success, or who fail entirely, share one fault—forgetfulness. Military supervisors associate memory failure directly with lack of dedication and disinterest. This may be medically unsound, but it is an opinion with which staff officers must live, and those who suffer the malady would be well advised to try the remedy—increased dedication and heightened interest—it often works.

Almost everyone can remember minute details about subjects which interest them: baseball fans have little trouble recalling statistics on their favorite teams; bridge players remember thousands of hands played in past games and tournaments; hobbyists' minds are virtual catalogues of trivia associated with their hobbies; financial interests, involving hordes of detailed market transactions and trends, evoke excellent memories in some; deeply religious people often have extraordinary recall of the teachings of their spiritual leaders. Yet many of these same people are unable to remember even the most pressing matters pertaining to their military duties. It is possible that supervisors and commanders are justified in suspecting that lack of dedication and disinterest contribute to the amazing discrepancies between on-duty and off-duty memories.

We do not recommend that young staff officers concentrate on their duties to the exclusion of all outside interests, but most successful staff officers try to exclude all extraneous interests from their minds when working on official business. True, staff work is often less interesting than baseball, bridge, or stamp and coin collecting. However, it is the business for which staff officers are paid and, even more importantly, it represents a voluntarily assumed, sworn commitment to the American people. These obligations warrant each officer's full attention and total concentration on his work.

Young staff officers' interests should be aroused when they consider that their combined responsibilities involve the health, morale and welfare of thousands of people; gathering, analyzing and evaluating information influencing national defense; obtaining, maintaining and employing millions of dollars worth of supplies and equipment; and helping supervise the operations of a multibillion dollar organization. It may stimulate them further to know that those interests increase in proportion with participation, and, as interest increases, memories are almost certain to improve.

Working Files

Administration and maintenance of record and official reference files are discussed in some detail in Chapter 7. These files usually are kept by administrators whose interests are completeness and mechanical perfection of the files. Material in those files is retained, retired or destroyed on fixed regulatory schedules. References are treated the same way, but procedures are locally established. Record and reference files are extremely useful and action officers engaged in specific projects or responsible for certain areas of interest should supplement the official files with personal records of their activities.

Military actions seldom consist of one-time papers, coordination efforts or briefings. Even the simplest letter, message or report is likely to have an impact on other areas of staff interest, affect related actions, influence operations, plans and resources at subordinate levels, and evoke unexpected reactions from higher commanders and their staffs. Because the military organization is stratified into many command levels, and because each level is constantly involved in many concurrent actions, the full scope of projects which begin as simple, one-time efforts may develop only over extended periods of time—weeks, months, even years. As these projects evolve the number of documents involved grows: internal memoranda, conference and briefing notes, directives and correspondence from and to higher and lower headquarters.

Most of these actions are recorded in the official files and, if remembered, can be retrieved with some effort. However, most good staff officers prefer to keep their own *working file* on each action until certain that the action is completed. This is a beneficial practice for several reasons: first, working files are informal and can be arranged to suit the mental processes of the action officer or to meet the requirements of each project; secondly, they are instantly available without searching through official files; thirdly, they are not subject to disposal when a prescribed date arrives or when a project is officially completed (dead actions often arise to haunt action officers long after their end has been officially declared); lastly, and most important, working files collect complete accounts of individual projects and put them under one cover.

Working files vary according to the personal characteristics of the action officers who maintain them. Officers with extraordinary memories may throw every document pertaining to a project into a drawer, *in* box, folder, or filing cabinet and, with amazing accuracy, select any piece of paper needed. To these fortunate few, the working file is a convenient double-check for material long since committed to memory. Other officers make elaborate productions of their working files, replete with hard covers, indexes and chronological summaries. Most are somewhere in between; neither so informal that their files are useless to all but those who have established and memorized them, nor so elaborate that the file requires more effort than the project. Each staff officer must choose the method best suited to his use, but should bear in mind that in his absence his project file should be useable by others.

Data Banks

Like reference material and files, each military headquarters maintains extensive "raw" data for each facet of its operations and, like references and files, these data are available and required information can be extracted when needed, albeit with some expenditure of effort and time.

To conserve both energy and time and to be more responsive to requirements, most effective staff officers maintain their own mini-data banks. Supply staff officers, for example, might keep close at hand lists of federal stock numbers, authorization documents such as Tables of Organization and Allowances, usage rates, storage space requirements, order and receipt times, etc. Transportation officers can often use time-distance charts, aircraft and vehicle hauling capacities, weights and cubes of common items, commercial shipping rates, common carrier schedules, etc. These personal data files are convenient; they also pose one major threat—data, like all information, change. Federal Stock Numbers are added, deleted and modified to reflect the acquisition of new equipment and the disposal or modification of older items; reorganizations scramble Tables of Organization and Equipment; and transportation data fluctuate with changing equipment, commercial scheduling, and economic factors. Outdated or incorrect data can be worse than no data. Therefore, considerable time and effort are needed to assure the validity of personal data files. Staff officers should accumulate only those data most frequently needed, and resist temptation to gather impressive but seldom used libraries of reference data.

Policy Files

The importance of command policy on staff operations was stressed in Chapter 8. From the action officer's point of view, however, the policies of many supervisors other than the commander come into play. An action officer's work could, as an extreme example, pass through a senior project officer, a section chief, a branch chief, a division chief, a deputy staff element chief, and the staff element chief before even starting its journey to the commander. To that action officer, the commander's policies are rather distant considerations compared to the much more proximate challenge of six local supervisors. To pass those six obstacles successfully, the action officer must carefully study the peculiarities, preferences and dislikes of each, and must remember everything learned for future reference.

Wise action officers maintain more extensive *policy files* than those kept by supervisors. In that file action officers maintain innumerable bits of information about those who approve their work and rate their effectiveness. If the section chief prefers the word *use* to *employ* that is certainly valuable information to be stored away and constitutes a typical policy file entry. Consider more examples:

1. The branch chief likes a small summary of each action for his working files.
2. The division chief will sign nothing that has not been coordinated with each branch chief.

3. The deputy staff element chief likes to read distribution, brief the boss, and plan his day during the first hour of each morning.
4. The chief is a speed reader; long, complex sentences without smooth transitions distract and annoy him.

While these examples may seem extreme, they demonstrate the value of maintaining detailed policy files. The examples themselves are extreme only in the unlikely coincidence of one action officer encountering all of these pitfalls with no kindly warnings along the way. Actually, each of the supervisor's personal whims were based on sound practices, and each was carefully selected because it represents the particular idiosyncracy of an outstanding officer with whom the authors have worked.

Sample Actions. Early in their tours of duty, staff officers should notice some very marked differences in the productivity and effectiveness of those around them. Almost every office in every headquarters has its share of those for whom nothing goes right. For them every action becomes a disaster, difficult to coordinate, impossible to sell; each paper bounces repeatedly at each level of supervision; every briefing becomes a nightmare of rehearsals, rewrites, more rehearsals and more rewrites; even their informal conversations generate controversy and confusion. Samples of their work would do little to help the beginner. In the same offices, however, are successful staff officers; those whose work is consistently acceptable and usually outstanding. Young staff officers would do well to compile a file of samples prepared by those coworkers and study, analyze, and use them.

Nothing can be more comforting to an inexperienced staff officer encountering a particular action for the first time, than to have before him samples of similar actions that have passed the test. Later, perhaps, those samples can be replaced by the staff officer's own papers which have proven especially successful.

Management

In recent years, management of resources has become an essential skill for all military leaders and for the staffs that assist and advise them. Since the beginning of warfare, commanders have been responsible for husbanding their assets and applying all human and physical resources with maximum effectiveness. Staff organizations have, since their inception, reflected those command responsibilities. However, from the late 1930's through the Vietnam conflict the U.S. Army had been either preparing for imminent combat, or was engaged in combat operations. In that environment economy was never ignored, but national defense through military preparedness and tactical victories were paramount considerations. During those critical years management of resources too often was interpreted to mean "be sure we have enough of everything" rather than "be sure we make the most of what we have."

However, as U.S. involvement in Southeast Asia has diminished, taxpayers quite properly insist that national defense be managed more efficiently. All military resources are becoming more austere, and commanders at all levels are faced with continuing their missions with an ever increasing paucity of funds, people, equipment, supplies, and services. In this atmosphere, the number of management experts is increasing in most headquarters. At the same time, management considerations have become vital facets of every staff function. Every staff officer must now understand and exercise accepted management practices. To better appreciate modern management, some understanding of its origins and its meaning as generally used in the military is necessary.

Management has long been a magic word in the business world. In the late twenties and early thirties it emerged as a separate entity and has been growing in stature ever since. As discussed here, management includes both the art or science of controlling resources, and the direction of those who do the controlling. Management enjoys the same respect in business as command does in the military. To succeed in business, one must aspire to positions in top management; in the military, to high command positions. This poses the question, How do management and command differ? Businessmen usually define management as the art or science of getting things done through and with people working in formally organized groups. The Army expands this definition to include the continuing actions of planning, organizing, directing, coordinating, and controlling the use of people, money, materials, and facilities to accomplish missions and tasks. By contrast, Army command involves the authority and the responsibility for executing these continuing actions and includes responsibility for health, welfare, morale, and discipline of assigned personnel.

The key distinctions between management and military command are the specifics of responsibility and authority not only as they apply to health, welfare, morale, and discipline but as applied to management itself. Management is primarily concerned with efficiency, although in recent years there has been a growing awareness of the close relationship between efficiency and the human concerns of work forces. To military commanders, missions come first but personnel are recognized as the most important resource. Next to the mission, their support and well being constitute the most important objectives. In the military, management is an inherent and indispensable facet of command, whereas command is neither inherent in nor a part of management. Command is all-inclusive and is established by virtue of grade and position, but management must be exercised by everyone who controls resources whether in command positions or not. All officers on their way up must master management techniques, for management ability becomes increasingly vital as the economics of national defense grow even tighter.

The business world runs on the profit motive. Ineffective management reduces profits and cannot survive. In the military, combat effectiveness replaces the profit motive, but good management and austerity dictate that this be achieved by the most economical means. Unfortunately, tools for measuring combat effectiveness are less precise than the black and red of profit and loss statements. However, improved methods are being developed so that commanders' effectiveness as managers can be weighed as accurately as their accomplishments as troop leaders.

The trend has been in that direction since the end of World War II. Prior to World War II the military slice of the national budget was modest compared to the huge military expenditures of recent years. The large percentage of federal revenue now being invested in national defense extends each citizen the right, if not the duty, to demand good management. These demands are being made loud and clear. Citizens are demanding a dollar's worth of defense for each dollar allocated to the military. This is evident in the serious consideration Congress gives to each military appropriations bill. It is even more apparent in the thoroughness with which the expenditure of funds already appropriated are audited. The General Accounting Office continuously monitors military management and reports the results of its audits to Congress. Good reports seldom make headlines, but front page attention given to cost overruns and other incidents of mismanagement reflects public interest and growing demands for better management. Admittedly, there have been disturbingly large numbers of these incidents. It seems that significant management failures since World War II have far exceeded all other types of serious command failures. Diligent efforts are being applied from the highest levels and throughout the Department of Defense to eliminate such failures (and those who cause them). Management is the watchword; those who do not heed will pay the penalty.

Management in the military is a challenge. Since World War II the military establishment has been constantly building up or cutting back its resources, often on a crash basis. As a result of these fluctuations the Army has undertaken several major reorganizations. Together these conditions have resulted in resource turbulence, making effective management of personnel and physical assets difficult at best, and occasionally causing unavoidable mismanagement. During the Vietnam action the requirement of combat caused personnel strengths to turn over as often as two and three times in one year in stateside divisions. In other instances stateside units were stripped of their equipment to fill requirements of higher priority organizations, while others retained all equipment but were without personnel to operate or maintain it. At local levels management under these conditions becomes little more than a holding action. Hopefully, the nation may now be approaching an extended, stabilized period of relative international quiet. In more stable periods, however, improved management is possible and is demanded.

Staff Management Responsibilities

The individual staff officer's questions at this point may be, How do I become personally involved? What do I manage? Most action officers work more or less independently under the direction of their immediate supervisor even though they may work with many people—sometimes assisting, sometimes being assisted. They usually have few supervisory responsibilities and little direct control over resources. Therefore, some staff officers, even some senior ones, probably would answer, You don't get involved, you manage nothing. They are wrong.

Staff officers become involved in management in two ways. First, as assistants to their commanders, they are involved because management responsibilities are an aspect of all command missions. Secondly, as trusted employees of the American public, each staff officer is obliged to protect that employer's interests, including husbanding of resources. Each staff officer must assist in managing all resources for which his commander is responsible—people, equipment, supplies, services, and money. He must also manage and conserve those resources which he personally controls, especially time—his own, and the time of those with whom he works. Army management responsibilities follow the chain of command and are inherent command responsibilities, but all Army members, not only commanders, must shoulder their share of management responsibilities. Staff officers as they advise, assist and act in the name of their commanders must reflect sound management considerations and insure optimum use of resources. Staff office chiefs, supervisors and action officers are responsible for the good management of resources within their own areas of operations as well. They must account for the use of all resources under their control. No one is excused; management is the concern of every staff member.

It should be obvious by now that management of resources has become, and will become even more, a key factor in every phase of staff work and in each staff officer's success. From the first, the wise staff officer will set about increasing his knowledge of management techniques, applying them to every task he undertakes. Studies and estimates must consider economic factors and give increasing weight to economics as a significant advantage or disadvantage of all proposals and recommendations; plans must continue to concentrate on mission accomplishment, but they must also devote more detail to resource management; orders and directives must efficiently restrict and limit resource use; and, above all, supervision by commanders and staffs must focus on optimum economy.

As individuals, action officers face more simple but equally important problems. Their primary jobs are problem solving. Their administrative support and most supplies and equipment come from the section or office administrative element. Normally, action officers have no one working directly for them and therefore have few personnel management duties. Management of resources is equally light, except for two very valuable assets—time and effort.

Personal time management is vitally important, and action officers should organize their approach to this issue—it will be one of their toughest problems. They never have enough time; deadlines close in, additional research must be performed, conferences cannot be avoided, phones will not stop ringing, the paper flow must be read (not just scanned), and some should be studied, not just read. So, demands on an action officer's time usually exceed the time available, and lost time can never be made up. If an action officer spends too much time on the wrong thing he is in trouble. The more important work he is expected to do probably will not get done, or will be done poorly. His effectiveness will be measured accordingly. To avoid this situation, action officers should examine their work requirements, arrange tasks in order of importance, and budget their time to cover all needs.

This approach is sound but realities must be recognized. Action officers may work independently but they are not independent. They are always involved in several actions at the same time. On some they are primary action officers, on others they assist other action officers, and on others they work as teams or committee members engaged in some major projects. These involvements limit staff officers' abilities to control their own schedules. Each is faced with numerous demands and diversions that arise quite apart from his regular staff actions. For example, an action officer might have to represent his boss on short notice at a conference, a briefing, or a staff meeting. He also could be given some special research or coordinating mission, or could find himself saddled with an additional duty detail—court member, project officer for the division picnic, etc.

Unpredictable demands can cause major adjustments to time management schedules though they do not detract from the need for such schedules. Even without the outside interferences, arranging an ironclad schedule is difficult. Officers with limited experience have difficulty gauging the time needed for different tasks, and since tasks and problems vary from day to day, estimating the necessary adjustments is not easy. The best approach is to plan a daily schedule covering all tasks on a priority basis, and try to stick to it, adjusting as necessary.

Experience is the best teacher, as far as time management is concerned. Like all teachers, however, experience imparts knowledge only to those who wish to learn, and learning comes from analysis of how time has actually been spent versus how it was scheduled to be spent.

Time usage logs can be valuable management tools. They can also present hazards common to all management tools—they tend to run wild, requiring more management than the management assistance they provide. During his career, every staff officer will encounter colleagues and supervisors who are aided by so many management tools (charts, data, fact sheets, reading files, etc.) that their entire efforts are required to maintain them. So before starting a time use log, the staff officer should consider the uses to which that tool will be put. The greatest benefit is that staff officers can learn to economize their time from these data showing how their time was spent or wasted.

Logs can be set up to suit individual action officers. Time can be broken into convenient intervals—15, 30, 60 minutes—or not broken into periods at all. Staff officers should devise the least demanding system for their purposes. Codes can be devised to denote different standard work items like writing, briefing, research, conference as well as some typical interruptions—phones, visits, etc. The important thing is a complete picture of time-consuming activities on a daily basis. This is not to say that the record must be analyzed on a daily basis, only recorded. It is more practical to examine logs on a weekly or even monthly basis after more data have accumulated. Theoretically, larger samples reflect truer pictures. The purpose is to get a grip on one's time, and when this is accomplished an action officer may decide that record keeping and analysis can be suspended as a full-time operation. Time logs are valuable, however, and most experienced officers resort to them periodically to keep their time in check.

Accurate worklogs often reveal surprises. It should not be difficult for the action officer to pinpoint his periods of low or questionable productivity and if a pattern develops, he has a starting point from which to make adjustments. The technique is simple, but successful application demands perseverance.

It probably will not take a log to identify one's daily period of peak productivity. Some are at their best at five o'clock in the morning, others do not reach their peak until evening. Recognize these periods and use them for the most difficult challenges in creative thinking. For example, most action officers consider problem-solving among their most difficult tasks; it calls for creative thinking of the highest order. Even after solutions have been reached they still must be sold. The solution must often be presented in writing, but sometimes verbal presentations like formal or informal briefings are more cogent. Finding the solution and selling it require sound, imaginative thinking. Action officers should conduct these heavy thinking sessions during peak productivity periods. Further analysis may identify distractions and interruptions that can be eliminated to further enhance the usefulness of these periods.

The only other thing the action officer manages is his relationship with other staff members and contacts. Although it has been suggested that he works independently, he could accomplish little completely on his own. True, solutions to his assigned staff problems should be the product of his own creative thinking, but creativity seldom flourishes without informal conversations with, and advice and assistance from, fellow staff officers. Often he may develop background information through discussions with contacts in higher and/or subordinate headquarters and he probably will need administrative help putting his product in final form. In short, he must have the cooperation of many others. Since cooperation means a joint effort toward a common objective, the action officer must manage his part of the relationships in a spirit that assures returns.

Management was defined earlier as the art or science of getting things done through and with people in formally organized groups. The action officer is not a professional manager in the strictest sense of the word, but management is becoming one of the most vital of the many skills and techniques he must master.

Completed Staff Work

The phrase *completed staff work* has been around for a long time. It is often used to mean submitting to the commander, for his approval, a recommended action that has been fully coordinated and for which implementing instructions have been prepared. To experienced staff officers, *completed staff work* means much more; it applies to all papers he prepares, not just those going to the commander, and it applies to every action he undertakes, whether or not it is reduced to writing. The vast majority of an action officer's efforts never go to the commander. They either go to other staff officers in his own headquarters, or to staff officers in another headquarters. Regardless of destination or degree of formality, each action should be complete within itself—it should be self-standing.

For major formal actions, completeness is assured, all conditions are met, and all questions are answered by use of organized, standard approaches and by reducing actions to prescribed formats. Chapters 4 and 5 discuss problem-solving approaches and formats for different standard staff actions. The thrust of these discussions was the commander's approach to problem-solving supported by the staff's assistance and advice. The object here is to stress the importance of completeness in *all* actions, not just those which come to command attention, and to suggest organized, standard approaches to even the most routine actions. Only disciplined, orderly thought processes can assure that every action is a professional, complete piece of work.

The staff study and estimate formats provide excellent check lists against which any action can be checked for completeness:

1. Has the problem been identified and addressed?
2. Have all possible influencing factors been considered?
3. Were all possible solutions or courses of action evaluated?

Personal Skills and Techniques 249

4. Has each possible solution been weighed against each possible influence?
5. Have all advantages and disadvantages been objectively compared?
6. Are all conclusions based on valid analyses?
7. Is the recommendation (or the action taken) valid and: Does it cover the entire problem? Is it compatible with all influences? Is it supported by analysis and comparison? Does it match the conclusions in substance? Is it sufficiently detailed (what, where, who, when, how, and why)?

If an action, simple or complex, minor or major, can meet the criteria of this test, it is conceptually complete, though not actually complete. Two other important steps must be taken—coordination and supervision. Coordination must be thorough and must include every staff element and staff officer with any possible interest before an action can be considered complete. When that has been accomplished an action can be considered a completed staff action to the extent that it is ready for dispatch or presentation to a commander. However, for the effective staff officer, one responsibility remains: seeing that the job gets done.

Consider the nature of military missions. Commanders are seldom charged with such tasks as merely planning and issuing orders for the capture of a tactical objective, preparing and issuing training programs, programming sufficient resources to operate an installation, designing and stocking a supply depot, or developing maintenance policies. Commanders are responsible for successful military operations; planning, ordering, preparing, programming, designing, and developing are only preliminary steps. The real efforts, and the payoff, lie in ensuring that subordinates follow those initial steps with positive action. Staff officers must follow-up each "desk" action, small and large, with staff supervision to assure positive and productive results.

Staff Supervision (Follow-through)

Staff supervision is discussed in detail in Chapter 4, "Staff Procedures." However, one facet of supervision deserves mention here. Staff actions are complex, detailed, time-consuming, and often nerve-racking experiences. When an action is finished, the officers involved usually are ready to file it away and forget it. Tempting as this may be, it cannot be done. Each action must be followed through; it must be checked on, additional actions taken, visits made, progress reports written, or whatever else is needed to assure that the actions really have been taken.

Summary

As indicated in the introductory comments in the beginning of this chapter, individual action officers are the heart of each staff. In many respects, they are the keys to our national defense effort. Most major military decisions announced by senior commanders, service secretaries, and even Department of Defense officials, originated at the desks of relatively junior staff officers. Commanders, particularly senior commanders, must trust their assistants to detect weaknesses and deficiencies in procedures and to identify changes and innovations for improving operations.

Every staff member assumes an awesome responsibility to support his commander with optimum professionalism, unlimited dedication, and undivided loyalty. Implicit in this obligation is the absolute responsibility to make every possible effort to improve personal skills, and to master the techniques necessary to meet the obligation. It is reemphasized that this chapter was not intended as a crash course on these skills and techniques. Hopefully, the discussions of a few of the important attributes of all successful staff officers will be sufficient to convince the beginner that these skills and techniques are so essential that he will be motivated to pursue additional study and research.

11.

Staff Assignments

Previous chapters explained what the staff is all about, its reason for existing, and its importance. We have traced the staff's evolution from its inception to the present, looked closely at staff organizations, examined some traditional policies that influence staff conduct, reviewed typical staff actions, and stressed the skills and techniques that are every staff officer's tools-of-trade.

The intent of those chapters was to orient the inexperienced staff officer to the nature of his new environment, familiarize him with the general nature of the work he can expect and advise him of the rules by which the staff game is played. These are all tangible aspects of staff life; it will be the objective of this chapter to present some of the less tangible, but nevertheless important concerns of the staff officer's job.

This chapter suggests ways to prepare for staff assignments, discusses the orientation process (those important first days on the job), covers some of the vital characteristics of life as a staff officer and concludes with what we consider to be the keys to success.

Normal Assignment Pattern

Staff assignments can come at any time, but most officers begin their active duty life assigned to troop units. In fact, this is the Army's general personnel assignment policy, and for a good reason. It is at the platoon level that the new lieutenant gains firsthand, face-to-face experience leading men—a necessary ingredient to professional development and career success. This is the bottom rung of the command ladder, a logical place to start. The platoon commander must not only become an expert in the operational functions of his platoon, he must also become an expert in the fundamentals of the many services and support functions that make the military machine run: training, supply, transportation, personnel management, food service, etc. What better basic training ground could be found for the future staff officer? Even more important, the platoon commander has the best opportunity to work with and become expert on the resource for which he will be held most rigidly accountable during his career, the Army's basic ingredient—*people.*

If an officer's career follows logical assignment patterns, the platoon commander could expect his next assignment would be as company commander, a job for which he should be well prepared. At the company level, his experience will broaden from the management of individual soldiers and the services and support functions as they apply to the individual, to the management of soldiers in subordinate groups who respond to him through intermediate commanders. As a company commander, his view of the operational functions of his command broadens from the more individually oriented platoon level perspective to encompass the capabilities of teams of men, weapons, and equipment. It is also at company level that the commander has his first experience of working directly with a staff (first sergeant, company clerk, mess sergeant, motor sergeant, etc.).

By the time the young officer reaches his next logical duty as a member of a battalion staff, his excellent experience as platoon and company commander should have been augmented by some military education. He is now prepared to become a staff officer at the lower levels of command. We hope this book may be of value to him as a guide and as a reminder of the importance of the trusted position he must fill. It should be of more use to those who skip some of those important developmental steps, but it can never replace the experience that comes with the logical progression through troop duties. This is the perfect foundation upon which other experience can be added.

Early Staff Assignments

The platoon-company-battalion route is the normal career progression. Unfortunately, not all careers develop normally. Some officers find themselves assigned to staff positions at the outset of their active duty tours. Even more find their normal career development interrupted by staff assignments after only brief experience with troops. These departures from the norm occur for many reasons. Some young officers are highly trained specialists whose skills can be fully used only in staff positions. More often, however, staff vacancies exist when appropriate troop positions are filled. Although these early staff assignments can be unfortunate, they are not entirely disastrous for those assigned to positions at the battalion or even group level headquarters. At these levels operations are less complex and staff procedures less mysterious, and the average officer can function and produce good work despite his lack of troop experience. But even here he will operate at less than his potential effectiveness, an obvious disadvantage to both the officer and the organization.

The truly difficult situation arises for new officers who find themselves assigned to the staffs of very senior commanders with large headquarters. Fortunately, except for the specialist, this is rare, but when it does happen the lieutenant needs all the help he can get. Only one step removed from these unfortunates are those who, after only one or two years with troops, unexpectedly find themselves ordered to large staffs, corps level or higher. This happens frequently and these officers also need help. It is hoped that this book can soften the shock and assist in preparing for those first staff assignments.

Proper preparation can be valuable—it can lessen the psychological shock inherent in first exposures to the apparent confusion of a large headquarters and, at the same time, increase self-confidence by strengthening professional qualifications. To begin with, newly selected staff officers should condition themselves for a change of pace, a new living and working environment.

While troop duty is demanding and rewarding, it offers a degree of simplicity. Missions are clear-cut and the challenges are personal, direct, and unmistakable. Every member of the unit plays a significant role in shaping the team into a winner. The results of their efforts are instantly visible, and recognition comes quickly for both outstanding performances and for those that leave something to be desired. There are no questions of "identity" for the individuals or for the organizations. Success in achieving common goals fosters *esprit de corps* and camaraderie. Furthermore, the young officer develops the aptitude most necessary for military success—leadership. With so many advantages, it is small wonder that most officers prefer troop assignments.

Peculiarities of Staff Assignments

First-time staff officers fresh from troop assignments will soon recognize the differences between troop and staff assignments. This will be particularly true for junior officers assigned to the large headquarters of a senior commander. The commanders' missions will be less clear-cut and, in most cases, will be stated in terms of broad areas of responsibility rather than the concise task assignments of the platoon, company, and battalion level mission. Even after these general responsibilities are understood, the young officer may have difficulty relating them to the functions of his lower-level position on the staff. Although the commander's mission may be broadly stated, the bottom rung action officer's position usually will be confined to narrow, specialized functions involving minutely detailed work. The challenge will be there and may well exceed that of the troop command. Too often, however, it may take the form of meeting suspense dates rather than accomplishing complete tasks which can be easily identified as major facets of the command mission. Larger staffs may consist of hundreds of action officers, all contributing small inputs to most of the major actions undertaken by the staff. Each input is important, but the beginner may feel that his efforts are very insignificant.

Failure to recognize the significance of one's efforts dulls the desire to work and leads to decreased or, in some cases, complete lack of contribution. A novice officer can easily be overcome by a feeling of lack of accomplishment, confirmed in his mind by lack of recognition. Gone is the instant visibility of results in troop command where both good work and mistakes became immediately apparent. There is precious little recognition for routine staff work accomplished at the action officer level of a large staff. It is an unusual officer who can attract early acclaim for his first minor staff actions.

Also missing in the staff job is the old team spirit found in the troop unit. While the staff is a single unit dedicated to a single goal, its members work in widely diversified fields. Each has his own small area of interest and, if he is good, has more than enough work in that small area to keep him busy. The newcomer may feel isolated and, to some extent, rejected by his fellow workers. Without an understanding coach, this can be a lonely feeling indeed.

Lack of contribution, lack of recognition, lack of identity, and lack of a team spirit all combine to portray a rather bleak picture to new staff officers. They may well ask, Where are the personal gratifications and opportunities for career enhancement? If the newcomer has prepared himself properly, he will soon recognize them. First, however, he must be prepared to overcome the initial feelings of inadequacy, loss of identity, and the loneliness of not belonging. Who has not heard the expression, "the best defense is a good offense?" Similarly, preparation provides the best chance to successfully start a staff career. Determine the objective and prepare to reach it.

Preparing for Staff Work

The ultimate goal of the troop commander is to be a successful leader. Attainment depends heavily on such qualities as physical and moral courage, stamina, and dedication. The goal of the staff officer should be expertise. This can only be achieved through knowledge and practice. Of course, the leadership qualities are still important, but something extra must be added—professional knowledge and skill, not only in military and technical matters but in the special skills and techniques of staff work. Obviously, preparation is the key. Regardless of experience and background, there are always additional techniques and skills that can enhance one's capabilities. The officer who attempts to master these skills is better prepared to step into his first staff assignment. The psychological shock will be less severe, and he will be capable of productive work much sooner than his unprepared counterpart.

Preparation means research and study. Obvious areas to attack are the new headquarter's organization, mission, and procedures. The mission and organization of all headquarters directly subordinate to the Department of the Army and of some installations are published in *Army Regulations.* Organization of types of field commands such as the field army, corps, and division are discussed in *Army Field Manuals.* Numerous field manuals have been published that discuss different types of commands in detail. The field manual index is found in Department of Army *Pamphlets.* Organization charts and mission statements of major overseas commands will be more difficult to acquire. Probably the best bet is to write to the particular command.

The value of this research should be apparent; arriving on the scene with some knowledge of the organization and purpose of the new headquarters provides some needed confidence. Additionally, it eradicates a frequent complaint of younger staff officers—lack of recognition. Senior supervisors will hardly fail to notice that the newcomer has taken the trouble to do his homework. If that homework has been extended to include subordinate units and activities, so much the better.

The standard reference on staff procedure is Field Manual 101-5, *Staff Officer's Field Manual.* To the seasoned staff officer it is an invaluable, comprehensive reference. The data are all there, but without some staff experience to relate them to, they may seem rather meaningless. For the beginner, *FM 101-5* presents a general overview of procedures and, if nothing else is available, can provide some help in visualizing the activities he might expect in his new home. If at all possible, the beginner should supplement official references with personal and less formal references. Correspondence with the new headquarters may be worthwhile, particularly if a friend or acquaintance is stationed there and is willing and qualified to discuss some of the procedures used by that headquarters, especially where they differ from the norm.

Two other valuable references to the officer preparing for his first staff assignment are AR 340-15, *Preparing Correspondence,* and AR 380-5, *Safeguarding Defense Information.* These supplement material presented earlier under *techniques* and deserve careful attention. These two publications treat the essence of staff work.

While the young staff officer may find that he is spending most of his time on "internally generated" tasks (those bits of paper that gyrate through the staff, never leaving the headquarters), the real meat of the staff's production are those papers that leave the headquarters. The final results of most staff actions are letters, messages, plans, orders, and other correspondence going to subordinates for action, to higher headquarters in response to directives, and to multiple addresses for information. It is helpful to know in advance how this correspondence must be prepared.

Closely allied to correspondence is the mandatory (and statutory) requirement to safeguard information which, if allowed to fall into the wrong hands, could be used to threaten national security. Perhaps no single blunder reflects as adversely on an officer's career as the inadvertent loss or misuse of classified information. The young staff officer will likely be working with many classified documents for the first time. It will be reassuring (to both the officer and his bosses) to know in advance the general rules which apply to this special type of information. A word of caution: both AR 340-15 and AR 380-5 prescribe broad rules and establish minimum standards, and most commanders have very strong ideas of their own as to the details of following those broad guides. Expect, therefore, to find additional guidance at the new headquarters. In fact, if it is not apparent, look for it.

It was stressed early in the previous chapter that communications are vital to every staff action. Anything officers can do in advance to sharpen their skills in this field will serve them well. Speed reading courses, charm schools for instructors, and effective writing courses are excellent possibilities. Another worthwhile asset is the ability to dictate. Time is the staff officer's nemesis; papers stack up and time flies, while bosses urge speed and demand results from what may seem to be unreasonable numbers of actions. In this atmosphere, nothing is more ulcer-producing than to laboriously write every communication in longhand. This can be particularly frustrating if a coworker (a competitor) is leaning back with his feet on the desk, drinking coffee, and producing twice one's work by dictating to a secretary. Dictation is not easy, but can be mastered through patient practice. Another time-saving skill is typing. The officer who can type has a distinct advantage. Although typists are provided, many officers must do their drafts in longhand. Even those who dictate often find all stenographers busy. This is slow, tedious, and less legible compared to typing. The effective staff officer must be able to communicate, and communicate expertly. Work on it, prepare in advance.

It is quite likely that an officer, through diligent effort, can obtain advance information on the mission and organization of the headquarters he is about to join. It is less likely that he will be able to gauge the character of the headquarters until he has joined. Every headquarters has its own character and personality, all organizations and institutions do. In the headquarters of two infantry divisions with the same missions and identical staffs, one would still sense differences in attitude, morale, and esprit. The differences probably can be accounted for in the commanders' personalities. It is a fact of life that a headquarters reflects the personality of the commander. Even if the commanders of these hypothetical infantry divisions stress the same things, they are certain to approach them differently and these differences will be reflected. Differences will be even more pronounced if the commanders stress different things (e.g. say spit and polish in one case, managerial efficiency in the other). Wherever it is focused, this emphasis will be mirrored in the headquarters.

In many cases the personality of the Chief of Staff may have a strong influence on the character of the headquarters. Some commanders give their chief a free hand in running the headquarters, while they concentrate on commandwide issues. This type of relationship will reflect the characteristics of both the commander and the chief.

The point of this discussion is to show that no two headquarters are the same, and working relationships and conditions will be influenced by the character of the headquarters. One headquarters may be "gung ho," the other academic. On the other hand, it is amazing how quickly the character of a headquarters can change with a change in commanders—it can happen overnight. This phenomenon is not limited to the military, but the military command system seems to accelerate the process. It should not take the new officer long to discern the type of team he is playing on.

Reporting to New Headquarters. No two headquarters are exactly alike, but the "reporting in" procedures are pretty much standard throughout the Army. While not required, it is still sound practice to report in early during a duty day, armed with orders and records and prepared to process. Unless told otherwise, the first stop should be at the Adjutant General's sign-in register. Finding that stop should be easy. Most military installations have gate guards or information activities near the entrance to the installations. Headquarters located off military installations have similar information activities near the entrance to the main headquarters building. These initial contacts have greeted many newcomers and are expert in the processing procedure. Once at the sign-in point, further directions and assistance will be available. The next stop after the sign-in probably will be the officers' personnel section, where the incoming officer's personnel records will be checked and filed.

From here the processing is time-consuming and tedious, but necessary. Most installations have now reduced the inconveniences of processing to a minimum by concentrating the processing services such as car registration, housing, transportation, etc. under one roof in a centralized facility. When the personal part of the process has been completed, the Adjutant General's representatives will direct the newly joined officer to his duty office. Whether it be intelligence, logistics, provost marshal, or whatever, the newly assigned officer should report to the administrative element of that office, where he will be assigned to a specific position and turned over to his office chief.

If a sponsor has been designated, and this is common but not universal practice, he will be eager to meet the newcomer when he arrives. He will assist as an escort to the duty office, and as a guide through the processing procedure. A reasonable amount of time is usually allowed for processing, say a day or two. On the other hand, new officers sometimes step into crisis situations on staffs that are critically shorthanded and may be put to work immediately, with processing being completed catch-as-catch-can.

Regardless of the time available, "reporting in" and "processing in" are routine operations and should not present any special challenge, although settling into the new position and duties may require some psychological adjustments.

Learning the Job. New staff officers start out as action officers. Just as platoon leaders represent the bottom rung of the command ladder, action officers represent the bottom rung of the staff ladder. An action officer may be located in any of the staff offices. In most large headquarters the major subdivisions—personnel, intelligence, operations, and logistics—are called staff offices. These are further subdivided into divisions, branches, and sections. Young officers are usually action officers and occupy desks at the section level and report to section chiefs. Not all action officers are lieutenants. In fact, grades of the action officers vary from lieutenant to colonel. The mix depends on the size of the headquarters, personnel authorizations, and personnel availability.

When the new action officer has been assigned a desk in his section, he is ready for the formal orientation which most headquarters provide. Formats vary, but the most common approach is the headquarters' briefing, usually staged monthly or as appropriate. These cover mission, organization, functions, goals, and accomplishments. The presentation will likely be highly professional, if not dazzling. The content, however, may leave one with that "drinking from a fire hose" feeling. Remember, the objective of this type of briefing is to give the "big picture." Most are eminently successful. Other orientation procedures may include guided tours and informational brochures. It is important that new staff officers understand the overall objectives and use that understanding as a basis for the more detailed orientations concerning their own working level and personal areas of interest.

At some point in this orientation period the newcomer will probably meet his office chief, his division chief, his branch chief, and other members of the office. Each of these may have some further words of orientation and welcome. Throughout this book we have stressed the vital importance of knowing the people with whom one must work. This is the place to start. Possibly even more important than the information received during the orientation process, will be the opportunity to meet other staff officers. Listen to what they have to say, and begin the process of identifying those who seem to be productive, energetic, and dedicated workers.

One of the most typical characteristics of outstanding officers, particularly staff officers, is the ability to remember people by name. True, the first few days in a large headquarters are confusing, and many people are met very briefly. There will be little time for becoming well acquainted with anyone, but the newcomer should have some gleaning of the caliber of the team and the atmosphere of the headquarteers.

In his office, the new staff officer should already have met the other members of his section. These typically include military or civilian administrative people and other action officers who, in some headquarters, may be civilian experts. These associates at section level can be very helpful in continuing the orientation process. They will have answers to many of the questions that arise, particularly those that relate to local customs and procedures. This is the most important orientation information which others can offer. It is here that departure is taken from the broader, more general nature of the headquarters and office level briefings and tours. The newcomer now discovers exactly what his job is and how it is done. If he is to succeed, it is in his own office that he must find his niche, discover his role, and establish his importance to the staff and the commander.

There are pitfalls. While the newcomer must be guided to some extent by those already on the job, he must also be guided by integrity and common sense. Just as any team has those who prefer to ride the bench rather than extend the effort and sweat required to become a starting player, each staff has a few who produce at less than maximum capacity. Beware of those who say, "There is very little to do here." There are always things that need doing, and there are always those who can avoid doing them. A good (but not infallible) rule is to identify the busiest action officer in the section and learn from him. Above all, learn from experience and observation. Put the most important of those communication skills to work—listen!

Continuing the Learning Process. Probably the most important part of the orientation process depends upon the individual. His curiosity and initiative should cause him to carry on long after the formal orientation has ceased. This is a matter of continuing study, of reading one's self into the situation. For starters, the fledgling should review the headquarter's table of organization or the table of distribution, as the case may be, to gain a working knowledge of the organization. Most large headquarters publish periodic desk top organization charts which include the names of incumbents, as well as their telephone, building, and room numbers. This personalized table of organization or authorization is a valuable tool to the new officer when he sets out to coordinate his first staff action.

Another document that should be scrutinized along with the organization table is the functions and organization manual. Most large headquarters publish one. This document itemizes functions by staff offices, broken down to branch level. It is a detailed presentation of the responsibilities of each staff element and is an invaluable orientation aid. Later it assists in determining responsibilities. Many questions arise in the minds of all staff officers as to which office should take an action. In fact, these questions quite often come up among older staff officers and are debated heatedly. The answers to these questions should come from the organization and functions manual. The responsibility question frequently results in a jurisdictional dispute between staff offices. Again, the organization and functions manual should provide the basis for settlement. If it does not the dispute could ultimately end up with the Chief of Staff who would rule on the matter and concurrently direct that the deficiency in the manual be corrected.

Obviously, staff officers have good reasons for knowing the organization and functions of their headquarters. They should know the same facts about the next senior headquarters in the chain of command and all subordinate headquarters. They should also learn the troop lists of subordinate units and, to the best of their abilities, everything there is to know about them. After all, the senior headquarters will be the source of all missions and tasks, and the lower organizations constitute the only resources available to accomplish the mission.

Policies

Most large headquarters publish command policies and operating procedures in some form. Headquarters memoranda are a common format. These usually cover most facets of headquarters' operation and may comprise a file of several hundred memoranda. Numbering systems normally are the same as those used for *Army Regulations*. The term *policy* infers *commander's policy* when applicable to the entire headquarters or to subordinate organizations. Though these policies often originate in the staff elements expert in particular areas of interest, when published they become the commander's policy and reflect his personal preferences. For this reason, policy memoranda are normally published by the commander, his deputy, or his chief of staff.

The different staff offices prepare and publish memoranda covering procedures in their areas of responsibility. The newly joined staff officer should find many of these of interest, such as "Office Hours," "Leaves, Passes, and Absence by Vocal Order of the Commanding General," and "Officer Efficiency Reports." Others, such as "Preparation of Correspondence" and "Message Preparation and Processing," are vital to his function as a staff member. In summary, the whole file of headquarters' policies and procedures should be reviewed, and those that are pertinent to the staff officer's position should be studied in detail.

In addition to the headquarters' policies and procedures, each major staff office chief normally establishes policies to convey his preferences in office matters, and the same can be true at division, branch, or even section level.

These policies are pertinent and applicable only to those specific levels. As with the headquarters, any division or branch chief may be authorized to prescribe procedures in his area of expertise. In any case, the action officer must be familiar with all and comply where appropriate.

After he has been around long enough, it is probable that he will contribute to improving procedures and possibly recommend policies. Sometimes even the newest officer can contribute to the commander's policies quite unintentionally. For example, after only two or three weeks on the job in a NATO headquarters, and having issued only one outgoing letter, a newly assigned British officer caused the following to be published over the signature of the commander (an American Lieutenant General): "The term—*in the fullness of time*—will not be used in correspondence leaving this headquarters."

Other files are important, namely the action files in the action officer's own office. Most "new" problems have some background material in these files. Additionally, a general review of the files in his assigned area should be valuable in reading into the situation. The files constitute a history of the actions that have been taken during the past few months. From them, the newly arrived officer can form a mental picture of the types of actions taken and the broad areas of interest of his section, the branch, the division, and the staff office. He also becomes familiar with the headquarters' position on a variety of actions. This will be valuable background for future actions in which he will participate. As a byproduct, he will gain familiarity with files' composition. Although the action officer will not be responsible for file maintenance, on occasion it will be necessary to retrieve material from the files. It helps to know where to look.

As noted earlier, the quality and quantity of orientations can vary widely. A good welcome and introduction certainly help to start a new staff officer off on the right foot. And what the introduction lacks, the initiate must provide himself.

The Chain of Command

One matter that may not be addressed in the orientation is the chain of authority. The new staff officer may ask, Who is my commander? For whom do I work? Several aspects of the answer are not as clear-cut as in a troop unit. First and foremost, it should be clear that the section chief is the immediate supervisor. He will assign most work and will rate performance, but he is not a commander. The commanding general is the commanding officer and commands all military personnel assigned to the headquarters. Even though there may be five or six levels of supervisors between the action officer and the commander, the commander alone is responsible for the administration of discipline. In some instances he may delegate specific authorities to his deputy, but in the last analysis *he* still is responsible. So, in the headquarters' hierarchy, the commander and his deputy are the only officers who can exercise disciplinary powers.

On the administrative side, office chiefs are delegated authority to grant leaves and passes, assign details, approve travel, and to perform certain other supervisory functions. They, in turn, may redelegate some of these tasks to their division chiefs. Normal administration of officers' records is performed by the Adjutant General, Officer Personnel Section, or by central personnel offices working through the administrative element in each staff office.

Though, the action officer's staff projects are assigned by his section chief, there are other duties that flow directly down the office chain. These are many of the same "additional duties" so familiar in troop units. Others may be peculiar to a headquarters, but they are still additional duties. Headquarters, wide duties, such as Staff Duty Officer, court martial detail, and Combined Federal Campaign details, are administered by the Adjutant General. Again, coming down the staff chain, each of the several offices may be required to run its own additional duty rosters for essential details at that level. Duties may be as varied as member of an office party committee, inventory officer for classified documents, building fire marshal, project officer for the Boy Scout Camporee, to name a few. Regardless of who maintains the roster, the duties are passed down through the office chain. These chores need doing and the duty roster is equitable. The outstanding officer will tackle these additional duties with the same vigor and purpose that he applies to his regular duties.

Social Duties

Additional duties constitute only one feature of staff line apart from the all-absorbing staff actions. Social duties, official and unofficial, constitute another such feature. The official social demands upon a junior officer in a large headquarters will be less than those in a company, battalion, brigade, or division. Like everything else, social programs depend upon the headquarters. In one large headquarters, he may not be required or have an opportunity to attend a single social event in the course of a year. In another headquarters, the newly joined officer and his wife may be expected at a welcoming reception shortly after arrival, and then attend quarterly headquarters-wide parties. In between, attendance at award and retirement ceremonies and other official functions may be mandatory or optional.

The most prevalent social gatherings at a large headquarters will probably be those sponsored by individual staff offices, or by divisions, branches, and sections within the office. Although there is no written rule, it seems the higher the level of sponsorship, the less frequent the parties. A major staff office that puts on a party more often than once a quarter is, in most headquarters, considered a real swinger. At division or branch level, some sort of monthly social function would not be too unusual. Few, if any, of the functions are put on a "command performance" basis, but attendance is encouraged for all. There is no question that a well balanced, lively social program enhances the esprit of the headquarters and lightens the load of grueling staff work. Social events afford the staff officer opportunities to know his associates better and to make new friends, and, of course, they can be fun.

Staff officers' wives can enjoy social life in the Officers' Wives Club. Most headquarters have one, and in a large headquarters, in addition to the headquarters club, there may be separate organizations for the distaff side of the different staff offices. For example, the officers' wives of the Operations and Training staff office may have a separate club. Furthermore, special groups, such as the wives of aviation officers within Operations and Training, may have their own club. The staff officer's wife can usually avail herself of as much or as little club activity as she might care for. Staff social life is similar to unit social life, except that there probably will not be as much of it, at least on an organized basis.

Characteristics of Successful Staff Officers

After the new staff officer has adjusted to his position and has been exposed to the different features of staff life, the rest is up to him. Presumably, he wants to succeed. Career officers must succeed, and success as a staff officer is as important, if not more so, as succeeding as a troop leader.

The ingredients for success as a staff officer probably differ little from those required for success in any endeavor. In oversimplified form they can be summed up as preparation, application, and attitude. Each warrants further comment.

The matter of advanced preparation was discussed earlier. The suggestions offered concerned the period prior to reporting for staff duty. Some officers may have little opportunity for preparatory study. Those who do should be off to a head start for an early advantage.

The preparation addressed here, however, relates to continued study after reporting. This is the preparation for the next day, the next week, and the next month. Knowledge is crucial to the success of the staff officer, and he should never cease his pursuit of it. There is no limit to the amount of knowledge to be attained, but priorities can be established. The local situation is a good place to start. This can be expanded to meet the next most pressing needs.

Books are valuable but not the only sources of knowledge. Observation helps, and on a large staff one has some excellent opportunities. It is likely that the commander has gathered about him, at least in key positions, the best pros he can find. The new staff officer would do well to study their approach and performance. Keen observation of a large staff should also reveal methods that are not so effective. For worthwhile results, observation requires acute awareness.

Conditioning for added responsibilities is another important preparatory element. The advancing officer should always be prepared to take on additional responsibilities. The smart officer will try to equip himself in advance to take on additional loads. He does this by seeking out and doing those knotty tasks that others avoid. It may be a tough briefing that no one wants to give or a matter to be coordinated with a particularly difficult staff officer. Often the very factors that make these tasks difficult are factors that can turn them into valuable learning vehicles. The briefing may be tough because of the subject matter—good. This will provide an opportunity to study new and more detailed material. More often, however, briefings are avoided because the person to be briefed is considered difficult—so much the better. Good quarterbacks do not develop the ability to withstand the onslaught of 280-pound linemen by playing touch football with the neighborhood Girl Scouts. The briefer who can handle the tough customers is destined to succeed.

The same reasoning applies to coordinating with those considered "hard to deal with." Those "disagreeable" persons are troublesome to the less professional staff members only because they are knowledgeable and have consistently done their homework. They ask questions, pry into background, prefer data to speculation, and they like to see references. They like to know the views of other experts. They dislike sloppiness and abhor incompleteness. Altogether boothersome people are exactly the type to be avoided, except by the staff officer who is prepared to meet their standards—in short, all but those who are themselves satisfied with nothing short of perfection. The officer who is looking for added responsibilities can find many opportunities. Of course, he must be unobtrusive in his approach and effective in his performance. He will grow with these responsibilities. In preparing for bigger things to come, be content to allow others to take the easy jobs. The tough ones are for the best ones.

The next key to success, obviously, is application. Nothing less than total commitment will do. This does not mean a twenty-four hour a day job to the exclusion of everything else. It does mean concentration on the job and a complete willingness to give the time and effort needed to do it well. The task at hand comes first, but balance must be preserved. Most officers are dedicated and approach their profession from the viewpoint of service rather than personal gain. The staff officer must add to his efforts and dedication an additional ounce of devotion. He must remember at all times that his mistakes, or anything short of his best efforts, may reflect more dramatically on others' reputations and careers than upon his. The staff officer is an extension of the commander's responsibilities, and all his actions reflect as though they were taken personally by the commander. This is a heavy responsibility and must be taken very seriously.

Total commitment is only a part of another essential attribute of successful staff officers, and this is attitude. Qualities other than dedication contribute to attitude. One of these is cooperation. Staff work is teamwork and the staff officer must be a team player. Almost every staff action undertaken will require cooperation from others. Conversely, fellow staff officers need assistance in their efforts. The staff has one purpose—to assist the commander—and nothing less than the full cooperation of every staff officer is required to insure optimum progress toward that goal.

Courtesy, of course, complements cooperation. It recognizes the dignity of an individual and usually evokes a positive response. It is easily given and gratefully received. No man is too big or too busy to practice ordinary courtesy in his daily relationships and his work. Military courtesy typifies the professional.

The successful staff officer must be creative as well as cooperative. He must exercise his imagination to the fullest and have the moral courage to stand behind his independent thinking. In most cases it would be much easier, when grappling with a tough problem, to polish up a solution that the boss wants to hear. The valuable staff officer, though, is the one who exercises his imagination and intellect to come up with his own solution, one that appears to be the best. Staff officers who present solutions borrowed from the commander make a very limited contribution. A parrot can say, "yes, sir." The best efforts of the staff can only be realized when all of its members have harnessed their brainpower and are putting forth fresh ideas. The fledgling staff officer may be reluctant to try out his ideas for fear of embarrassment. This is no excuse for holding back. Cut-and-try is part of the learning process. There is always room for creative thinking.

The staff officer's attitude must be "can do," and this is *sine qua non*. This approach is important in any field, but it is especially applicable to the staff officer, particularly the new staff officer. A "can do" attitude provides the necessary drive to get him through the early days of his assignment, when things can be confusing or even discouraging. Once he has adjusted, he needs a positive approach to face the many problems and situations that will confront him. Staff work consists primarily of problem-solving. Some problems are easy, but most are complex beyond description. A strong, affirmative state of mind is needed to meet these challenges. There is no room for wavering—only the positive will succeed.

A natural question might be, which of the keys is most important? None can be singled out as the most crucial. Some may have more application in different cases. The really important requirement is to keep all things in balance. If one goes overboard in a particular area, other areas of concentration are bound to get out of balance. All must be synchronized for smooth functioning.

The Rewards

A successful staff tour has its rewards, both personal and professional. Professionally, the new staff officer has mastered the rudiments of military staff work. He has qualified himself for further staff assignments of greater complexity and added responsibility. He has added to his background an understanding of the military staff system which will be of value in any future assignment. Most importantly, he has met and, hopefully, impressed superiors and coworkers. Those new associates will remember him in later years when key people are needed for bigger and better jobs. Furthermore, the contacts and friendships formed with associates can be valuable to him throughout his career.

From a personal standpoint the rewards are even greater. Many professional friendships are also personal friendships that can grow to be treasured through the years. Likewise, memories of the trials and triumphs have a way of hanging around for future reminiscence. The successful completion of a staff tour can also do wonders for an officer's self-confidence. This, of course, must be held in bounds, but it is a comforting feeling to know that the next staff assignment can be taken in stride. For most, however, the greatest satisfaction comes from knowing that a difficult assignment has been met and mastered. This strong sense of accomplishment whets the appetite for the next challenge.

12.

Staff Officers of Other Services

As stated at the outset, this book's primary goal is to help U.S. Army staff officers become better assistants and advisors to their commanders. It is particularly aimed at the younger officers whose backgrounds, training, and military experience have inadequately prepared them for staff assignments. To a large extent, the book reflects the authors' combined thirty years of Army experience on the staffs of many commanders at varying levels of responsibility. For that reason, some of the detailed procedures, office titles, and sample formats discussed in previous chapters may be inapplicable to the other military branches—Air Force, Navy, Marine Corps.

However, the fundamentals of good staff work are the same in all services and, for the most part, staff organizations, procedures, and typical actions vary little among the services. Most importantly the skills, techniques, and personal characteristics that mark the outstanding staff officer are common prerequisites for success regardless of uniform color. Staff officers from any service can profit from the guidance proffered in the preceding chapters. The following discussions are intended to highlight the similarities between the staffs of the several services and to provide a basis, or point of departure, for applying the material to the other services. First, all staff officers, regardless of service, must recognize and accept the fact that their respective service, while separate, is not truly independent. Each depends on, is obligated to, and must work closely with its sister services.

Interservice Relationships

Perhaps very early in the history of organized warfare, battles fought on land were completely independent from naval operations. However, it is difficult to imagine a time when navies did not depend on land forces to secure and hold bases from which their ships could operate. Even more difficult to imagine would be armies operating in foreign lands across the seas without depending on ships for transportation, resupply, and protection from seaborne attack. Of course, those who fight in the air have always depended on their ground and sea based counterparts to provide secure operating and living facilities. At the same time, Air Force missions have always been heavily oriented toward assisting their sister services.

Successful officers of all services always have been keenly aware of their dependence on and obligations to other services. In today's complex and sophisticated military profession, the officer who understands only his own service is, in effect, a professional cripple. Except for the most insignificant tasks, he cannot possibly perform effectively in even the smaller single service headquarters. Assignments to the challenging and professionally rewarding *joint* and *combined* staffs would be out of the question. In the space available a course of instruction on the staffs of each branch of the military services is impossible. Hopefully, however, sufficient information can be provided to stimulate interest in further research and study.

Purpose of Separate Services

For many years military leaders and civilian authorities have come along who advocated creating a single, all purpose defense force to replace the independent branches—Army, Navy, Air Force, Marine Corps and, in time of war, Coast Guard. Opponents have argued that basic differences in mission orientation and the unique environment for which each service is oriented make such a single service infeasible. The relative merits of these positions are not germane to the purposes of this book, but differences *do* exist, and they must be recognized by all staff officers. Those who defend their country face-to-face with the enemy on the ground form different philosophies from those who serve on the seas or engage the enemy in the air. Also, each arm has its own proud history of service to the country, and each is steeped in its own tradition of heroism, courage, dedication, and undivided loyalty.

The entire Department of Defense, each of its branches, and every uniformed member and civilian employee share a common overall mission—defense of the United States. At the highest levels of responsibility, however, that single mission divides into three major environmentally oriented facets: defense on the sea, defense in the air, and defense on the land. Where these responsibilities interface, additional factors require land forces (Marines) to operate on land in support of the waterborne operations, creating bridgeheads from the sea to the land, and sea forces designed and equipped to operate near the land (Coast Guard). It is apparent that this natural division of national defense forces along environmental lines must unavoidably lead to some divergence of philosophies and priorities of concerns.

Although dedicated to the same mission, each service must place major emphasis on its respective area of interest, thus assuring that each facet of defense receives adequate consideration. The minor differences in staff organizations, terminology, procedures and formats stem from the singular nature of each service's operating environment, its specialized equipment, and the peculiarities of the tactics and strategies employed to accomplish its missions, whether air, land, or sea oriented. Again, it is emphasized that these are *minor* differences. They are no bar to interservice cooperation, nor do they detract from the basic similarities between the staffs of the respective services. However, the Army or Air Force officer who must work with a Navy headquarters would certainly find a background knowledge of Navy customs, traditions, procedures and terminology helpful.

Service Similarities

Not even the strongest advocate of the single service concept would deny that differences exist among the services, and he would also concede that many of those differences would continue even if all military men wore the same color uniform. Conversely, the staunchest supporter of the multiservice defense force would admit that the differences are less significant than and far outweighed by the similarities.

Missions. Before making specific staff comparisons, it might be well to examine some of the common ground shared by the staffs of all services.

All share a common mission, the defense of the United States. Each has a separate role, but in modern warfare many areas overlap. This overlap sometimes attracts public attention when jurisdictional disputes arise. Forward area air defense for ground troops is a good example of a past jurisdictional controversy. The Army and the Air Force each believed, with some justification, that the air defense mission fell into its operational area. The Air Force maintained that combating its counterpart, enemy air forces, was clearly an Air Force mission of such importance that it should not be fragmented. The Army believed that its commanders should have the responsibilities, capabilities, and authority to protect the ground forces essential to their missions.

So, while all of the services are dedicated to the same mission, unanimity of opinion is not automatic. However, the fact that jurisdictional disputes can arise, emphasizes the extent to which technological advances have drawn the services' missions closer together. Disputes arise from similarities of missions, not from differences.

Command Channels. In addition to sharing a common mission, the services operate under the direction of the same Commander in Chief, the president. His authority to command is established by the Constitution and the American people. From the president, the chain of command leads downward through another common authority, the Secretary of Defense and his advisors, the Joint Chiefs of Staff, composed of the Army and Air Force Chiefs of Staff, the Chief of Naval Operations and, when appropriate, the Commandant of the Marine Corps.

At the top command echelon, therefore, all services share a common command authority, and their directives, regulations and guidance are formulated by the same staff, the Joint Chiefs and their assistants. Planning at the Joint Chief's level embraces an interacting defense concept, so here there are even greater interservice similarities. Most contingency plans for possible future combat operations are prepared in broad, conceptual format by the Joint Chiefs of Staff for the Secretary of Defense and are equally applicable to each service. Each service must prepare supporting plans compatible with, supporting, and supported by the plans of other services. Since these plans must be developed and coordinated at many levels of responsibility, mutual cooperation is essential, as is standardization of organizations and procedures.

Below the Office of the Secretary of Defense, lines of authority separate by services, starting at the Department level with the Secretaries of the Army, Navy and Air Force, then to the senior military officer in each service, and down the respective military chain of each service. The Joint Chiefs of Staff direct the operations of all unified commands which include forces from two or more of the services. Here the line of command is from the Chairman, Joint Chiefs of Staff to the Commander of the unified command, thence down the chain to the different service forces within the command. Chart 12.1 reflects this top level command organization.

Legislative and Judicial Controls. Command authority is undivided and rests entirely with the president as Commander in Chief, and is exercised through the agencies of the executive branch of the government. In their efforts to create checks and balances in our government, the framers of the Constitution gave the other branches authority to regulate and control the military establishment. All services are subject to the laws passed by the legislative branch, and their judicial systems must meet the requirements of the Constitution as interpreted by the U.S. Supreme Court.

The legislative branch exercises an additional, very powerful influence significant to all military activities—it controls the resources available for operations. Congress appropriates and allocates money for national defense, and it also sets the upper limits on military strengths, and approves development and acquisition of new equipment. These common controls also contribute to the standardization of procedures within the different services.

**Chart 12.1
Department of Defense
Command Structure**

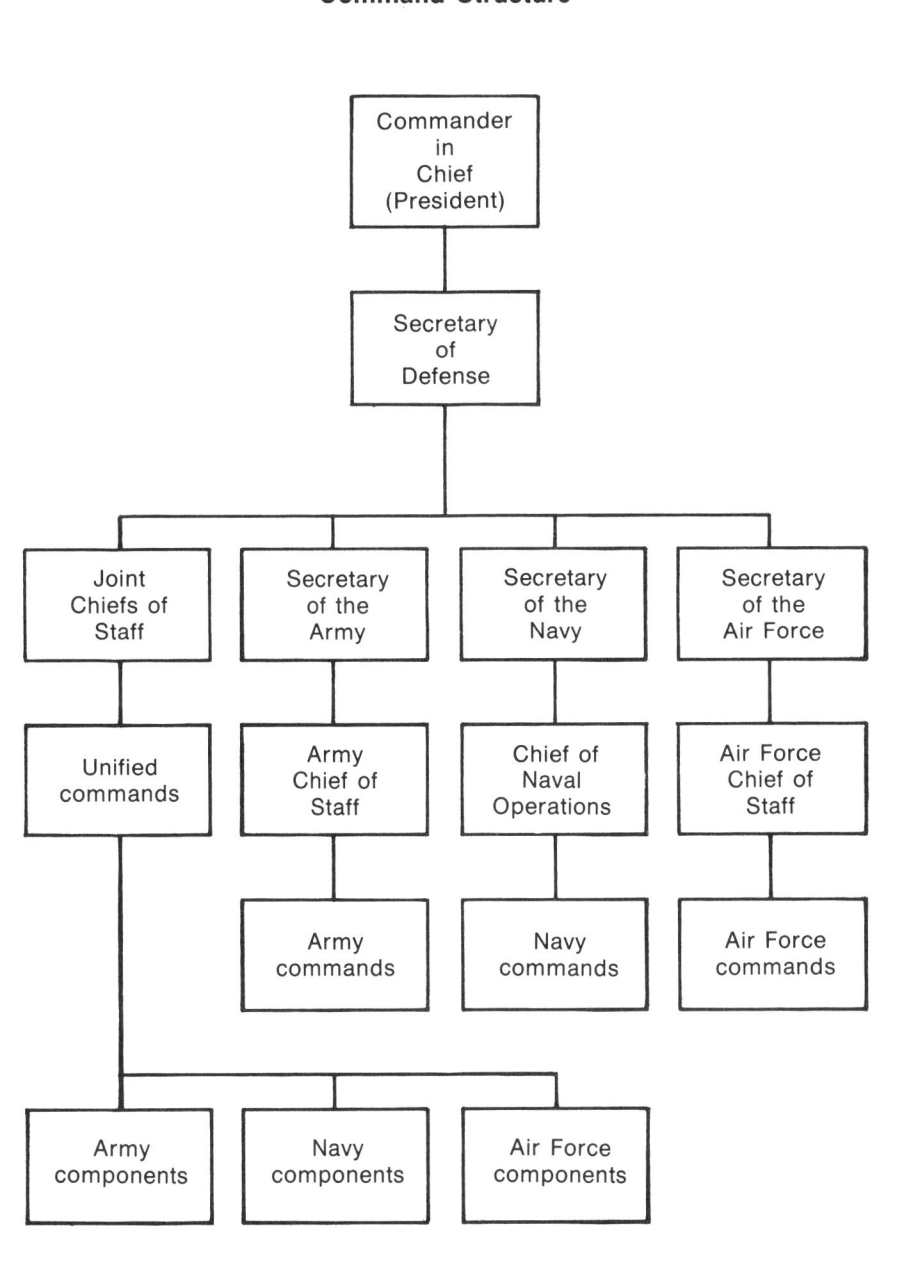

```
                    Commander
                        in
                      Chief
                   (President)
                        |
                   Secretary
                       of
                   Defense
                        |
  ┌─────────────┬─────────────┬─────────────┐
 Joint       Secretary    Secretary    Secretary
 Chiefs of   of the       of the       of the
 Staff       Army         Navy         Air Force
  |             |             |             |
 Unified     Army         Chief of     Air Force
 commands    Chief of     Naval        Chief of
             Staff        Operations   Staff
  |             |             |             |
             Army         Navy         Air Force
             commands     commands     commands
  |
  ├─────────────┬─────────────┐
 Army         Navy         Air Force
 components   components   components
```

Command Philosophy. Since command authority flows from and responsibilities are assigned by the Commander in Chief through a single staff, the services share common definitions and philosophy of command. In its simplest form, command is the authority exercised by a military commander over his subordinates by virtue of rank or assignment. Each service accepts the philosophy that, at each echelon, all responsibilities are charged to a single person—the commander. He alone is responsible for all that his subordinates do, and all that they fail to do. Commanders assign specific responsibilities to subordinate commanders, to staffs, and to individual assistants. With each assignment they delegate the authority necessary to get the job done.

Assigning responsibilities and delegating authority in no way alter a commander's position in the eyes of his superiors. He, and he alone, remains totally responsible. This includes the responsibility for properly exercising delegated authority. This philosophy engenders another which establishes a common point of departure for all staff officers' approach to their duties. Staffs and their members exist only to assist and advise their commanders. They have no other purposes.

Mission Orientation. Another philosophy common to all services concerns their devotion to mission accomplishment. All services are mission oriented. The mission comes first, regardless of costs or consequences. A moment's reflection should confirm the necessity for this obsession with mission in the military service. Anything less would completely undermine military effectiveness, and its soundness has been proven through the centuries.

Organization. The services share a common approach to command and mission, and to a large extent, to organization as well. The services are functionally organized. In fact, the Department of Defense is functionally organized for land, sea and air operations. Within the services, organizational units are similarly grouped by functions. Typical examples might include a troop carrier wing, a destroyer squadron or an armored division.

The same type of functional organization carries over into the staffs in the different services. First, all are organized to advise and assist the commander. In addition they are broken down into organizational groupings that represent the broad fields of command interest: personnel, intelligence, operations, logistics, comptroller, and communications. Furthermore, the larger staffs within each service (the staffs of general and flag officers) are made up of three components: personal staff, coordinating staff, and special staff.

Comparison of Staff Organizations

The similarities between staff organizations can best be illustrated by examining the organizational charts of representative headquarters of each service at several different levels of responsibility. Equating levels of responsibility among the services is difficult. The comparisons chosen are primarily based on the approximate grades of the commanders. Chart 12.2 depicts the organization of the U.S. Army Forces Command; 12.3 is the organization of

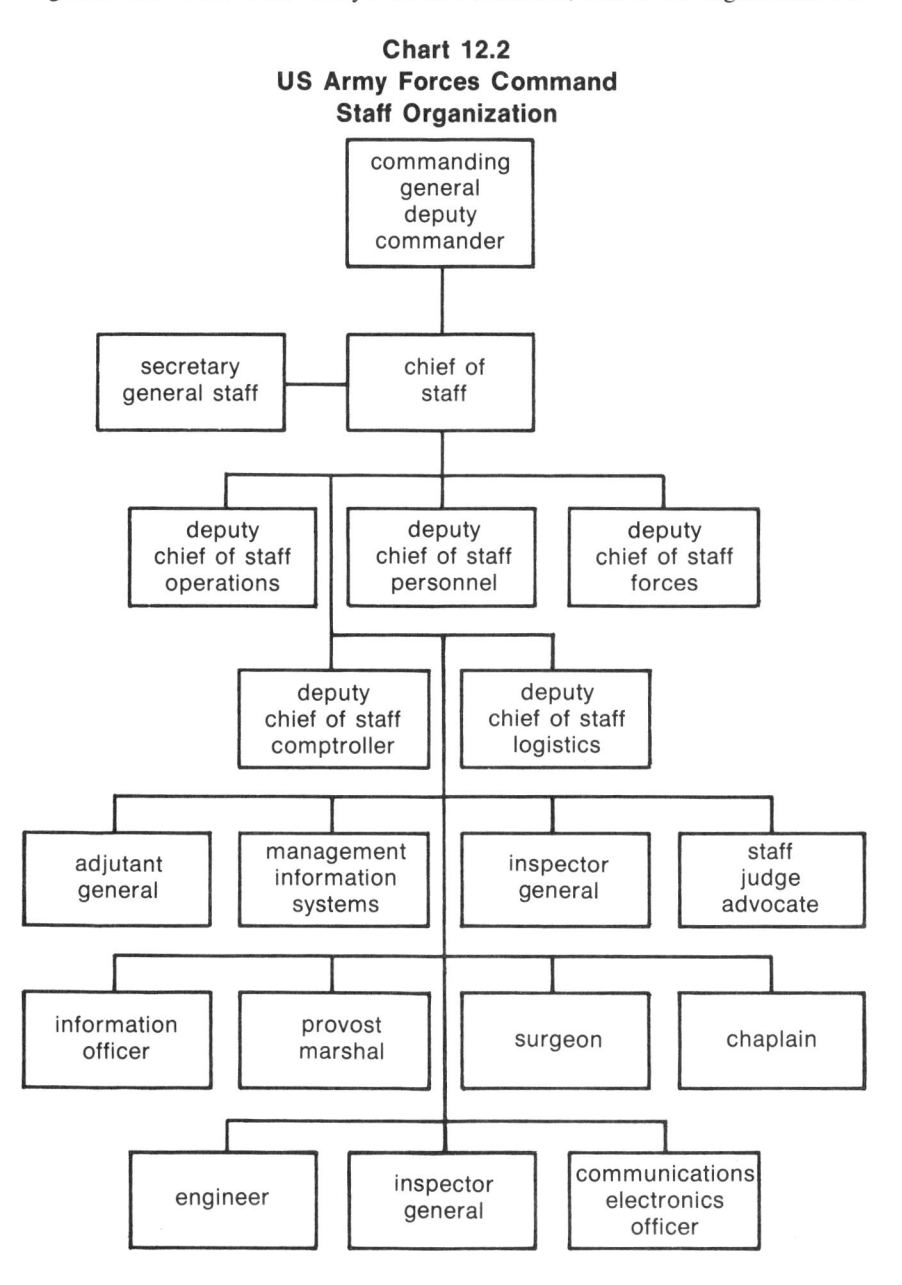

Chart 12.2
US Army Forces Command
Staff Organization

```
                    commanding general
                    deputy commander
                           |
        secretary ——— chief of staff
        general staff
                           |
        ┌──────────────────┼──────────────────┐
    deputy              deputy              deputy
    chief of staff      chief of staff      chief of staff
    operations          personnel           forces
                           |
                  ┌────────┴────────┐
              deputy              deputy
              chief of staff      chief of staff
              comptroller         logistics
                           |
    ┌──────────┬───────────┼───────────┬──────────┐
  adjutant   management   inspector            staff
  general    information  general              judge
             systems                           advocate
                           |
    ┌──────────┬───────────┼───────────┬──────────┐
  information  provost                          chaplain
  officer      marshal     surgeon
                           |
              ┌────────────┼────────────┐
          engineer      inspector    communications
                        general      electronics
                                     officer
```

Headquarters, U.S. Naval Training Command; and 12.4 shows the staff arrangement in the U.S. Air Force Strategic Air Command. The most cursory examination of these senior headquarters' staff structures reveals that they are virtually identical. Minor differences exist in the titles of major staff elements, and there is some variation in the organization of subelements. For

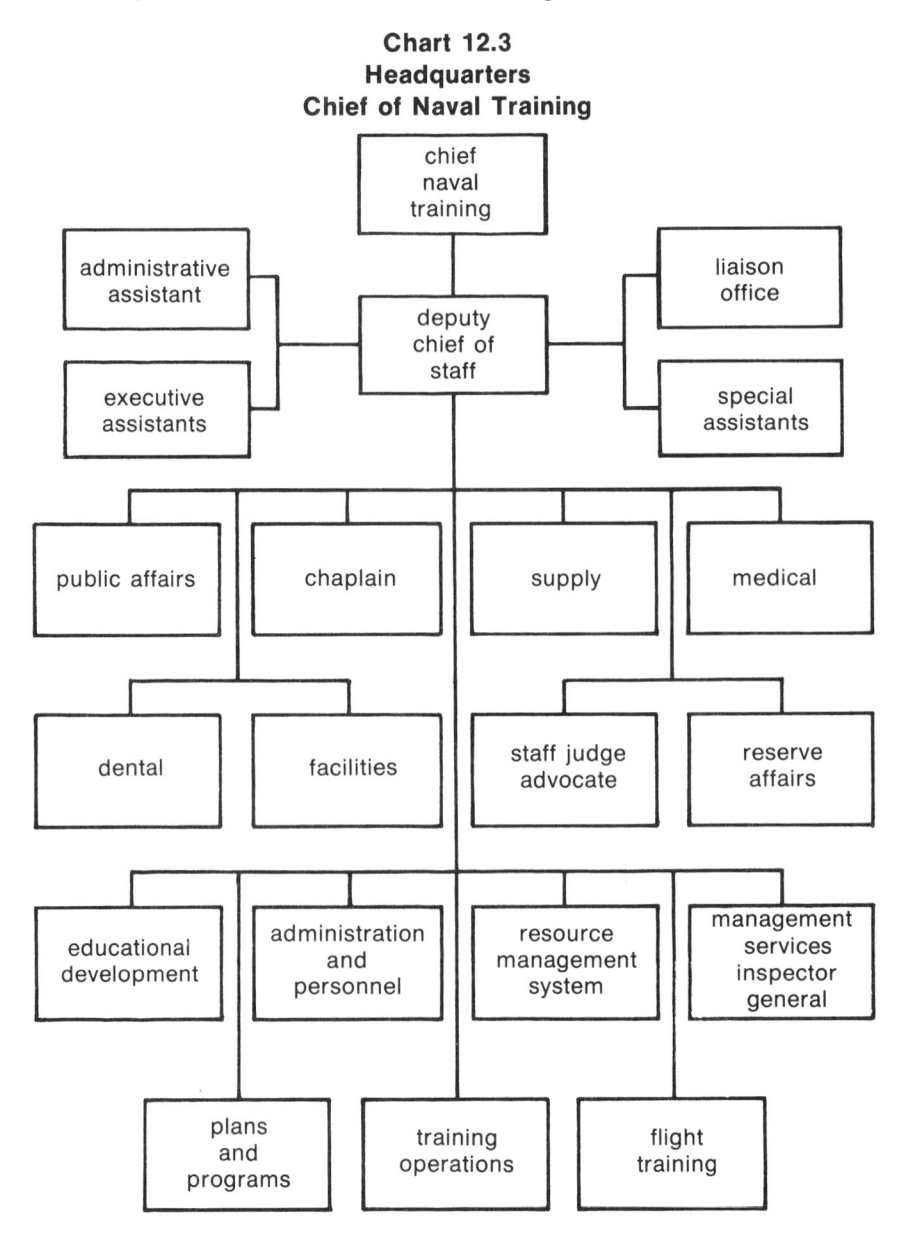

**Chart 12.3
Headquarters
Chief of Naval Training**

- chief naval training
  - administrative assistant
  - executive assistants
  - liaison office
  - special assistants
  - deputy chief of staff
    - public affairs
    - chaplain
    - supply
    - medical
    - dental
    - facilities
    - staff judge advocate
    - reserve affairs
    - educational development
    - administration and personnel
    - resource management system
    - management services inspector general
    - plans and programs
    - training operations
    - flight training

example, the Air Force Director of Administration does not have the military personnel functions performed by his Army counterpart, the Adjutant General. These differences are insignificant in view of the overriding similarities. Staff element titles are unimportant, as are minor variations in assignments of specific functions. The important comparison is in major areas of command interest reflected in the staff organizations.

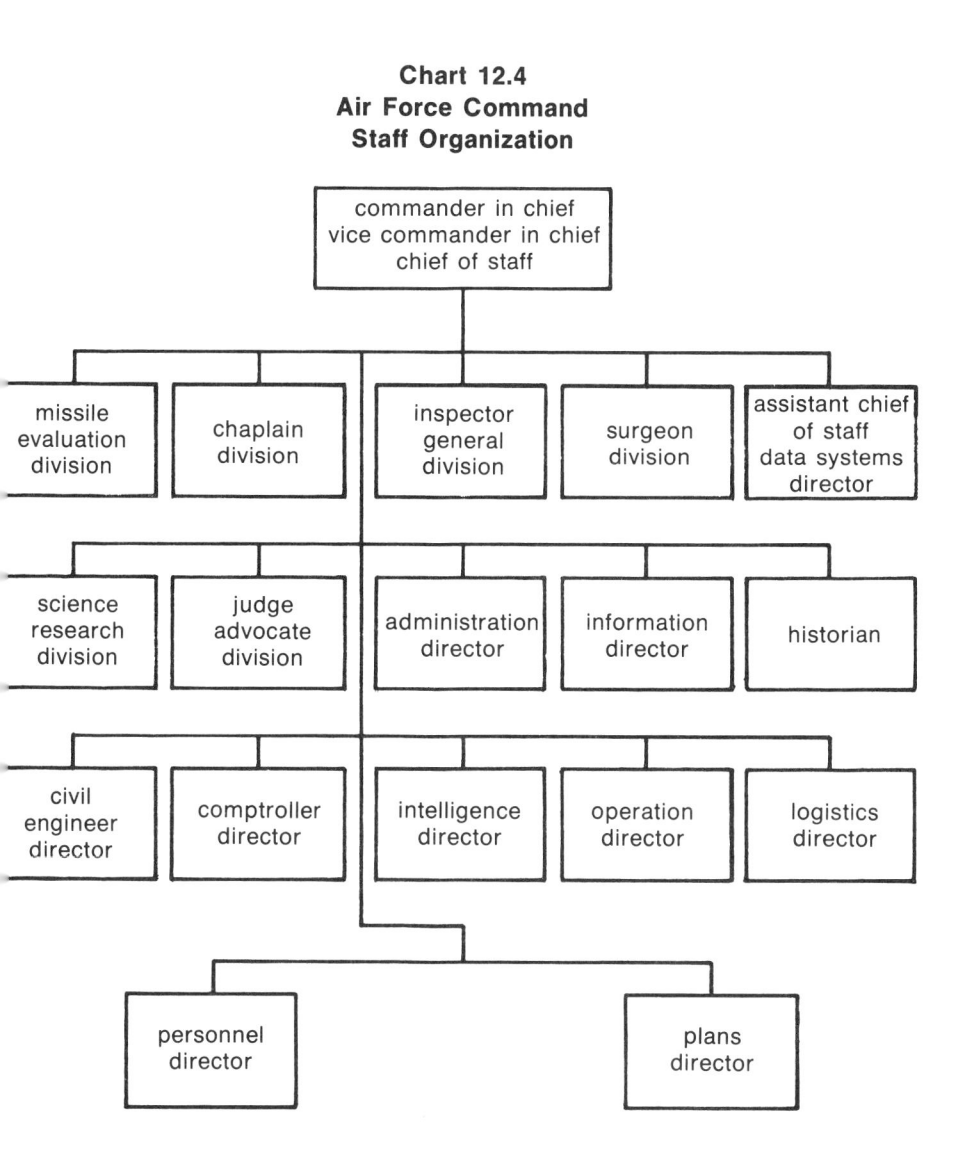

**Chart 12.4
Air Force Command
Staff Organization**

- commander in chief / vice commander in chief / chief of staff
  - missile evaluation division
  - chaplain division
  - inspector general division
  - surgeon division
  - assistant chief of staff data systems director
  - science research division
  - judge advocate division
  - administration director
  - information director
  - historian
  - civil engineer director
  - comptroller director
  - intelligence director
  - operation director
  - logistics director
  - personnel director
  - plans director

276   The Army Staff Officer's Guide

The similarities are further demonstrated by additional comparisons. Chart 12.5 is the headquarters organization for an Army Corps; Chart 12.6 shows the headquarters organization of Numbered Air Force; 12.7 reflects the staff organization for a Navy Fleet; and Chart 12.8 is a typical Marine

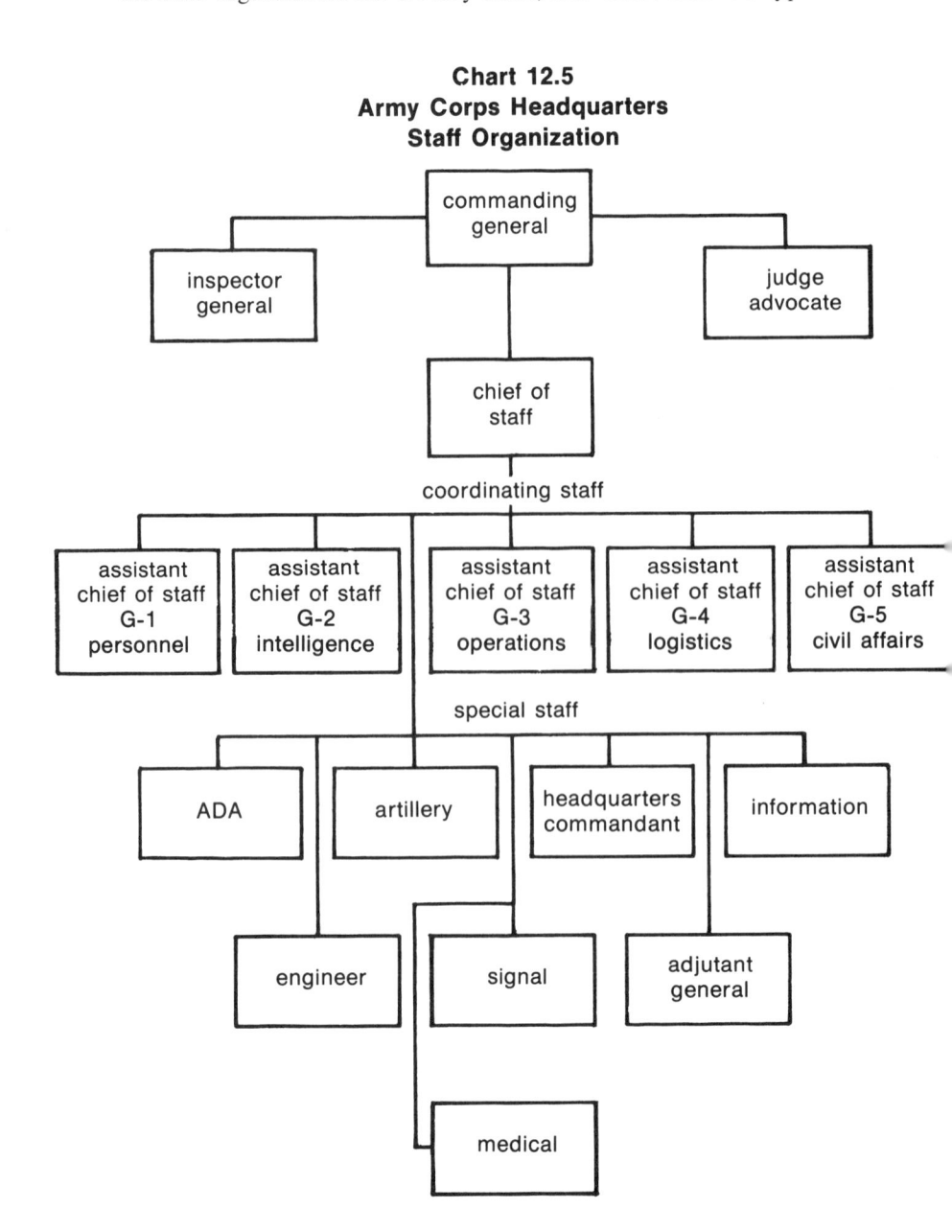

**Chart 12.5
Army Corps Headquarters
Staff Organization**

- commanding general
  - inspector general
  - judge advocate
  - chief of staff
    - coordinating staff
      - assistant chief of staff G-1 personnel
      - assistant chief of staff G-2 intelligence
      - assistant chief of staff G-3 operations
      - assistant chief of staff G-4 logistics
      - assistant chief of staff G-5 civil affairs
    - special staff
      - ADA
      - artillery
      - headquarters commandant
      - information
      - engineer
      - signal
      - adjutant general
      - medical

Corps staff organization. Again the similarities are obvious, further emphasizing the common command concerns around which all staffs are built—people, their health, welfare, training, and problems; information on wide ranges of influencing factors; the physical assets needed to accomplish the mission; and planning and supervision of operations, whether land, sea, or air.

(Text continued on page 279)

**Chart 12.6
Numbered Air Force
Staff Organization**

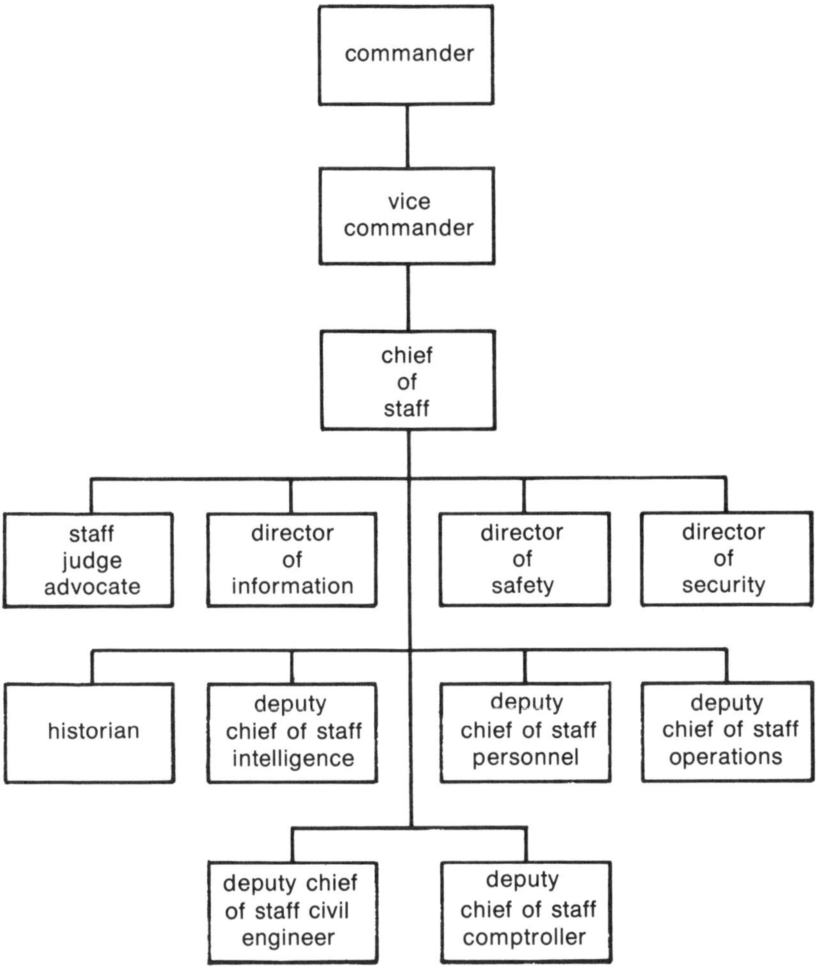

```
                    commander
                        |
                 vice commander
                        |
                   chief of staff
    _____|_____
   |            |              |             |
  staff      director      director      director
  judge         of            of            of
 advocate   information     safety       security
   |_____|_____|_____|
   |            |              |             |
historian    deputy         deputy        deputy
          chief of staff  chief of staff chief of staff
          intelligence    personnel      operations
                   |_____|
                   |              |
             deputy chief     deputy
             of staff civil  chief of staff
              engineer       comptroller
```

**Chart 12.7
Operational Staff
Commander in Chief
US Pacific Fleet**

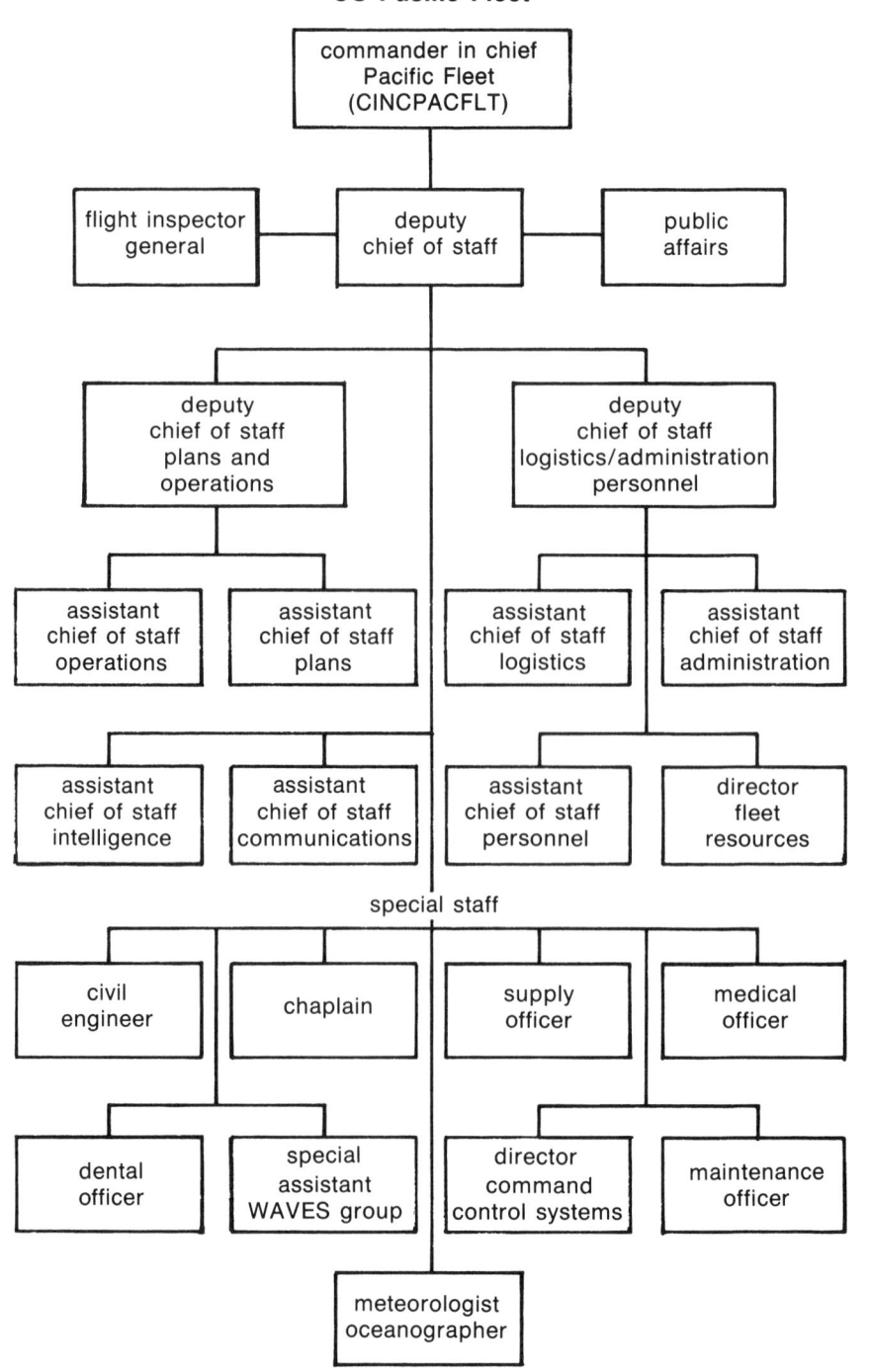

- commander in chief Pacific Fleet (CINCPACFLT)
  - flight inspector general
  - deputy chief of staff
  - public affairs
    - deputy chief of staff plans and operations
      - assistant chief of staff operations
      - assistant chief of staff plans
      - assistant chief of staff intelligence
      - assistant chief of staff communications
    - deputy chief of staff logistics/administration personnel
      - assistant chief of staff logistics
      - assistant chief of staff administration
      - assistant chief of staff personnel
      - director fleet resources

special staff

- civil engineer
- chaplain
- supply officer
- medical officer
- dental officer
- special assistant WAVES group
- director command control systems
- maintenance officer
- meteorologist oceanographer

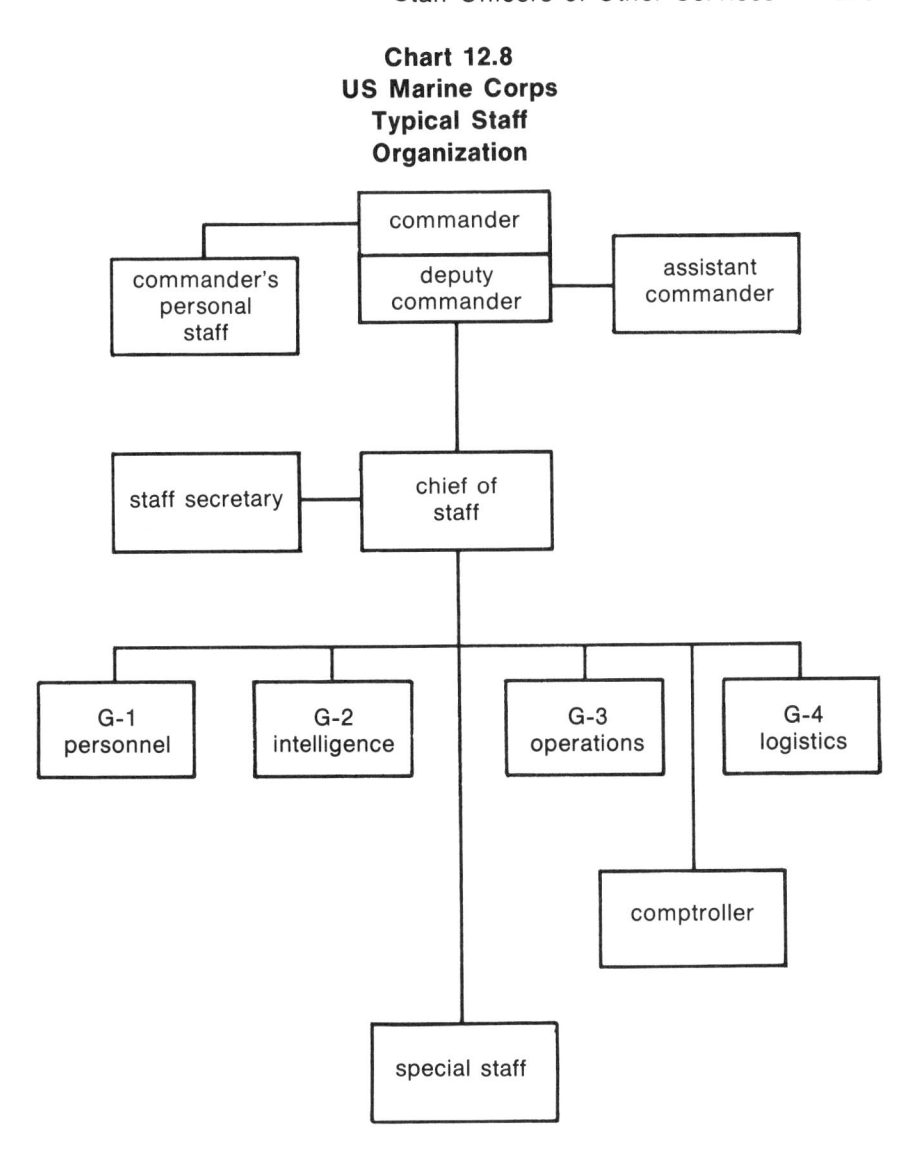

**Chart 12.8
US Marine Corps
Typical Staff
Organization**

```
                    commander
commander's         deputy          assistant
personal            commander       commander
staff

staff secretary     chief of
                    staff

G-1          G-2            G-3          G-4
personnel    intelligence   operations   logistics

                            comptroller

            special staff
```

Flexibility and Deviations. Although all services are prone to standardization in their staffs, considerable flexibility is available to meet unique situations and special mission requirements. This is particularly true for the Navy and Air Force because of the different combinations of units to be controlled and the wide variety of operations to be undertaken. Also, staffs of smaller unit commanders vary somewhat from the pattern of larger staffs. This reflects the more specialized, narrower missions of smaller units. The Air Force, for wing level and subordinate unit staffs, uses a dual deputy system rather than the multiple director system found in larger headquarters. Essentially, the dual deputy system breaks into two elements, operations and support. The Navy's shipboard staff is tailored to meet unique requirements, and the Army's staff for the commander of an installation varies from the standard pattern of larger organizations.

As a final comparison, charts 12.9 through 12.11 reflect the staff organizations of relatively small Army, Navy and Air Force headquarters: an Army Battalion; an Air Force Squadron; and a Navy Ship Staff. In the last analysis, all staffs are organized to deal with the same things—people, intelligence, operations, and physical assets. Because of their critical importance, money and communications often are managed by separate staff elements.

Common Policies. In the different services, command policies covering staff responsiveness and relationships with other commands have much in common. All commanders want to be informed of significant actions and to make the key decisions. They also want to be totally responsive to higher headquarters yet retain freedom of action. Lastly, they want to provide all possible support to subordinate commanders and permit full exercise of initiative within command policy or direction. All staffs must perform within these guidelines.

Staff Actions. To this point the common features of purpose, organization, functions, and policy have been reviewed. We have seen what the service staffs are, what they do and why they do it. The next matter to be addressed is *how* they do it. Here too, in the broad sense, many similarities exist. The staff officer's job, in all services, is problem-solving. Most of his time and effort will be consumed in identifying problems, developing solutions, getting agreement, selling the product, and insuring that the solution is carried out.

It should be evident from earlier chapters that the standard staff approach to the problem-solving process used by the Army is a *military* approach, not an *Army* approach. All services use staff studies, estimates, plans, orders, and reports. Certainly not all of the formats are identical in every detail, but the procedure is the same. Formats can be learned with minimum effort. The sophisticated steps of the procedure (research, analysis, evaluation, coordination, recommendation, and supervision) are not so easy. They require extensive training and practice to be mastered. Once learned, however, the professional skills can be applied in any staff situation, regardless of service.

The same can be said for the personal skills and techniques addressed in Chapter 10. Rare indeed is the officer who excels in all of the skills. Most are well aware of the time, the patience, and the effort required to master even

(Text continued on page 282)

Staff Officers of Other Services 281

Chart 12.9
Typical Army Battalion Staff Organization

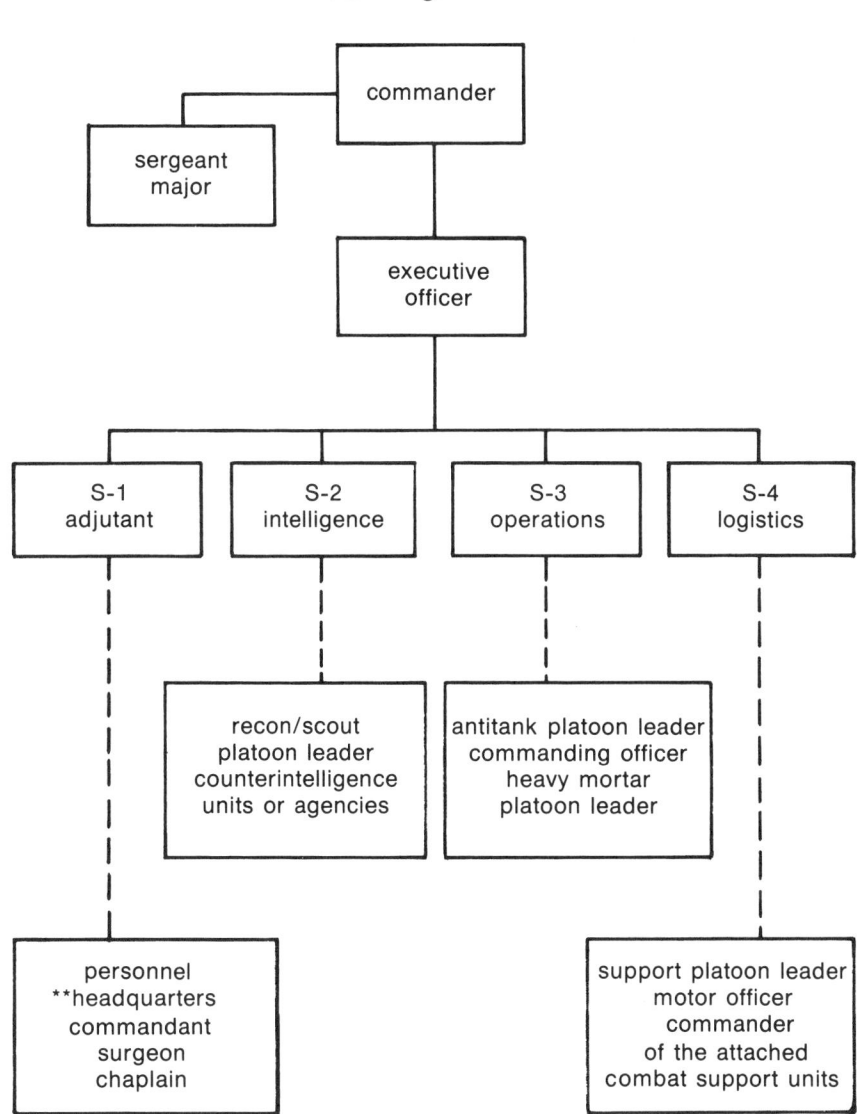

```
                        ┌──────────────┐
                        │  commander   │
        ┌───────────┐   │              │
        │ sergeant  ├───┤              │
        │  major    │   └──────┬───────┘
        └───────────┘          │
                        ┌──────┴───────┐
                        │  executive   │
                        │   officer    │
                        └──────┬───────┘
         ┌────────────┬────────┼────────┬────────────┐
    ┌────┴────┐  ┌────┴────┐ ┌─┴──────┐ ┌────┴────┐
    │  S-1    │  │  S-2    │ │  S-3   │ │  S-4    │
    │adjutant │  │intel.   │ │operat. │ │logistics│
    └─────────┘  └─────────┘ └────────┘ └─────────┘
```

recon/scout platoon leader
counterintelligence units or agencies

antitank platoon leader
commanding officer
heavy mortar platoon leader

personnel
**headquarters commandant
surgeon
chaplain

support platoon leader
motor officer
commander of the attached combat support units

composition of special staff varies to suit type of battalion
**headquarters company commander performs headquarters commandant functions.

**Chart 12.10
Standard
Ship's Organization**

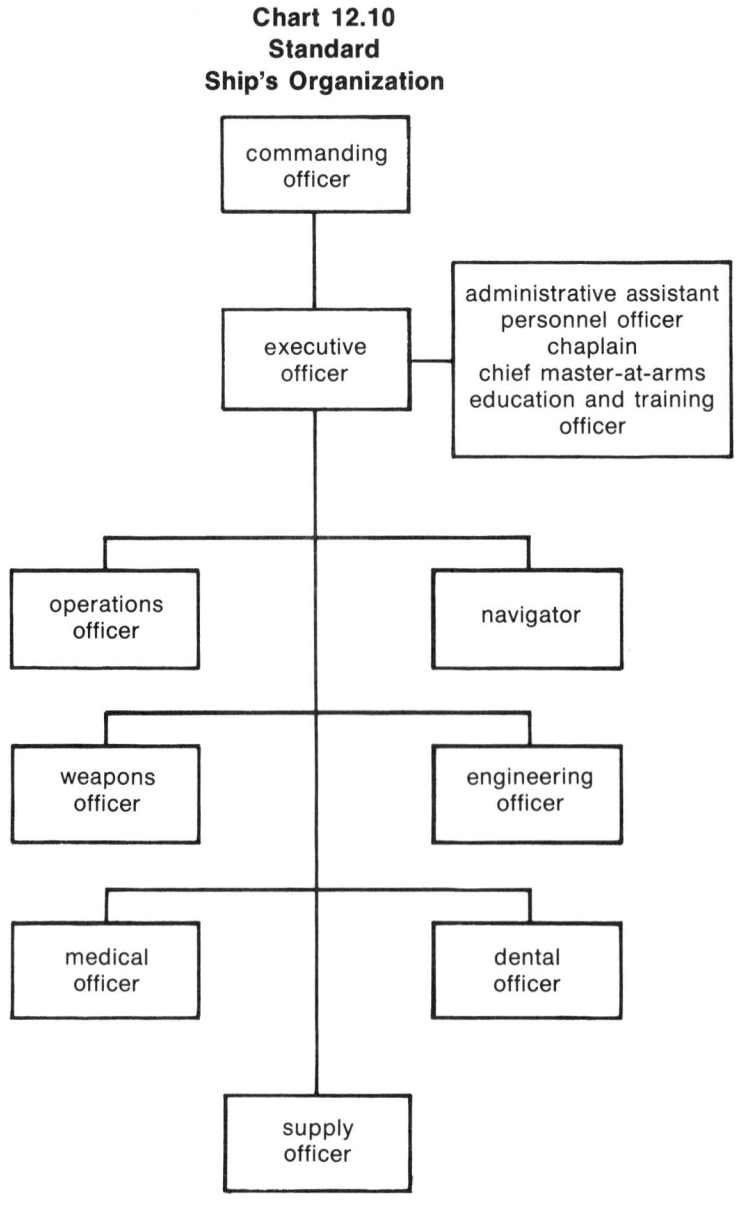

```
                    commanding
                      officer
                         |
                         |
                    executive          administrative assistant
                     officer           personnel officer
                         |             chaplain
                         |             chief master-at-arms
                         |             education and training
                         |             officer
        ┌────────────────┴────────────────┐
   operations                         navigator
    officer
   ┌────────────────────────────────────┐
   weapons                          engineering
   officer                            officer
   ┌────────────────────────────────────┐
   medical                            dental
   officer                           officer
                   supply
                   officer
```

one of the skills—writing, for example. The multiplicity of skills needed brings the scope of the task into focus. Mastery of the personal skills parallels that of the professional skills in effort and commitment required. These skills, too, can be put to work in any situation in any service. In fact this often happens, as officers of all services work side-by-side in the same headquarters.

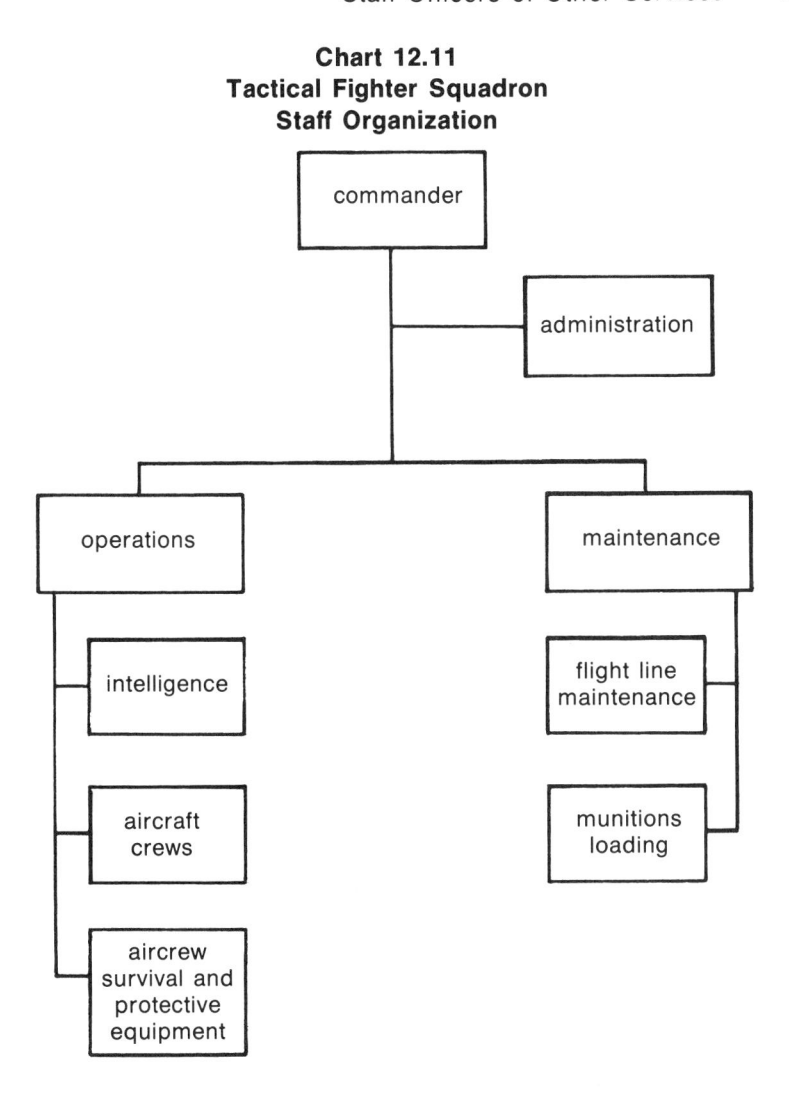

Chart 12.11
Tactical Fighter Squadron Staff Organization

```
                    commander
                       |
                       |—————— administration
                       |
          ——————————————————————
          |                    |
      operations          maintenance
          |                    |
      intelligence      flight line maintenance
          |                    |
      aircraft crews    munitions loading
          |
      aircrew survival and
      protective equipment
```

Joint Staffs

Joint staffs are organized to support commanders of unified commands. Such multiservice commands normally are established to accomplish long-term missions which require execution by forces from two or more of the armed services, and which require unified direction. Unified commands are also used for complex operations in a large geographical area by multiservice forces.

Commanders of unified commands are designated from one of the service components. In instances where the mission has equal air, ground, and water implications, the command may rotate among the services, with Army, Air Force and Navy alternately providing the commander for specified terms. More frequently the commander is selected from the service most directly involved in the mission. Regardless of service, the unified commander's role is identical to that of his single service counterpart. He has full and absolute direction over the forces and resources assigned to accomplish his mission—he is the boss.

His orders come directly from the Joint Chiefs of Staff where they are issued in the name and under the authority of the Secretary of Defense. The U.S. European Command and the U.S. Pacific Command are typical unified commands. Organizational structures of joint staffs closely parallel those of the larger service staffs as illustrated in the typical *Joint Staff* organization shown on chart 12.12. Procedures are also adapted from those used by the different service staffs. Estimates and staff studies are used to analyze and resolve problems, and plans and orders are used to implement solutions.

Combined Commands

Combined commands are similar to unified commands, but also include forces from allied nations. All that has been said about joint staffs could be said about combined staffs, with the additional dimension of international composition. However, one dimension is sometimes ommitted. Combined commands sometimes consist of a single service. In the North Atlantic Treaty Organization, for example, several combined headquarters have been established to control land forces, while others are responsible for air and sea operations. The separation of responsibilities and authority is somewhat deceptive. When three commanders must plan for possible massive military operations in one area—one responsible for land warfare, another for air operations, and the other for control of the seas—they obviously must work closely together. Their plans must be mutually supporting, and they must share the available resources to support contingencies. The staff officers who create and maintain the harmonious relationships which comprise this community of effort must be of the highest caliber.

The proceedings of joint and combined staffs are more formal than their service counterparts, and for good reasons. The scope and complexity of the operations, the divergence of interests, and the significance of the actions dictate that they be formalized and recorded.

Assignments to Joint and Combined Staffs. Duty with joint and combined staffs calls for the top professionals in the military business. Only those capable of eclectic, broad thinking and who can set aside single service prejudices can hope to succeed. Even in a single service headquarters, staff officers cannot entirely divorce their efforts from those of sister services. In

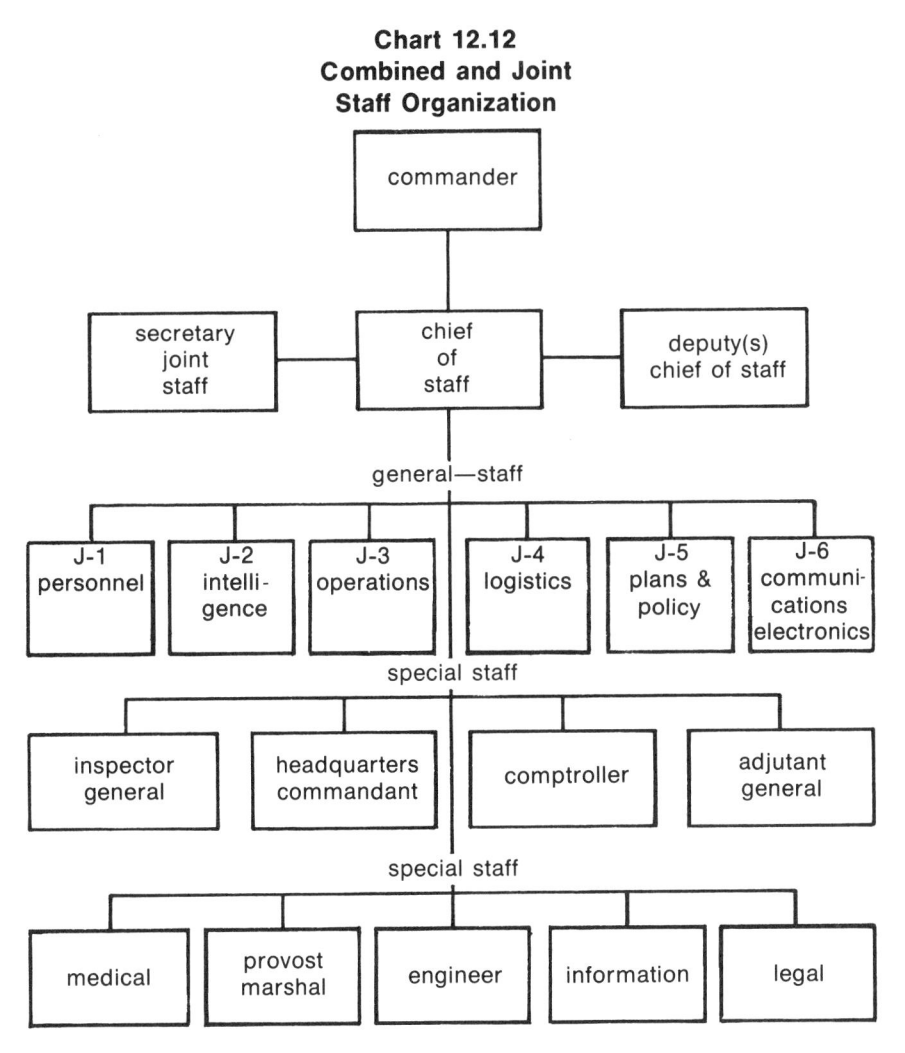

Chart 12.12
Combined and Joint Staff Organization

```
                          commander
                              |
    secretary ——— chief of staff ——— deputy(s)
    joint staff                       chief of staff
                              |
                        general—staff
   ┌──────┬──────┬──────┼──────┬──────┐
  J-1    J-2    J-3    J-4    J-5    J-6
personnel intelli- operations logistics plans & communi-
         gence                         policy cations
                                              electronics

                        special staff
   ┌──────────┬──────────┬──────────┐
  inspector  headquarters  comptroller  adjutant
  general    commandant                 general

                        special staff
   ┌────────┬────────┬────────┬────────┐
  medical  provost  engineer information legal
           marshal
```

*normally, two deputies: one for administration; one for operations.

general, however, staff officers in an air, ground, or sea headquarters are preoccupied with the concerns of their commanders' single service missions. In joint headquarters the commander's mission *is* multiservice and includes employing Army, Navy and Air Forces. His staff officers must have the professional knowledge and mental flexibility to advise and assist him in this multifaceted endeavor.

Equally important and, for some, more difficult, is the requirement to subjugate pride in one's own service sufficiently to concentrate objectively on the capabilities, limitations, and needs of all services. Criticality also is a factor Joint commands usually are assigned operational missions of high importance to our national defense. Staff performance, good or bad, at this level could have significant and immediate effects on that defense. The highest levels of professional competence, personal dedication and integrity are therefore demanded.

Joint and combined staff positions are reserved for the most capable officers each service has to offer, and normally these are officers in the higher grades. Their expertise and experience are needed to deal with problems at this level. The fundamental qualifications and the professional and personal skills needed are the same as those required to successfully perform any staff assignment. A solid foundation in organization, procedures, and techniques should qualify an officer to start up the staff ladder in any service.

Summary

Staff officers of the different services require many special skills relating to the mission's equipment, tactics, and operating procedures peculiar to their respective branches. They must master the terminology, internal operating procedures, and formats common to the headquarters to which they are assigned. In general, however, each will find his principle reasons for existing the same—to assist and advise a commander. Each will work in very similar organizational environments, follow similar procedures, and work on similar actions. Most importantly, each will find that the same personal skills must be mastered. While some of this book's examples may not be applicable to all services, and some of the detailed procedures discussed may vary from those prescribed by other services, the fundamentals are universal and should prove helpful to staff officers of any military service.

Index

Abbreviated staff studies, 153-54
Accuracy
  in speaking, 227
  in writing, 230
Action
  courses of, 110-11
Adjutants general
  administration of military personnel by, 65
  administrative responsibilities of, 63-65
  interface with personnel officers' functions, 65
  message center operations by, 192
  messenger service of, 192
Administration
  Adjutants' general responsibilities for, 63-65
  allowing time for, 191-92
  as internal support function, 189-90
  control of within headquarters, 64
  correspondence as function of, 191-92
  distribution of paper work, 191-92
  duty rosters, 197, 262
  files. See Files.
  of military personnel, 65, 198-200
  orders, 48, 141-42
  reproduction, 195-96
  routine orders, 197
  typing services, 195
Administrative controls, 64
Aides, 29
Analysis
  of area of operations, 126-27
  of available information, 97
  of missions, 7, 46
  of resources, 51
Appropriations, 59
Armored forces
  in World War I, 15
  in World War II, 16
  Panzer forces, German, 16
Army Regulations, 255-56
Assets. See Resources.
Assignment of missions, 7.
Assignments to staff positions, 251ff.
Assistance
  for newly assigned officers, 2, 259
  legal, 76
Assistant
  chiefs of staff, 22

commanders, 21
Assumptions in problem solving, 109, 118-19
Audio-visual aids, 196, 233-34
Authority of commanders, 7, 19, 174ff., 261
Authorizations
 for equipment, 51
 for personnel, 32
 for supplies, 51
Automatic data transmission, 201
Automatic voice network (AUTOVON), 200-01
Availability of resources, 9, 51, 94
Aviation staff officers, 78
Base operations
 funds for, 59
Basic concerns of commanders, 12, 17, 21
Basic elements of command organization, 21
Battle of Prairie Grove, Arkansas, 13
Beasts of burden, 12
Blunt, Major General, USA, 12
Briefings, 156ff.
 advantages of, 232
 catagorization of, 233
 formats for, 233
 purposes of, 232
 rehearsals for, 234
 skills for, 156
 techniques, 233-34
 visual aids and, 233
Budgeting, 59
Centers, emergency operations, 79
Centers, message, 192
Chain of command, 183-84, 261
Changes
 in missions, 179-80
 in organization, 181
 in planning factors, 132
 in resource availability, 181
Chaplains
 as staff officers, 70
 functions of, 23
Chiefs of staff
 assistants to, 22
 deputy, as staff element chiefs, 22
 early use of, 13-14
 use of by commanders, 30, 257
Chops. *See* Coordination.
Civil affairs
 as staff office, 23
 functions included in, 56
 psychological operations, 56
Civil War
 Battle of Prairie Grove, Arkansas, 13
 Blunt, Major General, USA, 12
 staff expansion during, 13
Classified information, 194, 256
Clearances
 security, 203
Clubs
 officers' wives', 203
Cold War, 18
Combined staffs, 284
Command, 174ff.
 chain of, 183-84, 261
 compared with management, 243
 groups, 31, 151
 interest items of, 154-55, 174-76, 192
 organization, basic elements of, 21
 policies. *See* Commanders.
 sergeants major, 23
Commandant, headquarters, 62-63
Commanders, 173ff.
 aides to, 29
 analysis of missions by, 7

Index 289

and chiefs of staff, 30, 257
and personal staff, 24
assistants to, 21
authority of, 7, 19, 174, 261
basic concerns of, 12, 17, 21
concepts of operations, 9
decisions of, 47, 96, 101, 116, 179
dependence on staffs, 6, 10, 20
guidance issued by, 95, 98, 134, 177
immediate associates of, 27
intelligence as major concern of, 37, 42
items of interest to, 154-55, 174-76, 192
personnel responsibilities for, 31, 35
policies of, 173ff.
  concerning chain of command, 183-84
  creative thinking, 181-82
  decisions-making, 179
  for issuing guidance, 178
  for working with other Services, 280
  general discussion of, 135, 173-74, 260
  in other Services, 280
  interheadquarters relationships, scope of, 182-83
  keeping commanders informed, 174
  matters for commanders attention, 176
  mission changes, 179-80
  negative responses, 180
  organizational changes, 181
  policy files, 241
  staff supervision, 186
  suspense dates, 184-85
prehistoric, 11
problem-solving. *See* Problem-solving procedures.
  matters to be brought to the attention of, 176
  missions of. *See* Missions
  responsibilities of, 6, 7, 31, 35, 75, 76
  special staffs, 23, 61
  supervision by, 48, 102
Commands
  specialized, 17
  support, 19
Communication
  as staff officer skill, 209ff.
Communications. *See also* Skills.
  as staff element, 23
  automatic data transmission, 201
  electronics in, 200
  messengers, 192, 200
  postal services, 200
  radio, 201-02
  staff officers' responsibilities for, 200
  technical advancements in, 19
  telephone, 200-01
Complaints. *See* Inspectors general.
Completed staff work
  importance of, 248-49
Comprehension, 212-13
Comptrollers, 22-23, 58
Concepts of operations, 9
Conclusions
  in problem-solving, 119
Conferences, 155ff., 234ff.
  conferees, selection of, 235
  defining objectives of, 236
  discussion, control of, 237
  follow-up actions, 237
  for coordination, 168
  leadership of, 236-37
  objectives of, 236
  opposing views, 236

planning for, 235
staff officers' functions in, 235
Construction, 53-54
  of facilities, 53
  relationship to other activities, 53
  repair of facilities, 53, 206
  See also Logistics
Control
  of administration within headquarters, 64
  of conference discussions, 237
  span of, 23
Controls
  administrative, 64
  judicial, 75-76, 270
  legislative, 270
  reports, 143-44
  telephone, 200-01
Conversations, 219
Cookbook method of instruction, 95
Coordination
  between Services, 18
  by special staffs, 24
  chops, method of obtaining, 18, 166
  conference method, 168
  formal, 166
  general discussion of, 164-65
  importance of, 56
  informal, 167
  interheadquarters, 164, 172
  nonconcurrences, 168-69
  protocol and, 166
Correspondence, 150ff., 235
  distribution of, 63-64, 191-92
  formats for, 152
  incoming, 151
  internal, 152-55
  management of, 190
  movement of, 190-91
  outgoing, 151, 192

preparation for, 150
sources of, 190
suspense controls for, 193
Counterintelligence, *See* Intelligence.
Courses of action, 110-11
Creative thinking
  commanders demands for, 181-82
Criteria for staff work, 105
Data
  automatic processing equipment for, 71
  automatic transmission of, 201
  processing of, 202-03
Data banks, 240-41
Decisions
  by commanders, 47, 96, 101, 116, 179
Deputy chiefs of staff, 22
Directives
  from higher headquarters, 135
Directorate staff. *See* Staffs.
Discipline
  mental, 214
Discussion
  control of in conferences, 237
  in problem-solving, 119
Distribution and allowance tables, 32
Duty rosters, 197, 262
Electronics, 200
Emergency operations centers, 79
Enemy capabilities, 39
Engineers. *See* Construction and Logistics.
Equipment
  authorizations for, 51
  automatic data processing, 71
  headquarters requirements for, 204-05
  impact of, 15
Estimates

as problem-solving tools, 99
formats for, 124-26
intelligence, 116
staff, 105-6
supporting, 100
Facilities
construction of, 53
headquarters' requirements for, 206
maintenance and repair of, 53, 206
Fact sheets, 155
Facts
use of in problem-solving, 109
Field manual
staff officers' (FM 101-5), 255
Files
policy, 241
retention of, 194-95
retirement of, 194
screening of, 194-95
working, 239
Filing, 189-90
increased requirements for, 63
magnitude of efforts, 64-65
Fiscal management, 58
Food services, 36
Formats
analysis of the area of operations, 126-27
briefings, 233
correspondence, 152
estimates
intelligence, 124-25
staff, 124
supporting, 125-26
fact sheets, 155
letters of instruction, 147-48
orders, 141
plans, 139-40, 145-46
reports, 144, 148-49
staff studies, 126

standing operating procedures, 128-30
summary sheets, 153
Fragmentary orders, 141
Funds
appropriations of, 59
budgeting for, 59
for base operations, 59
for headquarters operations, 196
for mission operations, 59
staff responsibilities for, 196
General staff organization
adoption by USA, 14, 22
German Great General Staff, 14
Grades
of personnel, 33
Grant, Ulyses S., General USA
use of staff, 14
Gustav, IV, Swedish King
originator modern staff, 14
Headquarters, 5-6, 204-6
commandant, 63
equipment requirements for, 204-05
facilities' requirements, 206
funds for operating, 196
housekeeping functions in, 206
physical plant operation of, 6
purposes of, 5-6
supply requirements for, 204-05
support requirements for, 205
utilities for, 206
Health, morale and welfare activities, 36
Helicopters, 18
Higher headquarters
directives from, 135
Information
analysis of, 97
classified, 194, 256
release of, 78
Interservice relationships, 267-68

Inspections, 162-63
  by inspectors general, 74
Inspectors general, 74-75
  complaints, 75
  functions of, 74
  inspections by, 74
  interface with other staff activities, 75
  investigations by, 74
  relationships with commanders, 24, 74-75
Instructions
  cookbook methods of, 95
Instructions
  letters of, 141, 147-48
Intelligence, 37-45
  as command concern, 37, 42
  as staff element, 22
  combined with operations, 49
  consideration of enemy capabilities, 39
  counterintelligence activities, 40
  estimates, 116
  internal security functions of, 203
  nontactical, 41
  outside influences, 9, 37, 41
  staff officers' responsibilities for, 42
  terrain, 40
  weather, 40
  weather officers, 72
Internal correspondence, 152-55
Investigations. *See* Inspectors general.
Joint staffs, 18, 283
Judicial controls, 75-76, 270
Judgement, 114
Korea
  U.S. military operations in, 18
Labor disputes, 41
Law enforcement, 66

Leadership
  and the staff officer, 254
  in conferences, 236-37
Letters of instruction, 141, 147-48
Liaison, 163-64
Legal assistance, 76
Legislative controls, 270
Logistics, 49ff.
  analysis of physical resources by, 51
  as staff office, 22, 49,
  construction function of, 52-53
  impact of tanks on, 16
  impact of new equipment on, 15
  in supported units, 49
  maintenance functions of, 52
  mortuary services as function of, 55
  orders, 48
  physical resources as function of, 51
  supply as function of, 51-55. *See also* Supply.
  transportation as function of, 55
Losses. *See* Personnel.
Maintenance, 52
Major staff elements, 21. *See also* Staff.
Management, 242-48
  and staff officers' responsibilities for, 245
  compared with command, 243
  data processing as tool of, 202
  engineering, 204
  fiscal, 58, 196-97
  information systems office role in, 70
  of correspondence, 190
  of resources, 242
  of time, 246
  of typing services, 197-98
  of visitors, 197-98

Material
  organization of, 216-18
Meetings, 163
Memoranda, 152
Memory, 238-39
Mental discipline, 214
Message centers, 192
Messenger services, 192, 200
Military occupational specialties (MOS), 33
Military schools, 17
Missions
  analysis of, 7, 46
  assignment of, 7
  changes in, 179-80
  commanders' responsibilities for, 31
  determining scope of, 134
  funds for, 59
  included tasks, 8, 134
  of other Services, 269
  outside influences on, 9, 37
  restatement of, 46
  sources of, 96
  statement of, 107
Mobility
  contribution of helicopters to, 18
Money. *See* Fiscal management.
Morale, 35
Mortuary services, 55
Motivation, 35
Negative responses, 180
Nonconcurrences, 168-69
Nontactical intelligence, 41
Nuclear weapons officers, 78
Objectivity
  in communicating, 227, 231-32
Observation, 214, 263-64
Officers' wives' clubs, 263
Official visits, 214-15
Operations, 43-51
  analysis of area of, 121
  as staff element, 22
  base funds for, 59
  combined with intelligence, 48
  concepts of, 9
  emergency centers, 79
  organization as function of, 49
  planning as function of, 48
  orders, 48, 139-40, 146-47
  psychological, 226
  training function of, 226
Opposing views
  objective consideration of, 236
Oral presentations, 226
Orders, 48, 140-42
  administrative, 48, 141-42
  as problem-solving step, 47, 96, 102
  formats for, 140-41
  fragmentary, 141
  from higher headquarters, 135
  logistical, 48
  operations, 48, 139-40, 146-47
  routine, 197
  warning, 141
Organization
  and equipment tables (TOE), 32
  as staff function, 49
  changes in, 181
  charts and, 25
  command, 21
Organizing material, 216-18
Other Services
  command channels, 226
  command policies, 280
  missions of, 269
  staff organization of, 269, 272-73
  working with, 280
Outside influences, 9, 37, 41
Paragraphs
  organization of, 229
  See also Writing.

Papers
  talking, 155
Paperwork
  distribution of, 191-92
Performance rating, 199
Personal skills. *See* Skills for staff officers.
Personal staffs, 21-24
  commanders use of, 24
  composition of, 21, 24
  functions of, 24
Personnel, 31-37
  administration of, 65, 198-200
  as commanders concern, 34
  as staff element, 22
  authorizations for, 32
  commanders' responsibilities for, 31, 35
  complaints by, 75
  categories of, 198
  expanded requirements for skills, 15
  functions of adjutants general and, 65
  grades of, 33
  headquarters assignment to, 198
  health, morale and welfare activities for, 36
  losses of, 33
  military administration of, 65, 198-200
  morale, 35
  motivation, 34
  performance ratings, 199
  qualifications, 15
  recreation activities, 16
  religious welfare, 70
  requirements, 16
  resources, 31
  strengths, 32
Planning, 131-40
  as problem-solving step, 47, 101
  as staff action, 131
  continuity of, 132
  factors and changes in, 132
  for conferences, 235
Plans
  formats for, 140
Policy files, 260
Policies. *See* Commanders.
Postal services, 200
Prehistoric commanders, 11
Preparation. *See* Assignments.
Preventive medicine, 12, 68
Primary programs
  funding, 59
Problem-solving procedures, 95-103
  assumptions in, 108-9, 118-19
  commanders' decision in, 47, 101
  commanders' guidance in, 95
  commanders' use of, 44
  conclusions, 119
  considering available information, 95, 97-98
  general approach, 95
  identifying problem, 95-97
  initial command guidance, 98
  orders and, 47, 96, 102
  planning and, 47, 101
  standardization of, 93, 104
  steps, 103
  studying problem, 95, 99
  summary, 123
  supervision and, 96, 102-03
  understanding problem, 96
Processing data, 202-03
Programs
  funding, 59
Property disposal activities, 55
Protocol
  in coordination, 166
Provost marshal, 66
Prussian Staff System, 14

Psychological operations, 56
Qualifications
  personnel, 15
Radio
  in communications, 201-02
Ratings
  performance, 199
Reading, 212. *See also* Skills.
Recommendations, 114
Recreational activities, 35
References, 2-3, 255-56
Regulations. *See* Army Regulations.
Rehearsals, 234
Relationships
  between chiefs of staff and staffs, 30, 257
  between commanders and inspectors general, 24
  between headquarters, 182-83, 185
  interservice, 267-68
Release of information, 78
Religious activities, 70
Repair of facilities, 206
Reporting to new headquarters, 227-28
Reports, 142
  control of, 143-44
  formats for, 144, 148-49
Reproduction, 195-96
Requisitioning
  equipment and supplies, 51
Research, 157, 237
Resources
  analysis of, 51
  availability of, 9, 51, 94
  changes in, 181
  establishing requirements for, 9
  evaluation of, 16
  management of, 242-43
Responses, negative, 180
Restatement of missions, 46

Retention of files, 194-95
Retirement of files, 194-95
Rosters. *See* Duty rosters.
Routine orders, 197
Screening of files, 194-95
Security
  internal, 203
Selecting best courses of action, 136
Sentences
  construction of, 228. *See also* Writing.
Sequences of planning steps, 132
Services
  food, 36
  legal, 76
  medical, 36
  messenger, 55
  mortuary, 55
  postal, 200
  reproduction, 195-96
  typing, 195
Skills
  briefing, 156, 232-34
  concentration, powers of, 210
  conducting conferences, 234
  listening, 210
  observation, 214
  reading efficiency, 212
  speaking, 219-21
  writing, 227-30
Smaller staff elements, 27
Social duties, 262-63
SOP (standing operating procedures), 99
Sources of background information, 157-58
Span of control, 23
Speaking, 219-27. *See also* Speeches.
  accuracy, 227
  affectation, 227
  audience contact, 226

clarity, 226
coherence, 227
completeness, 227
conversations, 219-20
emotional control, 221
formal presentations, 220-21
gestures and, 226
humor and, 226-27
language, 226
mechanics, 226
objectivity, 227
types of. See Speeches.
understanding listeners, 221-22
unity, 227
Special staffs. See Staffs.
Special studies, 120
Specialties
  military occupational, 33
Speeches
  extemporaneous, 224
  impromptu, 225-26
  memorized, 223
  reading prepared material, 222-23
Speed reading, 212, 256
Sponsors
  for newly assigned officers, 257
Staff
  actions, 104ff., 150ff. See also Planning and Orders.
  analysis of areas of operation, 121
  completeness in, 47
  criteria for, 105
  estimates. See Estimates.
  facts used in, 118-19
  forecasts in, 132
  letters of instruction, 141
  orders. See Orders.
  organizing material for, 216-18
  planning. See Planning.
  reports, 142
  standing operating procedures (SOP), 122
  studies. See Studies.
assignments, 251ff.
  background, 251-52
  importance of, 1
  normal pattern of, 251
  personal gratification from, 1, 266
  preparing for, 252-57
  to combined headquarters, 284
  to joint headquarters, 284
estimates, 112-13
expansion of, 14-15
officers
  ancient, 13
  additional duties, 197
  assistance, 2
  communication responsibilities for, 200
  field manual for, 255
  skills. See Skills.
organization
  adjutants general, 63
  aides, 29
  assistant Chiefs of Staff, 22
  aviation staff officers, 78
  chaplain, 70
  chiefs of staff, 30
  command groups, 31
  command sergeants major, 29
  communications and electronics, 23
  comptroller, 22-23, 58
  deviations in, 279
  engineer, 25-26. See also Construction.
  headquarters commandant, 62
  information, 78
  inspectors general, 24, 74-75

intelligence, 22, 37, 43
logistics, 22, 49, 55
major elements, 21
management information systems office, 70
nuclear weapons employment officers, 78
operations, 22, 44
other Services, 272
personnel, 21, 24, 31, 35, 74
provost marshal, 66
smaller elements of, 27
staff judge advocate, 75
standardization of, 93
surgeon, 55, 67
typical examples of, 26
relationships with chief of staff, 30, 257
responsibilities for use of funds, 196
studies. *See* Studies.
supervision, 48, 102, 158-62
work, 248-49
Staffs
at company level, 10
combined, 284
commanders' dependency on, 6, 10, 20
expansion of, 14
joint, 18, 283
purposes of, 7, 20, 188
requirements for, 10
Standing operating procedures (SOP), 99, 122, 135
Statement of mission, 107
Strengths
personnel, 32
Studies
abbreviated, 153-54
as problem-solving steps, 99
special, 120
staff, 117-20
supporting, 100

Summary sheets, 153
Supervision
as problem-solving step, 96, 102-03
by commanders, 48, 102
by correspondence, 164
interheadquarters, 165
reacting to, 164
staff, 158-59, 249
Supply
authorizations for, 51
headquarters, requirements for, 204-05
property disposal as, activity, 55
requisitioning of, 51
Support
administrative, 189-90
commands, 19
complexities of, 19
headquarters requirements for, 6, 188-89, 206-07
medical, 67
organizations, 19
to subordinate organizations, 185
estimates, 116
Surgeon, 60, 67
Suspense controls, 193
Suspense dates, 184-85
Tables of distribution and allowances (TDA), 32
Tables of organization and equipment (TOE), 32
Talking papers, 155
Tanks
impacts on logistics, 16
Techniques
briefings, 233-34
Telephones. *See* Communications.
Terrain, 40
Time, 246

Training, 49
Typing services, 195
Utilities
　headquarters requirements for, 206
Visitors, 197-98
Visits,
　official, 214-15
Visual aids, 233
Vocabulary, 228
Warning orders, 141

Weather, 40
Weather officers, 72
Wives' clubs, 203
Working files, 193-94
Working with other Services, 280
Writing, 227-31
　accuracy, 230
　brevity, 228-30
　clarity, 230-31
　coherence, 230-31
　completeness, 231
　objectivity, 231